Manchester Medieval Sources Series

series advisers Rosemary Horrox and Simon MacLean

This series aims to meet a growing need amongst students and teachers of medieval history for translations of key sources that are directly usable in students' own work. It provides texts central to medieval studies courses and focuses upon the diverse cultural and social as well as political conditions that affected the functioning of all levels of medieval society. The basic premise of the new series is that translations must be accompanied by sufficient introductory and explanatory material and each volume therefore includes a comprehensive guide to the sources' interpretation, including discussion of critical linguistic problems and an assessment of the most recent research on the topics being covered.

also available in the series

Mark Bailey *The English manor c. 1200–c. 1500*

Malcolm Barber and Keith Bate *The Templars*

Simon Barton and Richard Fletcher *The world of El Cid: Chronicles of the Spanish Reconquest*

Andrew Brown and Graeme Small *Court and civic society in the Burgundian Low Countries c. 1420–1520*

Samuel K. Cohn, Jr. *Popular protest in late-medieval Europe: Italy, France and Flanders*

Trevor Dean *The towns of Italy in the later Middle Ages*

P. J. P. Goldberg *Women in England, c. 1275–1525*

Martin Heale *Monasticism in late medieval England, c. 1300–1535*

Rosemary Horrox *The Black Death*

David Jones *Friars' Tales: Thirteenth-century exempla from the British Isles*

Graham Loud *Roger II and the making of the Kingdom of Sicily*

Simon MacLean *History and politics in Late Carolingian and Ottonian Europe: The Chronicle of Regino of Prüm and Adalbert of Magdeburg*

Anthony Musson with Edward Powell *Crime, law and society in the later middle ages*

I. S. Robinson *Eleventh-century Germany: The Swabian Chronicles*

I. S. Robinson *The papal reform of the eleventh century: Lives of Pope Leo IX and Pope Gregory VII*

Michael Staunton *The lives of Thomas Becket*

Craig Taylor *Joan of Arc: La Pucelle*

Elisabeth van Houts *The Normans in Europe*

David Warner *Ottonian Germany*

Diana Webb *Saints and cities in medieval Italy*

CHRONICLES OF THE INVESTITURE CONTEST

Manchester University Press

MedievalSources*online*

Complementing the printed editions of the Medieval Sources series, Manchester University Press has developed a web-based learning resource which is now available on a yearly subscription basis.

MedievalSources*online* brings quality history source material to the desktops of students and teachers and allows them open and unrestricted access throughout the entire college or university campus. Designed to be fully integrated with academic courses, this is a one-stop answer for many medieval history students, academics and researchers keeping thousands of pages of source material 'in print' over the Internet for research and teaching.

titles available now at MedievalSources*online include*

Trevor Dean *The towns of Italy in the later Middle Ages*

John Edwards *The Jews in Western Europe, 1400–1600*

Paul Fouracre and Richard A. Gerberding *Late Merovingian France: History and hagiography 640–720*

Chris Given-Wilson *Chronicles of the Revolution 1397–1400: The reign of Richard II*

P. J. P. Goldberg *Women in England, c. 1275–1525*

Janet Hamilton and Bernard Hamilton *Christian dualist heresies in the Byzantine world, c. 650–c. 1450*

Rosemary Horrox *The Black Death*

David Jones *Friars' Tales: Thirteenth-century exempla from the British Isles*

Graham A. Loud and Thomas Wiedemann *The history of the tyrants of Sicily by 'Hugo Falcandus', 1153–69*

A. K. McHardy *The reign of Richard II: From minority to tyranny 1377–97*

Simon MacLean *History and politics in late Carolingian and Ottonian Europe: The Chronicle of Regino of Prüm and Adalbert of Magdeburg*

Anthony Musson with Edward Powell *Crime, law and society in the later Middle Ages*

Janet L. Nelson *The Annals of St-Bertin: Ninth-century histories, volume I*

Timothy Reuter *The Annals of Fulda: Ninth-century histories, volume II*

R. N. Swanson *Catholic England: Faith, religion and observance before the Reformation*

Elisabeth van Houts *The Normans in Europe*

Jennifer Ward *Women of the English nobility and gentry 1066–1500*

Visit the site at *www.medievalsources.co.uk* for further information and subscription prices.

CHRONICLES OF THE INVESTITURE CONTEST
Frutolf of Michelsberg and his continuators
selected sources translated and annotated
by T. J. H. McCarthy

Manchester University Press

Copyright © T. J. H. McCarthy 2013

The right of T. J. H. McCarthy to be identified as the author of this work has been asserted by him in accordance with the Copyright, Designs and Patents Act 1988.

Published by Manchester University Press
Altrincham Street, Manchester M1 7JA
www.manchesteruniversitypress.co.uk

British Library Cataloguing-in-Publication Data
A catalogue record for this book is available from the British Library

ISBN 978 0 7190 8469 0 hardback
ISBN 978 0 7190 8470 6 paperback

First published 2013

The publisher has no responsibility for the persistence or accuracy of URLs for any external or third-party internet websites referred to in this book, and does not guarantee that any content on such websites is, or will remain, accurate or appropriate.

Typeset in Monotype Bell
by Koinonia, Manchester

In memoriam
Felix Alexander Ellis McCarthy

CONTENTS

List of maps, genealogies and tables	*page* ix
Acknowledgements	xi
Abbreviations	xiii
Maps	xv
Genealogy of the Salians	xix
Introduction	1
Frutolf of Michelsberg, *Chronicle* **(1001–1101)**	85
The *1106 Continuation* **of Frutolf's** *Chronicle* **(1096–1106)**	138
The *Anonymous imperial chronicle* **(1096–1114)**	187
Ekkehard of Aura, *Chronicle,* **book 5 (1106–16)**	219
Ekkehard of Aura, *Hierosolimita*	254
The *1125 Continuation* **of Frutolf's** *Chronicle* **(1117–25)**	261
Bibliography	286
Index	312

LIST OF MAPS, GENEALOGIES AND TABLES

Maps
1 The empire during the Salian period (the kingdoms of Germany, Italy and Burgundy)   *page* xv
2 Places mentioned in the text (Germany and northern Burgundy)   xvi
3 Places mentioned in the text (Italy and southern Burgundy)   xvii
4 Places mentioned in the text (Byzantium and Palestine)   xviii

Genealogies
1 Genealogy of the Salians, *c.* 936–1125   xix
After S. Weinfurter, *The Salian century: main currents in an age of transition*, trans. B. M. Bowlus (Philadelphia, 1999), pp. 184–6
2 Frutolf of Michelsberg's genealogy of the Ottonian dynasty   90

Tables
1 Outline of Frutolf of Michelsberg's *Chronicle*   23
2 Synchronous history in Frutolf of Michelsberg's *Chronicle*   28

ACKNOWLEDGEMENTS

In preparing this translation of Frutolf's *Chronicle* and its continuations I have benefitted greatly from the generosity and advice of several distinguished scholars. Professor William L. North (Carleton College) has been an enthusiastic supporter of the project: he kindly sent me his unpublished translations of part of Frutolf's *Chronicle* and has been unfailingly helpful on many points of detail. I also owe much to the friendly assistance of Dr Christian Lohmer of the *Monumenta Germaniae Historica*, whose forthcoming edition of Frutolf's *Chronicle* will put all scholars of medieval historical writing in his debt. Professor John France (Swansea University and the United States Military Academy, West Point) kindly read those sections of the translation dealing with the crusades. Drs Simon MacLean and Rosemary Horrox, the series editors of Manchester Medieval Sources, have been very helpful and encouraging during the preparation of this book. I must also thank Dr Joachim Ott of the Thüringer Universitäts- und Landesbibliothek in Jena, who shared with me his unpublished description of Frutolf's autograph manuscript, as well as Dr Kai-Michael Sprenger (Deutsches Historisches Institut in Rome) and Dr Lila Yawn (John Cabot University, Rome), with whom I discussed aspects of this project.

Generous support for my research was provided by New College of Florida, which I acknowledge with gratitude. Special thanks are due to the staff of the library at New College, who have been immensely helpful and courteous in assisting me with my studies. I am also grateful to the staff of the library at Columbia University, the Bodleian Library, the library of the American Academy in Rome and the Vatican Library, where much of the research for this book was undertaken. I should like to thank my research assistant, Gail Fish, as well as Danielle Fasig, Zachary Low and the students of my Salian Germany class, whose work with me on my draft translations was beneficial in improving this book. My friend and colleague, Professor David Rohrbacher, generously gave of his time and expertise to read and check long passages of my translation, for which I am especially grateful. While all my colleagues at New College have been supportive, I must thank in particular David Harvey, Robert Johnson and Nova Myhill, as well as Anne Latowsky and Gregory Milton of the University of South Florida at Tampa. My friends in York, Oxford and Dublin have been very encouraging: Dr Jacco Thijssen, Professor John Caldwell, Dr K. S. Houston, Mr A. C. S. Johnstone and Dr Helga Robinson-Hammerstein. I am most fortunate to benefit from the friendship and learned advice of Professor I. S. Robinson, with whom I have discussed many aspects of this project. Above all, I must record my heartfelt thanks to my wife, Professor Carrie Beneš, who has been a constant source of support, and without whose help I could not have completed this book.

T. J. H. McCarthy
New College of Florida
In festum sancti Augustini

ABBREVIATIONS

AA	Albert of Aachen, *Historia Ierosolimitana*, ed. and trans. S. B. Edgington, *History of the journey to Jerusalem* (Oxford, 2007)
CCSL	*Corpus Christianorum. Series Latina*
Chroniken	F.-J. Schmale and I. Schmale-Ott (ed. and trans.), *Frutolfs und Ekkehards Chroniken und die Anonyme Kaiserchronik* (Ausgewählte Quellen zur deutschen Geschichte des Mittelalters 15; Darmstadt, 1972)
CSEL	*Corpus scriptorum ecclesiasticorum Latinorum*
DA	*Deutsches Archiv für Erforschung des Mittelalters*
FC	Fulcher of Chartres, *Historia Hierosolymita*, ed. H. Hagenmeyer, *Fulcheri Carnotensis historia Hierosolymita (1095–1127)* (Heidelberg, 1913)
GF	*Gesta Francorum*, ed. and trans. R. Hill, *The deeds of the Franks and the other pilgrims to Jerusalem* (Oxford, 1972)
IL	T. E. Mommsen and K. F. Morrison, *Imperial lives and letters of the eleventh century* (New York, 1962; repr. 2000)
JL	*Regesta pontificum Romanorum*, ed. W. Wattenbach, S. Loewenfeld, F. Kaltenbrunner and P. Ewald, 2nd edn (Leipzig, 1885)
MBDS	*Mittelalterliche Bibliothekskataloge Deutschlands und der Schweiz*, 4 vols (Munich, 1918–79)
MGH	*Monumenta Germaniae Historica*
Briefe	*Die Briefe der deutschen Kaiserzeit*
AA	*Auctores antiquissimi*
Constitutiones	*Constitutiones et acta publica imperatorum et regum*
DD H. III	*Diplomata Heinrici III*
DD H. IV	*Diplomata Heinrici IV*
DD H. V	*Diplomata Heinrici V*
DM	*Deutsches Mittelalter. Kritische Studientexte*
Epistolae	*Epistolae selectae*
Fontes	*Fontes iuris Germanici antiqui in usum scholarum separatim editi*
Libelli	*Libelli de lite imperatorum et pontificum*
LibM NS	*Libri memoriales et necrologia. Nova series*

NecG	Necrologia Germaniae
Quellen	Quellen zur Geistesgeschichte des Mittelalters
SS	Scriptores (in folio)
SSrG	Scriptores rerum Germanicarum in usum scholarum separatim editi
SSrG NS	Scriptores rerum Germanicarum, nova series
NA	Neues Archiv der Gesellschaft für ältere deutsche Geschichtskunde
PL	J. P. Migne (ed.), Patrologiae cursus completus. Series Latina
RA	Raymond of Aguilers, Historia Francorum qui ceperunt Iherusalem, ed. J. H. Hill and L. L. Hill, Le «Liber» de Raymond d'Aguilers (Paris, 1969)
RHC Occ.	Recueil des Historiens des Croisades. Historiens occidentaux, 5 vols (Paris, 1844–95)
SC	I. S. Robinson, Eleventh-century Germany: the Swabian chronicles (Manchester, 2008)
WC	Würzburg Chronicle, ed. G. Waitz, 'Chronicon Wirziburgense ad a. 1057', MGH SS 6 (Hanover, 1844), pp. 17–32

Biblical references are given according to the Vulgate.

Map 1 The empire during the Salian period (the kingdoms of Germany, Italy and Burgundy)

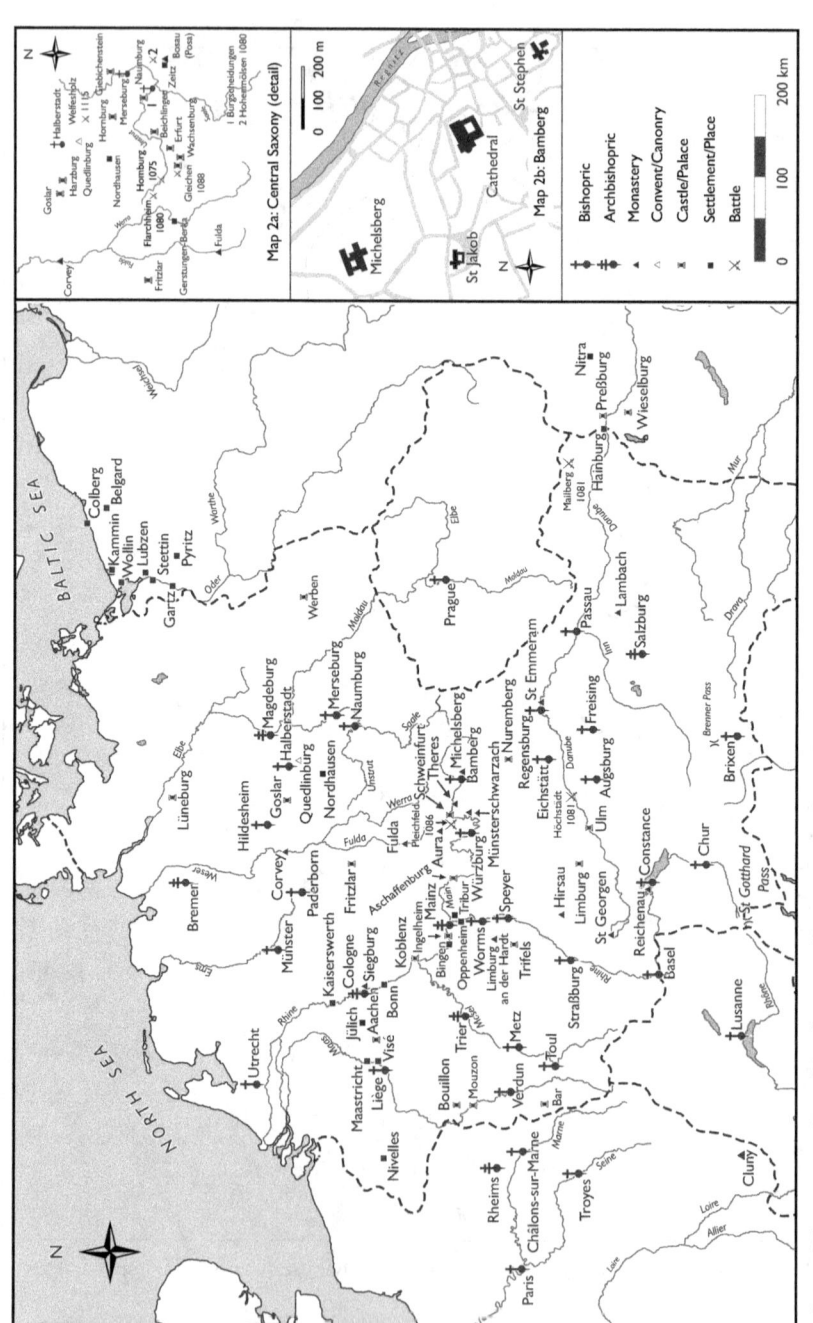

Map 2 Places mentioned in the text (Germany and northern Burgundy)

Map 3 Places mentioned in the text (Italy and southern Burgundy)

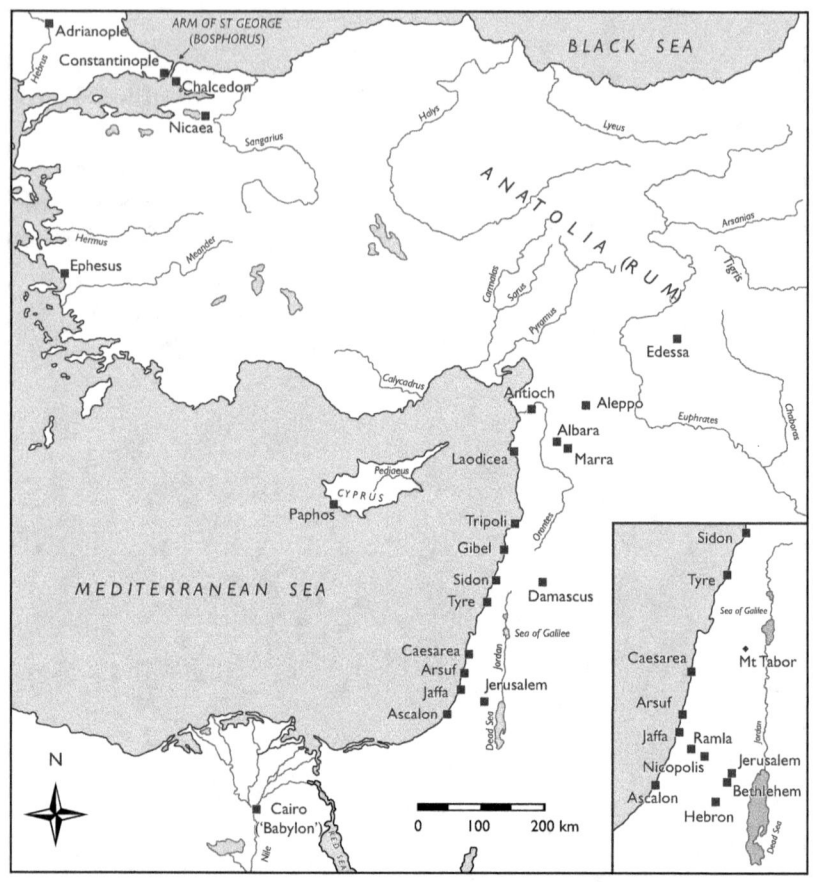

Map 4 Places mentioned in the text (Byzantium and Palestine)

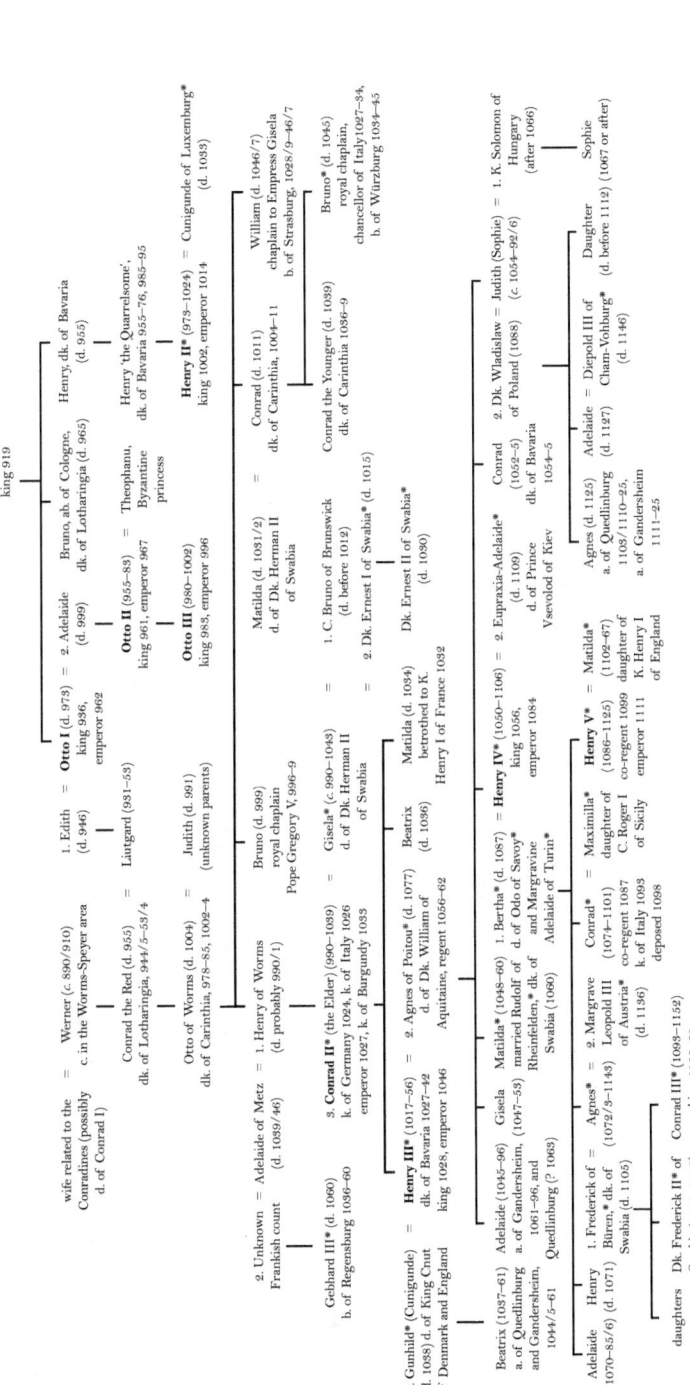

Genealogy of the Salians, c. 936–1125

INTRODUCTION

In 1015 Eberhard, the first bishop of Bamberg, founded a monastery dedicated to St Michael the Archangel and St Benedict of Nursia on a hill close by his fledgling city on the River Regnitz. It was not an isolated foundation. In 1007 the city of Bamberg itself and its cathedral had been established and lavishly endowed by King Henry II, while between 1007 and 1009 Eberhard had founded a house of canons regular dedicated to St Stephen at the behest of the king and his queen Cunigunde.[1] This programme of ecclesiastical foundations was interpreted by Frutolf of Michelsberg (d. 1103), writing at the very end of the eleventh century, as a deliberate effort by the last Ottonian emperor to provide for the well-being of his beloved Bamberg. The cathedral, endowed 'most copiously with rich estates and every appropriate adornment', was dedicated both to St Peter, 'the rock of apostolic strength', and to the heroic St George. In the southern part of the city the canonry of St Stephen provided a 'strong tower ... against the buffeting winds of vice', while in the northern part the other great military saint, Michael, stood guard against the 'cold wind' of evil.[2] For Frutolf and his contemporaries, who were keenly aware of the connexion between the physical and the metaphysical worlds, the spiritual armoury of Henry II's foundation augured well for its success: Bamberg was truly 'a safe refuge in the protection of angels'.

It was from Bamberg that Frutolf observed the momentous political and religious upheavals which began to engulf the kingdoms of Germany, Italy and Burgundy during the reign of Henry IV (1056–1106) and which continued into the reign of his son Henry V (1106–25). Historians frequently call this conflict of empire and papacy the 'Investiture Contest', a label that refers to the disputed practice of lay investiture, whereby the king appointed the bishops and the abbots of royal monasteries in his realm. At the heart of that practice was the ceremony of investiture itself, during which the king conferred upon the candidate the symbols of his office – the episcopal staff and ring in the case of a

1 See von Guttenberg (1937), pp. 33–6, 52–3; Göller (2007), p. 44.
2 See Frutolf, *Chronicle* 1001, below, p. 86.

bishop or the abbatial staff in the case of an abbot – with the words 'receive the church'; after this the recipient performed homage and swore fealty to the king.[3] Nevertheless, the term 'Investiture Contest' inadequately describes the conflict, for lay investiture only came to dominate it during the reign of Henry V.[4] As the narrative sources translated in this volume show, the conflict of empire and papacy was in reality a series of parallel conflicts that pitted the Salian rulers at times against sections of the imperial aristocracy, at times against elements within the church and still at other times against both together.

The origins of these conflicts lie partly in the history of the papal reform movement, which developed in the aftermath of Henry III's intervention in the politics of the Roman church in 1046. In the autumn of that year Henry III (1039–56) undertook his first expedition to his Italian kingdom with the intent of receiving imperial coronation but found a papacy in crisis as a result of tensions among the Roman aristocracy.[5] In September 1044 the powerful Crescentii family had orchestrated a rising against the rival Tusculani with the result that the Tusculan pope Benedict IX was briefly replaced by Silvester III (Cardinal Bishop John of Sabina) before regaining office. The severity of Benedict's rule seems to have contributed to the opposition he faced and may well have led to his eventual decision to resign in favour of his godfather John Gratian, the archpriest of St John at the Latin Gate, who took the papal name Gregory VI on 1 May 1045. Henry III's response to this crisis was to investigate the respective claims of the three popes, for it was both sacramentally and politically imperative that he receive the imperial crown from a pope whose title was beyond reproach. A synod at Sutri on 20 December 1046 confirmed Silvester's forfeiture of the papacy and also uncovered evidence that Gregory VI's accession had been tainted by some form of monetary transaction (the 'heresy of simony'); in the light of this evidence Gregory either resigned or, as some sources maintain, was deposed.[6] A synod in Rome on Christmas Eve condemned Benedict IX and elected Bishop Suidger of Bamberg as Pope Clement II (1046–7).

---

3 Schieffer (1981), pp. 10–13; Robinson (1999), pp. 114–15.

4 Robinson (1978a), p. 1; Robinson (1990), p. 421.

5 On the early eleventh-century papacy see Cushing (2005), pp. 17–24; Blumenthal (2004), pp. 9–13. On the crisis of 1046 see Zimmermann (1968), pp. 119–39; Herrmann (1973), pp. 151–65; Cowdrey (1998), pp. 4–8, 21–6.

6 Peter Damian, *Letter* 72, MGH *Briefe* 4/2, p. 363; trans. Blum 3 (1992), p. 145; *De ordinando pontifice*, pp. 80, 83. See Gresser (2007), p. 10.

INTRODUCTION 3

Henry's actions decisively re-oriented the papacy, for each of the three succeeding popes – Damasus II (1047–8), Leo IX (1048/9–54) and Victor II (1054–7) – was a German bishop and confidant of the emperor. But whereas the years 1046–57 were characterized by harmonious co-operation between empire and papacy, the years 1057–73 witnessed the gradual distancing of the imperial court and the papal reform movement. The premature death of Henry III in 1056, which left the kingdom in the hands of his six-year-old son Henry IV, robbed the papacy of its principal defender against the ambitions of the Roman families. The regency government of Empress Agnes (d. 1077), embroiled in unrest in Germany stemming from resentment against the policies of her late husband Henry III, lacked the resources to protect the papacy effectively. Thus, twice in three years the Roman aristocracy attempted to regain its hegemony over the Roman church by orchestrating its own papal elections: in 1058 the Crescentii and Tusculani joined forces to install Cardinal Bishop John of Velletri as 'Benedict X' and in 1061 the Roman aristocracy together with the bishops of Lombardy chose Bishop Cadalus of Parma as 'Honorius II'. On those occasions the reformers elected Nicholas II (1058–61) and Alexander II (1061–73) respectively.[7] The gravity of the situation was compounded when the imperial government – unaware of the election of Alexander II – recognized 'Honorius II' at the Council of Basel in October 1061. Schism followed and it was not until 1064 that the regency government, by then under the control of Archbishop Anno of Cologne (d. 1075), recognized Alexander as the lawful pope.

In these circumstances the papacy sought new alliances to replace those lost with the death of Henry III. The first was with the formidable new house of Canossa-Lotharingia, formed in 1054 when Godfrey 'the Bearded' (d. 1069), the deposed duke of Upper Lotharingia, married his cousin, the widowed Margravine Beatrice of Tuscany (d. 1076).[8] Although an opponent of Henry III, Godfrey had been reconciled with the imperial court shortly before the emperor's death through the efforts of Pope Victor II and proved a capable ally both of the minority government and of the reform papacy. It was hardly coincidental that in 1057 the reformers elected Godfrey's brother, Cardinal Frederick of

---

7 On the elections of 'Benedict X' and 'Honorius II' see Krause (1960), pp. 62–3, 107, 149; Jenal (1974), pp. 247, 263–7; Hüls (1977), p. 144; Schmidt (1977), pp. 72–80, 104–11, 117–18, 126–7; Tellenbach (1993), pp. 149–50, 158–60; Cowdrey (1998), pp. 49–53; Cushing (2005), pp. 68–70, 76–7.

8 On Godfrey see Boshof (1978), 63–100; Weinfurter (1999), pp. 104–7.

Lotharingia, as Pope Stephen IX, or that Stephen's successors Nicholas II and Alexander II were both Tuscan bishops with strong ties to the house of Canossa-Lotharingia.

The second new alliance, with the Normans of southern Italy, also seems to have been intended to counter the ambitions of the Roman families.[9] At the Treaty of Melfi in August 1059, Nicholas II recognized the claims of Richard of Aversa to the principality of Capua and Robert Guiscard to the duchies of Apulia and Calabria in return for promises to aid and defend the present pope and his successors. Although an older generation of historians saw these alliances as evidence of the papacy's efforts to liberate itself from imperial control, more recent scholarship has emphasized that in this period the papacy became independent against its will.[10] Even as the reformers sought new alliances, they recognized the importance of their traditional connexion with the imperial court.

The unintended distancing of empire and papacy for political reasons was paralleled by a series of important institutional and intellectual developments within the papal reform movement itself. These developments can in part be traced to innovations introduced during the pontificate of Henry III's cousin Leo IX (Bishop Bruno of Toul): first, the transformation of the cardinal deacons, priests and bishops from a body of clergymen whose primary function was to aid the pope in the liturgy to a body that constituted his principal advisers and seemed to Cardinal Peter Damian writing in 1063 as 'the spiritual senators of the universal church';[11] secondly, the filling of vacancies in the college of cardinals with distinguished non-Romans – many from Leo's Lotharingian homeland – who would articulate the essential tenets of papal doctrine in the coming years; thirdly, increased reliance upon papal representatives called legates, who had full authority to act for the pope and thus to deal with matters of church discipline at great distances from Rome; and fourthly, the innovation of papal councils in Italy, Germany and France to prosecute clerical abuses and to disseminate knowledge of papal legislation. These innovations began to transform

---

9 Bonizo of Sutri, *To a friend* 6, p. 593; trans. Robinson (2004b), p. 203. See Deér (1972), p. 87; Robinson (1990), pp. 367–70; Loud (2007), pp. 137–41.

10 For the older literature see Fliche (1924), pp. 323–5; Haller (1951), pp. 324–5. For a discussion of the historiography see Robinson (1999), pp. 38–41. See also Loud (2002), pp. 154–7; Loud (2007), pp. 139–40.

11 Peter Damian, *Letter* 97, *MGH Briefe* 4/3, p. 80; trans. Blum 4 (1998), p. 83. See Robinson (1990), pp. 33–9.

the papacy into what has been termed an 'effective supranational institution' no longer focused predominantly on Rome and its immediate surroundings.[12]

Leo IX's institutional reforms stemmed from a desire among reformers to combat the clerical abuses of nicholaitism and simony. Nicholaitism was understood in the eleventh century to refer to clerical marriage. It was not uncommon among the clergy: even up to the first quarter of the twelfth century at least a quarter of the canons of St Paul's Cathedral in London were married, for example.[13] To reformers, however, nicholaitism tied clerks to the corrupted secular world through fornication and endangered the church's material foundation since the children of priests sought to inherit church property.[14] Simony, named after the Simon Magus of Acts 8.9–24 who had attempted to buy the power of the Holy Spirit from St Peter, involved payment for ecclesiastical offices.[15] At the beginning of the eleventh century its meaning was generally restricted to a blatant attempt to buy an office – a good example is provided in Wipo's account of the simoniacal transaction that accompanied the appointment of the bishop of Basel by Conrad II in 1028 when 'the king and queen received an immense sum of money for the bishopric from a certain clerk, a nobleman by the name of Udalric'.[16] By the last quarter of the century, however, the definition of what constituted payment had been expanded by some reformers to include any form of gift or service.

An important articulation of changing attitudes to simony is provided by the writings of one of the reformers brought to Rome by Leo IX – Cardinal Humbert of Silva Candida (originally a monk of the Lotharingian monastery of Moyenmoutier). In his treatise *Against simoniacs* of 1057/8, Humbert fatefully connected simony with the practice of lay investiture. He took as his starting point Leo IX's dictum 'no one should be promoted to ecclesiastical government without the election

---

12 Cushing (2005), p. 55.

13 Brooke (1951), 125. The heresy nicholaitism was sometimes linked with the deacon Nicholas of Antioch (Acts 6.5), though the sect of the Nicholaites active in Ephesus is mentioned in Apocalypse 2.6 and 2.15. Nevertheless, even the Church Fathers seem to have had only vague notions of the heresy's substance.

14 See Brooke (1956), 3. On nicholaitism more generally in the eleventh century see Cushing (2005), pp. 98–9.

15 See Blumenthal (2004), pp. 13–14; Cushing (2005), pp. 95–8.

16 Wipo, *Deeds of Emperor Conrad* 8, p. 31 (*IL*, p. 74).

of the clergy and people'.[17] Lay investiture contravened canon law, which mandated that a bishop should be elected freely by the clergy and people of his diocese and then confirmed by the metropolitan; secular rulers, who were mere laymen, had no place in this process.[18] Although Humbert's radical views did not have an immediate impact upon the question of the legality of lay investiture, they would in time pose considerable difficulties for the Salian emperors, who frequently promoted to vacant bishoprics those clerks with a distinguished record of imperial service.[19] Thus when Henry IV attempted to invest bishops as his father had done he was implicated in simony, and the act of investiture itself came to signify to his critics not only the simoniacal aspects of that transaction but the enslavement of the church to secular authority.

Changing attitudes to simony were paralleled by changing attitudes to ecclesiology – the theory of the nature of church structure and governance. Here the crucial development was the gradual elaboration of the doctrine of papal primacy, which can be seen in the works of reformers such as Humbert and Peter Damian.[20] Humbert's treatise *Concerning the holy Roman church*, for example, asserted that the Roman church was 'head of all churches after Jesus Christ'.[21] The immediate context of this work was the need to refute the claim of the patriarch of Constantinople to equality with the pope arising out of the schism of 1054 between the Greek and Roman churches (which Humbert did by producing an effective distillation of earlier canonical collections).[22] But the doctrine of papal primacy would also have important consequences for the relationship of the Roman church with other churches in the West. It featured in Peter Damian's *Concerning the privilege of the Roman church*, a report of his legation to Milan in 1059 that stressed Rome's universality of jurisdiction.[23] As with simony and lay investiture, so too freshly articulated theories about papal primacy would influence the

17 Council of Rheims cap. 1, quoted in Anselm of St-Remi, *Historia dedicationis ecclesiae sancti Remigii* 16 (*PL* 142.1437A).
18 Humbert, *Against simoniacs* 3.6–9, 3.11, pp. 205–8, 211.
19 Schieffer (1981), 41–2, 44–7. More generally, Blumenthal (1988), pp. 89–92.
20 See Robinson (1988), pp. 266–79; Blumenthal (2004), pp. 14–16.
21 Humbert, *Concerning the holy Roman church*, p. 129.
22 On Humbert and the schism of 1054 see Hoesch (1970), pp. 11–16, 27–31; Robinson (2004b), p. 7.
23 Peter Damian, *Letter* 65, *MGH Briefe* 4/2, pp. 228–47; trans. Blum 3 (1992), pp. 24–39. See also Ryan (1956), pp. 60–8; Cushing (2005), pp. 74–6.

thought of Pope Gregory VII, who saw 'the holy Roman church' as the 'mother and mistress of all churches'.[24]

The doctrine of papal primacy made it imperative for the papacy to take the lead in reforming the church and thus the eradication of nicholaitism and simony became part of a campaign to secure the 'liberty of the church' (*libertas ecclesiae*). This was to be achieved by leading the church back to what Gregory VII described as the 'condition of ancient religion' – an idealized notion of the church's 'golden age' in the era of Constantine the Great (d. 337) or Gregory the Great (d. 604) when it was free from the debilitating effects of secular dominance.[25] What began in the 1040s and 1050s as an attempt to curb the individual abuses of nicholaitism and simony had, therefore, by the 1070s expanded into a broader campaign to free the church from secular 'interference'.

The gradual distancing of empire and papacy, both institutionally and intellectually, took place against a backdrop of political unrest in Germany. The origins of this unrest can be traced to the reign of Henry III (1039–56). While Henry III is frequently remembered for his piety, his commitment to rejuvenating church discipline and his efforts to introduce the Peace and Truce of God movements to Germany, the primary sources also speak of the increasingly autocratic nature of his rule and of growing dissatisfaction in the kingdom. 'At this time both the foremost men and the lesser men of the kingdom began more and more to murmur against the emperor and complained that he had long since departed from his original conduct of justice,' wrote the Swabian chronicler Herman of Reichenau in response to Henry III's deposition of Duke Conrad of Bavaria in 1053, while Otloh of St Emmeram in his *Book of visions* of c. 1063–5 recorded a nobleman's dream about God's damning judgement upon the emperor.[26] But while Henry III faced determined opposition in many parts of his kingdom, it was accumulating resentment in Saxony that would have the greatest consequences for his son. His frequent visits to the Saxon royal palace of Goslar, his increased exploitation of the silver mines in the nearby Harz mountains and the favour he showed to Saxon bishops were perceived by the Saxon nobility as a threat to their ancient freedoms and privileges. Such fears seem to have been the spur for a conspiracy reported by Lampert of

---

24 Gregory VII, *Epistolae vagantes* 54, p. 134.

25 *Ibid.* 2, p. 6. See Miccoli (1966), pp. 225–99; Robinson (2004a), pp. 284–9; Robinson (2004b), pp. 1–4.

26 Herman of Reichenau, *Chronicle* 1054, p. 132 (*SC*, p. 95); see Reuter (2006), pp. 376–7. Otloh of St Emmeram, *Book of visions* 15, pp. 87–8; see Weinfurter (1999), p. 103.

Hersfeld in which 'the Saxon princes frequently discussed the injustices that they had endured from the emperor and decided that there would be no sweeter vindication for their grievances than to snatch the kingdom away from his son'.[27]

Henry III died at the age of thirty-nine in 1056 and the nine years of Henry IV's minority until 1065 passed without any attempt to snatch the kingdom away from the Salian dynasty. Once of age, the early years of Henry IV's personal rule were dominated by his attempts to tighten his control over Saxony. Like his father he favoured the royal palace of Goslar and tended to side with bishops in their quarrels with the Saxon nobility. But he also embarked upon a programme of castle building such as had not previously been seen in Saxony – strongly fortified castles that were garrisoned with Swabians loyal to the king and that seemed to the Saxons to exist not for their protection but for their oppression. In the words of the annalist of Disibodenberg, 'King Henry planned to subject all the Saxons to servitude' by resolving 'first to despoil the princes of their honours and dignities and thereby to subject the rest of the people of the province to his lordship'.[28] Henry faced localized rebellions from Margrave Dedi I of the Lower Lausitz in 1069 and from Otto of Northeim (who had been deposed from the duchy of Bavaria) in 1070–1. But the accumulated resentment of the Saxons towards the king's policies displayed itself most clearly in the 'Great Saxon Rebellion' of 1073–5. Although Henry emerged victorious from this rebellion with a stunning victory at the Battle of the Homburg on 9 June 1075, he proved unable in the following years to maintain peace throughout the German kingdom. From 1076 onwards, as relations between Henry IV and the papacy deteriorated rapidly, some of his former allies, such as the eventual anti-king Rudolf of Rheinfelden, deserted him and increasingly made common cause with his ecclesiastical critics. By the late 1070s those who opposed Henry IV – though their motives were many and varied – frequently did so by claiming to fight for the liberty of the church.

While civil unrest in Germany was an important catalyst for the wider conflicts of Henry IV's reign, so too were the king's actions with respect to the church during the period 1065–76. Henry IV came of age amid high hopes on the part of reformers that his rule would bring about a rapprochement between the imperial court and the papacy.[29] The events

27 Lampert of Hersfeld, *Annals* 1057, p. 71.
28 *Annals of Disibodenberg* 1075, p. 6.
29 Peter Damian, *Letter* 120, *MGH Briefe* 4/3, p. 389; trans. Blum 4 (1998), p. 392.

of the subsequent years, however, served only to deepen the rift with Rome: in 1065 and 1067 royal expeditions to aid the papacy against its enemies came to nothing, while in 1069 the king began unsuccessful proceedings to obtain a divorce from his wife Bertha of Turin.[30] The damage done to Henry's reputation by the divorce proceedings was exacerbated by complaints about the king's personal life. Gregory VII claimed that 'shameful reports of the king's behaviour' had reached him on numerous occasions.[31] In 1073 the Saxon rebels demanded that the king should abandon his 'herd of concubines' and instead 'cherish and treat the queen as his wife'.[32] These charges would be repeated by Henry's opponents in the polemics of the 1080s and again by pro-Gregorian chroniclers in their accounts of the allegations made by Henry's second wife, Eupraxia-Adelaide, at the Council of Piacenza in 1095.[33] Although the truth of these allegations cannot be established (since they owe much to the efforts of Gregorian polemicists to portray Henry as the archetypal tyrant described by Isidore of Seville),[34] their very existence confirmed to Henry's opponents that he refused to live his life 'in ways befitting a king'.[35]

Equally as worrying in the eyes of many reformers was the poor quality of the king's early episcopal appointments. Although the deterioration began during Henry's minority when the kingdom's two leading churchmen – Archbishops Anno of Cologne and Adalbert of Hamburg-Bremen – had attempted to use episcopal appointments to expand their respective power bases, problems continued during the early years of the king's personal rule. Some royal appointees were resisted by the cathedrals on which they were imposed, most notoriously at Constance in 1070–1 when the chapter brought accusations of simony and theft of church treasure against Bishop Charles to the metropolitan, Archbishop

---

30 See Robinson (1999), pp. 107–12.
31 Gregory VII, *Register* 4.1, p. 290; trans. Cowdrey (2002), pp. 206–7; *Epistolae vagantes* 14, pp. 34, 38.
32 Lampert of Hersfeld, *Annals* 1073, pp. 151–2. Cf. Bruno of Merseburg, *Saxon war* 6–14, pp. 16–22.
33 Bernold of St Blasien, *Chronicle* 1095, p. 519 (*SC*, p. 324); *1106 Continuation* 1099, below, p. 159.
34 Isidore, *Etymologies* 9.3.20; trans. Barney (2006), p. 201: 'Now in later times the practice has arisen of using the term [tyrant] for thoroughly bad and wicked kings, kings who enact upon their people their lust for luxurious domination and the cruellest lordship.' See Robinson (1999), pp. 113–14.
35 Gregory VII, *Epistolae vagantes* 14, p. 34.

Siegfried of Mainz, and Pope Alexander II.[36] The Constance debacle seems to have alerted the papacy to irregularities within the imperial episcopate, for Alexander summoned to his Lenten synod of 1073 'many bishops from the land of Germany' who were 'polluted not only by carnal crime but also by the defilement of simony'.[37]

It was, however, Henry IV's actions with regard to the archbishopric of Milan that led to his first open breach with the papacy. The period 1057–75 witnessed a protracted and at times violent power struggle within the Milanese church between the supporters of the archbishop and the *Pataria*, a group that campaigned against clerical marriage and simony.[38] The reform papacy looked with interest upon the outcome and allied itself early on with the *Pataria*: not only might the crisis further reform, but it might also bring the proud and independent Milanese church firmly under Roman obedience. But Milan was also of interest to the German kings: it commanded the north of their Italian kingdom and its archbishop exercised considerable royal authority.[39] In 1070 Henry IV rejected Alexander II's call to recognize as archbishop the candidate of the *Pataria* and invested instead a noble Milanese sub-deacon named Godfrey. Alexander responded to Henry's actions by excommunicating five of the king's advisers in 1073. Henry's response, extant in a letter of that year, was to admit that 'through the seductive deception of those whose counsels we have followed … we have also sold churches to unworthy men'.[40] This capitulation was in large part dictated by political necessity, since 1073 also saw the outbreak of the 'Great Saxon Rebellion' and Henry feared an alliance of his political and ecclesiastical opponents. But when the king had emerged victorious from that rebellion in 1075, he no longer felt it necessary to conciliate the papacy and, turning again to Milan, disregarded the claim of the papal candidate by investing as archbishop a Milanese sub-deacon and royal chaplain named Tedald. He compounded the situation by investing bishops unknown to Gregory VII in Fermo and Spoleto, dioceses under the metropolitan jurisdiction of Rome. In the aftermath of his excommunication of Henry in the Lenten synod of 1076, Gregory would lament that 'the only thank-offerings which he [Henry] presented to God for the victory which he obtained [in 1075] were that he straightway

---

36 Fleckenstein (1968), pp. 228–30; Schieffer (1972), 46–50.
37 Gregory VII, *Register* 1.77, p. 109; trans. Cowdrey (2002), p. 80.
38 Cowdrey (1968), 25–48.
39 Cowdrey (1966), 1–15; Robinson (1999), pp. 123–4.
40 Henry IV, *Letter* 5, p. 9 (*IL*, p. 142).

INTRODUCTION 11

broke the promises of amendment which he had made and ... took the excommunicates back into his friendship and society'.[41]

For Gregory, the most frustrating aspect of Henry's behaviour was his unwillingness to use his royal authority to aid the cause of reform. On numerous occasions early in his pontificate Gregory had spoken enthusiastically about the role he envisaged Henry playing in the reform of the church. On 7 December 1074, for example, he wrote to Henry asking him to compel the bishops of Bamberg, Strasburg and Speyer to attend his forthcoming Lenten synod, while in a second letter of the same date he outlined grandiose plans to lead a crusade to the East and invited Henry not only to counsel him but to accept from him 'the Roman church so that you may both guard her as a holy mother and defend her to her honour'.[42] Gregory expected Henry IV to play the role that his father had played in the reform of the church. These hopes, which were conditioned by Gregory's personal experience of how the relationship between empire and papacy used to work, show that even at the beginning of his pontificate reformers did not desire independence from the empire. But the eventual realization that the king would not aid him in the type of reform he envisaged – starkly underlined by Henry's attack on Gregory at the Council of Worms in January 1076 – prompted the pope's unprecedented intervention in German politics: in his Lenten synod of 1076, Gregory excommunicated Henry and released German subjects from their fealty to him.[43] Two years later, at the November synod of 1078, Gregory's continued frustration with the king's behaviour resulted in the prohibition of lay investiture for the first time.[44] The synod's decree against lay investiture was an attempt to prohibit the means of simony and at last the theories of Humbert, which had seemed radical in the late 1050s, formed the basis of papal policy.

Despite the papal legislation of 1078, the events of the following years underline the fact that Henry IV's conflict with the papacy never explicitly centred on lay investiture. Worsening relations between empire and papacy saw the king and thirty imperial bishops renounce their allegiance to Gregory and elect Archbishop Wibert of Ravenna (d. 1100) as 'Clement III' at the Synod of Brixen in 1080. Henceforward the

41 Gregory VII, *Epistolae vagantes* 14, p. 36.
42 Gregory VII, *Register* 2.30, 2.31, pp. 164–5, 167; trans. Cowdrey (2002), pp. 121, 123. See Cowdrey (1982), pp. 27–40.
43 Gregory VII, *Register* 3.10a, pp. 268–71; trans. Cowdrey (2002), pp. 191–3.
44 Gregory VII, *Register* 6.5b, p. 403; trans. Cowdrey (2002), p. 283. See Schieffer (1981), pp. 114–52; Robinson (1990), p. 409.

empire was in a state of schism with competing parallel episcopacies – one Henrician and the other Gregorian – in many dioceses. The years following Gregory VII's death in 1085 were dominated by Henry's attempts to compel the submission of the Gregorian 'rebel' Urban II and his supporters, or – from the perspective of Urban II and his successor Paschal II – by the struggle of orthodox catholics to combat a schismatic emperor. When imperial and Gregorian bishops met to discuss the case of Henry and Gregory at Gerstungen-Berka in Thuringia on 20 January 1085, the debate centred not on investiture but on the lawfulness of the pope's excommunication and deposition of the king.[45] The unprecedented innovations of Gregory VII, the disastrous effects of his policies for the peace and unity of the empire and his assault on divinely ordained kingship are the chief concerns of imperial polemics composed during the reign of Henry IV; only Wido of Ferrara's *Concerning the schism of Hildebrand* (1086) and Sigebert of Gembloux's *Letter* against Pope Paschal (1103) specifically address lay investiture.[46] Although Urban II issued decrees against lay investiture at the Councils of Melfi (1089) and Clermont (1095), his priority was to end the schism in the church and restore obedience to the papacy by defeating Henry IV and his antipope 'Clement III'. This too was the primary concern of Urban's successor Paschal II during the early years of his pontificate: in his Lateran synod of 1102, the 'schism of our times was reckoned among the chief heresies and was condemned with perpetual anathema'.[47]

It was as a deliverer from the 'schism of our times' that the young Henry V presented himself to Henry IV's opponents when he defected from his father's side in December 1104. He immediately associated himself with the Gregorian party in Germany and promised 'due obedience to the pontiff of the apostolic see'.[48] He did not, however, renounce investiture. His reluctance to abandon the practice became apparent only in the aftermath of his father's death on 7 August 1106, which suddenly left him as the unopposed ruler of Germany. At the Council of Guastalla in October 1106, royal envoys asked Paschal II to recognize Henry V's 'right of kingship' – lay investiture – and this demand was repeated the following year at the Council of Troyes when the king's envoys announced that 'the power of constituting bishops had

---

45 Frutolf, *Chronicle* 1085, below, pp. 124–5. See Vollrath (1991), pp. 102–11; Cowdrey (1998), pp. 235–7.
46 Robinson (1999), p. 279; Robinson (2004a), pp. 292–5.
47 *1106 Continuation* 1102, below, p. 171.
48 *Ibid.* 1105, below, p. 177.

been given to Emperor Charles [the Great] by apostolic privileges'.⁴⁹ Paschal refused and in the diplomatic words of the anonymous chronicler writing for Henry V some seven years later, the pope 'promulgated judgement according to the decrees of his predecessors on the free election of bishops and on restraining the presumptuousness of the laity in ecclesiastical matters'.⁵⁰ The question of lay investiture, which had been overshadowed by more pressing concerns during the pontificates of Gregory VII and Urban II, now became the outstanding issue that separated empire and papacy. The point is encapsulated in a letter addressed to the cardinals of the Roman church by the reformer Bishop Bruno of Segni (d. 1123):

> there was no dispute between us and them about the heresy of simony, because that heresy was equally condemned by us and by them. And the king himself wanted to give us his full assurance that neither churches nor ecclesiastical dignities would ever be sold with his counsel or consent, if only we would grant him the investiture. All who were with him, since they wished to please him, affirmed that it was most just that what his predecessors had possessed for so long a time be granted to him as well. We, in contrast, put forward the canons and the emperors' constitutions themselves in which all secular powers and all laymen, although religious, are removed from the ordination and disposition of churches.⁵¹

Owing to the extensive political power exercised by German bishops, Henry V sought to control episcopal appointments as his father had done and extorted recognition of this right from a captive Paschal II in the Treaty of Ponte Mammolo in 1111. But Paschal's subsequent denunciation of the privilege he had conceded under duress, combined with the independent activities of papal legates who excommunicated the emperor, meant that Henry V, like his father, eventually faced an alliance of his ecclesiastical and secular opponents. He recognized that there could be no peace without a compromise on the matter of lay investiture. This compromise, which paralleled settlements that the papacy had reached with the English and French kings during the early twelfth century, came with the Concordat of Worms (23 September 1122).⁵²

The texts translated in this volume offer a variety of perspectives on the

---

49 Donizo of Canossa, *Life of Matilda* 2.17, p. 400; *Anonymous imperial chronicle* 1107, below, p. 209.

50 *Anonymous imperial chronicle* 1107, below, p. 208.

51 Bruno of Segni, *Letter* 4, ed. Fransen (1972), 529–32. The translation is that of Professor W. L. North, to whom I am grateful for drawing my attention to this letter.

52 Robinson (1990), pp. 420–41, with bibliography.

conflict of empire and papacy. The earliest – and the one which ties all the others together – is the *Chronicle* by the distinguished polymath Frutolf of Michelsberg (completed at the end of the eleventh century). This work is the product of immense learning and has been characterized as an attempt 'to describe in detail and bring together in a comprehensive presentation covering the entire course of time every conceivable piece of historical information known to him'.[53] Yet it is not merely a slavish compilation; Frutolf possessed an acute and sophisticated sense of history, and was willing to select, abridge and manipulate his sources accordingly. Frutolf's *Chronicle* was continued by others a number of times between 1106 and 1125, and the authors of these continuations brought to it their own preoccupations and concerns. Whereas Frutolf was suspicious of the innovations of the Gregorian papacy and condemned rebellion against Henry IV, the clerk who continued his chronicle to 1106 was more interested in the crusading movement and the pontificate of Paschal II. The author the *Anonymous imperial chronicle* of 1113/14, on the other hand, was guided by the need to produce a dynastic history honouring Henry V and so glossed over Henry V's conflicts with the papacy. Later continuations followed the fortunes of the papacy with considerable partisanship, featuring detailed reports of papal councils and portraying the Concordat of Worms as a papal victory over secular interference in the business of the church.

Frutolf's *Chronicle* and its continuations, therefore, offer a case study on the transmission of texts and ideas in the middle ages. On the one hand they show the enduring importance of compilation based upon authoritative models: each of the texts translated here is, to a greater or lesser extent, closely modelled on earlier narrative sources. On the other hand they show how freely medieval historians could adapt their models: diverse perspectives necessitated not only the writing of history but also the rewriting of history. It is somewhat paradoxical that Frutolf's *Chronicle*, which presents a measured defence of the traditional Ottonian-Salian view of kingship in the face of Gregorian 'innovations', should have been most widely disseminated in continuations sympathetic to the papal cause. This is in large measure due to the vicissitudes of manuscript transmission – to the needs and decisions of individual scribes. Ultimately, those scribes have shaped our knowledge of the past through their mediation of the sources. As this volume shows, questions of authorship, audience and manuscript transmission had a direct bearing on the portrayal of the conflict between empire and papacy.

53 Classen (1982), p. 400.

The *Chronicle* of Frutolf of Michelsberg, 1001–1101

Life and works

What little is known of Frutolf of Michelsberg's life and career must be deduced from clues within his own works as well as from surviving references to him in contemporary sources. That he was Bavarian is suggested by the form in which he rendered German names in his chronicle.[54] Other evidence points more specifically to the monastery of St Emmeram in Regensburg. Frutolf's music treatise is indebted not only to the earlier treatises by Abbot Bern of Reichenau (d. 1048) and Herman of Reichenau (1013–54), which were disseminated in southeastern Germany primarily through St Emmeram, but also to the treatise by the St Emmeram monk William (d. 1091), who later became abbot of Hirsau.[55] St Emmeram influence is evident too in parts of Frutolf's *Chronicle*: the report on Pope Leo IX's visit to Regensburg in 1052, for example, is closely based upon St Emmeram sources.[56] The textual evidence pointing to Regensburg is complemented by palaeographical evidence, for the similarities between the handwriting of Otloh of St Emmeram (c. 1010–c. 1072) and Frutolf have prompted the suggestion that Otloh taught Frutolf.[57] Finally, Frutolf's keen interest in the *quadrivium* (the mathematical arts of geometry, arithmetic, music and astronomy) might well have originated at St Emmeram, where in the mid-eleventh century Otloh and William pioneered quadrivial studies.[58]

If Frutolf was originally a monk of St Emmeram, he must have moved to Michelsberg at some point during the eleventh century. That such a move was possible is clear from Michelsberg's history in that period. Michelsberg was founded in 1015 by Bishop Eberhard of Bamberg and the following years saw the gradual development of the new monastery.[59] It is likely that its size in these early years was relatively small: the combined evidence of the monastery's necrology and other

---

54 *Chroniken*, p. 4; Märtl (1991), p. 342.
55 McCarthy (2009), pp. 30–1.
56 *Chroniken*, pp. 4, 10; Märtl (1991), p. 342 n. 67. See below, p. 100. Frutolf's report is based upon the *Notae Sancti Emmerani*, a late medieval collection of historical notes kept at St Emmeram from the tenth century onwards. The passage in Frutolf's chronicle is the earliest surviving version of this report and was presumably derived from a St Emmeram manuscript no longer extant.
57 Hoffmann (1986), p. 440; Hoffmann (1995), p. 179.
58 Märtl (1991), p. 342.
59 See Hallinger (1950), pp. 345–53.

sources puts the total number of recorded community deaths during Michelsberg's first 100 years at a few less than ninety.[60] The fledgling monastery depended in these years on longer established monasteries for personnel, particularly Fulda and Tegernsee. The arrival of Abbot Rupert in 1066, however, ushered in a period of forty-six years during which the monastery of St Emmeram in Regensburg seems to have become the primary influence on Michelsberg. The monastery's necrology charts this realignment by showing an increase in St Emmeram personnel during the second half of the eleventh century: in addition to Rupert, Abbots Thiemo (1086–94) and Gumpold (1094–1112) were also St Emmeram monks.[61] These years of St Emmeram influence coincide with Frutolf's lifetime and have led to the suggestion that he came to Bamberg with one of these abbots.[62]

Although Frutolf's date of birth is unknown, his death on 17 January 1103 is recorded in the necrologies of Michelsberg, Tegernsee and Fulda, which contain the additional information that he had been ordained priest.[63] Two Bamberg clerics, writing soon after his death, add that he was schoolmaster and prior of Michelsberg. The first, Heimo (d. 1139), was a canon of the collegiate church of St Jakob in Bamberg and knew Frutolf personally; in his computistical treatise *De decursu temporum* he described Frutolf as 'our master of pious memory'.[64] Heimo's description implies that Frutolf was indeed a schoolmaster, since in eleventh- and twelfth-century Germany the title *magister* denoted a practising teacher.[65] The second, Burchard (d. 1147), was the librarian and prior of Michelsberg; his early twelfth-century catalogue of the monastic library identifies Frutolf as the monastery's prior.[66]

While we know little of Frutolf's life, we know a great deal about his intellectual interests from his extant works, autograph manuscripts and Burchard's library catalogue (which contains an inventory of Frutolf's books). In addition to the chronicle, Frutolf's surviving works include a

---

60 Nospickel (ed.), *Das Necrolog*, pp. 100–2.
61 *Ibid.*, pp. 301, 304.
62 Märtl (1991), p. 342; Nospickel (ed.), *Das Necrolog*, pp. 302, 383. Hoffmann (1995), p. 74 suggests between 1050 and 1060.
63 Nospickel (ed.), *Das Necrolog*, p. 193; *MGH NecG* 3, p. 138; Schmid (ed.), *Die Klostergemeinschaft von Fulda* 1, p. 234.
64 Heimo of Bamberg, *De decursu temporum* 1.4, p. 139.
65 Barrow (1989), 118–20; McCarthy (2004), 157.
66 Ruf (ed.), *MBDS* 3/3, p. 360.

learned music treatise and tonary (*Breviarium de musica* and *Tonarius*),[67] and an unedited liturgical treatise in two books (*De officiis divinis*).[68] There are also good reasons for believing that he compiled a gloss on the Old and New Testaments (*Glosa in vetus et novum testamentum*),[69] while the question of his authorship of a treatise on the mathematical game rhythmomachia has not yet been resolved.[70] Three of the manuscripts that Frutolf copied survive today: his working copies of the *Chronicle* (Jena, Thüringer Universitäts- und Landesbibliothek, Bose q. 19) and *De officiis divinis* (Bamberg, Staatsbibliothek, Msc. Lit. 134), as well as his copy of Bern of Reichenau's *Prologus in tonarium* (Karlsruhe, Badische Landesbibliothek, 504, fols 1–14). That he copied many more books is evident from Burchard's library catalogue, which includes a list of the books bequeathed to Michelsberg by Frutolf, with the added observation that Frutolf copied most of them himself:

> Below are listed the books that Frutolf of blessed memory, prior of this monastery, brought together in this place, nearly all of which he copied in his own hand: two graduals; a gloss on the Psalter; a gloss on the Old Testament; a gloss on the Apostle; a gloss on the Old and New Testaments; a chronicle book; a book that is called *Pan*; a benedictional; the music treatise of Guido [of Arezzo]; Frutolf's *Breviarium de musica*; the tonary and music treatise of Bern [of Reichenau] and the dialogue of William [of Hirsau] in one volume; Priscian on accentuation and Bede on metre in one volume; the *computus* and measurement of the astrolabe by Herman [of Reichenau] in one volume; a book of the customs of the ancient Fathers; two [sets of] examples of the first steps in prose and poetic composition; Theodolus.[71]

The combined evidence of Frutolf's surviving autograph manuscripts and Burchard's inventory suggests that Frutolf was a leading figure in the Michelsberg scriptorium during the last third of the eleventh century. Burchard's inventory also reveals the practicality of Frutolf's

---

67 Ed. Vivell, 'Frutolfi *Breviarium de musica* et *Tonarius*', *Akademie der Wissenschaften in Wien. Philosophisch-Historische Klasse. Sitzungsberichte* 188/2 (1919). A facsimile edition of the tonary is: Maloy, *München, Bayerische Staatsbibliothek, Clm 14965b: the Tonary of Frutolf of Michelsberg* (Ottawa, 2006). See also Vivell (1913), 463–84; Maloy (2002), 641–93; McCarthy (2009), pp. 97–9.

68 Bresslau (1896), 226–34; Kennedy (1938), 313–15; Hoffmann (1995), p. 148.

69 See below, pp. 18–19.

70 Frutolf, *Rhythmomachia*, ed. R. Peiper, 'Fortolfi Rhythmimachia', *Zeitschrift für Mathematik und Physik 25. Supplement zur historisch-literarischen Abtheilung des XXXV. Jahrgangs* (1880), 167–227. Frutolf's authorship has been disputed: *Chroniken*, p. 7. See, however, McCarthy (2009), p. 42. For an introduction to rhythmomachia see Moyer (2001).

71 Ruf (ed.), *MBDS* 3/3, p. 360.

books: virtually all were designed to serve the needs of monastic life. Some point to Frutolf's activities as a teacher. Priscian, Bede, the composition primers and Theodolus (presumably the *Ecloga*) were probably used by Frutolf to teach Latin grammar, the foundation of monastic education.[72] Herman of Reichenau's *Computus* and *Mensura astrolabii* were the most advanced works available on the arts of calendrical computation and astronomy (necessary for understanding the liturgical year and monastic timetable),[73] while the numerous music treatises enabled Frutolf to instruct his brothers in the correct singing of the Divine Office, perhaps the most important element of monastic life. Similarly, the two graduals (books containing the Proper chants of the Mass) and the benedictional (a book containing different forms of blessings) were connected with duties of liturgical direction, duties frequently performed by a monastery's prior.

Frutolf's own works were also conceived as practical works relevant to the monastic life. *De officiis divinis*, for example, concerns itself with the organization of a central element of monastic life – the liturgy. Meanwhile, *Breviarium de musica* covers the technical elements of Gregorian chant that the singer must understand in order to sing the liturgy flawlessly and takes as its starting point the maxim that 'music is the science of singing well through long reflexion and constant practise'.[74] It is one of a number of similar works written by the 'south-German circle of music theorists', a group of monks and clerks based in the monastic and cathedral schools of southern Germany whose learned treatises reflect their keen interest in singing the music of the Divine Office and Mass correctly.[75]

Less well known to historians is Frutolf's interest in biblical studies. Burchard of Michelsberg recorded that Frutolf possessed four works of biblical exegesis: glosses on the Psalter, the Old Testament, the 'Apostle' (by which Burchard presumably means St Paul), and the Old and New Testaments. Since Burchard specified that Frutolf copied virtually all of his own books, it is probable that these glosses were Frutolf's autographs. While Burchard was not necessarily implying that Frutolf was their author, that conclusion is suggested by a later source. The 1483 library catalogue of Michelsberg unequivocally ascribes two of the four

---

72 On Theodolus's *Eclogues* in the medieval curriculum see Green (1982), 49–106.
73 On Herman see Cordiolani (1961), 167–90; Borst (1984), 379–477; McCarthy (2009), pp. 23–30.
74 Frutolf, *Breviarium de musica* 1, 26.
75 McCarthy (2009), pp. 1–53.

glosses from Burchard's inventory to Frutolf: the gloss on the Psalter, which it describes as 'Frutolf on the first fifty [psalms], Frutolf on the second fifty, Frutolf on the third fifty' (following the tripartite division of Cassiodorus' commentary on the Psalter), and the gloss on the Old Testament, which it describes as 'Frutolf on the Old Testament'.[76] The compiler of the 1483 catalogue had no reason to ascribe these works to a monk who had died almost 400 years earlier unless the manuscripts he saw clearly identified Frutolf as their author. These two manuscripts were surely the same ones that Burchard described as being 'copied in Frutolf's own hand' and warrant the suggestion that the other two glosses might also have been Frutolf's works.

Only one of these four biblical glosses has so far been discovered: the gloss on the Old and New Testaments (*Glosa in vetus et novum testamentum*), which exists not in Frutolf's copy, but in the copy that belonged to a fellow monk named Thiemo (d. 1119), who appears to have worked closely with Frutolf in the Michelsberg scriptorium.[77] The *Glosa in vetus et novum testamentum* is a work concerned with the explanation of problematic terms in the Bible. Although this might seem an elementary concern to the modern observer, it was of vital importance to medieval clerks since the Bible confronted them with a myriad of non-classical Latin words as well as words derived from other languages. The explanations in the *Glosa* are overwhelmingly terse and factual, ranging from single words to a few lines. It and the other three collections were probably the basis of Frutolf's teaching on the text of the Bible at Michelsberg: the compiler of a similar collection clearly identified the need of his 'less educated brothers' for instruction in Scripture, since they could neither comprehend its literal meaning nor understand even its words.[78] This was also the purpose of Frutolf's biblical glosses.

The *Chronicle*

Frutolf's *Chronicle* is a vast work covering history from the creation of the world until the end of the eleventh century (Georg Waitz's nineteenth-century edition occupies some 180 folio-sized pages). Like his other works, it is practical and didactic in conception. It was not designed to function as a manual for classroom instruction, however, but to provide its reader with an accurate chronology of history. It

---

76 Ruf (ed.), *MBDS* 3/3, p. 373.

77 MS Karlsruhe, Badische Landesbibliothek, 504, fols 119v–152r. See McCarthy (2008), 29–32.

78 Morin (1896), 68.

reflected Isidore of Seville's basic definition of the word 'chronicle' as the 'succession of times' and, following the example of Bishop Eusebius of Caesarea (c. 260–339), it sought to 'pursue the truth more diligently' so that 'any ancient event worthy of memory' could be recorded 'in its proper place'.[79] Frutolf's emphasis on order paralleled the didactic nature of his other works, for his *Breviarium de musica* and *De officiis divinis* sought perfection in Gregorian chant and in the liturgy through the proper ordering of their elements. The chronicle thus functioned as a reference work and could be used by a monk to provide historical context for the works he encountered as part of the *lectio divina*.[80] But it also offered moral instruction, for it provided examples (*exempla*) of good behaviour to be imitated and evil behaviour to be avoided. It thereby satisfied the need identified by Abbot Peter the Venerable of Cluny (c. 1092–1156), who bewailed the laziness of his contemporaries in allowing to die out the 'memory of everything that is happening in their times, which could be so useful to those who come after them'.[81]

The *Chronicle* was probably Frutolf's last work. Although he must have spent many years collecting materials for it, two pieces of internal evidence indicate that he copied the final version only towards the end of his life in 1099. In the annal for AD 46 Frutolf commented that, despite the difficulties he had encountered, he had endeavoured to record the papal succession until 1099, while in the annal for 1057 he stated that 'at the time of writing this' Henry IV had ruled for forty-two years.[82] The chronicle was known to Frutolf's pupil Heimo of Bamberg, who discussed its calculation of the date of creation in his own *De decursu temporum*, as well as to the twelfth-century author of the encyclopaedic *De scriptoribus ecclesiasticis*, who recorded that Frutolf 'was most acute in music just as in the other arts' and 'wrote, among other things, a chronicle'.[83] Nevertheless, the chronicle was altered and continued a number of times during the early twelfth century, with the result that Frutolf's authorship was forgotten until the pioneering work of Harry Bresslau in 1896.[84]

---

79 Isidore, *Etymologies* 5.28; trans. Barney (2006), p. 125; Frutolf, *Chronicle, MGH SS* 6, pp. 33, 34; cf. Eusebius, *Chronicle*, pp. 8, 19.

80 *SC*, p. 8.

81 Peter the Venerable, *On miracles* (*PL* 189.0908C).

82 Frutolf, *Chronicle* 46, *MGH SS* 6, p. 100; 1057, below, p. 104. See also Schmale (1966), 81–4.

83 Heimo, *De decursu temporum* 1.4, p. 139; Wolfger of Prüfening (?), *De scriptoribus ecclesiasticis* 103, p. 91.

84 See below, p. 42; Bresslau (1896), 197–219.

INTRODUCTION

Frutolf's autograph manuscript of his chronicle still survives: today it is Jena, Thüringer Universitäts- und Landesbibliothek, Bose q. 19. This manuscript remained in Michelsberg until at least the end of the fifteenth century: a fifteenth-century *ex libris* on fol. 1r reads 'Book of the monastery of St Michael on the Mount near Bamberg' (*Codex monasterii sancti Michaelis in monte prope Babenberg*) and it is probably to be identified with the work described as the 'Chronicle of Eusebius' (*Cronicam Eusebii*) in the 1483 Michelsberg catalogue.[85] (This description derives from the fact that the beginning of the chronicle reproduces large parts of Eusebius's chronicle.) In the mid-seventeenth century the manuscript was acquired by the antiquarian Johann Andreas Bose (1626–74) and passed to the University of Jena after his death.[86] Its format suggests that it was Frutolf's working copy, written up from materials he had been collecting for some time: the leaves measure 13.5 cm x 20.5 cm, thus making it a small-format book of the type common for personal or practical use. Nevertheless, the text has been very carefully copied and contains few corrections. That it is unfinished may be concluded from the blank spaces left for the annals for 1059 and 1061–3 on fol. 177r, which were obviously intended to be filled with relevant material at a later date. The manuscript also lacks perhaps as many as 110 folios, or nearly a third of its original text. In Waitz's 1844 edition, these gaps were reconstructed by using manuscripts of the twelfth-century continuations attributed to Ekkehard of Aura, since their archetype was copied from Frutolf's original before the losses occurred. A partial copy of the chronicle survives in another, contemporary, Michelsberg manuscript: Karlsruhe, Badische Landesbibliothek, 504, fols 187r–197v. This codex is a later binding of fourteen originally separate manuscripts, many of which emanate from the circle of Frutolf of Michelsberg and his colleague Thiemo.[87] It contains the annals for 1057–99 as well as annals for 1100 and 1101 not present in the autograph copy.[88]

The structure of the *Chronicle*

Frutolf's *Chronicle* is often cited as a classic example of 'universal

---

85 Bresslau (1896), 179; *MBDS* 3/3, p. 377.
86 Kappner (1931), 85.
87 See Bresslau (1896), 226–34; Dengler-Schreiber (1979), pp. 207–9; Hoffmann (1995), p. 179; McCarthy (2008), 4–11.
88 Frutolf's authorship of the 1100 and 1101 annals has been questioned: *Chroniken*, p. 8.

history'.[89] This genre had its origins in the work of early Christian writers, who perceived in the Bible a unity of intent that amounted to a universal history of salvation. These currents were followed and developed in Eusebius of Caesarea's *Chronicle* (composed in its final version *c.* 325). Eusebius wrote in Greek, and his work might not subsequently have been so influential in the Latin West had it not been for St Jerome (d. *c.* 419), whose Latin translation and continuation of Eusebius's *Chronicle* until 378 would determine the genre of universal history for the next thousand years.[90] But Frutolf was also influenced by other genres of historical writing. Late-antique and medieval histories of individual tribes or peoples – so-called 'national histories' – provided him with material for lengthy digressions that often interrupted his chronological scheme.[91] Thus, for example, material from Jordanes's *History of the Goths* (written in early 551), Paul the Deacon's *History of the Lombards* (left unfinished upon his death at the end of the eighth century) and Widukind of Corvey's *Deeds of the Saxons* (completed in three versions between 967 and 973) formed the basis of sections devoted to these groups.[92] Simultaneously, the chronicle has an annalistic structure, whereby its material is organized as a sequence of yearly reports or 'annals'. It is thus also heir to a practice that originated in Anglo-Saxon England and which was transmitted to the continent by missionaries during the seventh and eighth centuries. Annals were originally short historical observations added in the margins of manuscripts that already had an independent chronological function, such as liturgical calendars or Easter tables.[93] Sometimes these observations migrated from the margins of their host manuscripts to become self-standing historical works of varying levels of detail. Like the chronicles of his German contemporaries Herman of Reichenau, Berthold of Reichenau (d. 1088) or Sigebert of Gembloux (d. 1112), therefore, Frutolf's chronicle is a hybrid of different types of historical writing. The geographical scope of the *Chronicle* parallels the focus of Frutolf's chronology: beginning in the ancient Near East it moves first to the Greek and Roman Mediterranean and then to the Frankish kingdoms before concluding with the German empire of Frutolf's own day. The main focus of the

---

89 See Goetz (1999), pp. 114–15; Allen (2003), pp. 17–42.
90 Jerome, *Chronicle*, ed. Helm, *Die Chronik des Hieronymus*, 2nd edn (Berlin, 1956). See Allen (2003), p. 20.
91 On 'national history' see Pohl (1994), pp. 9–26; Pizarro (2003), pp. 43–5.
92 Frutolf, *Chronicle, MGH SS* 6, pp. 119–21, 141–50, 176–83.
93 See McCormick (1975).

Years (AD)	Synopsis (*italic font indicates Frutolf's own headings*)	Pagination (*MGH*)
	Preface from Eusebius-Jerome.	33
	Beginning of the chronicle from the creation of the world.	34
	History of ancient civilizations.	
	Harmonization of various ancient chronologies with biblical chronology.	
	The foundation of the city of Rome (hereafter used as a dating constant).	50
	An excerpt from the life of Alexander the Great.	62
	Concerning the marvellous things which Alexander is said to have seen.	70
	Continuation of synchronous history.	76
	End of the First Punic War.	80
	Imperial years of Augustus – imperial years recorded hereafter.	93
1	The Incarnation, dated by a variety of means – AD dating used hereafter.	95
46	Peter becomes first pope – discussion of the institution of the papacy and its early succession.	98
47–367	Chronology resumes.	100
	Concerning the origins of the Franks.	115
367–77	Chronology resumes.	119
	The history of the Goths.	119
	Concerning the Amazons.	121
	Concerning the origins of the Huns.	123
378–565	Chronology resumes.	130
	The history of the Lombards.	141
565–768	Chronology resumes.	150
	Description of the deeds of Charles the Great.	161
769	Chronology resumes. Regnal years of Charles the Great recorded.	165
800	Imperial coronation of Charles the Great and transfer of empire from Constantinople to the West – henceforward only the imperial years of western emperors are recorded.	169
919		175
	Genealogy of the Carolingians.	176
	Concerning the origins of the Saxons.	
920	Chronology resumes.	180
1001	The reign of Henry II.	192
1024	Genealogy of the Ottonians.	194
1099	*Chronicle* ends.	

Table 1 Outline of Frutolf of Michelsberg's *Chronicle*

eleventh-century material is thus the German kingdom, supplemented with occasional reports on affairs in the two other constituent kingdoms of the empire, namely, Italy and Burgundy (Table 1).

The sources and method of the *Chronicle*

Frutolf's chronicle relies upon an impressive range of sources, both ancient and medieval. They include the historical works of Eusebius-Jerome, Sallust, Pliny, Livy, Virgil, Orosius, Jordanes, Rufinus of Aquileia, Isidore, Bede, Fredegar, Josephus and Tertullian, as well as Augustine's *City of God*, Paul the Deacon's *History of the Lombards*, *Life of St Columbanus* and *Life of Gregory the Great*, Gregory I's *Dialogues*, Einhard's *Life of Charles the Great*, Widukind of Corvey's *Deeds of the Saxons*, Liutprand of Cremona's *Antapodosis*, the *Liber pontificalis*, the so-called *Würzburg Chronicle*, and eleventh-century papal and imperial letters.[94] Frutolf consulted some of these works in Michelsberg but others he probably found in the nearby cathedral library, where he must have been a well-known visitor (see Map 2b). This much is suggested by the evidence of surviving manuscripts and by internal evidence from the chronicle. An eleventh-century cathedral manuscript, for example, was the likely source for the material he took from Jordanes' *History of the Goths*, Paul the Deacon's *History of the Lombards* and the Archpriest Leo's *Life of Alexander the Great*.[95] The textual variants of Frutolf's quotations from the letters of Henry IV and Gregory VII show that his sources were those used in the *Codex Udalrici*, the famous letter collection compiled by the cathedral schoolmaster Udalric of Bamberg c. 1125.[96] Similarly, Frutolf's praise for Meinhard of Bamberg, the cathedral *scholasticus* from the 1060s until 1085, suggests a firm bond of friendship between two clerics.[97] The picture of Frutolf that emerges is not one of a cloistered monk working in isolation, but of an active researcher scouring libraries for material and eager to discuss his ideas with friends and colleagues.

The *Chronicle*, like Frutolf's other works, illustrates the centrality of compilation to eleventh-century composition. It skilfully weaves together material from its many sources just as his *Breviarium de musica* combines material from the works of Herman of Reichenau, William

---

94 See von den Brincken (1957), p. 189.
95 Bamberg, Staatsbibliothek, Msc. Hist. 3; see Leitschuh and Fischer (1887), pp. 119–28.
96 McCarthy (2011).
97 Frutolf, *Chronicle* 1085, below, p. 124.

of Hirsau, Guido of Arezzo and others.⁹⁸ In an age when so much of scholarship was cumulative in nature, Frutolf and his contemporaries saw compilation as a necessary compositional methodology. The author of the *Anonymous imperial chronicle*, for example, had no compunction in drawing the attention of Henry V, the recipient of his chronicle, to the fact that the work was 'excerpted' and commended it to the emperor 'if only for the authority of the ancient chroniclers and not of ourselves'.⁹⁹ So too when Ekkehard of Aura dedicated his chronicle to Abbot Erkembert of Corvey, he stated plainly that 'we have hurried through and abbreviated the narrations of various chroniclers from the beginning of the world'.¹⁰⁰ A further glimpse of the process, this time in the field of biblical scholarship, is afforded in the preface to a mid-twelfth-century revision of the *Glosa in vetus et novum testamentum* by a monk named Albert: frustrated by the contradictory definitions found in different glossaries, Albert decided to compile a new collection from the many existing biblical glossaries, omitting what was superfluous and drawing upon 'St Jerome, Isidore and Bede and all other suitable books'.¹⁰¹ Compilation, therefore, was not an uncritical act: it involved careful thought on what to include and exclude and, when sources disagreed, on how to resolve those contradictions. There is no better example of these critical decisions than one of Frutolf's most famous contributions to eleventh-century historical writing – his new calculation for the creation of the world.

In Eusebius-Jerome, Frutolf found not so much a written-out chronicle, as a comparative tabular representation of the chronologies of ancient civilizations accompanied by terse records of events such as the deaths of kings or the foundations of cities. Eusebius-Jerome, however, recorded nothing of the world's creation. St Augustine (d. 430), on the other hand, took a more metaphysical approach to history and in a number of works developed the concept of the 'six ages' of history.¹⁰² This theologically inspired paradigm reckoned the first age of the world (infancy) to extend from Adam to Noah, the second (childhood) from Noah to Abraham, the third (adolescence) from Abraham to King David, the fourth (youth) from David to the exile of the Jewish people in Babylon and the fifth (maturity) from the Babylonian exile to the preaching of

98 McCarthy (2009), pp. 94–108.
99 *Anonymous imperial chronicle*, below, p. 187.
100 Ekkehard, *Chronicle*, below, p. 219.
101 Morin (1910), 118. See also McCarthy (2008), 35–43.
102 Allen (2003), p. 31.

Christ. The sixth age (old age) had begun with Christ's preaching and was to end at some unspecified point, while the seventh and final age of rest was yet to come. In the seventh century Isidore of Seville (d. 636) combined these two traditions, adding material to Eusebius-Jerome for the two pre-Abrahamic ages while simultaneously using Augustine's paradigm as an overarching structure for cosmic history.[103] Isidore's work was taken further by the Venerable Bede (d. 735), who outlined the ages of the world in a more detailed manner in chapter 66 of his treatise *De ratione temporum*.[104]

The material that Isidore added for the first two ages of history was closely based on the genealogical chapters of Genesis (5 and 11), with some interpolations drawn from other chapters of Genesis, Jerome, Augustine and the Jewish historian Flavius Josephus (AD 37–c. 100). Frutolf took this as the basis of his pre-Abrahamic chronology, but skilfully interwove it with other material. He followed Bede in rejecting the chronology of the Septuagint for that of 'Hebrew truth' (St Jerome's translation of the Hebrew Bible into Latin – the Vulgate).[105] Using both Isidore and Bede as models, Frutolf then demonstrated this by tallying the ages of the Patriarchs when their sons were born (as given in the Vulgate). He added extra detail, however, inserting from Genesis 5 the age at which each of the Patriarchs died and also extrapolating from this other relative chronological information. He ended his computation with Noah who 'at 500 years begot Shem, Ham and Japheth, 100 years before the Flood, in which years he built the ark'.[106] Frutolf concluded that 'in the ten generations from the beginning of the world to the Flood' 1,656 years had elapsed, 'as St Augustine affirms', and contrasted this solution with those of the Septuagint and Josephus.[107] Frutolf also followed Bede in rejecting the Septuagint calculation for the second age: using precisely the same methodology he calculated 292 years, thereby giving 1,948 years in total from the creation to Abraham.[108]

In his calculation of the subsequent ages of history, however, Frutolf rejected Bede's solution in favour of calculations derived from Eusebius-Jerome. For the third and fourth ages he calculated 940 and 486 years

103 Isidore, *Chronica maiora*, pp. 426–31 (*CCSL* 112, pp. 7–29).
104 Bede, *De ratione temporum* 66, pp. 463–535.
105 Frutolf, *Chronicle*, *MGH SS* 6, p. 34; Bede, *De ratione temporum* 66, p. 463.
106 Frutolf, *Chronicle*, *MGH SS* 6, p. 35.
107 *Ibid.*
108 *Ibid.*, p. 36; Bede, *De ratione temporum* 66, p. 463.

respectively instead of Bede's 942 and 473.[109] Frutolf's decision seems to have been based on his preference for the authority of Jerome when possible: for the first two ages Jerome was silent and so he gave preference to Bede's calculations, but from the third age onwards he followed Jerome even though his reckoning was based on the Septuagint.[110] The result was that Frutolf calculated that creation took place 3,962 years before the birth of Christ.[111]

Synchronous history in the *Chronicle*

Frutolf also faced the task of harmonizing divergent historical material for much of the ancient period. Although the calculation of the ages of history – for which the Old Testament was the primary source – necessarily involved Jewish chronology, beginning with the third age of history the chronologies of other peoples, as outlined in Eusebius-Jerome, also demanded Frutolf's attention. From this point until the Incarnation, Frutolf was faced with the task of writing the synchronous history of different civilizations. From Eusebius-Jerome he took over the device of parallel chronological tables, giving the reigns of the kings or emperors of different civilizations in different columns (as shown in Table 2).

As with Eusebius-Jerome the number of columns varied according to the historical presence of the various realms: in places Frutolf's tables contained up to nine parallel columns.[112] He recorded important events in the margins or, if the reports were longer, by breaking up the tables with sections of text. Some of the longer reports developed into self-contained subsections of the chronicle: such are the sections headed 'An excerpt from the life of Alexander the Great' and 'The marvellous things that Alexander is said to have seen', which Frutolf inserted into his chronology of Alexander's rule.[113] Here, as elsewhere in the chronicle, chronological history was temporarily suspended.

Frutolf's wish to establish accurate chronology was not restricted to

---

109 Frutolf, *Chronicle*, MGH SS 6, pp. 45, 54; Bede, *De ratione temporum* 66, p. 463.
110 von den Brincken (1957), p. 189.
111 Disagreeing with Herman of Reichenau, who followed Bede in giving 3,952 years: Herman, *Chronicle* 1, p. 74.
112 Frutolf, *Chronicle*, MGH SS 6, p. 48, where there are columns for Judah, Israel, Medes, Egyptians, Albans, Athenians, Spartans, Corinthians and Macedonians. See also Goetz (2002), pp. 148–50.
113 Frutolf, *Chronicle*, MGH SS 6, pp. 62–76.

Hebrews	Assyrians	Sicyonians	Egyptians	Argives	Athenians	
58	1	3	29	14	1	Cecrops, the younger brother of Erectheus, ruled for forty years as Athens' seventh king.
59	2	4	30	15	2	
60	3	5	31	16	3	
61	4	6	32	17	4	
62	5	7	33	1	5	Acrisius, the fourteenth king of the Argives, ruled for thirty-nine years.
63	6	8	34	2	6	
64	7	9	35	3	7	
65	8	10	36	4	8	
66	9	11	37	5	9	
67	10	12	38	6	10	
68	11	13	39	7	11	
69	12	14	40	8	12	
70	13	15	41	9	13	
71	14	16	42	10	14	
72	15	17	43	11	15	
73	16	18	44	12	16	
74	17	19	45	13	17	
75	18	20	46	14	18	
76	19	21	47	15	19	
77	20	22	48	16	20	

Lamperes, the twenty-third king of the Assyrians, ruled for thirty years. In these times the kingdom of the Argives, which had stood firm for 452 years, ended with the death of Acrisius. Thenceforward, since power had been transferred to Mycenae, Eurystheus the son of Sthenelus reigned after Acrisius and then Atreus, Thyestes, Agamemnon, Aegistus, Orestes, Tsiamneus, Penthilus and Cometes until the descent of the Heraclidae in Peloponnesia.

78	1	23	49	17	21
79	2	24	50	18	22
80	3	25	51	19	23

Table 2 Synchronous history in Frutolf of Michelsberg's *Chronicle*

Source: Jena, Thüringer Universitäts- und Landesbibliothek, Bose q. 19, fol. 21r

his new calculation for the date of creation and the synchronous tables of pre-Incarnation history: this preoccupation suffuses the entire chronicle. In this respect a comparison with Herman of Reichenau's chronicle is instructive. Whereas Herman began his chronicle with the Incarnation and used *anno domini* dating throughout, the Incarnation did not mean for Frutolf the abandonment of other dating systems, since *anno domini* years appear side by side with imperial and regnal years from the Incarnation to the end of the chronicle. Similarly, Frutolf scrupulously recorded indiction cycles and olympiads throughout the chronicle.[114] In effect, therefore, the entire chronicle was conceived as a set of synchronous tables that achieves chronological unity with the Incarnation.

Frutolf and imperial history

For Frutolf, arguably the most important political event of ancient history was the foundation of Rome, which he recorded with great precision as having occurred on the 'tenth kalends of May [22 April], 429 years after the destruction of Troy, exactly 3,211 years from the beginning of the world'.[115] The foundation of Rome was significant for teleological reasons, for Frutolf's conception of history was influenced not only by the 'six ages' paradigm but also by that of the 'four empires'. This idea can ultimately be traced to the Old Testament and the Prophet Daniel's apocalyptic vision of four beasts, which mapped out the course of nations leading to the kingdom of God.[116] Although early Christian writers disagreed on the identity of the empires represented by the first three beasts, they agreed that the fourth and final empire was that of Rome and that the world's continued existence was contingent upon hers.[117] Hence, Frutolf uses *ab urba condita* ('from the foundation of the City') as a dating constant until the Incarnation and thereafter uses the imperial years of Roman emperors to complement *anno domini* dating. In 639 he made an important addition by introducing a column for the Carolingians. These three synchronous systems begin each annal until the death of the Byzantine emperor Constantine VI in 797. For

---

114 Indiction: a fifteen-year fiscal cycle in imperial Rome. Olympiad: the four-year cycle between the ancient Olympic games.
115 Frutolf, *Chronicle, MGH SS* 6, p. 50.
116 Daniel 7.
117 Jerome, *Commentariorum in Danielem* 7, identified the first three as Babylon, the Medes and Persians (counted together) and Macedonia; Orosius, *Historiae* 2.1.5–6, identified them as the Assyrians, Medes and Persians (counted together), Carthage and Macedonia. See Allen (2003), pp. 25–8.

Frutolf, this brought an end to the sojourn of the Roman empire in Byzantium: three years later, with the imperial coronation of Charles the Great, the empire was translated to the west and Charles became its seventy-third emperor after Augustus. Frutolf announced the translation of empire (*translatio imperii*) by commenting that 'hitherto, from the time of Constantine the Great, the son of Helen, the Roman Empire had remained in Constantinople with Greek emperors; henceforward it was transferred through Charles to the Frankish kings, or rather, emperors'.[118]

Frutolf was equally careful to note the dynastic transition from Carolingian to Ottonian rule. Although he admitted that 'some said' Ludwig the Child (893–911) was 'the last of the Carolingians to rule among the East Franks', he maintained that 'others counted Conrad, who ruled after him, as the last ... since his father Conrad ... is reckoned to have been the brother of Ludwig'.[119] By claiming King Conrad I (911–19) as a Carolingian, Frutolf was easily able to demonstrate a direct line to the Ottonians: 'King Conrad died and on his advice and command Duke Henry of Saxony was elevated to the kingship'.[120] The ensuing genealogy of the Carolingians, neatly rendered in black and red ink on fol. 152v of Frutolf's autograph manuscript, and lengthy excerpt from Widukind's *Deeds of the Saxons* were carefully placed by Frutolf to introduce the new dynasty:

> Since the line of the Carolingians ceased in the kingdom of the Franks, the kingship was transferred to the Saxons through Henry. We have briefly drawn a genealogy of the Carolingians for memory's sake and then we have described the origins of the Saxon people, about which there are different opinions, before pressing on to the beginning of the kingdom [of the Germans].[121]

Frutolf provided a similar genealogy upon the end of the Ottonian dynasty in 1024.[122]

That the Ottonians and Salians, like the Carolingians before them, were the true successors to Roman imperial power is evident not only from Frutolf's handling of *translatio imperii* and dynastic change, but also from the way in which he carefully dated the beginning of individual

---

118 Frutolf, *Chronicle* 800, *MGH SS* 6, p. 169. Goetz (1999), pp. 209–10.
119 Frutolf, *Chronicle* 912, *MGH SS* 6, p. 175.
120 *Ibid.* 919, p. 175.
121 *Ibid.*
122 Below, p. 00. See Schmid (1994a), pp. 478–81; Schmid (1994b), 196–225.

reigns from the founding of Rome and recorded their place in the succession since Augustus. This would have important consequences for his interpretation of eleventh-century history when the authority of the eighty-seventh successor to Augustus – Henry IV of Germany – was challenged. On the one hand, the concept of a continuing Roman empire allowed Frutolf to situate the history of his own time within the greater history of God's creation, while on the other it compelled him to defend that empire's legitimate ruler. His preoccupation with empire marks his chronicle as an 'imperial chronicle' and explains the centrality of the German kings and emperors to his narrative.

The *Chronicle* 1001–1101

The annals from 1001 onwards may conveniently be divided into two sections, pre- and post-1057. The structure of the pre-1057 portion is largely determined by the so-called *Würzburg Chronicle*, a set of terse annals covering the period AD 42 to 1057 preserved today in the Michelsberg manuscript Karlsruhe, Badische Landesbibliothek, 504, fols 171r–186r.[123] The *Würzburg Chronicle* owes its title to the fact that it carefully records the succession of the bishops of Würzburg from the mid-eighth century onwards. It is based upon a concise chronicle known variously as the *Swabian universal chronicle* (*Chronicon Suevicum universale*) or the *Reichenau imperial chronicle* (*Reichenauer Kaiserchronik*), which is itself probably a revised abridgement of Herman of Reichenau's *Chronicle* by his assistant Berthold of Reichenau.[124] While it is unclear whether or not the Karlsruhe manuscript of the *Würzburg Chronicle* was the actual manuscript used by Frutolf, it is certain that the text it preserves was Frutolf's most important source for the period 1000–57.[125]

The subject matter of the *Würzburg Chronicle* consists of the military expeditions of the German rulers, episcopal successions, notable occurrences and natural calamities such as famines or earthquakes. Frutolf copied the reports closely, though not always verbatim: he frequently altered the syntax, substituted synonyms and added qualifications or extra detail in a manner closely resembling the distinctive style of

---

123 Waitz's edition of the *Würzburg Chronicle* mistakenly attributed it to Ekkehard of Aura: *Ekkehardi Chronicon Wirziburgense, MGH SS* 6, pp. 17–32.
124 Robinson (1980), 84–136; Robinson (2008), pp. 11–12, 24.
125 See Buchholz (1879); Pokorny (2001), 63–93, 451–500.

copying evident in his *Breviarium de musica*.[126] Some of his additions reflect his interest in chronology – the noting of indiction cycles and olympiads – while others commemorate special events of local significance: his elaborate eulogy for Henry II (the founder of Bamberg), his detailed report on the consecration of the abbey church at Michelsberg or an elaborate story about how Bishop Eberhard of Bamberg and the ghost of Henry II saved Bamberg from the depredations of Bishop Bruno of Augsburg, for example.[127] Perhaps the most noticeable additions were dictated by Frutolf's need to adapt his source to his own imperially centred plan: he restructured the narrative of the *Würzburg Chronicle* into blocks devoted to the respective reigns of Henry II, Conrad II, Henry III and Henry IV, marking out all but one with a heading ('The years of Henry III', for example) and beginning each with an elaborate announcement of the accession of the new ruler.[128]

The post-1057 annals ceased to derive their structure from a single source. Until the mid-1070s they contains echoes of material from Berthold of Reichenau's *Chronicle*, a parallel that has recently been explained by the suggestion that Frutolf's copy of the *Würzburg Chronicle* may have continued until *c.* 1075.[129] As no single template has been identified for the post-1075 material, it is likely that Frutolf recorded the events of his own lifetime from a mixture of memory, oral reports and documentary sources. By far the longest annals are those from 1068 to 1085, a period of great crisis in the kingship of Henry IV. Frutolf treats in detail Henry's problems in Saxony, developing clerical opposition to the king, the conflict with Gregory VII, civil war in Germany, the triumphant assertion of royal authority with the imperial coronation of 1084, the death of Gregory VII in exile in 1085 and the subsequent papal succession. These annals show that Frutolf's most important concern was the defence of royal authority: Henry IV always remained central to his narrative. Nevertheless, the conflict that marked these years also led Frutolf to investigate the themes of rebellion and papal authority, and he devoted much effort to analysing the actions of important rebels and Pope Gregory VII.

---

126 McCarthy (2009), pp. 99–101.
127 Frutolf, *Chronicle* 1001, 1021, 1025, below, pp. 85–7, 89, 91–2. On the anecdote concerning Bruno of Augsburg see Goetz (1999), pp. 164–6.
128 Frutolf, *Chronicle* 1001, 1040, 1057, below, pp. 85, 95, 104. Frutolf's autograph manuscript does not transmit such a heading for Conrad II (probably an omission on Frutolf's part).
129 I am grateful to Dr Christian Lohmer for this suggestion.

INTRODUCTION

The detail in which Frutolf focused on the key years 1076–80 is reflected in his use of documentary sources to examine the conflict between Henry and Gregory. He cited the German bishops' renunciation of Gregory VII at the Council of Worms (24 January 1076);[130] Gregory VII's letter of 1076 to the faithful in Germany justifying his excommunication of Henry in the aftermath of the Council of Worms;[131] a letter Gregory wrote to the German princes in late January 1077 explaining why he had absolved Henry IV from his excommunication at Canossa;[132] the record of Gregory's Lenten synod of 1080, in which the pope attempted to explain with the benefit of hindsight what had been decided at Canossa four years previously;[133] the decree of the Council of Brixen (24 June 1080), in which Henry and thirty imperial bishops formally deposed Gregory VII;[134] and Bishop Anselm II of Lucca's *Book against Wibert*, an excoriating attack on the antipope 'Clement III' (Archbishop Wibert of Ravenna).[135] Frutolf consulted these sources in Bamberg, which often seems to have served as a staging point for imperial diplomatic missions and thereby accumulated copies of imperial and papal propaganda in its libraries.[136] But other material relevant to these years, which cannot be traced directly, must also have originated in reports that reached Frutolf in Bamberg: his account of the riot that accompanied the coronation of Rudolf of Rheinfelden as anti-king in Mainz and Rudolf's subsequent flight from the city (1077), his vivid anecdote about Rudolf's death after the Battle of Hohenmölsen (1080), or his thorough account of the debate that took place between imperial and papal bishops at Gerstungen-Berka (January 1085).

The annals from 1086 onwards are generally less detailed than those for the period 1068–85. Nevertheless, Henry IV still features as the central character in the annals for 1086–90, which record important events such as the Battle of Pleichfeld and subsequent siege of Würzburg (1086), the surrender of the new anti-king Herman of Salm (1087),

130 Henry IV, *Letters*, pp. 65–8 (*IL*, pp. 147–50). Frutolf, *Chronicle* 1076, below, p. 113.
131 Gregory VII, *Epistolae vagantes* 14, pp. 32–41. Frutolf, *Chronicle* 1076, below, p. 115.
132 Gregory VII, *Register* 4.12, pp. 312–14; trans. Cowdrey (2002), pp. 221–2. Frutolf, *Chronicle* 1076, below, p. 114.
133 Gregory VII, *Register* 7.14a, pp. 479–87; trans. Cowdrey (2002), pp. 340–4. Frutolf, *Chronicle* 1076, below, p. 115.
134 Henry IV, *Letters*, pp. 69–73 (*IL*, pp. 157–60). Frutolf, *Chronicle* 1080, below, pp. 118–19.
135 Anselm of Lucca, *Book against Wibert*, pp. 517–28. Frutolf, *Chronicle* 1080, below, p. 119.
136 Erdmann (1936), 30–4; McCarthy (2011).

the death of Empress Bertha and Henry's second marriage (1088 and 1089), the episcopal succession to various bishoprics and the emperor's unsuccessful siege of the Thuringian fortress of Gleichen (Christmastide 1089). Even shorter and more sketchy are the annals for 1090–7, which coincide with Henry IV's third Italian expedition. During these years Frutolf resorted to reporting events such as local feuds, the death of the Hungarian king or strange astronomical portents. The reason for the brevity of these annals was that the absence of Henry IV, the central figure in his narrative, robbed him of material worth reporting. (Evidently, Bamberg's wealth of sources relating to the 1070s and 1080s was not paralleled by sources relating to the 1090s.) Once the king returned from Italy so too did the detail in Frutolf's reports: after a gap of six years, the annals for 1097–9 again report the deeds of Henry IV.

A significant exception to the brevity of Frutolf's annals in the period 1090–7 is his report on the gathering of the First Crusade, which is one of the earliest and most valuable narrative accounts of the armed pilgrimage of 1096. Frutolf recorded the fervour that gripped people in the aftermath of Pope Urban II's speech at Clermont in 1095. He recalls how 'innumerable armed troops of kings, nobles and even common people of both sexes began to travel towards Jerusalem, passionately stirred up by repeated reports about the oppression of the Lord's Sepulchre'. He seems, however, to have cast a not-altogether-approving eye on the popular enthusiasm, observing that 'the majority set off hurriedly in different groups with different and unreliable leadership'. He reports the disastrous fate of the 'great multitude of both [sexes] ... seduced' by Count Emico of Flonheim and, with some ambivalence like other monastic chroniclers, the pogroms perpetrated by those led by the priest Gottschalk.[137] His interest in the fate of Jewish communities in German cities extended into subsequent annals, for he recorded that at Regensburg in 1097 the emperor 'allowed the Jews who had been coerced into baptism the use of their own laws' and held an investigation at Mainz the following year concerning the theft of Jewish assets.[138]

The reprehensible leadership and activities of the so-called 'People's Crusade' Frutolf contrasted with the contingent led by Duke Godfrey of Lotharingia, 'a man of most illustrious origin ... fortified with no little faith'. Frutolf took his lengthy report on the success of the First Crusade directly from the letter in which Archbishop Daimbert of Pisa,

---

137 Frutolf, *Chronicle* 1096, below, p. 130–1. Cf. the interpolation in Bernold of St Blasien's *Chronicle* 1096: *SC*, p. 331.

138 Frutolf, *Chronicle*, 1097, 1098, below, pp. 131, 132.

Duke Godfrey of Lower Lotharingia and Count Raymond of Toulouse announced to the 'lord pope of the Roman church, all bishops and the entirety of the Christian faithful' the success of the First Crusade.[139] This letter was written at the Syrian port of Laodicea in September 1099 and, as the author of the *1106 Continuation* informs us, was brought to Bamberg by Count Robert of Flanders on his return from the crusade.[140]

Frutolf and royal authority

In assessing Frutolf's attitude towards royal authority, the historian should not neglect the influence of Bamberg itself. This much is clear from the keen interest Frutolf showed in Henry II's foundation of the city. So important were Bamberg's imperial origins to Frutolf that he portrayed Michelsberg's foundation as an integral part of Henry II's plan, even though it had in reality been founded independently by Bishop Eberhard of Bamberg.[141] Frutolf seems, therefore, to have taken great pride in the imperial pedigree of his surroundings and this, when combined with the importance of a continuing Roman empire to his historical world-view, made for a chronicler who upheld the traditional rights of the German kings and emperors.

Frutolf's notion of kingship is rooted in Ottonian-Salian theories of the king as 'vicar of Christ' (*vicarius Christi*), 'a divinely ordained ruler, necessary to the good order of Christian society'.[142] In the words of the Mainz coronation *ordo* of c. 960, this king shared in the ministry of the bishops who consecrated him and defended the church against its external enemies.[143] The chronicle contains many *exempla* of kings ordering Christian society for the better, from Henry II restoring 'what had hitherto been dilapidated' and adding 'to whatever was less than sufficient' throughout his kingdom, to Henry IV ordering the affairs of the imperial church at Mainz in May 1085.[144] In a period that witnessed frequent challenges – actual and ideological – to royal authority, Frutolf never questioned the legitimacy of Henry IV's rule. Whereas the Gregorian polemicist Manegold of Lautenbach would advance a contractual theory of kingship (whereby a king who oppressed his

---

139 Ed. Hagenmeyer, *Die Kreuzungsbriefe*, pp. 167–74. Frutolf, *Chronicle* 1098, below, pp. 133–6.

140 *1106 Continuation* 1099, below, p. 154.

141 On the foundation of Michelsberg see Hallinger (1950), pp. 345–53.

142 Kost (1962), pp. 43–54; Robinson (1978a), pp. 70–5; Robinson (1999), pp. 13–14.

143 Coronation prayer, *Roman-German Pontifical* 1, p. 257. See Nelson (1988), p. 243.

144 Frutolf, *Chronicle* 1001, 1085, below, pp. 86, 123–4.

subjects forfeited his office),[145] Frutolf maintained that kingship was inviolable, even in circumstances where its effectiveness was doubtful. Hence his portrayal of Henry IV's mother and regent, the Empress Agnes, as a virtuous woman who 'ruled wisely and vigorously' until she was thwarted by the jealousy of the princes.[146] Frutolf's favourable assessment of Agnes contrasts sharply with that of many of his contemporaries. According to the south-German chronicler Berthold of Reichenau, for example, her favouritism towards Bishop Henry of Augsburg 'greatly displeased some of the princes of the kingdom, who would not tolerate his arrogance'.[147] The anonymous annalist of Niederaltaich blamed Agnes for precipitating the schism of 1061–2, misogynistically commenting that, 'as is often the case with women', she 'was easily swayed by advice from all sorts of people'.[148]

Respect for kingship also explains why Frutolf records Henry IV's political miscalculations but at the same time refuses to condone rebellion. Frutolf's critique of the king's oppression of the Saxons mirrors the allegations of Henry's Saxon opponents of the 1070s.[149] Nevertheless, rebels such as Margrave Dedi I of the Lower Lausitz, who revolted in 1069 in support of territorial claims in east Saxony, were 'quickly checked by divine and earthly majesty'.[150] A similar pattern is evident in the account of Otto of Northeim's downfall in 1070: Frutolf emphasized that Otto – 'a man of the highest nobility who had few equals in prudence and in matters of war' – was deprived of the duchy of Bavaria not because he was guilty of the unjust treason charges brought against him, but because he was guilty of contumacy. For Frutolf, therefore, rebellion was a form of tyranny against the 'Roman empire' and the king dealt with Otto 'as with a true enemy of the commonwealth (*res publica*)'.[151]

Frutolf illustrates the futility of rebellion most effectively with a carefully constructed portrait of Rudolf of Rheinfelden (d. 1080), the deposed duke of Swabia who was elected anti-king by a group of princes opposed to Henry IV at Forchheim on 14 March 1077. Frutolf perceived

145 Manegold of Lautenbach, *Liber ad Gebhardum*, pp. 308–430.
146 Frutolf, *Chronicle* 1056, below, p. 104.
147 Berthold, *Chronicle* 1058 (first version), p. 185 (*SC*, p. 102).
148 *Annals of Niederaltaich* 1060, p. 56. See also the hostile accounts of Lampert of Hersfeld, *Annals* 1062, 1064, pp. 79, 92. Robinson (1999), pp. 28–43; Weinfurter (1999), pp. 112–19.
149 Frutolf, *Chronicle* 1068, below, p. 108.
150 *Ibid.* 1070, below, p. 109.
151 *Ibid.* 1071, 1072, below, p. 109, 110.

the granting of Swabia to Rudolf in 1057 as a decisive moment in the history of resistance to Henry IV because it was 'an important source of the confusion through which the kingdom was disturbed'. Simultaneously, Rudolf was betrothed to Henry IV's sister Matilda; Frutolf construed this as a sinister development and – probably repeating royal propaganda intended to discredit Rudolf – suggested that Rudolf had effectively kidnapped Matilda in order to gain Swabia.[152] His claim about Rudolf's nefarious acquisition of the duchy stands in sharp contrast to the analysis offered by the anti-Henrician historian Lampert of Hersfeld, who saw the marriage as a means by which a powerful lord 'might be the more completely won over and be all the more faithful to the realm in those dangerous times'.[153] Frutolf's anecdote is best read side by side with his claim that Rudolf was 'completely unconnected with the royal lineage'.[154] This was intended to demonstrate the absurdity of Rudolf's election as anti-king, since royal lineage was an important consideration in determining suitability for German kingship. Rudolf's unsuitability manifested itself in events, for his coronation at Mainz sparked a riot in which the anti-king and 'all who had come with him were driven out'.[155] (Conversely, the Gregorian chronicler Berthold of Reichenau emphasized Rudolf's suitability for kingship by presenting this riot as a miraculous victory for the anti-king.[156]) Royal lineage was also the qualification that Rudolf's successor as anti-king, Count Herman of Salm, lacked: 'although in his own parts ... no one could equal him in martial prowess or in wealth, once he assumed the name of king his own people as well as outsiders soon began to despise him'.[157]

Rudolf 'to his own damnation, turned against the empire and sought to kill or depose his lord the king; but the success he had in this plan is not even hidden from peasants'. With these wry words, which conclude the annal for 1057, Frutolf skilfully presaged Rudolf's death from wounds received at the Battle of Hohenmölsen in 1080. A similar interpretation of Rudolf's treachery was put forward c. 1094/5 by Bishop Walram of Naumburg, who pointed out to Count Ludwig of Thuringia that 'assur-

---

152 *Ibid.* 1057, p. 105. See Maurer (1978), pp. 21–2; Schmid (1988), p. 190; Black-Veldtrup (1995), pp. 78, 108–9; Robinson (1999), pp. 33–4.
153 Lampert, *Annals* 1057, p. 73.
154 Frutolf, *Chronicle* 1077, below, p. 115. Contrary to Frutolf's claim, Rudolf was a kinsman of the Salians: Hlawitschka (1991), pp. 175–220.
155 Frutolf, *Chronicle* 1077, below, p. 116.
156 Berthold, *Chronicle* 1077, p. 269 (*SC*, p. 168).
157 Frutolf, *Chronicle* 1082, below, p. 121.

edly the beginning must have been evil when it was followed by so bad an end'.[158] In particular it was the loss of Rudolf's right hand – the hand with which he had sworn fealty to Henry IV – that proclaimed to Frutolf and others the futility of rebellion. The anonymous biographer of Henry IV, writing after 1106, claimed that it was 'a demonstration of the most just punishment for perjury', while the clerical authors of Henry IV's letters cited the fact that 'the Lord has destroyed our vassal, the perjurer' as proof that God had ordained Henry king.[159] Frutolf's account of Rudolf of Rheinfelden thus repeats the main themes of royal polemic against the anti-king. It may usefully be contrasted with the efforts of Gregorian commentators to explain the theodicean problem of Rudolf's death by portraying him as a martyr: Bernold of St Blasien, for example, saw Rudolf not as a perjured traitor but as 'another Maccabeus' who 'deserved to fall in the service of St Peter'.[160]

Frutolf and the papacy

Frutolf used the arrival of St Peter in Rome, which he dated to AD 46, as a convenient opportunity to embark upon a lengthy discussion of the papal succession.[161] This excursus offers a revealing glimpse of Frutolf the historian attempting to reconcile contradictory historical traditions in an effort to provide an accurate account of papal succession until the end of the eleventh century. Nevertheless, although Frutolf was – like Herman of Reichenau before him – fascinated by the papal succession, for most of the eleventh century he showed no special interest in papal history.[162] When he did, his reports tended to note events of local significance – the Bamberg visits of Popes Benedict VIII in 1020 and Leo IX in 1052, for example. This seeming contradiction is in keeping with the traditional practice of German chroniclers, who were – by and large – far more interested in the deeds of the king and emperor or in the careers of native churchmen than in the far-off bishop of Rome.[163] Hence, Frutolf devotes much more attention to the careers of Archbishops Anno of Cologne (d. 1075) or Siegfried of Mainz (d. 1084) than he does to most popes. In this respect his *Chronicle* differs strikingly from the chronicles

---

158 Walram of Naumberg, *Letter*, p. 287. See Robinson (1978a), pp. 93–5.
159 *Life of Henry IV* 4, p. 19 (*IL*, p. 111); Henry IV, *Letter* 17, p. 25 (*IL*, p. 164).
160 Bernold, *Chronicle* 1080, p. 426 (*SC*, p. 266).
161 Frutolf, *Chronicle* 46, *MGH SS* 6, pp. 99–100.
162 On Herman see *SC*, p. 8.
163 See McCarthy (2011).

by his contemporaries Berthold of Reichenau, Bernold of St Blasien and Hugh of Flavigny.[164] These monks, uncompromising champions of Gregory VII, redefined the traditional imperially-oriented chronicle by making the pope and not the emperor the focal point of their works.

From 1073 onwards, however, Frutolf was forced to address the papacy in more detail because of the escalating conflict between Gregory VII and Henry IV. Thus Gregory VII appears more frequently than any other eleventh-century pope, although that greater frequency does not translate into the reverential treatment accorded him by Gregorian writers.[165] Whereas Frutolf describes Gregory's predecessor Alexander II as a man of 'blessed memory' and successor Victor III as 'a true servant of God', he remembered Gregory as the pope who endangered 'the Roman commonwealth and the whole church ... through new and unheard-of errors'.[166] Frutolf's opinion of Gregory was partially coloured by the complaints of German bishops who resented the pope's sometimes high-handed interventions in the affairs of the imperial church. In a well-known letter of 1075 addressed to Bishop Hezilo of Hildesheim, Archbishop Liemar of Bremen described Gregory as a 'dangerous man' who wished 'to order bishops about as if they were his bailiffs'.[167] (Liemar was in fact articulating the clash between Gregory's ecclesiology of papal primacy and his own Gelasian ecclesiology, which saw the church as a fraternity of bishops.) Papal respect for episcopal rights is the theme of the lengthy *exemplum* in the annal for 1053 in which Frutolf pointed to the model behaviour of Leo IX, who deferred 'to the metropolitan in his own diocese'; the object of this *exemplum* must surely have been Gregory VII.[168] Other important influences were the decrees issued at the Councils of Worms (24 January 1076) and Brixen (25 June 1080). The first, a letter in which twenty-six imperial bishops withdrew their obedience from 'brother Hildebrand', painted Gregory as a 'standard-bearer of schism ... eager for profane innovations'[169] – a probable reference to Gregory's 'new counsels', which entailed not only

---

164 On Berthold and Bernold see *SC*, pp. 20–57; on Hugh see Healy (2006).

165 *SC*, pp. 33–6, 52–6. See also Bonizo, *To a friend*; Paul of Bernried, *The life of Pope Gregory VII*, trans. Robinson (2004b), pp. 158–261, 262–364.

166 Frutolf, *Chronicle* 1074, 1085, below, pp. 112, 126. Negating the suggestion of Stoclet (1984), 200–9.

167 Liemar of Bremen, *Letter*, p. 34. Robinson (1978b), 103–31.

168 Frutolf, *Chronicle* 1053, below, p. 101. McCarthy (2011).

169 Henry IV, *Letters* (Appendix A), pp. 65–8. On the Council of Worms see Cowdrey (1998), pp. 135–8; Robinson (1999), pp. 143–6.

the rejection of the sacraments of unchaste or simoniac priests, but the debarring of 'such men from serving at the holy mysteries, even by force if necessary'.[170] The decree of the Council of Brixen amplified many of these complaints and claimed that on the death of Alexander II 'this oft-mentioned plague bearer [Gregory] ... occupied the Lateran Palace with warlike hostility', thereby ignoring the provisions of the Papal Election Decree of 1059, which granted the imperial court the right of approving the pope elect.[171] For Frutolf, Gregory's accession was tainted by electoral irregularity, as were the elections of the unfortunate Victor III and his successor Urban II; they were made pope by Gregory's Norman allies, Matilda of Tuscany and 'all those of this sort emulating that sect'.[172]

Like others in Germany, therefore, Frutolf's objections were not to church reform but to Gregory's unorthodox methods of implementing it.[173] Indeed, at no point does Frutolf identify Gregory as a 'reformer' – the conflict of empire and papacy remained for him a conflict of authority. Nevertheless, he maintained a certain even-handedness in his treatment of Gregory. He acknowledged that among Gregory's supporters were churchmen of irreproachable character and holiness: one such person was the distinguished canonist Bishop Anselm II of Lucca, whose *Book against Wibert* Frutolf cited to counterbalance the accusations levelled at Gregory in the decree of the Council of Brixen.[174] Similarly, Frutolf's examination of papal letters led him to exonerate Gregory from complicity in the election of Rudolf of Rheinfelden as anti-king at Forchheim in 1077.[175] While Frutolf saw that Gregory VII was a polarizing figure, he also seems to have concluded that the pope was not solely responsible for the conflicts of Henry IV's reign. Gregory had become involved in an already volatile situation in Germany and, as the annals for 1057 to 1101 show, Frutolf also blamed German churchmen and princes for the breakdown of political order.

Whereas some medieval chroniclers wrote on a year-by-year basis, Frutolf constructed his account of the eleventh century in 1099/1100.

170 Gregory VII, *Register* 2.45, p. 184.
171 Henry IV, *Letters* (Appendix C), p. 71. On royal rights in the Papal Election Decree see Peter Damian, *Letter* 88, *MGH Briefe* 4/2, p. 526; trans. Blum 3 (1992), p. 319. See also Hägermann (1970), 161; Robinson (1999), p. 39.
172 Frutolf, *Chronicle* 1085, below, p. 126.
173 See Robinson (2004a), pp. 281–4.
174 Frutolf, *Chronicle* 1080, below, p. 119.
175 *Ibid.* 1076, below, p. 115.

INTRODUCTION

This temporal perspective afforded him the opportunity to look back with hindsight on the conflicts of the previous fifty years and to develop his interest in historical causation. Accordingly, the last fifty years of his *Chronicle* represent an attempt to answer a question that bewildered many of his contemporaries: what was the reason for the conflict that had endangered the unity of the *res publica*? His answer to that question differs considerably from the answers provided by Gregorian partisans like Berthold of Reichenau or Bernold of St Blasien. On countless matters of detail and interpretation his chronicle and theirs offer contradictory perspectives, providing the student of the period with a useful guide to the claims and preoccupations of each side.

The continuations of Frutolf's *Chronicle*

Frutolf's *Chronicle* was continued a number of times during the first quarter of the twelfth century. The key to understanding these continuations is Frutolf's autograph manuscript – Jena, Thüringer Universitäts- und Landesbibliothek, Bose q. 19. Around 1105/6 someone at Michelsberg continued Frutolf's autograph of his *Chronicle* to the beginning of 1106. This new composite text – Frutolf's original plus the continuation to 1106 – provided the basis for a chronicle of 1113/14 dedicated to Henry V, as well as for further continuations to 1125.

The existence of multiple continuations of the *Chronicle* obscured Frutolf's authorship of his own work: from the middle of the twelfth century until the end of the nineteenth not only the various continuations, but also the original *Chronicle* itself, were attributed to Abbot Ekkehard of Aura (d. 1126). In his 1844 edition for the *Monumenta Germaniae Historica*, Georg Waitz perpetuated this misattribution by editing the *Chronicle* and its continuations as works of Ekkehard. Waitz classified the manuscripts known to him into six distinct groups – A, B, B*, C, D and E – which, he argued, represented six different versions of the chronicle produced by Ekkehard at various points during his career.[176] In Waitz's scheme A was the partial copy of 'Ekkehard's' *Chronicle* in the Michelsberg manuscript Karlsruhe, Badische Landesbibliothek, 504;[177] B was the full text transmitted in the Jena manuscript, which Waitz mistakenly believed to be Ekkehard's autograph;[178] the

---

176 Waitz, *MGH SS* 6, pp. 4–16.
177 See above, p. 21.
178 *Ibid.*

related B* comprised a group of ten manuscripts that continued the B text to 1125; C was a much abridged version of the *Chronicle* beginning with the origins of the Franks and ending in 1114; D and E were very similar but yet distinct versions of the *Chronicle*, which continued to 1125 like B* but which also made various alterations to the earlier part of the text.

Waitz's analysis of the manuscript tradition of what he believed to be Ekkehard's chronicle produced a highly complex structure that was not entirely harmonious in all its parts. The first challenge came in 1896 when Harry Bresslau brilliantly identified Frutolf of Michelsberg as the author of a chronicle and the Jena manuscript as Frutolf's autograph of that chronicle.[179] Bresslau turned Waitz's analysis of the Jena manuscript on its head by showing that the pre-1099 material was Frutolf's and arguing that only the post-1099 material was by Ekkehard. A more wide-ranging reassessment of Waitz's conclusions came in a series of studies from 1956 to 1971 by Irene Schmale-Ott and Franz-Josef Schmale.[180] Their work re-classified the continuations of Frutolf's *Chronicle* into four distinct recensions, which they attributed to Ekkehard of Aura, plus an anonymous *Kaiserchronik*, which they attributed to a different author:

- Recension 1. Schmale and Schmale-Ott designated the minor revisions to Frutolf's autograph and its continuation to early 1106 as Recension 1. They argued that this continuation was Ekkehard's first historical work, copied in his own hand and that Ekkehard composed it *c.* 1106, when he was a monk of Michelsberg. The last datable event in this version is the election of Henry V as king at Mainz on 5 January 1106 and the formation of a high-powered legation of princes and bishops to go to Rome 'to consult wisely on all things for the benefit of the church'.[181] The continuation was finished, they suggested, because of circumstances: namely that Ekkehard himself took part in that embassy.[182]
- Recension 2 is no longer extant. Nevertheless, Schmale and Schmale-Ott were confident it once existed because of the survival of a letter of dedication to Henry V in a later continuation (see Recension 3 below). The beginning of this letter unequivocally identifies the sender as Ekkehard.[183] According to Schmale and Schmale-Ott, the letter originally prefaced a version of the chronicle presented to Henry V at the beginning of his

179 Bresslau (1896), 197–219.
180 Schmale-Ott (1956), Schmale-Ott (1971), Schmale (1971).
181 *1106 Continuation* 1106, below, p. 186.
182 *Chroniken*, p. 33.
183 See below, p. 220.

reign. This version, putatively dated to late 1106, would essentially have comprised the text of Frutolf's *Chronicle* and the *1106 Continuation*.[184]
- Recension 3. Unlike Waitz, Schmale and Schmale-Ott believed that there were no significant differences between the manuscripts of D and E. They grouped them together and called them Recension 3. This version owed its existence to Abbot Erkembert of Corvey, who asked Ekkehard for a chronicle in preparation for a pilgrimage to Jerusalem, which he undertook along with many others from Saxony in 1117.[185] Schmale and Schmale-Ott believed that Recension 3 was compiled in 1116/17 from Ekkehard's earlier reworkings of Frutolf's *Chronicle* and, for the period after 1106, from the *Kaiserchronik*.[186]
- Recension 4 – the equivalent of Waitz's B* – was Ekkehard's final continuation of Frutolf's *Chronicle*, which extended the text until 1125. This recension appeared to Schmale and Schmale-Ott to be an amalgamation of Ekkehard's earlier continuations and the *Kaiserchronik*.[187]
- The *Kaiserchronik*. Schmale and Schmale-Ott were sceptical of the claim that Ekkehard was responsible for Waitz's C recension.[188] Noting the very different political attitudes of its author and Ekkehard – he was pro-imperial while Ekkehard was pro-papal – they concluded that C could not have been written by Ekkehard. Schmale-Ott christened it the *Kaiserchronik* ('imperial chronicle') and although she initially believed it to have originated in Würzburg, she eventually identified it as a work written in the circle of Bishop Otto of Bamberg.[189]

Schmale and Schmale-Ott concluded, therefore, that Ekkehard of Aura was responsible for all the continuations of Frutolf's *Chronicle* except the *Kaiserchronik*. Their research formed the basis of an interim edition, which presented a newly edited Latin text of Frutolf's *Chronicle* for the years 1001–1101, followed by selections from the four recensions they attributed to Ekkehard and part of the *Kaiserchronik* for the years 1095–1125.[190] For historical and textual reasons, however, the present translator doubts whether Ekkehard was responsible for all the continuations attributed to him by Schmale and Schmale-Ott. While the present introduction cannot hope to provide a detailed critique of their theory or offer a full alternative in its place, it will discuss outstanding problems as they arise in relation to the individual continuations. At the very least, the doubts raised here should encourage readers to think

184 *Chroniken*, p. 34.
185 *Annals of Hildesheim* 1117, p. 64.
186 *Chroniken*, pp. 34–6.
187 *Ibid.*, pp. 36–7.
188 Meyer von Knonau (1907), p. 7 n. 1; Wattenbach and Holtzmann (1948), p. 502 n. 208.
189 Schmale-Ott (1956), 379–87; Schmale-Ott (1971), 449–57.
190 See below, p. 82

about the material factors that influence medieval historical writing, since our understanding of the continuations hinges upon questions of authorship and textual transmission.[191]

This translation refers to Recension 1 as the *1106 Continuation* and tentatively suggests – based upon content and palaeographical evidence – that its author was also the author of what the 1972 edition called the *Kaiserchronik* and this translation calls the *Anonymous imperial chronicle*.[192] As there are good reasons to believe that Ekkehard's letter to Henry V was the prologue to Book 5 of his *Chronicle* for Erkembert of Corvey rather than the dedicatory letter to a now-lost 'Recension 2', it has been placed accordingly.[193] Recension 3 of the 1972 edition is the only work that can be attributed to Ekkehard with confidence: the portion translated here is entitled Book 5 of Ekkehard's *Chronicle*. Finally, this translation refers to Recension 4 as the *1125 Continuation*; its author may well have been Ekkehard, though this has not yet been established with certainty.[194]

The *1106 Continuation*, 1096–1106

Probably in 1106 or shortly thereafter someone at Michelsberg – usually identified as Ekkehard of Aura – took up the autograph manuscript of Frutolf's chronicle and continued it to January 1106. The continuator had a different background from Frutolf. He had taken part in the crusade of 1101 and on his return to Germany via Italy had seen and heard Pope Paschal II solemnly pronounce the sentence of excommunication against Henry IV in the Lateran basilica on Maundy Thursday 1102 (3 April).[195] His experience of hearing and seeing Paschal II in Rome must have confirmed and strengthened his regard for the reform papacy, for he expressed opinions that differed from those of Frutolf: he was more critical of Henry IV and showed a keen interest in the reforming measures and councils of Paschal II. The *1106 Continuation*, therefore, is dominated by its author's concern with the crusading movement and the reform papacy. Unlike Frutolf, he had no particular interest

---

191 I intend to pursue a full study of the continuations in the future.
192 See below, pp. 48, 54–5, 57–8.
193 See below, pp. 68–9.
194 See below, p. 74.
195 *1106 Continuation* 1102, below, pp. 171–2.

in chronology and dispensed with the regnal years, imperial years, indiction cycles, olympiads and other dating systems that punctuate Frutolf's *Chronicle*. The annals are dated only by *anno domini* and are much longer than Frutolf's, suggesting that the continuator saw his continuation as a strictly contemporary account of political events.

Before extending Frutolf's *Chronicle* the continuator made various changes to its final annals. In the annals for 1096 and 1097 he underlined a few phrases (possibly signalling an intention to delete) and occasionally supplied alternative wordings between the lines. His greatest intervention, however, was in the annal for 1098. As Frutolf had written it, this annal contained an extended quotation from the letter sent by Archbishop Daimbert of Pisa, Duke Godfrey of Lower Lotharingia and Count Raymond of Toulouse to the pope in September 1099, which recounted the progress of the crusade from its arrival in Asia Minor (1097) until the capture of Jerusalem (15 July 1099) and the subsequent Battle of Ascalon (12 August 1099).[196] Frutolf's use of this letter in the 1098 annal pre-empted the actual end of the crusade in 1099, a chronological disjunction that seems to have upset the continuator. On fol. 184r of Frutolf's autograph he began drawing a line through the text and then, beginning on fol. 184v, scraped clean (erased) the subsequent folios in order to write his own version of events. The result was a greatly shortened annal for 1098. These changes were probably the result of the continuator's greater knowledge of the crusading movement, for he reused portions from the crusading princes' letter in what must have seemed to him a more appropriate place – the annal for 1099.[197]

Other changes reflect the continuator's interests in the reform papacy and in opposition to Henry IV. In erasing and rewriting the annal for 1099, he excised Frutolf's report about the imperial council in Bamberg at which Henry IV proclaimed the Peace of God and replaced it with an effusive defence of the emperor's son Conrad (1074–1101), who in 1093 had rebelled against his father and made common cause with the Gregorian party in Italy.[198] The reason for the continuator's eulogy was the disinheriting of Conrad as a result of the coronation of his younger brother Henry at Aachen at Epiphany 1099. While in reality Conrad's rebellion probably owed more to political calculation than to reforming sympathies, he was hailed as the champion of the reform papacy by its

---

196 Ed. Hagenmeyer, *Die Kreuzungsbriefe*, pp. 167–74; see above, p. 35, below, pp. 133–6.
197 *1106 Continuation* 1099, below, pp. 154–8.
198 Frutolf, *Chronicle* 1099, below, pp. 136–7; *1106 Continuation* 1099, below, pp. 141–2.

supporters.[199] For the continuator he possessed the essential qualities of a righteous king: he was 'a thoroughly catholic man who was most obedient to the apostolic see'.[200] In a similar fashion, whereas Frutolf tersely noted the death of Pope Urban II and remained ambivalent towards the succession of Paschal II (since, as he commented, Clement III was still alive), the continuator added an obituary for Urban and was careful to emphasize that Paschal's succession was not only unanimous but was 'additionally indicated by other revelations'.[201]

The identity of the continuator

Since the nineteenth century the continuator of the Jena manuscript has been identified as Abbot Ekkehard of Aura. The most detailed treatment of this subject is provided by the studies of Franz-Josef Schmale and Irene Schmale-Ott, who argued that the *1106 Continuation*, which they called Recension 1, was the first of four continuations of Frutolf's *Chronicle* undertaken by Ekkehard.[202] Their studies also resulted in the following biography. Ekkehard, born c. 1080, was a member of the Bavarian nobility (his lengthy digression on the family history of the Aribones suggested to Schmale and Schmale-Ott that he might have been a kinsman of that powerful Bavarian dynasty).[203] He went on crusade – not the victorious First Crusade but the disastrous follow-up crusade of 1101, in which he was a member of the contingent under the command of Duke Welf IV of Bavaria. Although that crusade was a failure, Ekkehard managed to reach Jerusalem by early autumn 1101. He did not remain there long; on 24 September 1101 he embarked upon the voyage home and reached Rome during Holy Week 1102 (30 March–5 April). From Rome, Ekkehard returned to Germany and about 1102/3 was a monk at the Bavarian monastery of Tegernsee. Probably about 1105/6, he moved to the monastery of Michelsberg in Bamberg, where he seems to have come into contact with two figures who would be instrumental in his subsequent career: the young Henry V and Bishop Otto of Bamberg. Ekkehard approved of Henry V for championing church freedom and for opposing Henry IV, while his friendship with the saintly – and powerful – Otto would last

---

199 Robinson (1999), pp. 286–8.
200 *1106 Continuation* 1099, below, p. 141.
201 *Ibid.*, below, p. 159.
202 Schmale-Ott (1971), 403–11; *Chroniken*, pp. 22–31; Schmale (1980), cols 443–7; Schmale (1986), cols 1765–6.
203 Schmale-Ott (1971), 405. *1106 Continuation* 1104, below, pp. 175–6.

until his death. Ekkehard, therefore, was something of a well-connected man of affairs who in 1106 twice accompanied Bishop Otto on diplomatic missions to Italy. In 1108 Bishop Otto founded a new monastery, dedicated to St Laurence, on his personal estates at Aura in the diocese of Würzburg and made Ekkehard its first abbot. The monastery was part of the Hirsau network of reform monasteries, but it took until 1113 for it to be completed and settled with monks from Hirsau.[204] Ekkehard's whereabouts during these five years are uncertain. He seems, however, to have spent time in Würzburg, for he wrote a *Life of St Burchard* which he dedicated to the abbot of St Burchard in Würzburg in thanks for the hospitality he had frequently been shown there.[205] Ekkehard's death on 20 February in some following year – usually reckoned as 1126 – is recorded in the necrologies of Michelsberg, Tegernsee and Lambach.[206] This biography of Ekkehard has superseded the older work of Georg Waitz who, relying heavily on the *Annales Hirsaugienses* by the early modern Benedictine abbot and historian Johannes Trithemius (1462–1516), believed that Ekkehard had himself been a monk of Hirsau before going on crusade.[207] (The *Annales Hirsaugienses* make additional claims rejected by Waitz, including the claim that Ekkehard began his career as schoolmaster of the cathedral at Worms.[208])

Schmale and Schmale-Ott's theories about Ekkehard and his involvement with Frutolf's *Chronicle* are not unproblematic. Their conclusion that Ekkehard produced four continuations encouraged the assumption that those continuations were consistently pro-Gregorian in their sympathies. There is, however, nothing in the Jena manuscript to identify Ekkehard as the author of the *1106 Continuation* and, as this translation suggests, there are important differences of outlook between it and later continuations.[209] Problematic, too, is the claim that Ekkehard was at Michelsberg, which plausibly allowed him to be the author of the *1106 Continuation*. Evidence for that claim might be adduced from the monastery's necrology, which records the death of 'Ekkehard, abbot of St Laurence in Aura, full brother'.[210] Nevertheless, this entry does

204 On Otto and the Hirsau reform see Jakobs (1961), pp. 140–5.
205 *Vita posterior sancti Burchardi*, pp. 50–2.
206 Michelsberg: Nospickel (ed.), *Das Necrolog*, p. 204; Tegernsee: *MGH NecG* 3, p. 140; Lambach: *MGH NecG* 4, p. 410.
207 G. Waitz, *MGH SS* 6, pp. 1–4.
208 Johannes Trithemius, *Annales Hirsaugiensis* 1 (St Gallen, 1690), p. 344.
209 See below, pp. 54–5.
210 Nospickel (ed.), *Das Necrolog*, p. 204.

not definitively prove Ekkehard's presence at Michelsberg, since monks were frequently remembered in the necrologies of communities with which their monasteries merely shared confraternity arrangements. (The claim that he had also been a monk of Tegernsee must be suspect for the same reason.[211]) Furthermore, a study of the Michelsberg necrology suggests that the designation 'full brother' (*plenus frater*) usually implied the member of another monastery, whereas monks of Michelsberg were normally described as being 'of our congregation' (*nostrae congregationis*).[212]

The difficulty with the theory that Ekkehard was at Michelsberg is that there is very little evidence for his life before he became abbot of Aura in 1108, and it is during this poorly documented period that he is supposed to have first begun continuing Frutolf's *Chronicle*. All that is known for certain about him dates from after 1108: namely, that he was abbot of Aura, spent time in Würzburg, wrote a *Life* of St Burchard, and compiled a chronicle based on Frutolf's and its continuations for Abbot Erkembert of Corvey. But what can be concluded with certainty about his involvement with Frutolf's *Chronicle* before 1108 is much more meagre than Schmale and Schmale-Ott believed.

Consequently, the present study refers to this author as the 1106 continuator. The only firm evidence for his identity derives from the continuation itself. He identifies himself as a participant on the crusade of 1101 and as a monk (presumably of Michelsberg, though he does not specify).[213] The exact nature of his participation on the crusade is also unclear, though his autobiographical comment about reading a 'little book' on the history of the First Crusade in Jerusalem as well as his repeated references to conversations he had with churchmen there suggests that he might already have been a cleric at that time.[214]

The 1106 continuator as an historian of the crusades

The First Crusade and its aftermath fills most of the annals for 1099–1101, while supplementary reports on the kingdom of Jerusalem appear in 1102 and 1105. The year 1099 was the moment for the continuator to survey the progress of the First Crusade from the time crusading enthusiasm began to grip great swathes of Europe late

211 See also the objections of Hoffmann (1995), p. 60.
212 Nospickel (ed.), *Das Necrolog*, pp. 301–32, 335–6.
213 *1106 Continuation* 1099, below, p. 149.
214 *Ibid.* 1099, 1101, below, pp. 153, 169, 170.

in 1095 to the victorious capture of Jerusalem and establishment of European principalities in the Holy Land in 1099. His history of the crusade was in part an attempt to counter antipathy and even hostility towards the movement in much of Germany: he writes of his desire 'to refute the imprudence – or more correctly the impudence – of some who, persevering always in old error, with rash speech presume to criticize the novelty of something so necessary to an ageing and declining world'.[215] It was with considerable regret that he identified the reason for German suspicion of the crusade as the 'schism between kingdom and priesthood', which has made 'us as hated and offensive to the Romans as the Romans are to us'. German antipathy towards the crusade because of its clearly perceived connexion with the reform papacy is a useful indicator of how low Gregorian fortunes in Germany had sunk in the 1090s and corroborates the gloomy assessment of the subject by the south-German chronicler Bernold of St Blasien.[216]

That the crusade 'was ordained not by men but by God' was evident to the continuator not only because of papal direction of it but also because of the many omens and prodigies that accompanied its proclamation.[217] His preoccupation with signs and portents derived not from credulity in the occult but from his reading of Isidore's *Etymologies*.[218] Portents, according to Isidore, seem to be contrary to nature but in reality are not since they are created by divine will and nothing created by divine will can be contrary to nature: they are merely contrary to human knowledge of nature, which is incomplete. Portents are also called 'signs, omens and prodigies, because they are seen to portend and display, indicate and predict future events'.[219] While the appearance of signs in the sky, the birth to a woman of a son who could speak or of 'foals that possessed great teeth' simultaneously foretold the crusade and proclaimed its truly extraordinary qualities, the continuator was also aware that many had been led astray through false omens. He severely criticized the 'false prophets' who were responsible for the perpetration of so much destruction in Germany and Hungary in 1096.[220]

The false prophets and their followers, 'shaken from the threshing-floor

---

215 *Ibid.* 1099, below, p. 142.

216 Bernold, *Chronicle* 1100, p. 539 (*SC*, p. 336).

217 *1106 Continuation* 1099, below, pp. 143, 149–50.

218 Isidore, *Etymologies* 11.3.1–4.

219 *Ibid.* 11.3.2, trans. Barney (2006), pp. 243–4.

220 *1106 Continuation* 1099, below, pp. 151–2. See Riley-Smith (1984), 51–72; Tyerman (2006), pp. 100–6.

of the Lord by the winnowing-fan', stood in sharp contrast to 'the true leaders of the army of the Lord' – Duke Godfrey of Lower Lotharingia and the other princes. Godfrey is the hero of the continuator's narrative of the First Crusade and its aftermath. With customary western prejudice against the Byzantine emperor, the continuator alleges that the earliest contingents to reach Constantinople would 'all have been killed by trickery ... had not Godfrey watched over the Lord's flock with care and caution'.[221] After the successful capture of Jerusalem 'the magnanimous duke, whose equal in piety can scarcely be found, began to undertake great things for the Lord despite his limited resources'.[222] There follows in this and the succeeding annal an extensive panegyric that lists Godfrey's achievements as Advocate of the Holy Sepulchre. Like Henry IV's son Conrad, Godfrey was obedient to the church and thus possessed the ideal qualities of a ruler.

Upon his death in 1100 Godfrey was succeeded by his brother Baldwin. Not only by his military prowess but also by his respect for the church did Baldwin seem to the continuator a worthy successor to his brother: upon becoming ruler of Jerusalem he 'bowed his head over the tomb of the Lord and submitted himself to His personal service'. But he also received royal benediction so that 'even greater fear of the Christians would be instilled in the pagans'.[223] With this portrayal of Baldwin's accession the continuator showed his view of kingship to be thoroughly Gregorian and quite unlike Frutolf's: kings existed to do the bidding of the church. The continuator's interest in the exemplary kingship of Baldwin, which he saw as a kingship dedicated to the defence of the church, is underlined in subsequent annals by his accounts of Baldwin's victories at the First Battle of Ramla (1101), the Battle of Jaffa (1102) and the siege of Acre (1104).

Of particular interest for students of the crusading movement is the continuator's eyewitness account of the crusade of 1101, a largely ignored addendum to the First Crusade.[224] The crusade of 1101 was born partially out of enthusiasm following the successful capture of Jerusalem in 1099 and partially out of the papacy's ongoing efforts to ensure that those who had deserted the First Crusade fulfilled their vows of pilgrimage. Already in 1099 Pope Urban II had threatened

---

221 *1106 Continuation* 1099, below, p. 153.
222 *Ibid.*, below, p. 158.
223 *Ibid.* 1100, below, p. 161.
224 See Cate (1969), pp. 342–67; Riley-Smith (1986), pp. 120–34; Mulinder (1996); Mulinder (1998), pp. 69–77.

deserters with excommunication and this threat was renewed several times by his successor Paschal II.[225] But the papacy also took steps to extend the preaching of the crusade to those who had largely ignored the earlier expedition. During the first half of 1099 Urban II commissioned Archbishop Anselm of Milan to preach the crusade in Lombardy and in the second half of 1100 papal legates preached the crusade at councils at Valence, Limoges, Poitiers and elsewhere. The results, according to the narrative sources, were as impressive as those for the First Crusade: armies from Germany, Burgundy, Lombardy, Aquitaine and France were led by illustrious noblemen and accompanied by three archbishops and at least eight bishops.[226] The Lombard army departed in September 1100 and was the first to reach Constantinople; it was destroyed by a coalition of Turkish princes somewhere near Merzifon in early August 1101.

The continuator set out in a German contingent independent of that led by Welf IV of Bavaria; it was only at Constantinople that he was 'joined by the contingents of Duke Welf, the army of William [Duke William IX of Aquitaine] and other groups'.[227] It is clear from his account that the crusaders were ferried across the Bosphorus – probably, though the continuator does not specify, to Kibotos on the opposite side from Constantinople. From the experiences of the Lombard contingent and the contingent led by Peter the Hermit during the First Crusade, it seems that Kibotos was Alexius's preferred sequestering point for crusaders: it enabled the Byzantines to reduce the rioting and skirmishing that usually attended the arrival of western contingents in Constantinople. Once over the Bosphorus, the crusaders 'waited with great suspense to know the outcome of the princes' daily meetings and their discussions with the emperor'. It was during this period of waiting, according to the continuator, that rumours began to spread about the 'faithless Alexius' who wished to 'let the Franks fight with the Turks so that they might tear each other apart like dogs'.[228] From what follows it seems that there was at this point a crisis of confidence within the continuator's contingent: some wished to continue to Palestine by land through Anatolia and others by sea. In a vivid passage the continuator recalls the consternation that gripped his comrades as those who had planned a sea voyage hastily abandoned their plans at

---

225 Ed. Hagenmeyer, *Die Kreuzungsbriefe*, pp. 174–6.
226 Riley-Smith (1986), p. 126.
227 *1106 Continuation* 1101, below, p. 163. A point confused by Cate (1969), pp. 350, 359.
228 *1106 Continuation* 1101, below, p. 164. See Neocleous (2010), 258.

great financial loss (panicking at rumours that the emperor planned to ambush them). He admits that he himself was 'vexed long and hard by the same indecision' but that finally, after taking ship, he 'reached the port of Jaffa after six weeks'.[229]

The continuator, therefore, left the main army early and so escaped its fate. For the Aquitanians and the rest of the Germans, along with an escort provided by the emperor, had turned aside from the main southerly road leading to Syria and headed 'north against the land of Gorrizim', where they met with incessant harrying from the Turks.[230] Although the continuator's comment about this diversion is contradicted by his contemporary Albert of Aachen, who states that the crusaders continued to march south towards Heraclea,[231] both historians agree that the crusaders fled and were wiped out. The continuator's account of what befell his comrades must have been based on the reports of the survivors he saw 'afterwards with hardly anything clinging to their bones at Rhodes, Paphos and other ports, or even occasionally at Jaffa'.[232]

The continuator spent only about two months in the Holy Land, from late summer to 24 September 1101, when he took ship at Jaffa and began his voyage home.[233] He recorded King Baldwin's victory at the First Battle of Ramla (6–7 September 1101), probably on the basis of an eyewitness account from Abbot Gerard of Schaffhausen, who carried the Lord's cross beside the king. During the battle the continuator seems to have been at Jaffa, which about the same time was blockaded by Egyptian ships; the blockade was broken by the arrival of a European fleet on 8 September.[234]

The continuator's accounts of the First Crusade and the crusade of 1101 are tinged with hostility towards the Byzantine emperor Alexius Comnenus. As in most western crusading sources, Alexius is portrayed as a wolf in sheep's clothing who befriended the crusaders 'with utterly feigned kindness'.[235] The recriminations against Alexius intensify during the narrative of the 1101 crusade, with the continuator blaming

229 *1106 Continuation* 1101, below, p. 165.
230 *Ibid.*
231 *AA* 8.37–8, p. 628.
232 *1106 Continuation* 1101, below, p. 166.
233 *Ibid.* 1102, below, p. 172.
234 Cf. *AA* 9.9–11, pp. 646–50.
235 *1106 Continuation* 1099, below, p. 153.

the emperor in large measure for the crusade's failure. Above all, the Alexius portrayed by the continuator is the 'faithless Alexius', the 'perjured Alexius' and the 'treacherous Alexius' who imprisoned the people of God in areas 'narrow, impassable and uninhabitable, known to the enemy but unknown to us'.[236]

The 1106 continuator, the papacy and the kingdom of Germany

Though the continuator would provide updates on the kingdom of Jerusalem in 1102 and 1105, his principal concerns after 1101 were the papacy and political developments in Germany. By Holy Week 1102 (30 March–5 April) he was in Rome and attended Paschal II's Lateran council, while the following year he noted Henry IV's public announcement of his intention to go on pilgrimage to Jerusalem, by which 'he gained great applause from the people'.[237] The annals for 1103 and 1104 witness the continuator's concern with growing evils in the German kingdom. Conrad of Beichlingen, the son of Otto of Northeim (d. 1083), was attacked and murdered 'as he travelled by night', only two years after his brother, Margrave Henry of Frisia, had been murdered.[238] Margrave Henry's death was, according to the continuator, 'felt deeply by the whole German kingdom; and this sorrow was ... doubled by the murder of his brother'. In 1104 Count Sigehard of Burghausen was killed in a riot that the continuator believed to have been linked to the Christmastide court in Regensburg. The continuator's interest in and outrage at the death of Sigehard might well have been on account of Sigehard's membership of the illustrious Bavarian family of the Aribones. The death of the aged Count Boto of Pottenstein in 1104 provided the opportunity for a detailed account of that family's history, an account that has led to the suggestion that the continuator was himself a kinsman of the Aribones.[239] If this is so, then his attitude towards Henry IV reflects the concerns of the nobility in a manner parallel to Herman of Reichenau's criticisms of Henry III towards the end of his chronicle.[240]

'In the bishop's palace in Speyer blood was seen flowing from bread

---

236 *Ibid.* 1101, below, pp. 164, 165, 166. Hostility to Alexius Comnenus in western sources: Erdmann (1935), p. 365; Becker (1988), pp. 414–16; Neocleous (2010), 253–9.

237 *1106 Continuation* 1102, 1103, below, pp. 171–2, 173.

238 *Ibid.* 1103, below, p. 174.

239 *Chroniken*, pp. 20–1, though the editors' assumption is that the continuator was Ekkehard of Aura.

240 Robinson (2008), pp. 16–18.

and prodigious edible lentils were discovered, which were interpreted as a portent of civil, or rather internal, war according to the ancient pattern of Roman history.' In his final report for 1104 (a quotation from Orosius's *History against the pagans* probably taken from an earlier part of Frutolf's chronicle), the continuator again saw omens as an indication of the troubled last two years of Henry IV's reign. The central focus of the annal for 1105 is the rebellion of Henry V. Like his brother Conrad before him, the young king was seen as a long-awaited saviour by Gregorians. For the continuator, Henry also possessed the ideal qualities of a Christian king: he 'promised due obedience to the pontiff of the apostolic see'.[241] The continuator was careful to emphasize the young king's respect for church authority: at the Synod of Nordhausen (21 May 1105), Henry V was 'present at the meeting of the servants of God only by request' and 'showed appropriate respect for the priests of Christ'.[242] This portrayal stands in stark contrast to Frutolf of Michelsberg's customary portrayal of Henry IV as the organizer of synods within his realm and reflects again the continuator's Gregorian sympathies.

Whereas Frutolf of Michelsberg was suspicious of the Gregorian papacy, the 1106 continuator supported the reforming measures of Urban II and Paschal II. Nevertheless, he maintained a measured tone towards Henry IV and never approached the level of excoriating polemic achieved by Gregorians such as Berthold of Reichenau or, perhaps, Ekkehard of Aura. Each of the annals from 1102 to 1105 begins in the traditional manner of an imperial chronicle by recording where the emperor spent Christmas. In all but one instance the continuator refers to Henry IV as emperor and expresses no doubts about the legitimacy of his rule. Only in the context of the Council of Mainz (December 1105–January 1106) does he refer to Henry IV as the 'so-called emperor': it was at this council that the emperor's opponents forced him to resign and hand the symbols of royal authority to his son.[243] The continuator was also measured in his assessment of the antipope 'Clement III' (Archbishop Wibert of Ravenna), whom he portrayed as a tragic figure helplessly caught in a situation not of his own making.[244] His respect for Clement might well have been the result of meeting him in person – as the continuator informs us he did – and contrasts starkly with

---

241 *1106 Continuation* 1105, below, p. 177.
242 *Ibid.*, below, p. 178.
243 *Ibid.* 1106, below, p. 185.
244 *Ibid.* 1100, below, pp. 161–2.

INTRODUCTION

the black-and-white distinctions drawn by staunch Gregorians such as Bernold of St Blasien, who invariably accompanied mention of the antipope with an opprobrious epithet such as 'heresiarch'.[245] It is also far removed from the vitriolic denunciation of Clement in Ekkehard of Aura's *Chronicle* and provides good reason for questioning the claim that Ekkehard wrote the *1106 Continuation*.[246]

The continuator's Gregorian sympathies are identifiable, therefore, not through denunciations of Henry IV or 'Clement III' but through the attention he devotes to the activities of Henry's opponents such as King Conrad, Urban II, Paschal II and the Gregorian bishops of Germany. His sympathies are most evident in the 1105 and 1106 annals, which are almost exclusively concerned with Henry V's rebellion against his father. It is in these annals that the continuator reaches his most polemical and consistently portrays Henry V as the defender of the church. For the continuator, the church's well-being was central to the kingdom's well-being and so it is that Henry V's religious motivations are made to outshine any political motivations he may have had. The continuator was at pains to stress that Henry V's rebellion stemmed 'not out of lust for power' but from a wish that his 'father would submit to St Peter and his successors according to Christian law'.[247] Similarly, at a stand-off between father and son at Mainz in the last week of June 1105, the continuator claims that Henry V's demands were 'nothing less than submission to the pope and the accomplishment of unity in the church' and, on the eve of battle on the River Regen, portrays the son offering to end his rebellion if only his 'father obediently submits himself to the yoke of the pope'.[248] The Lotharingian chronicler Sigebert of Gembloux, however, remained unconvinced by Henry V's pious credentials: 'the son of Emperor Henry opposed his father ... and rebelled under the guise of improving the commonwealth and restoring the church'.[249] It was a judgement shared by the author of the *1125 Continuation*, who complained that Henry V 'deprived his excommunicated father of the empire under the guise of religion'.[250] The 1106 continuator's panegyric of Henry V also fails to mention important developments concerning the practice of lay investiture. For, in early November 1105, Paschal II

---

245 *SC*, p. 53.
246 Ekkehard, *Chronicle* 1106, below, p. 223.
247 *1106 Continuation* 1105, below, p. 178.
248 *Ibid.*, below, p. 181.
249 Sigebert of Gembloux, *Chronicle* 1105, p. 368.
250 *1125 Continuation* 1125, below, p. 285.

had written to Archbishop Ruothard of Mainz insisting that investiture was the chief cause of simony and had thus reopened an issue that had been pushed to the background by the exigencies of the struggle with Henry IV.[251] Although lay investiture was poised to become the outstanding issue dividing empire and papacy in the coming years, for the 1106 continuator the conflict between the royal and priestly powers remained primarily a conflict over authority and schism that centred on the person of Henry IV.

The *Anonymous imperial chronicle*, 1096–1114

Closely related to Frutolf's *Chronicle* and the *1106 Continuation* is the *Anonymous imperial chronicle* composed in 1113/14. It survives today in one manuscript – Cambridge, Corpus Christi College, MS 373 – and covers history from the origins of the Franks to 1114. The Cambridge manuscript holds the key to understanding the purpose of the *Anonymous imperial chronicle*. This small book of ninety-six folios – the leaves measure 21.6 cm × 14.3 cm – has the chronicle as its only contents. Most of it has been copied by one scribe; only the preface, which dedicates the work to Henry V, and the last three-and-a-half folios have been copied by others. The manuscript also contains portraits, executed in red and black ink, of Carolingian, Ottonian and Salian kings from Pippin III (d. 768) to Henry V.[252] By far the most elaborate of these depicts Henry V's coronation – whether royal or imperial is debated – and introduces the last section of the chronicle.[253] A final illustration depicts the marriage feast of Henry V and Matilda of England, placed so as to accompany the account of their nuptials in the annal for 1114.[254] This carefully worked out illustration programme, the extreme diligence and neatness with which the main text has been copied and the conclusion of the original text with the royal marriage suggest that the Cambridge manuscript was the dedication copy of the chronicle presented to Henry V as a wedding present.

---

251 Paschal II, *JL* 6050, 174D–175D.

252 Cambridge, Corpus Christi College, MS 373, fols 14r, 24r, 28r, 31r, 33v, 34v, 36v, 39r, 40r, 42v, 47r, 48v, 51r, 53r, 55v, 60r, 83r. See Dale (2011), 557–83.

253 Cambridge, Corpus Christi College, MS 373, fol. 83r. Royal coronation: Schmid (1994a), pp. 487–8; imperial coronation: Schramm (1983), p. 145.

254 Cambridge, Corpus Christi College, MS 373, fol. 95v.

INTRODUCTION

The question of the chronicle's authorship is entangled with the historiography of the continuations to Frutolf's *Chronicle*. As mentioned above, Georg Waitz believed it to be the work of Ekkehard of Aura.[255] Waitz's ascription of authorship was bolstered when Harry Bresslau concluded that the main hand of the Cambridge manuscript was identical to that of the *1106 Continuation* in the Jena manuscript.[256] Since Ekkehard was then presumed to be the 1106 continuator, he also had to be the author of the *Anonymous imperial chronicle*. Irene Schmale-Ott, however, challenged this consensus on palaeographical, stylistic and textual grounds. She argued that the main scribe of the Cambridge manuscript was not the scribe of the *1106 Continuation* in the Jena manuscript, that there were clear stylistic differences between the Latin of the two texts and that the political outlook of each work was so different – the *1106 Continuation* being pro-Gregorian and the *Anonymous imperial chronicle* being pro-imperial – that they could not be the work of a single author.[257] She believed that the *Anonymous imperial chronicle* had been excerpted from 'Ekkehard's Recension 2' until 1106 and was thereafter based upon the author's personal knowledge and research.[258] On the grounds of its preoccupation with events in the bishopric of Würzburg, she first suggested that its author might be the Irishman David, the *scholasticus* of Würzburg mentioned in the annal for 1110.[259] She later revised this theory, arguing that the author must have been a close friend of Bishop Erlung of Würzburg – owing to his sympathetic treatment of Erlung's loyalty to Henry IV – and identifying him as Bishop Otto of Bamberg. The chronicle, concluded Schmale-Ott, was Bishop Otto's wedding present for Henry V, though she was not always consistent in stating whether she believed Otto to have written it himself or merely commissioned a Bamberg cleric to do so for him.[260]

The origins of the *Anonymous imperial chronicle* are not as straightforward as Schmale-Ott maintained. Hartmut Hoffmann has convincingly reaffirmed the former opinion that the hands of the *Anonymous imperial chronicle* and the *1106 Continuation* are the same, thereby negating the most important piece of material evidence for her claim that the two

255 See above, pp. 41–2.
256 As reported in *NA* 27 (1901), 5; *NA* 41 (1919), 329. See also Meyer von Knonau (1907), p. 7 n. 1.
257 Schmale-Ott (1956), 363–87; *Chroniken*, pp. 39–41.
258 *Chroniken*, pp. 34, 41.
259 Schmale-Ott (1956), 379–87.
260 Schmale-Ott (1971), 450; *Chroniken*, p. 42.

works could not have been produced by one person.²⁶¹ Furthermore, the present study suggests that the political stances of the two works are much more consistent than Schmale-Ott admitted and that their divergences can be explained by their differing purposes. In terms of content and outlook, therefore, it would seem more logical to suggest that the *1106 Continuation* and the *Anonymous imperial chronicle* are the work of a single author, who was not Ekkehard of Aura. Although the question of authorship can only be resolved by an in-depth re-evaluation of the manuscript sources, this tentative explanation finds support in Hoffmann's research and, paradoxically, in Schmale-Ott's own eventual conclusion that the *Anonymous imperial chronicle* was written in the milieu of Bishop Otto of Bamberg.²⁶²

The structure of the *Anonymous imperial chronicle*

The *Anonymous imperial chronicle* is organized into three books prefaced by a letter of dedication to Henry V: book 1 begins with the origins of the Franks and ends with the imperial coronation of Charles the Great on Christmas Day 800, book 2 begins in 801 with Charles's emperorship and continues until the end of Henry IV's rule in 1105, while book 3 is devoted to the reign of Henry V from 1106 to 1114.

The chronicle's most important sources are Frutolf of Michelsberg's *Chronicle* and the *1106 Continuation*, though it is not yet clear whether its author worked directly from the Jena manuscript or from an intermediate version.²⁶³ These are supplemented with material from Sigebert of Gembloux's *Chronicle*, which was completed *c.* 1112 (the final appearance of material from Sigebert occurs in the annal for 1081). Yet in his sources the author of the *Anonymous imperial chronicle* found much more than he needed and, by his own admission, he often excluded material not relevant to his purpose of providing an imperial history from the time of Charles the Great to Henry V: the annal for 1104, for example, omits the long genealogy of the Aribones.²⁶⁴ One of the most striking

---

261 Hoffmann (1995), pp. 56–62.

262 Schmale-Ott (1971), 455–7, pointed to stylistic parallels between the *Anonymous imperial chronicle* and Otto's letters.

263 My preliminary study of the manuscript variants shows that the *Anonymous imperial chronicle* is consistently closest to the manuscripts of Ekkehard's *Chronicle* (Schmale and Schmale-Ott's Recension 3) and hints at the presence of an intermediate source. Whether that source pre-dates or post-dates the *Anonymous imperial chronicle* is as yet unclear.

264 *Anonymous imperial chronicle* 1104, below, p. 194; cf. *1106 Continuation* 1104, below, pp. 175–6.

differences of content, however, is the absence in the *Anonymous imperial chronicle* of the extensive crusading material in the *1106 Continuation*: 'we refrain from reporting more about this journey since it demands so great a treatment and we already have enough other elegant accounts of it', wrote the author.[265]

For Henry V's Italian expedition of 1110–11, the anonymous chronicler relied on a history of 'all the events of this expedition in three books in so simple a style that it hardly differs from the common speech' by an Irish clerk named David, sometime *scholasticus* of Würzburg and royal chaplain.[266] The English historian William of Malmesbury, who had also read a copy of that history, identified its author as the David who later became bishop of Bangor.[267] David's history has not been identified, although the anonymous chronicler's comments were at one time interpreted to be autobiographical – namely, that David's history in three books was the *Anonymous imperial chronicle*.[268] This, however, cannot be so because William, who stated that he copied 'word for word from David's book', reproduced parts of that work not present in the Bamberg chronicle.[269] Whether or not the anonymous chronicler based more than his account of the Roman expedition on David's history cannot be known, although it is certainly possible.

The *Anonymous imperial chronicle* as panegyric

While the exact identity of the anonymous chronicler is unknown, the content of his chronicle allows the historian to form a picture of his political and religious views. As the letter of dedication to Henry V makes clear, the chronicle's purpose was 'to serve the honour both of the Roman empire and the German kingdom, the union of which began with Charles of the Franks'.[270] Imperial ideology permeates the chronicle and, like Frutolf, its author records each new ruler's place in the succession since Augustus. The work is above all a panegyric in chronicle format, casting Henry V as the most recent in a line of illustrious kings and emperors and a worthy successor to Charles the Great. Nevertheless, its author faced the considerable difficulty of providing

---

265 *Anonymous imperial chronicle* 1096, below, p. 188.

266 *Ibid.* 1110, below, p. 212.

267 William of Malmesbury, *Deeds of the English kings*, p. 421.

268 Schmale-Ott (1956), 379–87.

269 William, *Deeds of the English kings*, pp. 421–6.

270 *Anonymous imperial chronicle*, below, p. 187.

Henry V with an illustrious father in the person of Henry IV while simultaneously excusing Henry V's rebellion against his father in 1105. Whereas the *1106 Continuation* says little of Henry V's initial motives for rebelling other than that he had acted on the advice of a group of Bavarian noblemen, the *Anonymous imperial chronicle* casts the rebellion as a provident move designed to perpetuate Salian rule: Henry V foresaw the likelihood of a dynastic struggle after his father's death and so decided to become the focus of attention for dissatisfied elements within the empire before another could step into that position.[271] Henry V's motives, therefore, were primarily altruistic, and with an allusion to Cicero the author claims that the young king's first action was 'to take counsel for the commonwealth'.[272] The chronicler follows this with an even more startling claim – that Henry IV planned the ruse himself in order to neutralize objection to continuing Salian rule. In concluding that 'all these things undoubtedly happened through divine dispensation', the chronicler managed not only to exonerate Henry V but to do so in a way that preserved his father's honour intact.

While the *1106 Continuation* was never overly hostile to Henry IV, the author of the *Anonymous imperial chronicle* chose to portray him in a more favourable light. Gone, for example, is the reference to the 'many abominable things' of which Queen Adelaide had accused Henry IV at the Council of Piacenza (1095).[273] The most obvious example, however, is the chronicle's elaborate obituary for Henry IV. Here there is no hint of criticism. With the comment that Henry IV resisted 'the ungrateful who attempted to humble the royal power in Germany', the author at one stroke dispensed with the civil and religious conflicts that had dominated Henry IV's long reign.[274] He concentrated instead on the dead emperor's virtues, praising his vigorous and warlike nature, his learning, his interest in psalmody and the liberal arts, and his devotion to the cathedral of Speyer (the mausoleum of the Salian dynasty). This enthusiastic account of Henry IV's achievements stands in stark contrast to the bitter denunciation of the dead emperor that Ekkehard of Aura would later provide in his *Chronicle*.[275] The favourable portrayal of Henry IV in the *Anonymous imperial chronicle* is explained not only

271 *Ibid.* 1105, below, p. 195. Weinfurter (1999), p. 165, characterizes Henry V's rebellion as an implementation of 'the Salian principles of dynastic thinking'.
272 *Anonymous imperial chronicle* 1105, below, p. 195.
273 *Ibid.* 1099, below, p. 190; cf. *1106 Continuation* 1100, below, p. 159.
274 *Anonymous imperial chronicle* 1106, below, p. 205.
275 Ekkehard, *Chronicle* 1106, below, pp. 231–2.

by the work's purpose as panegyric, but also by the fact that it was written in 1113/14. For although Henry IV had died excommunicate and had been denied burial in consecrated ground for five years, on 7 August 1111 – the fifth anniversary of his death – he was with papal permission and great solemnity interred by Henry V next to Henry III and Conrad II in the cathedral crypt in Speyer. The *Anonymous imperial chronicle* thus belongs to the period when Henry IV's image had been rehabilitated by his son, who was now proud to count him among the illustrious successors of Charles the Great.

The principal theme of book 3 of the *Anonymous imperial chronicle* is praise of Henry V, with the author indulging in extensive panegyrics in 1105 (Henry V's rebellion against his father), 1106 (the forced abdication of Henry IV), 1110 (Henry V's announcement of his plans to seek imperial coronation in Rome), 1111 (the events surrounding the Treaty of Ponte Mammolo and the imperial coronation) and 1114 (Henry's wedding to Matilda of England). These eulogies consistently portray Henry V as a wise and provident ruler, a defender of the church favoured by God. In the 1105 and 1106 annals the chronicler repeated much of the praise heaped upon Henry V in the *1106 Continuation* while adding further encomiums about his reform credentials: 'the vile scandals of schisms that were everywhere round about were eliminated' and 'the bad fish were thrown out of Peter's net'.[276]

The chronicler's praise of Henry V was shaped not only by religious concerns but also by his conscious use of 'Romanizing' political terms. The letter of dedication opens by adducing the authority of Cicero – the epitome of political *Romanitas* – to extol the ruler who is good and wise and versed in all that contributes to the advantage of the state; it is this image of Henry that the chronicle seeks to portray. In 1110, for example, when Henry V announced an expedition to Rome to receive imperial coronation, the chronicler expressed it as a desire 'to bring the extensive Italian provinces into fellowship with the German kingdom through fraternal peace with ancient justice and laws'. He also praised Henry, 'the provident consul who undoubtedly loved his country', for 'knowing that the Roman republic was formerly accustomed to being governed not so much by arms as by wisdom', and for providing himself 'with the necessary protection not only of armed men but also of educated men'.[277] Classical too – and therefore authoritative

---

276 *Anonymous imperial chronicle* 1106, below, p. 203.
277 *Ibid.* 1110, below, p. 211.

– is the repeated use of the term 'commonwealth' (*res publica* in Latin) to describe the western empire. Although the chronicler was not the first author to use *res publica* in this way – Frutolf and Sigebert of Gembloux used it occasionally, as did Wipo in his *Deeds of Emperor Conrad* – the frequency with which he employs it is significant.[278] For, even more than Frutolf, the anonymous chronicler was eager to portray the empire of Henry V as the living continuation of the Roman empire. His emphasis on the wisdom and laws of ancient Rome differs in many respects from the notions of kingship usually employed by contemporary historians – drawn as they were from the writings of pseudo-Cyprian and Isidore of Seville – which emphasized the king's duty to defend strangers, orphans and widows, to judge impartially and to punish criminals.[279] Yet although it is tempting to see in the chronicler's smattering of classical allusions a conscious effort to outline new modes of political thought, caution is advisable. The 'Ciceronian' allusion that opens the letter of dedication is not in fact Ciceronian at all, but drawn from a reference to Plato in Boethius's *Consolation of philosophy*.[280] In an age when classical quotations could come from intermediary sources and not necessarily from direct engagement with the originals themselves, it is possible that the chronicler merely saw classicizing terminology as the appropriate accoutrement of a Roman emperor.

That God favoured Henry V was evident to the chronicler not only because of the successful outcome of the young king's rebellion against his father in 1105–6, but also because of the failure of numerous rebellions against him in 1113. The idea that God intervened on behalf of the righteous, so common in eleventh- and twelfth-century historical writing, nevertheless presented problems for the chronicler when he tried to account for Henry V's military failures. During Lent 1106 the young king faced opposition in Lotharingia from his father's allies and on Maundy Thursday (22 March) sent a force of 300 knights to seize the bridge over the River Maas at Visé. Henry V's forces, however, were heavily defeated by a force under the command of Duke Henry of Lotharingia and Count Godfrey of Namur. The anonymous chronicler accounted for this defeat in two ways. In Isidore's *Etymologies* he found a discussion of the goddess *fortuna*, 'who is called blind because she bears down upon people at random, without any consideration of merits, and

---

278 *Ibid.*, below, pp. 188, 192, 195, 202, 204. Cf. Frutolf, *Chronicle* 1072, 1074, below, pp. 110, 112; Sigebert, *Chronicle* 1105, p. 368; Wipo, *Deeds* 25, p. 43 (*IL*, p. 85).
279 Robinson (1999), pp. 347–8.
280 *Anonymous imperial chronicle*, below, p. 187.

comes to both good people and bad'.[281] This he applied to the defeat at Visé, for there Henry V 'felt the wheel of fortune spin to his disadvantage'. The concept of *fortuna* seems to have interested the chronicler, for he used it on four separate occasions in book 3. Nevertheless, he does not seem to have been entirely comfortable with the goddess's pagan origins and on two of the four instances he quickly equated the vagaries of fortune with the will of God, which is not always apparent to humans. It was precisely his desire to Christianize *fortuna* that led to his second manner of accounting for Henry V's defeat. He used a technique frequently employed by Gregorian apologists and compared the fallen soldiers to the Maccabees of the Old Testament.[282] The additional comment that these martyrs 'would acquire forgiveness of their former sins on this day of indulgence' suggests that he may also have been influenced by developing crusading theology.[283] If we accept that the chronicler also wrote the *1106 Continuation*, then his ideas may well owe much to his own experiences of crusading.

The anonymous chronicler continued the interest of the *1106 Continuation* in the fortunes of the reform papacy. Nevertheless, his account of the Council of Guastalla (October 1106) presents only a rapid and somewhat general sketch of the proceedings by portraying Paschal II as an amiable and skilful physician of the soul. His vagueness may have been intended to hide the reality of what happened at Guastalla, for other narrative accounts describe a much less congenial synod: the *Annals of Paderborn*, for example, record the condemnation and excommunication of many Italian bishops and the suspension from office of Bishops Frederick of Halberstadt and Widelo of Minden.[284] As the *Anonymous imperial chronicle* was written in the fraught aftermath of Henry V's dealings with Paschal II in 1111 – Henry's actions had been widely condemned at the Lateran synod of 1112 and he had been excommunicated by papal legates – it is worth considering that the chronicler was attempting to balance the competing demands of his own Gregorian sympathies and the need to address the expectations of his royal audience.

Similar concerns are obvious in the chronicler's portrayal of the king's

281 Isidore, *Etymologies* 8.11.94, trans. Barney (2006), p. 189.
282 Bernold of St Blasien used this technique to account for the death of Rudolf of Rheinfelden: *Chronicle* 1080, p. 426 (*SC*, p. 266). See above, p. 38.
283 *Anonymous imperial chronicle* 1106, below, p. 204. Cf. Bernold, *Chronicle* 1080, p. 426 (*SC*, p. 266).
284 *Annals of Paderborn* 1106, p. 116.

Italian expedition of 1110–11 and the Treaty of Ponte Mammolo. Although both the *1106 Continuation* and the *Anonymous imperial chronicle* praised Henry V as a champion of church liberty, the fact remained that the king was as reluctant to give up the right of investing bishops as his father had been. Despite the repeated efforts of Paschal II to prohibit lay investiture, Henry V managed successfully to prevaricate on the issue for the first five years of his reign. At the Council of Guastalla Henry V's chief negotiator, Archbishop Bruno of Trier, had asked unsuccessfully for the right of lay investiture; yet the council refrained from condemning either the king or the bishops he had invested since 1105.[285] Perhaps the need to seek reconciliation with the German church outweighed the need to press the prohibition of investiture at that point. Almost a year later, when Paschal II again prohibited lay investiture at the Council of Troyes (23 May 1107), Henry V replied 'that the power of constituting bishops had been given to Emperor Charles [the Great] by apostolic privileges' (a reference to a spurious investiture privilege of Pope Hadrian I, 772–95). Henry was then 'granted a deferral so that he might come to Rome within the next year and discuss the same matter in a general council'.[286] When he approached Rome for imperial coronation in February 1111, therefore, it was inevitable that the pope would seek resolution of the investiture matter. Paschal II, however, tried to take a more imaginative approach to the question of investiture than his predecessors. Realizing that it was no simple matter for a German king to renounce investiture – since bishops and royal abbots were such an integral part of political society – he suggested that churchmen should themselves renounce the *regalia*, that is, the secular lands, monies and privileges that they administered and received on behalf of the king. Paschal's idea did not involve a total renunciation of wealth by the church – as older generations of historians believed – but merely the clear separation of what belonged to the church by right and what belonged to the kingdom.[287] Prelates would retain control over church lands (the *ecclesiastica*). This was the basis of an agreement negotiated between royal and papal legates on 4 February at the church of S. Maria in Turri (a small church in the Old St Peter's complex). When the proposals were read to the assembled crowd on the morning of the planned imperial coronation (12

---

285 Blumenthal (1978b), pp. 64–5, 73.

286 *Anonymous imperial chronicle* 1107, below, p. 209.

287 Tierney (1964), pp. 87–8; Zerbi (1965), pp. 207–29; Werner (1978), p. 169; Wilks (1971), pp. 81–4; Blumenthal (1977), pp. 9–12.

February) there was uproar, mainly it seems from the German prelates accompanying Henry V. They did not recognize Paschal's distinction between *regalia* and *ecclesiastica*, fearing the economic ruin – and consequently the practical viability – of their churches.[288] In the turmoil that followed, Henry V took Paschal II and those cardinals who were with him into custody. In a public justification of his actions he claimed that this was for their protection, though his claim is contradicted by the papal version of events.[289] Two months of captivity wore down Paschal, who conceded to Henry the privilege of lay investiture in the Treaty of Ponte Mammolo (11 April 1111), promised never to excommunicate him and crowned him emperor on 13 April.

These events posed a considerable problem for the author of the *Anonymous imperial chronicle*, who seems to have been a moderate Gregorian. He resorted to the technique he had used in his description of the Council of Guastalla – a rapid summary of events, which he derived from the history written by the royal chaplain David.[290] The result is a slick and rosy account of the whole expedition in which the chronicler somewhat incongruously presents the Treaty of Ponte Mammolo and subsequent imperial coronation as the triumphant and definitive ending of the conflict between empire and papacy. (Conspicuous by their absence are any mentions in the subsequent annals of the backlash against Henry V at the 1112 Lateran synod or the excommunications pronounced against him by Paschal II's legates.[291]) The official 'imperial' account, however, did not impress all readers. William of Malmesbury, who had read David's history of the expedition independently, characterized it as a 'flimsy' work that showed 'more prejudice in favour of the king than is proper for an historian'. Yet William understood something of David's predicament and, 'rather than seem to condemn a good man out of hand', chose to 'be lenient with him, on the ground that he was writing panegyric and not history'.[292]

The fact that the anonymous chronicler, like David, was writing panegyric makes it difficult for the historian to assess his true attitude towards lay investiture. Sometimes he seems to disapprove of inves-

---

288 Fried (1973), 478–9, 505–6.

289 Henry V: *MGH Constitutiones* 1, p. 151; Paschal II: *MGH Constitutiones* 1, pp. 147–50. See Blumenthal (1977), pp. 13–15; Robinson (1990), pp. 425–6.

290 *Anonymous imperial chronicle* 1111, below, pp. 213–15.

291 See Ekkehard, *Chronicle* 1112, below, pp. 242–3.

292 William, *Deeds of the English kings*, p. 421.

titure from Henry IV while tolerating it from Henry V, but there are also many instances where he is inconsistent. There is no hint of disapproval at the appointment by Henry IV of Bishop Otto of Bamberg in 1102 – in fact, the chronicler commends Otto's steadfast loyalty to the emperor 'even through great danger'.[293] Similarly, his account of Henry IV's appointment of Erlung to the bishopric of Würzburg in 1105 does not criticize the practice of investiture and, in fact, attempts to legalize it by stressing that Erlung 'obtained the bishopric with the consent of the people and clergy'.[294] At least in the cases of Otto and Erlung the chronicler may well have had personal motives for his circumspection. He greatly admired Otto, who may well have commissioned him to write the chronicle, while the learned Erlung had been educated at the cathedral of Bamberg by Meinhard of Bamberg (who was in fact Erlung's uncle) and thus may also have been personally known to the chronicler. He was certainly not the only medieval author to have refrained from criticizing those whom he admired. In the end, the irreconcilability of the chronicler's views on lay investiture is a consequence of his success as a skilful panegyrist of Henry V.

Ekkehard of Aura, *Chronicle*, 1106–16

Probably sometime in 1117, Amel, prior of the monastery of Aura in the diocese of Würzburg, journeyed to the venerable Saxon monastery of Corvey and brought with him a chronicle that his abbot, Ekkehard, had written for the abbot of Corvey. The document that tells us of this visit is the letter of dedication that prefaces the chronicle in question.[295] It indicates that the work was commissioned by Abbot Erkembert of Corvey in advance of a pilgrimage to Jerusalem and clearly identifies its author as Ekkehard of Aura. The letter also enables the chronicle's precise dating, for its reference to the forthcoming pilgrimage implies that Ekkehard wrote the dedication before Erkembert set out for Jerusalem at some unspecified date in 1117.[296]

The letter of dedication survives only in a thirteenth-century copy of

---

293 *Anonymous imperial chronicle* 1102, below, p. 193.
294 *Ibid.* 1105, below, pp. 197–8.
295 Ekkehard, *Chronicle*, below, pp. 219–20.
296 *Annals of Hildesheim* 1117, p. 64: 'Abbot Erkembert of Corvey and many from Saxony left for Jerusalem.'

INTRODUCTION   67

Ekkehard's *Chronicle* from Saxony.[297] This manuscript is itself a direct copy of a twelfth-century manuscript from the monastery of Berge in Magdeburg.[298] Although the Berge manuscript is today incomplete – the text begins halfway through the annal for AD 6 – the manuscript containing the letter of dedication must have been copied from it before the losses occurred and so we can be confident that it originally transmitted the letter of dedication as well.[299]

The letter of dedication also contains valuable clues as to how the chronicle was composed. Ekkehard stated plainly that he had 'hurried through and abbreviated the narrations of various chroniclers from the beginning of the world and supplied with our own pen the deeds of our times'.[300] The narrations upon which he most relied were Frutolf of Michelsberg's *Chronicle*, the *1106 Continuation* and the *Anonymous imperial chronicle*, though it is as yet unclear whether he worked from those texts directly or from an intermediate source that had already abbreviated them. In either case, Ekkehard's *Chronicle* for Erkembert of Corvey differs from its *fontes formales* in important structural ways. To begin with, its text is divided into five books as follows:

Book 1: The creation of the world to the foundation of Rome (753 BC).
Book 2: Roman history until the Incarnation.
Book 3: AD 1 to Charles the Great's imperial coronation (Christmas Day 800).
Book 4: 801 to the beginning of Henry V's reign (1105).
Book 5: The reign of Henry V (beginning in 1106).

The chronicle also omits most of the material from the histories of

297 Paris, Bibliothèque nationale, MS lat. 4889a. See *MGH SS* 6, pp. 10–11, 16; *Chroniken*, p. 36.
298 Berlin, Preußischer Kulturbesitz, Staatsbibliothek zu Berlin, lat. fol. 295. See *Chroniken*, pp. 35–6; Fingernagel (1991), pp. 4–6.
299 There is some disagreement as to whether Ekkehard's *Chronicle* for Erkembert is transmitted only in two manuscripts. Schmale and Schmale-Ott argued that it is also to be found in the twelfth-century Paris, Bibliothèque nationale, MS lat. 4889 and its fourteenth-century copy Paris, Bibliothèque de l'Arsenal, MS lat. 1081 (see *Chroniken*, p. 36, where they refer to the Arsenal manuscript as 'MS 6'). Their claim contradicts the earlier conclusions of Georg Waitz, who believed that Paris lat. 4889 and Paris, Arsenal, lat. 1081 – which he labelled recension D – transmitted a version of Ekkehard's *Chronicle* not intended for the abbot of Corvey (*MGH SS* 6, pp. 9–11, 15–16). Waitz's conclusions were based upon textual differences between the two sets of manuscripts as well as upon the fact that only Berlin lat. fol. 295 and Paris lat. 4889a – which he labelled recension E – transmitted the letter of dedication and other references to Erkembert. The significance of these differences is not yet fully understood and will be examined in my future study of the texts.
300 Ekkehard, *Chronicle*, below, p. 219.

Alexander the Great, the Franks, Goths, Lombards and Saxons that Frutolf had inserted into his chronology.[301] Another important structural change relates to the crusading material of the *1106 Continuation*: Ekkehard excised the lengthy crusading reports from the annals in which they occurred and reconstituted them as an appendix, which he entitled '*Hierosolimita*, concerning the oppression, liberation and restoration of the holy church of Jerusalem'. (The opening of the *Hierosolimita* indicates that this change was in response to Abbot Erkembert's commission: Ekkehard hoped that it would function as a sort of historical guidebook and provide solace on Erkembert's pilgrimage to the Holy Land.[302]) Perhaps the most peculiar structural feature of Ekkehard's *Chronicle*, however, is that in none of its manuscripts does it end in 1117, the date of composition implied by the letter of dedication. Each contains annals for the years 1117–25 that are largely identical to the corresponding annals of the *1125 Continuation*. The significance of this is not yet fully understood and in the absence of a detailed study we can only conclude, as Georg Waitz did in the nineteenth century, that the surviving manuscripts do not transmit the version produced for Abbot Erkembert, but a version that was somehow combined with the later continuation.[303]

The fifth book of Ekkehard's *Chronicle* translated in this study is prefaced by a letter addressed to Henry V of Germany. Franz-Josef Schmale and Irene Schmale-Ott argued that this was the letter of dedication to Ekkehard's now lost 'Recension 2': 'after returning from the Synod of Guastalla', they claimed, 'Ekkehard prepared a copy of a chronicle based upon the partially corrected chronicle of Frutolf until 1097 and his own continuation, which in this copy, however, was continued to the end of the year 1106'.[304] The way in which this letter appears in the Berlin manuscript, however, suggests a different conclusion. It is found on fol. 99v, following immediately overleaf from a full-page drawing of Henry IV handing the *regalia* to Henry V (fol. 99r). The illustration depicts the deposition of Henry IV at Ingelheim (31 December 1105), at which he gave the imperial insignia 'into the hands of his son, praying for his prosperity and commending him to the foremost princes with many tears'.[305] The letter to Henry V is denoted with a

---

301 See above, pp. 22–3.
302 Ekkehard, *Chronicle*, below, p. 219.
303 *MGH SS* 6, p. 11.
304 *Chroniken*, p. 34.
305 Ekkehard, *Chronicle* 1106, below, p. 222.

large decorated initial capital and majuscule letters for its first line. At its conclusion, again in majuscule letters, is the following rubric: 'Here ends the prologue. Here begins the fifth book.' Then follows the 1106 annal, also with a large decorated initial capital and majuscule letters for the first line. This presentation is consistent with the usual way in which prologues are indicated in manuscripts of the period. Taken together with Ekkehard's own comment about his decision 'to inscribe the fifth book with his [Henry V's] name', it implies that the 'letter' is in fact a prologue to the chronicle's fifth book and not the dedicatory letter for a lost chronicle.[306] This interpretation is confirmed by the evidence of Helmold of Bosau (c. 1120–c. 1177) who – in the context of his discussion of the Concordat of Worms (1122) – wrote that 'whoever would know more about … the ending of this schism may read the fifth book of the history of Master Ekkehard, which he dedicates to the younger Henry'.[307] Clearly Helmold, writing c. 1170, understood well the function of this prologue; equally clear is the fact that the copy of the *Chronicle* he saw had the extra annals for 1117–25.

Content and themes, 1106–16

Although Ekkehard's *Chronicle* is largely compiled from pre-existing sources, the manner in which he revised those sources allows us to identify his distinctive historical voice. That voice reveals him to be a staunch Gregorian for whom Henry IV was an 'apostate and persecutor of souls'.[308] A comparison of Ekkehard's annal for 1106 with that of the *Anonymous imperial chronicle* reveals that Ekkehard's text contains no fewer than nine denunciations of Henry IV entirely absent from the anonymous chronicle. The first discrepancy occurs after the account of the Council of Mainz (Christmastide 1105–6), at which Henry V was elected king. The *Anonymous imperial chronicle* followed its account of the proceedings at Mainz with an elaborate eulogy of Henry V, the 'exquisite flower of the world' who mended 'the rent garment of Christ'.[309] Ekkehard's *Chronicle*, however, excises the encomiums of Henry V and instead concentrates on the triumphant victory of the 'Roman church' over the 'heresy of Wibert, or of Henry'. In bloodthirsty language that recalls the more vitriolic passages of the eleventh-century chronicler Berthold of Reichenau, it rejoices in the removal of 'pseudo-bishops'

---

306 *Ibid.* letter of dedication, below, p. 219.
307 Helmold of Bosau, *Chronicle* 40, pp. 82–3; trans. Tschan (1966), pp. 137–8.
308 Ekkehard, *Chronicle* 1106, below, p. 231.
309 *Anonymous imperial chronicle* 1106, below, p. 203.

from their graves and the scattering of the bones of their leader, the 'apostate invader', 'Clement III'.[310] Further hostile reports follow: an account of Henry IV's support for the antipope 'Silvester IV'; the accusation, absent from the *Anonymous imperial chronicle*, that Henry IV had ordered the kidnapping of the ill-fated Italian embassy of February 1106; the attempt to leave the reader in no doubt that resistance to Henry V in Alsace and Cologne originated in the 'machinations of his father'; the use of Henry IV's letters 'to attest to the manifold evasions of this man'; and the report about the cruel treatment of Henry V's messengers at the hands of the 'gathering of evildoers' in Henry IV's camp.[311] Ekkehard's attack culminates in his obituary for Henry IV which, in contrast to the sympathetic treatment of the emperor in the *Anonymous imperial chronicle*, is an assessment of excoriating severity. Its language is remarkably intemperate: Henry IV was an 'archpirate and heresiarch', a 'vile man' who had 'degenerated and surrendered in the battle with vice'.[312] The tirade vividly recapitulates the standard accusations that had been levelled at Henry IV by his opponents since he first gained a reputation for tyranny and immorality in the early 1070s – accusations intended to demonstrate that he was the archetypal tyrant of Isidore's *Etymologies*.[313] It is another reminder that at the time of Henry's death in 1106, the focus of the conflict between empire and papacy was not lay investiture but the emperor himself.

Although Ekkehard may have dedicated the fifth book of his *Chronicle* to Henry V, his attitude towards the last Salian emperor was more ambivalent than that of the 1106 continuator or the author of the *Anonymous imperial chronicle*. Reservations about Henry V first surface in the aftermath of his high-handed dealings with Pope Paschal II during the Italian expedition of 1110–11. The annal for 1112, for example, is dominated by an account of Paschal II's Lateran synod and repeats the accusations made there that the emperor was a 'tyrannical devastator of the commonwealth and destroyer of the churches'. Ekkehard provides a much less favourable account of the Saxon rebellion of 1112 than does the author of the *Anonymous imperial chronicle* and, moreover, plainly identifies the emperor's attempts to claim the inheritance of Count Udalric of Weimar as the catalyst for rebellion.[314] The year 1113

310 Ekkehard, *Chronicle* 1106, below, p. 223.
311 *Ibid.*, below, pp. 223–4, 225–6, 227–8, 230.
312 *Ibid.*, below, pp. 231–2. See Robinson (1999), p. 345.
313 Isidore, *Etymologies* 9.3.20, trans. Barney (2006), p. 201.
314 Ekkehard, *Chronicle* 1112, 1113, below, pp. 243–4.

also saw an uprising by Count Rainald of Bar and Mousson,[315] while the following year witnessed rebellion in Cologne and the Rhineland. By 1115 the emperor perceived clearly 'that Saxony had defected from him' and appeared in the province 'as well armed as he was angry'.[316] Ekkehard's interest in Saxon affairs here and in subsequent annals is perhaps explained by the Saxon audience of his chronicle. He gives some credence to the claim that the Saxons were acting in self-defence: they sought 'not to fight against their lord out of audacity, but to defend themselves out of necessity'. In the aftermath of defeat at the Battle of Welfesholz (11 February 1115), the emperor 'turned back to the Rhine not a little embittered, while the resolve of the Saxons to resist him was strengthened more and more'.[317] Their resolve expressed itself in the excommunication of the emperor by Cardinal Theoderic of S. Grisogono at the royal palace of Goslar on 1 September.[318]

The growing ineffectuality of Henry V's rule is a theme of the annals 1112–16. Ekkehard noted that a proposed general council for 1 November 1115 in Mainz failed because 'excepting a few of the bishops none of the princes had come'.[319] This failure was rendered all the more ignominious when the citizens of Mainz stormed into the royal palace and forced the emperor on pain of death to release Archbishop Adalbert of Mainz, who had been imprisoned on treason charges since 1112.[320] Adalbert immediately joined with Henry's enemies and attended a meeting 'with many other bishops at Cologne', while the emperor was forced to celebrate Christmas at Speyer 'with few bishops and princes'.[321] Most indicative of the emperor's increasing isolation, however, is the poignant account of his desertion by Bishop Erlung of Würzburg (Ekkehard's own diocesan bishop), who 'departed secretly, sorrowful unto death ... and thenceforward forfeited Caesar's confidence and grace'. Ekkehard's picture of Henry in these years is of a man beset by his enemies on all sides and forsaken by the imperial church. Nowhere is this more aptly summed up than in his analysis of the reasons for Henry V's second Italian expedition in 1116: although the emperor travelled to Italy to secure the vast

315 See Stroll (2004), pp. 207–9.
316 Ekkehard, *Chronicle* 1115, below, p. 246.
317 *Ibid.*
318 See Meyer von Knonau (1907), pp. 330–1.
319 Ekkehard, *Chronicle* 1115, below, p. 247.
320 Meyer von Knonau (1907), pp. 259–63; Weinfurter (1999), pp. 174–5; Stroll (2004), pp. 211–14.
321 Ekkehard, *Chronicle* 1116, below, p. 247.

inheritance of his kinswoman Matilda of Tuscany, Ekkehard portrayed his departure as an attempt 'to avoid the outcry of the princes'.[322]

Ekkehard's despondence concerning Henry V was counterbalanced by renewed emphasis on the affairs of the reform papacy. The Treaty of Ponte Mammolo had precipitated a crisis in the papacy, as several prominent reformers denounced the privilege of lay investiture that Paschal II had been forced to confer upon Henry V as the price of his freedom. A letter from Bishop Azo of Acqui informed the emperor of a forthcoming synod in Rome 'in which they say Pope Paschal is to be deposed and another elected'.[323] The rumour that the Lateran synod of 1112 sought to depose the pope may well have originated in the accusations of heresy that surfaced in the polemical literature generated by the Treaty of Ponte Mammolo: Gregory VII and Urban II had defined lay investiture as heresy and thus Paschal II was a heretic for conceding it to the king in direct contravention of their decrees.[324] Ekkehard's comment that 'the lord pope had to endure many injustices from the Roman church' suggests, however, that he did not share that view and is in keeping with his usual reverential attitude towards Paschal. His account of the 1112 Lateran synod, like his account of Guastalla in 1106, benefitted from access to synodal *acta*. (His annal for 1106 provides the text of the conciliar decree on the status of clerks ordained by schismatics, a text absent from the *1106 Continuation* and *Anonymous imperial chronicle*.[325]) Ekkehard concentrates on the profession of faith that the synod compelled Paschal to make 'so that no one should doubt his faith'.[326] The accusations of heresy against the pope are treated more explicitly in Ekkehard's account of the 1116 Lateran synod. Here Ekkehard identifies Paschal's accuser as Bishop Bruno of Segni, a veteran cardinal and protégé of Gregory VII.[327] While Bruno has sometimes been seen as an intransigent leader of opposition to Paschal II, it is more likely that he was deeply conscious of the need for

---

322 *Ibid.* below, p. 248.

323 *Codex Udalrici* 2, no. 258, ed. Jaffé, p. 288.

324 Josceran of Lyons, *Letter*, p. 656; Bruno of Segni, *Letters* 1, 4, pp. 563, 565; Guido of Vienne, *Synodal letter* (*PL* 163.0465C–0466C). See McKeon (1966), 3–12; Blumenthal (1978a), 82–98; Servatius (1979), pp. 309–20; Robinson (1990), pp. 128–30.

325 Ekkehard, *Chronicle* 1106, below, pp. 233–4.

326 *MGH Constitutiones* 1, pp. 571–2; Ekkehard, *Chronicle* 1112, below, p. 242.

327 *Ibid.*, below, p. 250. On Bruno see North (2000), pp. 203–20; Robinson (2004b), pp. 88–93.

a unified approach to the question of lay investiture from the church.[328] In 1112, at least, Bruno could not countenance Paschal's deposition and accepted that the pope considered the Treaty of Ponte Mammolo as odious as he did.[329] But while some clearly desired a unified front against lay investiture – and consequently against Henry V – the pope felt himself bound by his promise of 1111 never to excommunicate the emperor. Ekkehard charts this conflict between what W. L. North has termed 'public and private orthodoxy' by focusing on the efforts in the synod of Cardinal Bishop Conrad of Palestrina, the papal legate in Germany, to compel Paschal to excommunicate Henry as he had done in 1115.[330] Ekkehard's interpretation of the proceedings of 1112 and 1116 seems also to have been guided by a realization of the need for a unified policy, though for him one that saw the church act under the guidance of the pope. Hence his condemnation of Archbishop Guido of Vienne's independent excommunication of Henry V in 1112, an attempt 'to sow a new schism in our land' that 'lacked any papal authority and consequently any church authority'.[331]

As outlined above, a distinctive structural feature of Ekkehard's *Chronicle* for Erkembert of Corvey is that the crusading reports of the *1106 Continuation* appear in a separate appendix entitled *Hierosolimita*. While this appendix reproduces the original reports virtually word for word, it also adds short passages of connecting material, a confused report about the marriage of King Baldwin I of Jerusalem and an impassioned conclusion defending the crusading movement. The *Hierosolimita* has generally been seen as Ekkehard's own account of the crusading movement, based in part upon his personal experiences of the crusade of 1101. This claim is based upon the belief that Ekkehard was the author of the original reports in the *1106 Continuation*. If, as the present study suggests, Ekkehard was not the 1106 continuator, then the *Hierosolimita* is not substantially his own work but, rather, his rearrangement of 'the memorable accounts of different chronicles from the beginning of time until our own rotten times'.[332] This in turn implies that Ekkehard's

---

328 McKeon (1966), 5; Blumenthal (1978a), 89, 91; but see the critique of North (2000), pp. 209–11.

329 Bruno of Segni, *Letter* (to Paschal II), p. 565: 'That pact, so foul and violent, made with so much treachery, so contrary to all piety and religion, I do not praise. Nor do you, as I have heard from many people who have spoken to me'; translation from North (2010), p. 210.

330 North (2000), p. 211.

331 Ekkehard, *Chronicle* 1112, below, p. 243.

332 Ekkehard, *Hierosolimita*, below, p. 254.

involvement with the crusading movement was less extensive than has hitherto been believed.

The *1125 Continuation*, 1117–25

The *1125 Continuation* – designated B* by Georg Waitz and 'Recension 4' by Franz-Josef Schmale and Irene Schmale-Ott – is the most widely disseminated continuation of Frutolf's *Chronicle*.[333] Its text is an amalgamation of earlier sources. From the creation of the world until 1105 it reproduces Frutolf's *Chronicle* and the *1106 Continuation* more or less exactly. Its annals from 1106 to 1116 are very similar to the corresponding annals in the *Anonymous imperial chronicle* and Ekkehard's *Chronicle* for Erkembert of Corvey (believed to have been written in 1116/17). From 1117 onwards, however, its relationship with the last of these sources – Ekkehard's *Chronicle* – is less clear. Both works contain virtually identical annals from 1117 to 1125. This feature has been explained by the assumption that the *1125 Continuation* represents the original version of those annals and that Ekkehard's earlier *Chronicle* for Erkembert was at some point conflated with it.[334]

The presumed author of the *1125 Continuation* is Ekkehard of Aura, although there is nothing in the manuscripts to corroborate that presumption. Schmale and Schmale-Ott were aware of this difficulty and so looked to the continuation's internal features to bolster its connexion with Ekkehard. They observed a continuity in style and content between the *1125 Continuation* and the earlier recensions they attributed to Ekkehard. The continuation's detailed report on the disputed episcopal election in Würzburg (1122) suggested to them that its author must have lived in eastern Franconia, while its lengthy treatment of Bishop Otto of Bamberg's first mission to the Pomeranians (1124 and 1125) indicated that he had connexions in Bamberg.[335] The only person who fulfilled these criteria, they argued, was Ekkehard of Aura. Though there remain problems with this thesis, for want of a more detailed study the presumed author of the *1125 Continuation* remains Ekkehard of Aura.[336]

333 See Schmale (1971), 117–25. Other manuscripts have been discovered since Schmale's study.
334 *MGH SS* 6, p. 11; *Chroniken*, p. 36. See above, p. 68.
335 *Chroniken*, pp. 36–8.
336 Some of the internal evidence could point to Bamberg. The comment that 'our most

The *1125 Continuation* seems to have been completed in the second half of 1125. Its *terminus post quem* is provided by the death of Henry V on 23 May 1125 while the *terminus ante quem* of the material up to the year 1122 is provided by the author's comments on the disputed episcopal succession in Würzburg. Upon the death of Bishop Erlung of Würzburg on 28 December 1121, Henry V invested the young and still unordained Count Gebhard of Henneberg with the bishopric. Simultaneously, the cathedral chapter elected one of its number, the deacon Rugger, who was supported by Archbishop Adalbert of Mainz and the emperor's enemies. Rugger was consecrated by Adalbert at the monastery of Münsterschwarzach but could not gain control of the city, which was held by Gebhard. The chronicler's comment in the annal for 1122 that 'since then, Rugger has held that part of the bishopric around the River Neckar for his own use, while Gebhard has securely possessed the city and its surrounding area' must have been written before the end of 1125, for Rugger died that year and Gebhard resigned. While we cannot be certain about the date of composition for the remaining annals, they give the impression of being a current account of events.

The content of the *1125 Continuation*

The annals for 1117–25 provide the principal surviving narrative source for the final years of Henry V's reign. These years were dominated by continuing struggle with the papacy over the issue of lay investiture and domestic unrest at home. Like his father before him, Henry V faced a coalition of his ecclesiastical and secular enemies and it was this coalition that forced him to come to terms with the papacy in the Concordat of Worms of 1122.

The continuator's portrayal of events leading up to the Concordat of Worms was shaped by his avowedly pro-papal sympathies. He carefully recorded the papal succession from Paschal II's death in 1118 to the accession of Honorius II in 1124. The care he took to emphasize the legitimacy of Gelasius II, Calixtus II and Honorius II was necessitated by the existence of the imperial antipope 'Gregory VIII'. In 1117, during his second Italian expedition, Henry V travelled to Rome to pursue personal negotiations with Paschal II. He sought, as he outlined

---

longed-for steward sent from heaven, Bishop Otto, revisited the flock entrusted to him' at Easter 1125, might suggest that the continuator was a Bamberg cleric: below, p. 282. In addition, a number of the documentary sources used by the continuator were available in Bamberg during the first quarter of the twelfth century: see below, pp. 266 n. 45, 276 n. 113, 284 n. 158.

in a letter to Bishop Hartwig of Regensburg, recognition of 'our right to grant our *regalia* to anyone by means of staff and ring'.[337] Although he had been granted this right in the Treaty of Ponte Mammolo six years earlier, the pope had repudiated the treaty in the Lateran synods of 1112 and 1116. For Henry, the problems created by this *de facto* impediment to investiture were compounded by the subversive activities of papal legates in Germany: for while Paschal refused to excommunicate the emperor – because he had sworn never to do so in the Treaty of Ponte Mammolo – he also refused to nullify the excommunications imposed on the emperor by his legates Conrad of Palestrina and Theoderic of S. Grisogono. Henry never managed to meet Paschal because the curia withdrew to Benevento before his arrival in March 1117. Paschal's death on 21 January 1118, however, presented Henry with an opportunity to press his claims on the pope-elect, Gelasius II (the papal chancellor John of Gaeta). Again, the curia narrowly escaped southwards and, according to the *Chronicle of Monte Cassino*, Henry sought as the price of his support the confirmation of the Treaty of Ponte Mammolo.[338] It was in these circumstances that the emperor turned to the Spanish prelate Archbishop Maurice of Braga, the only churchman in Rome prepared to compromise with him, and enthroned him as 'Gregory VIII' on Easter Day 1118.[339] Thus the 1125 continuator was keen to stress that Gelasius II was elected 'with the unanimous consent of all catholics', whereas the emperor's 'shameless seizure' of the papacy 'cruelly revived the schism'.[340] He delegitimized the antipope by characterizing him as Henry's idol and in subsequent annals publicized his ineffectuality and eventual deposition.[341]

The continuator was similarly eager to emphasize the unanimous nature of the election of Gelasius's successor, Calixtus II. Here the complicating factor was that Gelasius, unable to establish himself in Rome, had died in exile at Cluny. He was succeeded by Archbishop Guido of Vienne, a Burgundian and kinsman of Henry V, but equally an implacable opponent of the emperor (in fact, Guido had already excommunicated the emperor independently in 1112).[342] The continuator cited a letter from Calixtus to Archbishop Adalbert of Mainz, the emperor's

---

337 Henry V, *Letter* (*Codex Udalrici* 2, no. 318, ed. Jaffé, p. 315).
338 *Chronicle of Monte Cassino* 4.64, p. 526.
339 Robinson (1990), pp. 431–2.
340 *1125 Continuation* 1118, below, p. 264.
341 *Ibid.* 1118, 1119, 1121, below, pp. 264, 267, 269–70.
342 Ekkehard, *Chronicle* 1112, below, p. 243.

chief ecclesiastical opponent in Germany, informing the archbishop of the manner of his election: the letter was careful to stress that Calixtus had been elected legally by the cardinal bishops and acclaimed unanimously by the Roman people.[343] In 1124, three years after the capture and deposition of the antipope 'Gregory VIII', the succession to Calixtus II was marred by disagreement when the election of the elderly Cardinal Theobald of S. Anastasia as 'Celestine II' was set aside in favour of the election of Cardinal Lambert of Ostia as Honorius II owing to the intervention of the powerful Roman family of the Frangipani. Although the 1125 continuator erroneously believed Archbishop Walter of Ravenna to have been Lambert's opponent, and glossed over the contentious nature of this election by claiming a unanimity that in reality was absent, he was probably correct in identifying an important qualification possessed by Lambert: he had been among the cardinals who had negotiated the Concordat of Worms and his German experience may have recommended him to a faction within the college of cardinals who favoured better relations with the empire.[344]

The emperor's enthronement of 'Gregory VIII' precipitated the papal excommunication that Paschal II would not countenance: 'Gelasius and the cardinals who were with him ... condemned the emperor and his idol.'[345] The change in papal policy also led the papal legate Conrad of Palestrina to renew his earlier excommunication of Henry at synods in Cologne and – ignominiously for the emperor – at the royal estate of Fritzlar. Conrad's actions seem to have galvanized domestic opposition to Henry, for his proposal that the emperor should 'explain himself ... or be deposed from the kingdom' at an early autumn assembly in Würzburg brought Henry's unexpected return from Italy. At Tribur on 24 June 1119, the emperor gave in to his opponents, abandoned the antipope and 'promised to make satisfaction for everything of which he was accused according to the advice of the senate'.[346] It is likely that at Tribur the princes imposed upon the emperor the duty of reconciliation with the papacy. A papal council held in October 1119 at the French archiepiscopal city of Rheims, close to the German border, presented the opportunity for that reconciliation.

---

343 *JL* 6682; *1125 Continuation* 1119, below, p. 265.
344 *1125 Continuation* 1124, below, p. 282; Klewitz (1957), pp. 243–7; Schmale (1961), pp. 120–3.
345 *1125 Continuation* 1118, below, p. 264.
346 *Ibid.* 1119, below, p. 266.

Prior to the Council of Rheims, Henry V met with two intermediaries – Abbot Pontius of Cluny and William of Champeaux, the bishop of Châlons-sur-Marne – at Strasburg to discuss the terms of a compromise on the matter of lay investiture. The envoys had been chosen carefully to be acceptable to both sides: Pontius of Cluny had previously acted on behalf of Henry V while the distinguished scholar William of Champeaux could explain the workings of the compromise on investiture that had already been reached with the French king. William assured the emperor that he would suffer no diminution of authority by renouncing investiture and both sides seem to have agreed on a basis for moving forward. The 1125 continuator derived much of his information about the negotiations at Strasburg and the subsequent Council of Rheims from the *Narrative of the Council of Rheims* by Hesso, the *scholasticus* of Strasburg.[347] This work, however, is heavily prejudiced against Henry V and Hesso's bias was also transferred to the *1125 Continuation*. The chronicler claimed that the decision to hold the Council of Rheims was taken at Tribur and that 'the king promised to participate personally and to be reconciled to the universal church'.[348] That Henry agreed personally to attend the council is doubtful. As with the Council of Troyes (1107), it is likely that Henry 'could not permit this question to be decided in a foreign kingdom'.[349] Moreover, Calixtus II had arranged to travel to the border fortress of Mouzon in the Ardennes during the interval between the second and third sessions of the council to meet Henry. Following Hesso, the chronicler blamed Henry for the failure of the negotiations. He saw the matter in black-and-white terms: the emperor would not give up investiture even though he had 'agreed to the making of a concordat between the royal and priestly powers'.[350] Although historians still debate the exact reasons for Henry's change of heart, it is likely that he and the papal negotiators left Strasburg with different understandings of what had been agreed: when the emperor saw the draft version of the treaty drawn up by the papal curia he realized he had been under a misapprehension.[351]

The failure of these negotiations hardened the continuator's attitude towards investiture and the emperor, for in the following annals he reported three episcopal successions that vindicated the principle of

347 Hesso, *Narrative of the Council of Rheims*, pp. 21–8.
348 *1125 Continuation* 1119, below, p. 266.
349 *Anonymous imperial chronicle* 1107, below, p. 209.
350 *1125 Continuation* 1119, below, p. 266.
351 Robinson (1990), pp. 495–6.

free election. Archbishop Adelgoz of Magdeburg was succeeded by a member of the cathedral chapter named Rugger 'after a canonical election', while Bishop Theoderic II of Münster succeeded Burchard by 'ecclesiastical election'.[352] The case that the continuator reported in greatest detail, however, was that of Würzburg in 1122. Upon the death of Bishop Erlung on 28 December 1121 the cathedral chapter elected the deacon and canon Rugger; Henry V, however, 'raised up through episcopal investiture a certain youth named Gebhard'.[353] The emperor's interest in Würzburg was undoubtedly dictated by the bishopric's wealth and key strategic value: its bishop customarily administered the duchy of Franconia, and Henry's recent quarrel with Bishop Erlung, which had resulted in his attempt to reassign the administration of the duchy to his nephew, Conrad of Staufen, made him keenly aware of the need to place this vital bishopric in the hands of an amenable candidate.[354] The Würzburg incident was symptomatic both of Henry's determination to maintain the right of investiture and of the level of opposition he faced from the German princes, for Archbishop Adalbert of Mainz and 'several of the Saxon princes ... confirmed the episcopal election and investiture of the aforementioned Rugger against the will of the king'.[355] As in 1119, it was this opposition that forced Henry to negotiate with the papacy; the emperor perceived that a resolution of the investiture issue was the most effective way of dividing his ecclesiastical and secular enemies.

The continuation's brief account of the agreement reached between Henry V and the papal legates on 23 September 1122 – the Concordat of Worms – is the most detailed account to survive. Like the account of the failed negotiations of 1119, it adopts a pro-papal stance and, furthermore, portrays the concordat as a victory for the church: divine intervention 'bent all the impetuosity of the emperor into obedience to the reverend pope for the cause of Mother Church'.[356] The account emphasizes the concessions made by the emperor more than those made by the pope and ignores the fact that in 1122 Henry obtained a better resolution than that on offer in 1119. For in 1119 the papal representatives would not concede that episcopal and abbatial elections should take place at court or that the emperor should confer the *regalia* on

352 *1125 Continuation* 1119, 1121, below, pp. 267, 269.
353 *Ibid.* 1122, below, p. 273.
354 Ekkehard, *Chronicle* 1116, below, p. 248.
355 *1125 Continuation* 1122, below, p. 273.
356 *Ibid.*, below, p. 275.

the elect with the sceptre and receive homage in return.[357] Neither did the continuator mention the criticisms that Calixtus II faced because of the concordat at the First Lateran Council (1123): he presented as a definitive victory what was from the papal perspective a temporary compromise.[358]

The chronicler's interest in reform also led him to include personal eulogies for pious figures associated with the reform movement. He records the death in 1120 of Bishop Theoger of Metz, who 'had many injuries inflicted upon him by the king's followers' and the martyrdom in 1123 of Bishop Dietrich of Zeitz-Naumburg, 'always a champion for the catholics against the schisms that sprouted forth at various times in his day'.[359] Their piety and loyalty to the papacy stood in stark contrast to the behaviour of Frederick of Somerschenburg, the Saxon count palatine and a supporter of Henry V, who was 'revealed to a certain servant of God' to have been 'carried down to the place of punishment'.[360] The *1125 Continuation* thus continued the pattern of the earlier chronicle by Bernold of St Blasien, which accorded Gregorians heroic status while confining their enemies to hell.[361] The author's most detailed personal biography and eulogy, however, was for Bishop Otto of Bamberg, whose first missionary visit to Pomerania is featured in the annals for 1124 and 1125.

The picture of Henry V presented by the *1125 Continuation* differs markedly from that of the *1106 Continuation* and the *Anonymous imperial chronicle*, and amplifies many of the reservations expressed in Ekkehard's *Chronicle* of 1116/17. The 1125 continuator censured the emperor for his involvement with the antipope 'Gregory VIII' and for his repeated attempts to retain lay investiture; a recurrent theme is that the emperor's obdurateness was the reason for the strife that endangered the kingdom. The 1120 annal was the occasion for a bitter polemic against Henry V that recalls the more vitriolic outbursts of eleventh-century chroniclers against his father Henry IV: 'the emperor un-imperially celebrated' Christmas at Worms; he was driven from Saxony because 'the bishops of that region abstained from communion with him'; in Franconia he was 'welcomed by some but detested by

---

357 Robinson (1990), pp. 437–8.
358 *Ibid.*, pp. 439–41; Stroll (2004), pp. 406–9.
359 *1125 Continuation* 1120, 1123, below, pp. 268, 279.
360 *Ibid.* 1120, below, p. 268.
361 *SC*, p. 53.

most'.³⁶² Like Berthold of Reichenau, who complained of Henry IV's 'savage and unjust rage' in subduing his opponents, the 1125 continuator also repeatedly criticized the anger of Henry V towards his enemies.³⁶³ Both authors were drawing on Isidore's definition of the tyrant – 'thoroughly bad and wicked kings who enact upon their people their lust for luxurious domination and the cruelest lordship'.³⁶⁴ As a foil to Henry's cruel domination, the chronicler gave an increasingly prominent place to the emperor's enemies, particularly Archbishop Adalbert of Mainz and the Saxon princes. Adalbert, that 'eloquent man holding primacy ... north of the Alps', appears as a champion of church liberty as well as the leader of the opposition to Henry V. The Saxon princes who with 'zeal were zealous for the Lord God of Hosts',³⁶⁵ displayed the essential characteristics of pious laymen: they performed the bidding of the church, agreeing that the bishops of Worms and Speyer should be restored to their bishoprics, aiding Adalbert's attempt to lift the siege of his archiepiscopal city and attempting to enforce the canonical election of Rugger of Würzburg.

The clearest indication of the continuator's attitude to Henry V is provided by the obituary in which he accused the last Salian emperor of duplicity and avarice. 'He deprived his excommunicated father of the empire under the guise of religion', wrote the continuator, 'but once confirmed in the honour he changed his behaviour'. This is a bitter reference to the disappointed hopes of Gregorians in Germany, who in 1106 had seen the young Henry V as the champion of ecclesiastical liberty. Reformers had assumed that the young king's opposition to his father entailed his subscription to all of their aims, but the one thing that Henry V would not relinquish was lay investiture. There could be no greater contrast between this obituary and the prologue to the fifth book of Ekkehard's *Chronicle*: the Henry V of 1116 appeared to the 'servants of God everywhere bursting from their hiding places' as '*a light shining in darkness*' (Ps. 111.4; John 1.5), whereas the Henry V of 1125 inflicted 'injuries on the Apostolic See' and 'always treated it as inferior to himself'. If indeed Ekkehard of Aura was the author of the *1125 Continuation*, then its gloomy character testifies to his bitterly disappointed hopes.

362 *1125 Continuation* 1120, below, p. 267. Cf. Berthold, *Chronicle* 1078, 1079, pp. 313, 345 (*SC*, pp. 198, 219).
363 Berthold, *Chronicle* 1076, p. 235 (*SC*, p. 142). See *1125 Continuation* 1119, 1121, 1122, below, pp. 265, 271, 274.
364 Isidore, *Etymologies* 9.3.20, trans. Barney (2006), p. 201.
365 3 Kings 19.14.

A note on the texts

This translation is based upon the composite edition of Frutolf's *Chronicle* and its continuations by Franz-Josef Schmale and Irene Schmale-Ott: *Frutolfs und Ekkehards Chroniken und die anonyme Kaiserchronik* (Darmstadt, 1972). This edition partially replaces the older edition of Georg Waitz, which attributed Frutolf's *Chronicle* as well as the continuations to Ekkehard of Aura: *Monumenta Germaniae Historica, Scriptores in folio* 6 (Hanover, 1844), pp. 33–267. The 1972 edition presents a newly edited Latin text for the last hundred years of Frutolf's *Chronicle*, selections of the four recensions the editors attributed to Ekkehard and part of the *Anonymous imperial chronicle (Kaiserchronik)* as follows:

> Frutolf, *Chronicle*: 1001–1101
> Ekkehard, *Recension* 1: 1096–1106
> Ekkehard, *Recension* 2: comprising only the 'letter of dedication' to Henry V
> *Kaiserchronik*: letter of dedication, annals for 1095–1114
> Ekkehard, *Recension* 3: letter of dedication, annals for 1106–16
> Ekkehard, *Hierosolimita*: those parts independent of *Recension* 1
> Ekkehard, *Recension* 4: 1117–25

In order to avoid the excessive duplication of recycled text, Schmale and Schmale-Ott presented the recensions partially and sequentially. Thus their edition of Recension 4, for example, presents only the annals for 1117–25 and not those for the years before 1117. While this has the disadvantage of hiding the differences between the unprinted parts of the recensions and other recensions – and thus of impeding the reader's appreciation of how they might be related – it did, within the bounds of practicality, make available a continuous text from 1001 to 1125. Schmale and Schmale-Ott never completed their planned full edition of Frutolf's *Chronicle* and its continuations, and so Waitz's edition must still be used for the pre-1001 material. A new edition of Frutolf's *Chronicle* is being prepared for the *MGH* by Christian Lohmer, but his edition will not include the continuations.[366]

The present translation is the first English translation of Frutolf's *Chronicle* and its continuations, apart from the short extracts that have sometimes appeared in crusading anthologies. Schmale and Schmale-Ott's 1972 edition contains a facing-page German translation of the annals for 1001–1125. An earlier German translation covering the

---

[366] Frutolf, *Chronicle*, ed. C. Lohmer, *MGH SS* 33 (forthcoming).

period 1001–1125, but based upon the text of the 1844 edition, is that of W. Pflüger: *Die Chronik des Ekkehard von Aura* (Leipzig, 1879).

Somewhat unusually for an English translation – as opposed to a critical edition – the introduction to this volume has devoted a great deal of attention to manuscript sources and their relationship with one another. This was not the original intention of the study, which began from the assumption that the important work of Schmale and Schmale-Ott represented a definitive solution to the textual problems surrounding Frutolf of Michelsberg's *Chronicle* and its continuations. Over the course of preparing the translation, however, it became increasingly apparent that the status of the continuations – and by extension the question of their authorship – was far from certain. In short, the manuscript transmission of the continuations is so complex that in some cases we cannot be sure to what extent their surviving manuscripts reflect the originals themselves.

A detailed textual study and critical edition of the continuations of Frutolf's *Chronicle* remains an urgent *desideratum*.[367] The tasks faced will be considerable. Among them will be the necessity of establishing whether Ekkehard's *Chronicle* for Erkembert of Corvey survives in two or four manuscripts. Clarity regarding the relationship of Ekkehard's *Chronicle* and the *Anonymous imperial chronicle* will result in more certainty about which work was written first. This in turn will affect our understanding of passages that claim to be eyewitness accounts, such as the account of the ill-fated Italian embassy of early 1106 or the account of the Council of Guastalla in late 1106.[368] Also needing re-examination is the significance of the *1125 Continuation*, for it is unclear whether or not it is merely a later amalgamation of already existing continuations. Any study will entail a thorough reassessment of the career of Ekkehard of Aura, which will have a direct impact upon the question of his authorship of the continuations. The introduction to this volume cannot take the place of these studies. It has, however, sought to draw attention to uncertainties where they exist and thereby to encourage the reader to think about their implications for our understanding of the texts. In the mean time, it is hoped that readers will feel free to draw their own conclusions regarding the involvement of Ekkehard of Aura with Frutolf's *Chronicle*.

---

367 I intend to pursue this study in the future.
368 See below, pp. 203, 206–7, 224–5, 232–4.

FRUTOLF OF MICHELSBERG, *CHRONICLE* (1001–1101)

The years of Henry II.

1.[1] In the one-thousand-and-first year of the Lord's Incarnation and the one-thousand-seven-hundred-and-fifty-second year since the founding of the city [Rome], Henry II,[2] formerly duke of Bavaria, who after Otto III[3] had died childless became the foremost in the kingdom, accepted the kingship and ruled in the eighty-fourth place since Augustus for twenty-three years and five months, twelve years with the title of king and eleven with the dignity and title of emperor. Having been elevated to the throne of the kingdom, having overcome Margrave Henry[4] and others who had resisted him at the beginning of his reign, and having subjugated Italy, Bohemia and Boleslav[5] together with the whole of the Slavic people, he was granted rest by the Lord.[6] Considering that he would have no sons because, as many attest, he never knew Cunigunde[7] his consort in the kingdom but loved her like a sister, he made the Lord, the giver of all good things,[8] his heir; and in the sixth year of his reign on wise counsel he founded the bishopric of Bamberg in honour of St Peter and St George, and endowed the place itself most copiously with rich estates and every appropriate adornment, as can still be seen today. By building a monastery in the southern part of the city for the order of canons in honour of St Stephen[9] the first martyr and founding another

1 The regnal years of Henry II. See above, p. 29.
2 Henry II (973–1024), king 1002, emperor 1014.
3 Otto III (980–1002), king 983, emperor 996. Otto III and Henry II were second cousins.
4 Henry of Schweinfurt, margrave of the Bavarian Nordgau (980–1017).
5 Boleslav Chrobry, duke of Poland 992–1025, king 1025.
6 A faint echo of 4 Esdras 2.34.
7 Cunigunde (d. 1033), queen and empress (Luxemburg family).
8 See James 1.17.
9 The collegiate church of St Stephen, founded by Bishop Eberhard of Bamberg on behalf of Queen Cunigunde and King Henry between 1007 and 1009. See Göller (2007), p. 44. Canons regular: clerics who followed a rule, lived a common life and served collegiate churches (usually, but not exclusively, in towns). In the later eleventh century, through the influence of the reform papacy, they would come to follow the *Rule* of St Augustine: Tellenbach (1993), pp. 120–1.

monastery in the other, that is the northern part, for regular monks in honour of St Michael the Archangel and St Benedict the abbot,[10] he provided also for himself and his city – founded on the rock of apostolic strength[11] and fortified and adorned with the walls and ramparts of the merits of St George and other saints – a *strong tower*[12] in Stephen against the buffeting winds of vice, and against that cold wind which has set its seat in the *north* – whence *all evil breaks forth*[13] – a safe refuge in the protection of angels, so that being surrounded *from right and left by the arms of justice*[14] in nothing was the waylayer[15] able to prevail. And where there was need in other places of the saints throughout the breadth of the kingdom he bestowed the largess of his munificence in no less measure, restoring what had hitherto been dilapidated to a better state and adding to whatever was less than sufficient.

The king's brother Bruno,[16] the bishop of the diocese of Augsburg, *envied his* brother's *propitious acts*[17] and inflicted as many injuries upon him as he might or, when he could not do so himself, supported wrongdoers or exhorted others to wrongdoing by his enthusiastic encouragement. Not only did his brother not respond with vengeance but, truly imbued with brotherly love, he passed over and patiently endured everything, busying himself *overcoming* him *with good*.[18]

Their sister, the lady Gisela[19] of happy memory, was sought out in marriage by the king of the Hungarians who was called Stephen;[20] but he was not worthy to marry her until he promised that he would accept the precepts of the Christian religion and the sacrament of holy baptism along with all his people. Once he did what he had promised, he remained afterwards pious and devoted to the Lord in the execution of

10 Michelsberg.
11 In Latin, a play upon the word *petrus* ('rock'), referring to St Peter and by extension the papacy. See Matthew 16.18.
12 Psalm 60.4.
13 Jeremiah 1.14.
14 2 Corinthians 6.7.
15 The Devil.
16 Bishop Bruno of Augsburg, 1006–29. For contemporary accounts of Bruno's quarrels with his brother see Thietmar, *Chronicle* 5.32, 5.38, 6.2–3, pp. 257, 263, 277–8; trans. Warner (2001), pp. 226, 230, 238–9.
17 Sulpicius Severus, *Vita sancti Martini* 2.5.
18 Romans 12.21.
19 Gisela (*c.* 985–1060).
20 Stephen I, king of Hungary 1001–38. The marriage took place in 995/6.

good works, which divine mercy demonstrated after his death through the evident sign of the occurrence of miracles at his grave.

After King Henry had spread the odour of his good reputation far and wide by bringing the place he loved[21] as well as other churches to perfection through enrichment, adornment and cultivation, at divine calling he went *the way of all flesh*[22] and joyfully returned his soul to God, as we believe, *on the third Ides of July* [14 July] in the twenty-fourth year of his reign, the eleventh of his emperorship and the fifty-second of his life. *He was buried in the bishopric of Bamberg which he founded, in the church of St Peter.*[23]

2. The year of the Lord 1002. *King Henry attacked Margrave Henry with an army and others who were resisting him.*[24]

3. The first year of the indiction.[25] The year of the Lord 1003. *King Henry subjugated Italy,*[26] *Bohemia*[27] *and Duke Boleslav as well as all the people of the Slavs.*[28]

4. The year of the Lord 1004. *There was a great famine.*[29]

5. The year of the Lord 1005.

6. The year of the Lord 1006. *The bishopric of Bamberg was founded by King Henry and Eberhard was* installed *there as bishop.*[30]

---

21 Bamberg.
22 See 3 Kings 2.2.
23 *WC*, p. 30. The cathedral at Bamberg, dedicated to Sts Peter and George.
24 *WC*, p. 29. Herman of Reichenau dates this expedition to 1003: *Chronicle* 1003, p. 118 (*SC*, p. 58).
25 A Roman fiscal cycle of fifteen years beginning in AD 312. See Cheney (2000), pp. 2–4.
26 *WC*, p. 29. On 14 May 1004 Henry was crowned king of Italy at Pavia. Violence ensued between the Pavians and the members of Henry's entourage. See Thietmar, *Chronicle* 6.6–7, pp. 281–2; trans. Warner (2001), pp. 241–2; Herman, *Chronicle* 1004, p. 118 (*SC*, p. 59).
27 In autumn 1004 Henry II restored the exiled Duke Jaromir of Bohemia: Thietmar, *Chronicle* 6.10–14, pp. 286–93; trans. Warner (2001), pp. 244–7. Like Thietmar, Herman of Reichenau dates this restoration to 1004: *Chronicle* 1004, p. 118 (*SC*, p. 59).
28 The expedition to Poland took place during August and September 1005: Thietmar, *Chronicle* 6.22, 26–7, pp. 300–1, 305–6; trans. Warner (2001), pp. 252, 254–6.
29 *WC*, p. 29.
30 *WC*, p. 29. Bishop Eberhard of Bamberg, 1007–40; Henry II's German chancellor

7. The year of the Lord 1007.

8. The year of the Lord 1008. *Bishop Bruno,*[31] formerly *a monk, journeyed to heaven: he had been afflicted with many tortures by the Prussians, having had his hands and legs hewn off and afterwards his head cut off. Bishop Eberhard was consecrated.*[32]

9. The year of the Lord 1009.

10. The year of the Lord 1010.

11. The year of the Lord 1011.

12. The year of the Lord 1012.

13. The year of the Lord 1013. *Henry was crowned and received imperial consecration from Pope Benedict in Rome.*[33]

14. The year of the Lord 1014. *Duke Ernest was killed while hunting.*[34]

15. The year of the Lord 1015.

16. The year of the Lord 1016. *Bishop Henry of Würzburg died.*[35]

17. The year of the Lord 1017.

1006–8/9; Italian chancellor until 1012/13; Italian arch-chancellor until 1024. The bishopric of Bamberg was founded at the Synod of Frankfurt on 1 November 1007. See Thietmar, *Chronicle* 6.30–2, pp. 310–13; trans. Warner (2001), pp. 257–9. On the foundation see Weinfurter (1986), 277–8; Arnold (1997), pp. 140–1; Störmer (1997), 443.

31 *WC*, p. 29. Bruno of Querfurt (*c.* 974–1009), missionary and martyr. See Thietmar, *Chronicle* 6.95, trans. Warner (2001), pp. 300–1.

32 *Chroniken*, p. 52, assigns the report of Eberhard's consecration to 1009. Frutolf's autograph manuscript (Jena, Thüringer Universitäts- und Landesbibliothek, Bose q. 19, fol. 171r), however, places it in 1008 and in this is followed by all manuscripts of the *1125 Continuation*. Dr Christian Lohmer's forthcoming edition for the *MGH* also assigns the report to 1008.

33 *WC*, p. 29. Pope Benedict VIII, 1012–24. The coronation took place on 14 February 1014: Thietmar, *Chronicle* 7.1, pp. 396–7; trans. Warner (2001), pp. 306–7.

34 *WC*, p. 29. Duke Ernest I of Swabia, 1012–31 May 1015. Thietmar, *Chronicle* 7.14, p. 414, trans. Warner (2001), p. 316, blames the accident on one of his knights; Herman of Reichenau identifies an otherwise unknown Count Adalbero as the culprit: *Chronicle* 1015, p. 119 (*SC*, p. 62).

35 *WC*, p. 29. Bishop Henry of Würzburg, 995/6–14 November 1018.

18. The year of the Lord 1018. The first year of the indiction.

19. The year of the Lord 1019. *Pope Benedict came to Bamberg and dedicated the church of St Stephen.*[36] *In the same year Bishop Werner of Strasburg fought with the Swabians against the Burgundians and was victorious.*[37]

20. The year of the Lord 1020. *There was a great earthquake on the fourth Ides of May* [12 May], *a* Thursday. In the same year *Archbishop Heribert of Cologne died. Pilgrim succeeded him.*[38]

21. The year of the Lord 1021. In the fifth year of the indiction, on Thursday the fourth Nones of November [2 November], in the twenty-first year of the glorious reign of the Emperor Henry and the ninth year of his emperorship, with the emperor himself presiding and overseeing, Eberhard, the first bishop of the church of Bamberg, in the thirteenth year since his installation, dedicated the church of St Michael on the Mount in honour of the same saintly archangel and St Benedict the abbot.[39] Many bishops took part in this consecration, namely Aribo of Mainz,[40] who dedicated the altar of St Martin, and Pilgrim of Cologne, who consecrated the altar of St Peter, along with many others. Rato,[41] the first father of this monastery, began to live in this same place in the year of the Lord's Incarnation 1015, and in that same year the foundations of the monastery were begun; and the church was dedicated in the second year of Henry,[42] the second abbot.

22. The four-hundred-and-fiftieth olympiad.[43] The year of the Lord

---

36 *WC*, p. 29. Benedict came to Bamberg on 24 April 1020, at which time Henry II placed his foundation under papal protection.

37 Bishop Werner I of Strasburg, 1001–28. Herman of Reichenau dates this expedition, which was provoked when King Rudolf III of Burgundy rescinded his promise of Burgundian succession to Henry II, to 1020: *Chronicle* 1020, p. 119 (*SC*, p. 62).

38 *WC*, p. 30. Archbishop Heribert of Cologne, 999–1021; Archbishop Pilgrim of Cologne, 1021–36.

39 St Benedict of Nursia (d. *c.* 550). Michelsberg was founded in 1015 by Bishop Eberhard of Bamberg. See Hallinger (1950), pp. 345–53.

40 Archbishop Aribo of Mainz, 1021–31.

41 Abbot Rato of Michelsberg, 1015/17–20.

42 Abbot Henry of Michelsberg, 1020–39.

43 The four-year cycle between the ancient Olympic games. See Isidore of Seville, *Etymologies* 5.37.1; trans. Barney (2006), p. 129.

1022. *Emperor Henry received the surrender of Troia,*[44] *and there was great loss of life in the army. Bishop Gebhard of Regensburg died; in his place another Gebhard was appointed.*[45]

23. The year of the Lord 1023.

24. The year of the Lord 1024. Emperor Henry II departed [this life].[46]

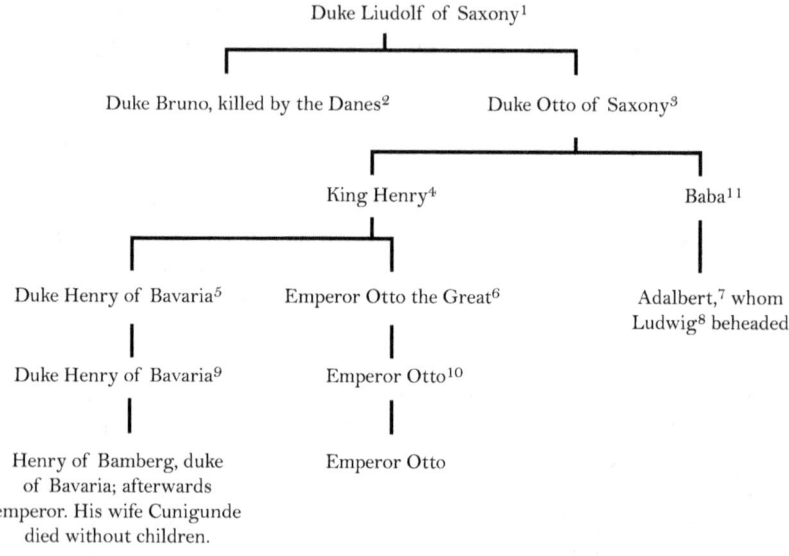

Genealogy 2 Frutolf's genealogy of the Ottonian dynasty.[47]

44 *WC*, p. 30. Troia surrendered in June 1022. See Holtzmann (1941), pp. 477–8; Deér (1972), pp. 26–7; Bloch (1986), pp. 14–18.

45 Bishop Gebhard I of Regensburg, 994–1023; Bishop Gebhard II of Regensburg, 1023–36.

46 13 July.

47 Frutolf's genealogy of the Ottonian dynasty. Cf. *WC*, p. 28. 1: Duke Liudolf of Saxony (d. 866). 2: Duke Bruno of Saxony, 866–80. 3: Duke Otto 'the Illustrious' of Saxony, 880–912. 4: Henry I, 'the Fowler' (876–936), duke of Saxony 912, king 919. 5: Duke Henry of Bavaria (d. 955). 6: Otto I 'the Great' (d. 973), king 936, emperor 962. 7: Adalbert of Babenberg, *fl.* late ninth century–early tenth century. 8: Ludwig (Louis) IV 'the Child' (893–911), king of East Francia and Lotharingia 900. 9: Henry 'the Quarrelsome', duke of Bavaria 955–76, 985–95. 10: Otto II (955–83), king 961, emperor 967. 11: Baba is probably apocryphal. Duke Otto's daughter was Oda, who married King Zwentibald of Lotharingia (d. 900): Regino of Prüm, *Chronicle* 897, trans. MacLean (2009), p. 221. Baba also appears in a catalogue of kings and emperors that survives in an early twelfth-century manuscript (Admont, Stiftsbibliothek, Cod. 735): '[Duke Otto] had a son who was called Henry the Humble and a daughter named Baba, from whose name the hill of Babenberg [Bamberg] is taken; she was the mother of Adalbert, whom Emperor Ludwig beheaded on account of the

In the year of the Lord's Incarnation 1025 and from the foundation of Rome 1,776, Conrad,[48] who although one of the foremost in the kingdom had opposed the previous king by rebelling, succeeded to the kingdom amid dissent among the princes over his election but with the support of Archbishop Aribo of Mainz and Bishop Eberhard of Bamberg; he ruled for fifteen years in the eighty-fifth place after Augustus.[49] Having been elevated to the seat of kingship, he planned on the advice of Bishop Bruno of Augsburg – the brother of Emperor Henry who, as mentioned above, *always envied his* brother's *propitious acts*[50] – to destroy the bishopric of Bamberg, since that same Bishop Bruno promised Queen Gisela[51] that he would transfer all the riches that had come to him by hereditary right to her son Henry.[52] Accordingly, the place and time of the meeting to which the king was to be conducted were fixed. But the night before that meeting was to occur Bishop Eberhard went secretly to the tent of the said Bruno and, sitting on his bed, admonishing and beseeching him greatly on this matter, he impressed the memory of his brother on his soul with equal solicitude. When Eberhard had spent many hours there he departed and Bishop Bruno, affected by the things he had heard, fell into a dream in which he saw his brother Emperor Henry – whose face had been disfigured through half its beard having been plucked off – standing by his bed and confronting him. Whereupon, much perturbed and puzzled, Bruno demanded who had the brazenness to presume [to disfigure Henry] in such a way. 'You have done this', came the reply, 'because you have dared to despoil me and the saints of God whom I have endowed with the things that God granted to me. Beware of this and further brazenness so that what you have begun is not repaid with great misery.' At this Bruno bolted up, since not only did the vision terrify him but it also

---

    murder of his brother Conrad' (*MGH SS* 10, p. 137). A possible source is Widukind of Corvey's *Deeds of the Saxons* 1.22, p. 31. See also Hlawitschka (2006), p. 46.

48 Conrad II (990–1039), king 1024, emperor 1027. Conrad was a kinsman of Henry II: Weinfurter (1999), pp. 5–17; Wolfram (2006), pp. 15–30.

49 The royal election took place on 8 September 1024. See Wipo, *Deeds of Emperor Conrad* 1, 2, pp. 8–20 (*IL*, pp. 57–66).

50 Sulpicius Severus, *Vita sancti Martini* 2.5.

51 Gisela (989/90–1043), queen and empress. Daughter of Duke Herman II of Swabia and Gerberga, the daughter of King Conrad of Burgundy (937–93). Married Count Bruno of Brunswick (date unknown), Duke Ernest I of Swabia (*c.* 1010) and Conrad II (1016/17). See Wolfram (2006), pp. 31–41.

52 Henry III (1017–56), king 1028, emperor 1046. The 'riches that had come to him by hereditary right': the inheritance of Henry II, much of which had formed the endowment for Bamberg.

made his limbs shake with horror and fear. Morning came and although he was expected for a long time at the assembly of the princes he did not appear; so the queen, worried for the sake of her son, besought him through messengers to appear so that he might fulfil his promise. But he protested that he was so ill that he could neither rise from his bed nor move on his feet. When it was suggested that he should be carried to the assembly in his bed so that what he had promised might be fulfilled, he utterly refused and declared openly that he had *sinned against God*,[53] against His saints and against his own brother. Thus divine mercy – on account of the merit of his family, lest the hope which He had placed in it be cheated – prevented all those shameful plots and conspiracies, so that what began well by this would be confirmed and always become more perfect.

In the second year of his reign, therefore, *King Conrad made his son Henry king and himself travelled to Rome* to receive *imperial* coronation.[54] After this he married his son to Cunigunde,[55] the daughter of Cnut, king of the Danes,[56] binding him to himself eagerly for good relations. In his own castle called Limburg, which before he had used for other purposes, he established a monastery, enriching it with many treasures and introducing there a congregation of monks under an abbot.[57] He also decided to exalt the bishopric of Speyer, but because his lifetime was not long enough, it fell to his son Henry to carry out his will, so that what began with magnificence his son Henry completed still more magnificently.[58]

1.[59] In the first year of King Conrad *a great dissention was* fomented *against* him *in the kingdom*, but it was with divine aid quickly calmed.[60]

---

53 An echo of Exodus 10.16.

54 *WC*, p. 30. See the annal for 1026, below.

55 See n. 79 below.

56 Cnut II 'the Great' (d. 1035), king of Denmark 1017/18–35, king of England 1016–35, king of Norway 1028–35.

57 The Salian family monastery of Limburg on the Hardt, founded in 1025 (diocese of Speyer). See Hauck (1954), 3, p. 1009.

58 On the restoration of the cathedral of Speyer see Kubach and Haas (1972); Weinfurter (1999), pp. 35–43, 111.

59 The regnal years of Conrad II.

60 *WC*, p. 30. This rebellion was led by Conrad 'the Younger' (d. 1039), Duke Ernest II of Swabia, 1015–30, and Duke Frederick II of Upper Lotharingia (d. 1026/7). Conrad the Younger was Conrad II's first cousin and the defeated candidate in the royal election of 1024. Ernest II was the king's stepson, the son of Queen Gisela by her second marriage. Frederick II was the stepfather of Conrad the Younger. On the rebellion see Wipo, *Deeds* 10, p. 32 (*IL*, p. 75); Bresslau (1879), pp. 57–8, 92–4.

2. The year of the Lord 1026. *Henry, son of King Conrad, was made king.*[61] Conrad *went to Rome* and was promoted to the *imperial* dignity.[62]

3. The year of the Lord 1027. *Bishop Bruno of Augsburg and Count Welf*[63] fought *against each other with plunder and arson.*

4. The year of the Lord 1028. *Duke Ernest* of Swabia[64] and *Count Welf came to surrender to Emperor Conrad.*[65]

5. The year of the Lord 1029. *Bishop Bruno of Augsburg died;*[66] *Eberhard* succeeded him.[67]

6. The year of the Lord 1030. *Emperor Conrad led an army against King Stephen of Hungary.*[68] *Meanwhile in Swabia Duke Ernest, Count Werner*[69] *and many others were killed on the sixteenth Kalends of September* [17 August].

---

61 *WC*, p. 30. Both Wipo and Herman of Reichenau date the coronation to 1028: Wipo, *Deeds* 23, p. 42 (*IL*, p. 84); Herman, *Chronicle* 1028, p. 121 (*SC*, p. 65).

62 Conrad was crowned emperor by Pope John XIX on Easter Day 1027 (26 March). Present were King Rudolf III of Burgundy and King Cnut of Denmark.

63 *WC*, p. 30. The Swabian Count Welf II (d. 1030). Herman of Reichenau identifies Welf among the ringleaders of the 1025 rebellion: *Chronicle* 1025, p. 120 (*SC*, p. 64). On the feud between Bishop Bruno and Count Welf see Wipo, *Deeds* 19, p. 38 (*IL*, pp. 80–1). According to Wipo, the bishop of Augsburg resorted to imperial aid to end the feud satisfactorily.

64 *WC*, p. 30. Duke Ernest II of Swabia, 1015–30. See n. 60 above.

65 Ernest and Welf surrendered at Ulm in July 1027. Ernest was imprisoned in the Saxon fortress of Giebichenstein: Wipo, *Deeds* 25, p. 43 (*IL*, p. 82).

66 *WC*, p. 30. Bruno died on 24 April.

67 Eberhard, bishop of Augsburg 1029–47.

68 *WC*, p. 30. See n. 20 above. Conrad's unsuccessful expedition was in response to Stephen's plundering raids into Bavaria. Wipo blames the Bavarians for provoking these raids: *Deeds* 26, p. 44 (*IL*, pp. 85–6). See Bresslau (1879), pp. 298–300.

69 Werner (Wezilo), count of Kyburg and Thurgau (d. 1030), vassal of Ernest II. Wipo, *Deeds* 25, p. 43 (*IL*, p. 85), relates that Duke Ernest was released from captivity and restored to his duchy on condition that he 'would pursue his knight Wezilo, who had disturbed the kingdom with many seditions, as an enemy of the commonwealth with all his followers, and confirm that he would do so with an oath'. When Ernest refused and renewed his opposition to Conrad II he was deprived of his duchy again. Ernest and Werner were apprehended by imperial forces under the command of Count Manegold, whom Wipo described as 'a vassal of the emperor and holding a great benefice from the abbey of Reichenau': *Deeds* 28, p. 46 (*IL*, p. 87). All three died in the skirmish. Bresslau (1879), p. 302 suggested that Manegold was from the house of the counts of Nellenburg.

7. The year of the Lord 1031. *King Stephen made peace with the emperor* through *emissaries.*[70]

8. The year of the Lord 1032. *King Rudolf of Burgundy died and sent his crown to Emperor Conrad.*[71]

9. The year of the Lord 1033. *Bishop Meinhard of Würzburg died.*[72] *Emperor Conrad advanced into Burgundy in winter.*[73] *An eclipse of the sun occurred on the third Kalends of July* [29 June] *at the sixth hour.*[74] The first year of the indiction.

10. The year of the Lord 1034. The emperor *advanced* into France against *Odo.*[75] He *also laid waste to Burgundy.*

11. The year of the Lord 1035. *The castle of Werben,* located *on the borders of Saxony, was captured by the pagans who are called the Liutizi,*[76] *and many of the Christians were killed and captured. Whereupon* the emperor *led an expedition against them.*[77]

12. The year of the Lord 1036. *Bishop Gebhard* II *of Regensburg died and Gebhard* III[78] succeeded *in his place.* The daughter of Cnut, the king of the Danes, was married to Henry, the son of the emperor.[79] The Liutizi *paid tribute* to the emperor. Arch*bishop Pilgrim of Cologne died* and was replaced by *Herman.*[80]

---

70 *WC*, p. 30. Cf. Wipo, *Deeds* 26, pp. 44–5 (*IL*, pp. 85–6); Herman, *Chronicle* 1031, p. 121 (*SC*, p. 66). Bresslau (1879), pp. 312–13.

71 *WC*, p. 30. Rudolf III (993–1032) died on 6 September. Wolfram (2006), 239–46.

72 *WC*, p. 30. Bishop Meinhard I of Würzburg, 1019–34 (d. 22 March).

73 To secure his accession to the kingship against Count Odo of Blois-Champagne: Wolfram (2006), pp. 239–42.

74 The sixth hour after daybreak: noon.

75 *WC*, p. 30. Odo II, count of Blois-Champagne (995–1037), nephew of King Rudolf III. Odo claimed the Burgundian throne on kinship: Wipo, *Deeds* 29, p. 47 (*IL*, p. 87); Wolfram (2006), p. 239.

76 *WC*, p. 30. The Liutizi: a confederation of Slavic tribes comprising the Zirzipani, Tollensi, Kessini and Redarii living between the Elbe and Oder. See Reuter (1991), pp. 178–9, 213, 256–7, 260, 262; Wolfram (2006), pp. 210–12.

77 Cf. Wipo, *Deeds* 33, p. 53 (*IL*, p. 92). See Wolfram (2006), pp. 222–4.

78 *WC*, p. 30. Gebhard III, 1036–60, half-brother of Conrad II (from the second marriage of Conrad's mother, Adelaide of Metz).

79 Gunhild (d. 1038), known as Cunigunde in Germany. She was married to Henry III at the end of June 1036 in Nijmegen: Bresslau (1884), pp. 169–70.

80 Archbishop Herman II, 1036–56, son of Otto II's daughter Matilda (d. 1025) and Ezzo, count palatine of Lotharingia.

13. The year of the Lord 1037. *Emperor Conrad led an army into Italy and took the bishop of Milan into custody;*[81] *he then escaped and rebelled against the emperor. Odo, prince of the Carolingians, was defeated by Duke Gozelo of Lotharingia*[82] *and was killed by a certain knight while fleeing.*

14. The year of the Lord 1038. *Stephen, the* pious *king of the Hungarians, died.*[83]

15. The year of the Lord 1039. Empress Cunigunde, mother of the poor though rich herself, departed [this life] for the riches of Christ on the fifth Nones of March [3 March].[84] *Duke Herman* of Swabia, the son of Empress Gisela, *died.*[85] *Emperor Conrad died on the second Nones of June* [4 June] *and was buried at Speyer.*[86] *Bishop Reginbold of Speyer*[87] *died on the third Ides of October* [13 October]. *An eclipse of the sun* occurred *on the eleventh Kalends of September* [22 August]. The five-thousandth year since the beginning [of the world].[88]

The years of Henry III.

1.[89] The year of the Incarnation of the Lord 1040 and from the foundation of Rome 1,791. Henry III, the son of Emperor Conrad, who had already been made king in his father's lifetime,[90] succeeded his father and ruled for seventeen years in the eighty-sixth place since Augustus. Eberhard, the first bishop of Bamberg, died.[91]

81 *WC*, p. 30. Archbishop Aribert II, 1018–45. The events took place in March 1037: Wipo, *Deeds* 35, pp. 54–5 (*IL*, pp. 94–5). See Cowdrey (1966), 10–11; Wolfram (2006), pp. 122–7.

82 At the Battle of Bar (15 November). Gozelo I, duke of Lower Lotharingia 1023–44, duke of Upper Lotharingia 1033–44. Cf. Wipo, *Deeds* 35, p. 55 (*IL*, p. 94). See Bresslau (1884), pp. 269–72; Wolfram (2006), pp. 326–7.

83 *WC*, p. 30. Stephen died on 15 August.

84 The dowager Empress Cunigunde died on 3 March 1033. Frutolf perhaps misunderstood the *Würzburg Chronicle*, which records the death of 'Queen Cunigunde' in the fourteenth year of Conrad II's reign (1038) – a reference to the death of Henry III's first wife Gunhild on 16 July (Herman of Reichenau) or 18 July (Wipo). Cf. Herman, *Chronicle* 1038, p. 123 (*SC*, p. 71); Wipo, *Deeds* 37, p. 57 (*IL*, p. 96).

85 *WC*, p. 30. Duke Herman IV of Swabia, 1030–8 (d. 28 July). Cf. Herman, *Chronicle* 1038, p. 123 (*SC*, p. 71).

86 Conrad died at Utrecht on Whit Monday. Burial: 3 July. See Wolfram (2006), pp. 341–7.

87 Bishop Reginbold of Speyer, ?1032–9.

88 On Frutolf's interest in chronological reckoning see above, pp. 25–9.

89 The regnal years of Henry III.

90 In 1028. Henry succeeded in 1039.

91 13 August.

2. The year of the Lord 1041. *King Henry waged war on Duke Bretislav of Bohemia,*[92] *but since many nobles and knights were killed or captured in the thickets of the forests over there and beyond, he could achieve nothing worthy of remembrance. King Peter of the Hungarians also aided that same duke against the king.*[93]

3. The year of the Lord 1042. *The Hungarians made a certain Ovo*[94] *king and expelled Peter their own king. This fugitive and exile sought and received the protection of King Henry, against whom he had rebelled the previous year.*[95]

King Henry entered Bohemia and destroyed everything with fire and pillage, forcing the rebellious duke to give hostages and afterwards to come before him in person at Regensburg to make humble submission and to swear an oath of fealty and service.[96]

King Ovo of Hungary, on account of King Henry's support for Peter, whom he had deposed, plundered and laid waste to the borders of Bavaria;[97] *but the greater part of his army was destroyed by Margrave Adalbert.*[98]

4. The year of the Lord 1043. *King Henry entered Hungary, destroyed its two most populous cities and captured others subjecting them to himself.*[99] *Empress Gisela died on the sixteenth Kalends of March* [14 February] *and was buried at Speyer.*[100]

5. The year of the Lord 1044. *King Henry again invaded Hungary and, having received satisfaction, hostages, tribute and sworn promises of peace, moved on. He returned from there and participated in a synod at Constance*

---

92 *WC*, p. 30. Bretislav I, 1037–55.

93 Peter (d. 1059), king 1038–41, 1044–6. Frutolf, following the *Würzburg Chronicle*, conflates events that Herman of Reichenau reports for 1039 and 1040: *Chronicle* 1039, 1040, p. 123 (*SC*, p. 72).

94 *WC*, p. 30. Ovo (Aba/Samuel), king of Hungary 1041–4.

95 Herman of Reichenau reports these events for 1041: *Chronicle*, p. 123 (*SC*, p. 73).

96 Henry campaigned in Bohemia between 15 August and 29 September. Bretislav surrendered in October 1041, and received Bohemia and two Polish provinces: Steindorff (1874), pp. 107–13.

97 Ovo's expedition began on 13 February: *Annals of Niederaltaich* 1041, p. 28. See Steindorff (1874), pp. 149–51.

98 Adalbert (of Babenberg), margrave of the East March (Austria) 1018–55.

99 *WC*, p. 30. The cities of Hainburg and Pressburg. This expedition happened in 1042 according to Herman, *Chronicle* 1042, p. 124 (*SC*, p. 73).

100 15 February according to the Speyer necrology: Steindorff (1874), p. 173 n. 1.

where *he forgave all* who had opposed him and their *crimes, settled all violent feuds and proclaimed a peace unheard of until then in all of Swabia and in all other provinces of his kingdom, and confirmed it by royal authority.*[101] *Thereafter Agnes,*[102] *the daughter of Prince William of Poitiers,*[103] *was anointed queen at Mainz and he* [Henry] *was joined to her at Ingelheim in a royal wedding.*[104] *There the great throng of players and jesters was* not only *dismissed empty-handed and lamenting without payment,* but also without *food* and drink.[105]

Liutpold, the son of Margrave Adalbert and a great scourge of the Hungarians, died much too young.[106] *A great pestilence of cattle. The winter was hard and snowy.*

6. The year of the Lord 1045. *Bishop Bruno of Würzburg died on the sixth Kalends of June* [27 May].[107] Adalbero was appointed in his place.[108]

King Henry made his third expedition into Hungary and with God's help was victorious,[109] *driving out Ovo, who took flight together with his wife, children and followers. Henry restored Peter to the kingship, subjected the Hungarian kingdom to himself and returned home with great honour.*[110]

---

101 *WC*, p. 30. Henry proclaimed a peace edict, perhaps influenced by the Peace of God movement, at the cathedral of Constance in the second half of October 1043. Cf. Herman, *Chronicle* 1043, p. 124 (*SC*, pp. 74–5). See Steindorff (1874), pp. 185–7; Hoffmann (1964), pp. 88–9; Ladner (1968), pp. 70–8; Wadle (1973), pp. 159–62; Weinfurter (1999), pp. 101–3.

102 Agnes of Poitou (?1025–77), queen 1043, empress 1046.

103 William V, duke of Aquitaine-Poitou 995–1029.

104 The coronation probably took place in mid-November and the wedding in late November: *MGH DD H. III*, pp. 112–18. See Steindorff (1874), pp. 192–3.

105 Compare Donizo of Canossa's account of the wedding of Margrave Boniface of Canossa and Beatrice of Lotharingia (perhaps 1037), *Life of Matilda* 1.10, p. 368: 'Drums resounded here together with citharas and lutes and the renowned duke gave very great rewards to the actors.'

106 9 December 1043: Steindorff (1874), p. 195.

107 *WC*, p. 30. Bruno, son of Duke Conrad I of Carinthia (d. 1011), bishop of Würzburg 1034–45. Bruno was mortally wounded at Persenbeug (the residence of Richlind, widow of Count Adalbero II of Ebersberg) when a balcony he, Henry III and others were standing on collapsed: Herman, *Chronicle* 1045, p. 125 (*SC* pp. 77–8). Herman dates the accident to 26 May.

108 Bishop Adalbero of Würzburg, 1045–90.

109 A reference to the Battle of Menfö on 5 July 1044. Cf. Herman, *Chronicle* 1044, pp. 124–5 (*SC*, pp. 75–6).

110 At a ceremony in the church of St Mary at Stuhlweissenburg (Székesfehervar) according to the *Annals of Niederaltaich* 1044, p. 37.

Duke Godfrey of Lotharingia[111] *rebelled against King Henry; he was forced to surrender and was held in the castle of Giebichenstein until he made reasonable satisfaction.*[112]

7. The year of the Lord 1046. *King Henry entered Italy and was received peacefully by the Romans.*[113] *In a synod he deposed three popes*[114] *who had not been properly made and appointed Suidger,*[115] *the second bishop of the church of Bamberg, as pope, by whom he and his consort Agnes were raised to the imperial dignity* on the holy day of the Lord's birth.[116] On her return journey from there *the Empress Agnes gave birth to a daughter at Ravenna.*[117] *The emperor, however, successfully led his army through Apulia and many other provinces and returned with great honour. Pope Suidger died on the seventh Ides of October*[118] *[10 October]* and Patriarch *Poppo* of Aquileia *was appointed in his place.*[119]

8. The year of the Lord 1047. *King Peter of Hungary was captured and blinded by a certain Hungarian tyrant,*[120] *who then expelled him and began to rule.*

111 Godfrey III 'the Bearded', duke of Upper Lotharingia 1044–7, duke of Lower Lotharingia 1065–9, margrave of Tuscany 1054–69. Godfrey rebelled in 1044 in pursuit of his claim to succeed his father, Gozelo I, to both Lotharingian duchies. Cf. Herman, *Chronicle* 1044, p. 124; *Annals of Niederaltaich* 1044, p. 34 (*SC*, p. 75 and n. 167).

112 Godfrey was imprisoned in Giebichenstein (near Halle) in July 1045 and released on Whitsun 1046 (18 May), at which point he was restored to the duchy of Upper Lotharingia: Herman, *Chronicle* 1045, 1046, pp. 125–6 (*SC*, pp. 78–9); Lampert of Hersfeld, *Annales* 1045, p. 59. See Boshof (1978), 84–6.

113 *WC*, p. 30. Henry entered Italy in October and arrived at Rome in the week before Christmas.

114 At Sutri on 20 December. Three popes: Benedict IX (Theophylact of Tusculum), elected December 1032, resigned 1 May 1045, deposed 20 December 1046; Silvester III (Cardinal Bishop John of Sabina), elected 10 January 1045, deposed 10 March 1045; Gregory VI (John Gratian, archpriest of St John at the Latin Gate), elected 1 May 1045, deposed 20 December 1046. See Schmale (1979), 55–103.

115 Bishop Suidger of Bamberg, 1040–7, Pope Clement II, 24 December 1046–9 October 1047. Clement was consecrated on 25 December. See Gresser (2007).

116 The coronation ceremony: *Die Ordines für die Weihe und Krönung des Kaisers und der Kaiserin*, no. 13, pp. 34–5; Robinson (1999), pp. 230–1.

117 Gisela (d. *c.* 1053). See Black-Veldtrup (1995), pp. 19, 109–10.

118 9 October 1047. Clement was poisoned with lead: Gresser (2007), pp. 108–14.

119 Poppo, bishop of Brixen ?1039–48, Pope Damasus II, 1047–8; appointed by Henry III at Pöhlde in December 1047, consecrated in Rome on 17 July 1048. Frutolf confused Poppo of Brixen with Poppo, patriarch of Aquileia 1019–42.

120 *WC*, p. 30. Andreas I, 1046–60, nephew of King Stephen I of Hungary (see n. 20 above). This took place in 1046 according to Herman of Reichenau: *Chronicle* 1046, p. 126 (*SC*, p. 79).

9. The first year of the indiction. The year of the Lord 1048. *Pope Poppo died* less than a *year* after *he had been appointed.*[121] In his place Bishop *Bruno of Toul,* who was afterwards called *Leo, was appointed pope.*[122] *Duke Otto of Swabia*[123] *died and in his place another Otto,* count *of Sweinfurt, was raised up* [by the king].[124]

10. The year of the Lord 1049. *In the* fourth *year of his emperorship, Emperor Henry invaded certain parts of France against* Dukes *Godfrey and Baldwin.*[125] *He forced them into submission, pacified the kingdom in those parts and returned victorious with honour.*[126] *A synod was held at Mainz,*[127] *in which Pope Bruno and Emperor Henry* took part.

11. The year of the Lord 1050. *The Hungarians rebelled again. Bishop Gebhard of Regensburg,* who was the emperor's uncle, advanced to *oppose them himself in place of the emperor and put many of them to flight.*[128] Moreover, he repaired the buildings of the border town of Hainburg and secured it with a garrison and, having established complete peace, returned home.

12. The year of the Lord 1051. *Archbishop Bardo* of Mainz departed life in peace.[129] He was succeeded by *Luitpold,* the provost of Bamberg.[130] *Emperor Henry* went *again into Hungary and, dividing his host of knights*

---

121 *WC,* p. 31. Damasus II died on 9 August 1048.

122 Bruno, bishop of Toul 1026–51, Pope Leo IX, 1048/9–54. Leo was elected at an assembly in Worms in December 1048 and consecrated on 12 February 1049: Robinson (2004b), pp. 33–5, 57.

123 Otto II, count palatine of Lotharingia 1035–46, duke of Swabia 1045–7.

124 Otto III (of Schweinfurt), duke of Swabia 1048–57 (Babenberg family). Otto was appointed during an assembly at Ulm in late January: cf. *MGH DD H. III* 209 (25 January).

125 *WC,* p. 31. Baldwin V, count of Flanders 1035–67. Godfrey 'the Bearded' renewed his rebellion in 1047 and was joined by Count Baldwin.

126 Godfrey surrendered in July 1049, having been pursued by the forces of the bishops of Liège, Utrecht and Metz. Baldwin surrendered at Aachen after the king's expedition. Cf. Herman, *Chronicle* 1047–9, pp. 126–9 (*SC,* pp. 82–6). See Boshof (1978), 94–6.

127 19–26 October. See *MGH Constitutiones* 1.51, p. 97; Munier (2002), pp. 130–1.

128 *WC,* p. 31. According to Boshof (1986), 184, the conflict was provoked by Gebhard. See Herman, *Chronicle* 1050, p. 129 (*SC,* p. 87).

129 *WC,* p. 31. Bardo, monk of Fulda, abbot of Hersfeld, archbishop of Mainz 1031–51 (d. 10 or 11 June). His sanctity and posthumous reputation: Herman, *Chronicle* 1051, p. 130 (*SC,* p. 89).

130 Luitpold, archbishop of Mainz 1051–9.

in two parts,[131] *invaded the land, which is surrounded and protected by forests and above all by many lakes, and occupied it. Those people are hardier than others and their king acted cunningly, destroying their property and everything else, and evading* the army of the emperor, *which was weakened through hunger, thirst and many casualties. The knights of the emperor therefore destroyed a great part of the province, killed many in that place besides and returned unmolested, but without success, along with the emperor.*[132]

13. The year of the Lord 1052. *The emperor again attacked Hungary and returned without achieving anything.*[133] *He*[134] *was joined by Bruno, bishop of the apostolic see. When the pope had come to Regensburg,*[135] *in the presence of emissaries from Paris he examined the authenticity of the relics of the blessed martyr Dionysius*[136] *that they had there, which had long been in doubt, and confirmed their legitimacy.*[137] *He also took up St Wolfgang,*[138] *a bishop of that city, from his tomb.*[139] From there he travelled with the emperor to Bamberg where he caused the privileges of that place to be examined and read aloud by his chancellor Frederick,[140] who afterwards succeeded him, and by his own authority he confirmed them.[141] From there they travelled together into the country of the Rhine and celebrated the birth of the Lord at Worms.

131 The king attacked from the south through Carinthia while Bishop Gebhard of Regensburg, Duke Welf of Carinthia and Duke Bretislav of Bohemia attacked from the north: Herman, *Chronicle* 1051, p. 130 (*SC*, p. 89).

132 Cf. *Annals of Niederaltaich* 1051, p. 47. Steindorff (1881), p. 158, saw the expedition as a practical defeat.

133 *WC*, p. 31. Summer 1052. Leo IX, at the request of King Andreas, persuaded Henry to call off his siege of Pressburg, though Herman of Reichenau comments that Andreas had deceived the pope: *Chronicle* 1052, p. 131 (*SC*, pp. 92–3).

134 *Notae S. Emmerani*, pp. 1095–6. Frutolf makes a number of changes to this passage, including the alteration of the incorrect St Dionysius (Denis) 'the Aeropagite' to St Dionysius 'the martyr'.

135 7 October.

136 Dionysius/Denis (d. *c.* 250), bishop of Paris.

137 See Schmid (1989), pp. 119–21.

138 Wolfgang, bishop of Regensburg 972–99, abbot of St Emmeran 972–5. Wolfgang split the offices of bishop and abbot in 975 and introduced Gorze-style monastic reforms to St Emmeram. See McCarthy (2009), pp. 11–12.

139 That is, he canonized Wolfgang. On the canonization and its political significance see McCarthy (2009), pp. 27–8.

140 Frederick of Lotharingia, brother of Duke Godfrey 'the Bearded' of Lower Lotharingia, later Pope Stephen IX.

141 *JL* 4283 (6 November). See Steindorff (1881), pp. 186–7.

14. The year of the Lord 1053. The pope and emperor celebrated Christmas at Worms with divine and royal celebrations. The pope celebrated Mass on the holy day and, as was fitting, he asked Archbishop Luitpold of Mainz, as the foremost in his diocese, to perform this service the following day. After the procession and the saying of the collect, the archbishop took his seat and one of his deacons, Humbert by name,[142] sang the lesson as many were accustomed to do in celebration of this feast.[143] Several of the Romans who were assisting the pope disapproved of this; they complained to the pope that things were not being done according to Roman custom and, persevering, persuaded him to dismiss the deacon and to stop the chanting. Since the deacon scorned that in his youthful way, the pope again forbade him to continue. Then in an even and audible voice, where he had previously sung, he read the lesson properly through to the end. Once this was finished, the pope called him into his presence and demoted him for his contemptuous disobedience. The archbishop, however, demanded that the pope should restore his rank to him. When the pope refused, the archbishop, who was of the old discipline, permitted this with reluctance, for the time being remaining silent. After the Gospel had been read, the Offertory had been sung and the moment of the Consecration neared, the archbishop took his place again and declared it for a truth that neither he nor anybody else would complete the Consecration unless the pope received his minister back into the procession. When the pope considered this he deferred to the archbishop, and sent the minister back immediately once again in vestments. And having received what was owed, the prelate rejoined the service. In this incident both the authority of the bishop and the humility of the pope are worthy of recognition, because the former was trying to preserve the dignity of his office, while the latter, although he had been granted a higher dignity, came to realize that he nevertheless ought to defer to the metropolitan in his own diocese.[144]

After[145] *this the pope returned to Rome accompanied by many knights from different provinces who had been supplied through the help of his allies and imperial command. And after Easter he led an expedition to Apulia and fought against the Normans,*[146] *who had at some time come into that land from*

---

142 Not to be confused with Cardinal Humbert of Silva Candida, 1050–61.

143 Presumably, he sang the lesson very melismatically.

144 Steindorff (1881), pp. 188–9, and Tellenbach (1993), p. 190, have questioned the anecdote's factuality. On its context and purpose see above, p. 39; also McCarthy (2011).

145 *WC*, p. 31.

146 The Battle of Civitate (18 June), fought against Count Humphrey of Apulia, Count

abroad, but who had then invaded papal possessions and *were enemies of the Roman empire. After both sides had suffered immense losses the pope and a few followers turned back and fled without victory, leaving there the bravest knights from Swabia and Bavaria; he took up position in the city of Benevento,* since there Udalric,[147] a Bavarian, held the bishopric.

15. The year of the Lord 1054. *The most religious pope Bruno, also called Leo, ended his life gloriously* on the thirteenth Kalends of May [19 April] *and was buried* with magnificence *at Rome in the church of St Peter;*[148] and he was rendered famous through miracles.[149]

Duke Conrad of Bavaria[150] *allied himself with the Hungarians and led a large rebellion, as did Baldwin and Godfrey.*[151]

16. The year of the Lord 1055. Bishop *Gebhard* of Eichstätt, *who was also called Victor, succeeded Leo as pope.*[152] *Margrave Adalbert died.*[153] *There was a great famine.*

Emperor Henry led an army into Italy, established all in peace there and on his return brought with him his niece Beatrice,[154] *the mother of Matilda,*[155] *treating her harshly because of a certain insolence towards him in her behaviour after the death of her husband, Duke Boniface.*[156]

Richard of Aversa and Robert Guiscard. See Steindorff (1881), pp. 245–50; Taviani-Carozzi (1996), pp. 181–211; Munier (2002), pp. 212–15; Loud (2000), pp. 110–21.

147 Archbishop Udalric of Benevento, 1053–69. Leo arrived in Benevento on 23 June and remained there until 12 March 1054. See Steindorff (1881), pp. 251, 266; Munier (2002), pp. 247–56; Loud (2007), pp. 69, 208–9. Cf. Herman, *Chronicle* 1053, pp. 132–3 (*SC*, pp. 95–6).

148 *WC*, p. 31. Leo was buried next to the tomb of Pope Gregory I: Herman, *Chronicle* 1054, p. 133 (*SC*, p. 98).

149 See Tritz (1952), 310–11, 321–53.

150 Conrad I, 1049–53, from the Ezzonid family (Lotharingia). Conrad was deposed during an assembly at Easter 1053 in Merseburg: Weinfurter (1999), pp. 109–10. Cf. Herman, *Chronicle* 1053, p. 132 (*SC*, p. 95), who saw the deposition as a sign of Henry III's increasingly autocratic rule.

151 The renewed rebellion of Godfrey 'the Bearded' was a response to royal displeasure over his marriage to the widowed Beatrice of Lotharingia, margravine of Tuscany (d. 1076). See Weinfurter (1999), pp. 106–7.

152 *WC*, p. 31. Gebhard I, 1042–57, Pope Victor II, 1055–7.

153 See n. 98 above.

154 Beatrice of Lotharingia, margravine of Tuscany (d. 1076), daughter of Duke Frederick II of Upper Lotharingia; married (1) Margrave Boniface of Tuscany (see n. 156 below); (2) Godfrey 'the Bearded' (see n. 111 above).

155 Matilda, margravine of Tuscany (1046–1115). See Hay (2008).

156 Boniface II of Canossa, margrave of Tuscany 1030–52. The expedition was intended

*Duke Welf of Carinthia died.*¹⁵⁷ *Conrad, the former duke of Bavaria, who had been expelled by the emperor* for being guilty of treachery, *died horribly* and as an exile *in Hungary. Conrad succeeded Bishop Arnold of Speyer.*¹⁵⁸

17. The year of the Lord 1056. *Count Herman of the East Franks*¹⁵⁹ *died on the sixth Kalends of February* [27 January]. *Bishop Gebhard of Regensburg, the uncle of Emperor Henry and a secret enemy of the worst sort, was seized, convicted and held in custody; but he was dealt with mercifully, released from exile and restored to his former position.*¹⁶⁰

Duke Godfrey came to surrender [to the emperor].¹⁶¹ *The Liutizi perpetrated a great slaughter against the Christians, some of whom perished by the sword and others by fleeing into the water. Among them Margrave William was killed.*¹⁶²

In these times many of the princes in the various provinces perished. Famines afflicted many regions, grave poverty and scarcity prevailed all over and *much evil was done at that time. Emperor Henry who was deeply affected in his heart* by these things, *began to be ill and, taking wise council on the threshold of death, requested pardon of all as far as he could; whosoever's possessions he had taken away he returned and those who had committed dastardly crimes against him or against the kingdom he forgave. He* also *saw to it that his son Henry was elected king by the Roman pontiff,* and all *the bishops and the princes* of the kingdom.¹⁶³ *Having arranged these and other*

---

to punish Godfrey 'the Bearded', who had married Beatrice without the emperor's knowledge: Weinfurter (1999), p. 106.

157 Welf III, duke of Carinthia 1047–55, margrave of Verona, died on 13 November: Steindorff (1881), p. 320 n. 4.

158 Conrad, 1056–60; Arnold I, 1054–5 (d. 2 October).

159 *WC*, p. 31. Count Herman remains unidentified.

160 In the fortresses of Wülflingen and Stoffeln according to Berthold of Reichenau, *Chronicle* (first version) 1056, p. 179 (*SC*, p. 101). Berthold's annal for 1055, pp. 177–8 (*SC*, p. 100), suggests that the conspiracy was undertaken by vassals of Gebhard and Duke Welf III without their lords' knowledge; the *Annals of Niederaltaich* 1055, p. 51, ascribe full responsibility to Gebhard and Welf. See Steindorff (1881), p. 323; Boshof (1991), p. 125.

161 Probably in May or June, when Henry III was in Lotharingia (*DD H. III* 372). See Steindorff (1881), pp. 353–4.

162 William, count of Haldensleben, margrave of the Saxon North March. See Fenske (1977), p. 23; Robinson (1999), pp. 24, 63. The defeat added to Saxon discontentment with the rule of Henry III.

163 Victor II met with Henry III at Goslar in September: Steindorff (1881), p. 350. Herman, *Chronicle* 1053, p. 133 (*SC*, pp. 96–7) reports that Henry IV was elected at Tribur in 1053.

things as far as he could, he cheerfully finished this present life in God on the third Nones of October [5 October].

After the emperor's death, since his son Henry was yet but a little boy, the lady Agnes,[164] the empress and mother of the boy, took the kingdom under her care and ruled wisely and vigorously until certain of the princes, tempted by envy, kidnapped the boy from his mother and stole from her the authority to rule over the kingdom. Archbishop Anno of Cologne[165] collaborated with them, since at a place called Kaiserswerth[166] he embarked the boy upon a ship and abducted him from his mother.[167] What intention he had in so doing or whether it pleased divine judgement we cannot tell: we can, however, be certain that from that moment on many calamities arose and thereafter increased. From that many dissensions in the kingdom, disturbances in the church, destruction of monasteries, contempt of the clergy, all injustices and treading underfoot of religion began and remain to this day. The empress herself, considering these changing fortunes, removed herself to Italy and led a religious life for a considerable time at the monastery which is called Fruttuaria.[168] She died afterwards in Rome and was buried with honour in the church of St Petronilla.

The years of Henry IV.

1.[169] The year of the Incarnation of the Lord 1057 and from the foundation of the city 1,808. *Henry*[170] *IV, the son of Emperor Henry, although yet a boy,* succeeded his father and *began to rule* and, at the time of writing this, has reigned for forty-two years in the eighty-seventh place since Augustus.

Empress Agnes, his own mother, assumed control of the duchy of Bavaria.[171]

Gebhard, the Roman pontiff, who was also known as Victor, having arranged

164 Agnes as regent: Robinson (1999), pp. 27–37, 42–4.
165 Anno, archbishop of Cologne 1056–75.
166 On the Rhine, south of Duisburg.
167 In 1062, probably soon after Easter (31 March). Lampert of Hersfeld identifies Count Ekbert I of Brunswick (the king's cousin) and Duke Otto of Bavaria as Anno's accomplices: *Annals* 1062, p. 80. See Robinson (1999), pp. 43–5; Weinfurter (1999), pp. 118–19.
168 See n. 207 below.
169 The regnal years of Henry IV.
170 *WC*, p. 31.
171 Agnes had been given Bavaria by Henry III in 1055; this was confirmed at an assembly in Regensburg at Christmas 1056. See Meyer von Knonau (1900), pp. 19–20.

many things well in Germany and in the other parts of the Roman kingdom with the counsel of the bishops and the secular princes, returned to Rome in peace at the beginning of Lent this year. There also in the same year he finished his life;[172] in his place Frederick, then a monk, the brother of Duke Godfrey, was made pontiff by the Romans and was called Stephen.[173]

The Saxons gathered an army, aggressively attacked the savage people of the Liutizi and inflicted various misfortunes upon them. They subjected them to Roman dominion and, accepting hostages and tribute, returned home.

At the same time a certain Frederick and his brothers,[174] who were raising up tyranny against the Roman empire in parts of Germany, were defeated by the Empress Agnes and the princes of the kingdom and came to surrender.

Otto of Sweinfurt,[175] *the duke of Swabia, died on the fourth Kalends of October* [28 September] and Rudolf of Rheinfelden,[176] who afterwards strove to be king, accepted the duchy – that was an important source of the confusion through which the kingdom was disturbed. Indeed, in the lifetime of Duke Otto, Emperor Henry had promised that same duchy to Count Berthold[177] (who later accepted the duchy of Carinthia), and had given him his ring as a memento of this matter. Berthold, diligently attending to this after the death of both parties, namely the emperor and the duke, presented the same ring to the Empress Agnes, who was then governing the empire, and reminded her that it symbolized the duchy he had been promised. But since the aforementioned Rudolf had entrusted the emperor's daughter[178] to Bishop Rumold of Constance[179] soon after the emperor's death – whether through advice or cunning is unfortunately unknown – and took her as his wife, the empress, for her daughter's sake, received him into favour and gave him that same duchy, about which Berthold's soul was not a little disquieted.[180] In order to calm this disturbance he was given the duchy

172 28 July.
173 Frederick of Lotharingia, chancellor of the Roman church (1051), abbot of Monte Cassino (1057), Pope Stephen IX, 1057–8. See n. 140 above.
174 Frederick of Gleiberg, a kinsman of Duke Frederick II of Lower Lotharingia (Luxemburg family). See Meyer von Knonau (1890), p. 43 n. 87.
175 See n. 124 above.
176 Rudolf of Rheinfelden, duke of Swabia 1057–79, anti-king 1077–80.
177 Berthold I of Zähringen ('the Bearded'), duke of Carinthia 1061–78.
178 Matilda (1048–60).
179 Rumold, bishop of Constance 1051–69.
180 Matilda and Rudolf were betrothed in 1057. The wedding took place at Christmastide 1059. Most scholars have characterized Frutolf's anecdote as propaganda

of Carinthia and afterwards, at Berthold's request, King Henry made it over to Berthold's son[181] of the same name. But later still, on the instigation of certain persons, the king gave that same duchy to his kinsman Liutold,[182] and thereby offended father and son by slighting them. Whence Duke Berthold, deeply agitated as if by the repetition of a former injustice, directed all his capacities for plotting – for which he was quite famous – to one end: that he be avenged upon both men, that is the king and Rudolf, for the latter had supplanted him from the duchy he had been promised and the former had deprived him of the duchy he had received. Meanwhile, many things that were managed rashly at this time converged around him and offered opportunities for these schemes: Duke Otto of Bavaria was deposed;[183] Conrad,[184] a Swabian, was killed by the king's knights and it was alleged that the king himself ordered the sentence. Thereafter, Otto conspired in Saxony and Berthold in Swabia, and there were disturbances and assemblies in both places in which hatred and envy of the king were aroused. In the mean time, many things happened in the kingdom that made it seem to both peoples that there were just and necessary reasons for not adhering to the king and for deserting him. Finally it went so far that Rudolf, to his own damnation, turned against the empire and sought to kill or depose his lord the king; but the success he had in this plan is not hidden even from the peasants.[185]

2. The year of the Lord 1058. The Roman pontiff Frederick, who was also called Stephen, ended his life and Alexander,[186] the bishop of Lucca,

---

    against Rudolf: Maurer (1978), pp. 21–2; Schmid (1988), p. 190; Black-Veldtrup (1995), pp. 78, 108–9. But Goez (1962), pp. 76–7 and Klewitz (1971), pp. 258–60, believe it a plausible account of the Swabian succession problem.

181 Berthold II of Zähringen, margrave, duke of Swabia 1090–8, duke of Zähringen 1098–1111.

182 Liutold of Eppenstein, duke of Carinthia 1077–90, who shared a great-grandfather with Henry IV (Duke Herman II of Swabia): Meyer von Knonau (1900), p. 21 n. 26. Berthold was deposed before the rebel assembly at Forchheim in March 1077. See Klaar (1966), pp. 108–9.

183 Otto I, count of Northeim, duke of Bavaria 1061–70 (d. 1083). On his deposition see below, pp. 109–10.

184 Otherwise unidentified. See Bruno of Merseburg, *Saxon war* 11, p. 19.

185 An ironic reference to Rudolf's death from wounds received at the Battle of Hohenmölsen (1080).

186 Anselm I, bishop of Lucca 1057–73, Pope Alexander II, 1061–73. Frutolf gives the wrong date and omits the pontificate of Nicholas II, 1058–61 (Bishop Gerard of Florence).

succeeded him. At this time Hildebrand,[187] who later became pope, began to discharge the office of archdeacon at Rome.[188]

3. The year of the Lord 1059.

4. The year of the Lord 1060. Archbishop Luitpold of Mainz died[189] and was succeeded by Abbot Siegfried of Fulda, who afterwards conspired with others against the lord king.[190]

5. The year of the Lord 1061.

6. The year of the Lord 1062.

7. The four-hundred-and-sixtieth olympiad. The year of the Lord 1063. The first year of the indiction.

8. The year of the Lord 1064. Bishops Siegfried of Mainz, Gunther of Bamberg[191] and William of Utrecht,[192] as well as several other bishops and nobles, journeyed to Jerusalem with many followers.[193] They endured many attacks from the barbarians but finally they reached their hoped-for destination, returning home far fewer in numbers and possessions.

9. The year of the Lord 1065. Bishop Gunther of Bamberg, returning from Jerusalem, died in Hungary and was taken to Bamberg where he was buried. After him Herman was appointed.[194] Count Gozwin,[195] who

---

187 Hildebrand, archdeacon of the Roman church, Pope Gregory VII, 1073–85.
188 Gaps left at the end of this annal and the 1059–63 annals in Frutolf's autograph manuscript indicate that he intended to supply reports for those years.
189 7 December 1059 according to Lampert of Hersfeld, *Annals* 1059, p. 77.
190 Siegfried of Eppenstein, abbot of Fulda 1058–60, archbishop of Mainz 1060–84. Siegfried's conspiracy: his coronation of Rudolf of Rheinfelden as anti-king in 1077. See below, pp. 115–16.
191 Gunther, bishop of Bamberg 1057–65.
192 William, bishop of Utrecht 1054–76.
193 The pilgrimage took place between November 1064 and summer 1065. It is also reported by other contemporary sources: *Annals of Niederaltaich* 1065, p. 66; Berthold, *Chronicle* 1065, p. 199 (first and second versions) (*SC*, pp. 106, 118–19). See Meyer von Knonau (1890), pp. 390–4, 445–50; Joranson (1928), pp. 3–43.
194 Herman, bishop of Bamberg 1065–75 (d. 1084). See n. 237 below.
195 Gozwin, count of Grabfeld (d. 1065): Meyer von Knonau (1890), pp. 272 n. 65, 453.

had tyrannically attacked the bishopric of Würzburg, was killed by the followers of Bishop Adalbero.[196]

10. The year of the Lord 1066. A comet was visible for a long time throughout the whole world.[197] In the same year England was pitifully attacked and eventually conquered by the Norman William, who was made king.[198] Soon afterwards he sent virtually all the bishops of that kingdom into exile and the nobles to their deaths. Those of the middle rank he forced into the service of his knights and all the wives of the natives into marriage with the newcomers.[199]

11. The year of the Lord 1067. King Henry took as his wife Bertha,[200] the daughter of Odo,[201] a certain Italian, and Adelaide,[202] and celebrated the wedding at Tribur.[203] The four-hundred-and-sixty-first olympiad.

12. The year of the Lord 1068. Taking advantage of the freedom of youth, King Henry began to reside solely in Saxony out of all parts of the Roman empire, to despise the princes, to oppress the nobles, to exalt inferiors (as it is alleged), to devote more time to hunting, games and other such pastimes than to the administration of justice, to marry the daughters of the illustrious to all manner of those of obscure birth, and to install his own garrisons because he did not trust the magnates of the kingdom sufficiently.[204] Since he had not yet fully reached the years of maturity, there were some who placed the blame not on him but on Archbishop Adalbert of Bremen,[205] for he did all these things on the

---

196 Adalbero, bishop of Würzburg 1045–90.

197 Halley's Comet, seen in western Europe from 24 April to 6 June: Yeomans (1991), p. 392.

198 William II, duke of Normandy 1035–87 and William I 'the Conqueror', king of England 1066–87. Coronation: 25 December 1066.

199 On German perceptions of the Norman conquest see van Houts (1995), 836–43.

200 Bertha of Turin (1051–87), queen 1066. On the strategic value of this marriage see Robinson (1999), pp. 25, 108.

201 Count Odo of Savoy (d. 1057/60).

202 Adelaide of Susa, margravine of Turin (1015–91).

203 South of Mainz on the eastern side of the Rhine.

204 The charges recorded by Frutolf were those discussed by Saxon magnates at the assembly of Hoetensleben in 1073 and recorded in the Saxon polemic of the 1070s: Lampert, *Annals* 1073, pp. 140–1, 146, 147–50; 1074, pp. 177–8; Bruno, *Saxon war* 8, 21, 25, pp. 18, 26–7, 29–30. Cf. *Annals of Niederaltaich* 1072, p. 84.

205 Adalbert, archbishop of Hamburg-Bremen 1043–72. From the summer of 1065 Adalbert became the king's principal adviser and used his position to enrich the

archbishop's advice.²⁰⁶

13. The year of the Lord 1069. The Empress Agnes, the mother of King Henry, overcome by weariness, or perhaps divinely impelled, relinquished the duchy of Bavaria and the governance of the kingdom out of penitence for Christ's sake and moved herself to Rome, where in marvellous humility she applied herself to the worthy fruits of penance and, after a number of years, finished this present life in the Lord.²⁰⁷

14. The year of the Lord 1070. Margrave Dedi, not without the advice of the Saxon princes, launched a rebellion against the royal lands.²⁰⁸ He was quickly checked, however, by both divine and earthly majesty, since his castles of Beichlingen and Burgscheidungen were destroyed by the king, his son²⁰⁹ – an equally warlike man – was done away with by one of his own servants and he himself was finished soon afterwards by an ordinary death.

15. The year of the Lord 1071. Duke Otto of Bavaria lost his duchy. He was of Saxon origin, a man of the highest nobility who had few equals in prudence and in matters of war. He was thought so excellent by all the leading men that the king – since he was already suspected and detested by the entirety of the Saxons – dreaded that Otto might be elevated against him to the summit of kingship if his own affairs went badly.²¹⁰ Then a certain Egino²¹¹ – of mediocre birth and of very little wealth,

---

church of Hamburg-Bremen. He was toppled from power by a conspiracy of bishops and princes at Tribur in January 1066, but had recovered much of his former influence by 1069. Hostility to Adalbert in the narrative sources: *Annals of Weissenburg* 1066, p. 53; Lampert, *Annals* 1065, 1066, pp. 88–90, 100–2; Bruno, *Saxon war* 5, 8, pp. 16–18.

206 Adalbert's role in formulating Henry IV's Saxon policy: Bruno, *Saxon war* 16, p. 22; Lampert, *Annals* 1072, p. 134.

207 14 December 1077. Agnes was driven from power in a coup orchestrated by Archbishop Anno of Cologne in 1062. She probably did not leave Germany until the summer or autumn of 1065: Struve (1985), 1–29; Black-Veldtrup (1995), pp. 27–36, 92–4.

208 Dedi I, margrave of Lower Lausitz 1046–75. The rebellion took place in 1069 in support of Dedi's claim to the benefices of Margrave Otto of Meißen, whose widow he had married. Dedi attempted to draw the Thuringian nobility into his rebellion: Lampert, *Annals* 1069, pp. 106–8. See Fenske (1977), pp. 34–6; Robinson (1999), pp. 64–5.

209 Dedi II (d. 1069) fought on the side of the king against his father in 1069.

210 The claim that Henry IV feared Otto's power was voiced by Bruno, *Saxon war* 19, p. 25, and seems to have been current in contemporary Saxon polemic.

211 The identity of Egino has never been fully established. Lampert, *Annals* 1070, 1072,

but of such audacity and wickedness as to be of great infamy – seized upon the opportunity for evil. Being protected by certain of the king's vassals, he insinuated himself into court and alleged that that great hero, whom he had never known, had suborned him to murder the king. Furthermore, he availed himself of the power of royal protection, as is the custom, until such time as he proved the truth of his accusation in a duel with the duke.[212] What more? Royal courts and councils having been arranged – one at Mainz, the other at Goslar – Otto refused to fight with Egino (or rather the duke with the brigand, the foremost with the ignoble);[213] yet Otto's own innocence and Egino's wickedness were little hidden. Thus Otto lost the duchy of Bavaria through being guilty of contumacy,[214] which duchy Welf,[215] an illustrious, harsh and warlike man who was a native of Swabia, then received. It was there that the seeds of such terrible discord sprouted and flourished into such lamentably permanent fruits – alas! – battles and seditions, plunder and arson, even schisms and heresies, as well as death.

16. The year of the Lord 1072. The king pursued Otto at every possible juncture, destroyed many of his fortresses, laid waste to his possessions and, as with a true enemy of the commonwealth, sought to ruin him entirely. On the other side Otto, supported by selected knights, with immense courage and exceedingly fierce spirit, busied himself avenging these injustices in whatever way he could – sometimes by pillage, sometimes by arson and yet other times even by the sword, for he was unable to contend with the resources of the king.[216] In fact, owing to Otto's collaboration the hard-spirited Saxon people did not cease to

---

1073, pp. 113–14, 135, 172, described him as a nobleman who lived by theft and highway-robbery. Egino's infamy is a prominent theme in anti-Henrician narrative sources, particularly Bruno, *Saxon war* 19, p. 25.

212 A nobleman accused of treason had the option of clearing himself by fighting a judicial duel against his accuser.

213 Otto was accused at the assembly of Mainz (mid-June 1070). The trial at Goslar was arranged for 1 August 1070. According to Bruno, *Saxon war* 19, p. 25, Otto refused to fight having been warned by his supporters at court that 'he would never escape with his life, even if he defeated his adversary'. On the trial, deposition and subsequent rebellion see Lange (1961), 33–7; Robinson (1999), pp. 65–70.

214 2 August 1070.

215 Welf IV, duke of Bavaria 1070–1101, and Otto's son-in-law. Welf was invested with the duchy at Christmastide 1070. On his family connexions see Robinson (1999), pp. 70–1.

216 With the exception of Magnus Billung, duke in Saxony 1073–1106, Otto failed to attract support among the Saxon princes. His rebellion ended with a negotiated settlement on Whitsunday 1071 (12 June). See Robinson (1999), p. 71.

plot against the king by uniting in conspiracy,[217] by relaying blasphemous and unheard-of accusations against him to the apostolic seat,[218] and by enticing confederates from the whole German kingdom through letters and messengers. First they turned Siegfried, the metropolitan of the see of Mainz,[219] Adalbert of Worms,[220] Adalbero of Würzburg, Gebhard of Salzburg[221] and many other bishops into their supporters and through them, as they say, even Pope Alexander. They won even a man of the greatest sanctity, Archbishop Anno of Cologne, as an accomplice in the same conspiracy. Terrified by their plots the king retreated from Saxony and dedicated himself to his duties in other parts of the kingdom.

17. The year of the Lord 1073. Archbishop Anno of Cologne and Bishop Herman of Bamberg were sent to Rome to collect money that was owed to the king.[222] Having carried out their mission they returned bringing letters from Pope Alexander, calling on the king to make satisfaction for simoniacal heresy as well as for certain other things in need of improvement, which had been heard by the pope in Rome.[223] After that the Saxons rose up and also built numerous fortifications because Saxony did not have many strongholds.[224] Moreover, they tore down the fortresses that the king had recently erected,[225] among which they

---

217 Frutolf is conflating the events of Otto's rebellion of 1070–1 and the Saxon rebellion of 1073–5, in which Otto played a leading role.

218 Accusations of sexual depravity which circulated as a consequence of the king's attempted divorce from his wife in 1069. According to Lampert, *Annals* 1073, pp. 152–2, 162, the Saxon rebels demanded that the king should abandon his concubines and live with his wife. See Robinson (1999), pp. 112–14; Althoff (2006), pp. 269–73.

219 Siegfried of Mainz's relationship with Rome and the reform papacy: Robinson (1999), pp. 110–12.

220 Adalbert, bishop of Worms 1070–1107, expelled from Worms in 1073.

221 Gebhard, archbishop of Salzburg 1060–88.

222 Frutolf is the only observer to mention this mission. Erdmann (1938), pp. 223–4, saw in this report a reference to a mission of 1070.

223 Berthold of Reichenau reports that in 1070 Alexander II wrote a letter, no longer extant, to the archbishop of Mainz concerning charges of simony against Bishop Carloman of Constance: *Chronicle* (second version), p. 210 (*SC*, p. 124). Schmale, *Chroniken*, p. 83 n. 49, suggested that the report could refer to letters sent by the pope after the Lenten synod of 1073, at which five of the king's advisers were excommunicated.

224 The Saxon rebellion of 1073–5. The rebellion broke out because of the east-Saxon nobility's accumulated resentment of the king's Saxon policy: Robinson (1999), pp. 72–104.

225 Peace had been negotiated between the king and the rebel leaders on 2 February

demolished the most important of those castles, which is called the Harzburg.[226] The church and dwelling house of the canons that was there they razed to the ground with great reckless fury and – in an act sacrilegious to say – they pulled from their grave the bones of the king's innocent son,[227] who was buried there, in order to insult his father.[228]

18. The year of the Lord 1074. Pope Alexander of blessed memory died[229] and was succeeded by Hildebrand,[230] who was afterwards called Gregory, by profession a monk[231] and archdeacon of the Roman church. Under him the Roman commonwealth and the whole church began to be endangered by schism through new and unheard-of errors.[232] Since he had climbed to this summit without the consent of the king and with only the favour of the Romans,[233] some assert that he was not canonically appointed, but that he tyrannically usurped the papacy for himself. On this account he was deposed by some bishops.[234] Through messengers and letters he frequently and repeatedly called King Henry to answer before a synod.[235]

1074 (the Peace of Gerstungen), in which the king promised to dismantle the recently erected fortifications in Saxony. According to Lampert, *Annals* 1074, pp. 183–4, the Saxon rank and file were not satisfied with the settlement and broke the peace by attacking royal fortresses as soon as the king withdrew.

226 March 1074.

227 Henry (d. 1071), the first-born son of Henry IV. Also interred in the royal grave was Conrad (d. 1055), the younger brother of Henry IV.

228 The desecration of the royal graves created widespread revulsion and was the turning point for the king's fortune in the Saxon rebellion: Lampert, *Annals* 1074, pp. 184–5.

229 21 April 1073.

230 Elected 22 April 1073.

231 Possibly at the monastery of St Mary on the Aventine Hill: Cowdrey (1998), pp. 28–9.

232 The theme of Gregory VII as schismatic appears frequently in the Henrician polemics of the 1070s and 1080s: Robinson (1978a), pp. 95–8.

233 A reference to the fourth clause of the Papal Election Decree of 1059, conceding an effective veto to the imperial court. Gregory's election: Cowdrey (1998), pp. 71–4. The Papal Election Decree of 1059: Stürner (1972), 37–52; Jasper (1986); Robinson (1999), pp. 37–9.

234 A reference to the Synod of Brixen (1080). Frutolf may also have intended the Synod of Worms (January 1076) during which the German bishops attempted, at the behest of the king, to compel Gregory to resign but stopped short of deposing him.

235 Perhaps an allusion to Gregory's letter of summer 1076 to 'all the faithful in Germany', in which the pope wrote that while still archdeacon of Rome he had 'frequently admonished him [Henry VI] by letters and messengers to cease from his wickedness'. Gregory, *Epistolae vagantes* 14, p. 34. Frutolf quoted from this letter

19. The year of the Lord 1075. With powerful forces that he had gathered from Swabia as well as from Bavaria, Franconia and Bohemia, King Henry advanced against the Saxons and engaged them by the River Unstrut.[236] Not without great slaughter on both sides, he at last attained victory and returned home. There Rudolf, duke of Swabia as well as Burgundy, who afterwards attempted to take possession of the kingdom, was observed to fight bravely for the king with his men.

Bishop Herman of Bamberg was deposed for simoniacal heresy on the authority of Pope Hildebrand[237] and in his place Rupert was nominated by the king.[238]

Archbishop Anno of Cologne, full of the merit of holiness, died and was buried in the monastery of Siegburg,[239] which he had constructed. He was succeeded by Hildulf.[240]

20. The year of the Lord 1076. A council was held at Worms[241] where in the presence of King Henry virtually all of the German bishops (except those from Saxony) deposed Pope Hildebrand, sending him a letter which, after hurling many complaints at him, concluded thus: *'Since, therefore, your accession was begun by so many perjuries, and the church of God is endangered by so grave a tempest arising from your abuses and novelties, and your life and conduct are dishonoured by such infamy, we renounce the obedience that we have not promised you and furthermore will never show you; and since none of us, as you have publicly declared, has hitherto been a bishop for you, you also will now be pope for none of us.'*[242]

In the same year, around the eighteenth Kalends of October [14

---

elsewhere in his *Chronicle*: see n. 252 below. Henry IV's 'wickedness': his failure to do penance for his guilty lifestyle, his association with excommunicates and his simoniac dealings with the imperial church.

236 The Battle of Homburg on the River Unstrut, 9 June 1075. Cf. Lampert, *Annals* 1075, pp. 217–22; Bruno, *Saxon war* 46, pp. 44–5; Berthold, *Chronicle* 1075, pp. 225–7 (*SC*, pp. 135–6). See Giese (1979), pp. 159–61; Robinson (1999), pp. 100–2.

237 At the Lenten synod of 1075: Gregory VII, *Register* 2.52a, p. 196; trans. Cowdrey (2002), p. 145. See Schieffer (1972), 22–46; (1975), 55–76; Cowdrey (1998), pp. 113–14, 124–7.

238 Rupert, bishop of Bamberg 1075–1102.

239 Anno died on 4 December. He had founded Siegburg in 1064: see Wisplinghoff (1975), pp. 21–8; Semmler (1959).

240 Hildulf, archbishop of Cologne 1076–8.

241 24 January 1076. See Cowdrey (1998), pp. 135–8; Robinson (1999), pp. 143–6.

242 Henry IV, *Letters* (Appendix A), p. 68 (*IL*, p. 149).

September], a great conference took place at Oppenheim,²⁴³ where virtually all the princes of the kingdom, but especially the Saxon and the Swabians, renounced their obedience to the king, pressing the case that, having already been called to make satisfaction by two popes, he had refused; and for that contempt the sentence of excommunication was imposed by the pope in a Roman synod.²⁴⁴ The king, however, being absent was not heard.²⁴⁵ Impelled by this commotion, the king, though his enemies did not expect it, set out for Rome intending humbly to ask forgiveness of the pope. Finding the pope *in*²⁴⁶ *the fortress of Canossa,*²⁴⁷ *he remained outside the gate of the castle for three days, putting aside all trappings of royalty, with bare feet and dressed in woollen clothes.*²⁴⁸ *And he did not cease to implore the apostolic mercy, help and consolation with great weeping until at last, with the prayers and lamenting intercessions of all those who were there,*²⁴⁹ *the bond of anathema was released and he was received into the grace of communion and the bosom of Mother Church having made* many *promises* to correct his future life.

Meanwhile the whole world bore witness to these things through its disorder. But since some say that Rudolf was elevated to the kingship²⁵⁰ on the authority and counsel of that same pope, and since some even deny that King Henry had been excommunicated by him,²⁵¹ it will not

243 The assembly of Tribur, 16 October–1 November 1076. The king encamped on the opposite side of the Rhine at Oppenheim: Berthold, *Chronicle* 1076, p. 286 (*SC*, pp. 152–3); Lampert, *Annals* 1076, p. 278; Bruno, *Saxon war* 88, p. 82. See Erdmann (1940), 486–95; Hlawitschka (1974), 25–45; Cowdrey (1998), pp. 150–3; Robinson (1999), pp. 155–8.

244 The Lenten synod of 1075.

245 A reference to the canon-law principle that the absent cannot be judged. The *Dictatus papae* – a papal memorandum entered into the *Register* of Gregory VII in 1075 – sought to claim this prerogative for the pope in special cases: Gregory VII, *Register* 2.55a, p. 201; trans. Cowdrey (2002), p. 149. See Cushing (1998), pp. 38, 108–9.

246 Gregory VII, *Register* 4.12, p. 313; trans. Cowdrey (2002), p. 222.

247 January 1077. Canossa: the family fortress of Countess Matilda of Tuscany (1046–1115), Gregory VII's staunchest secular supporter. On Matilda see Struve (1995), 41–84; Hay (2008).

248 Henry probably began his display of penance on 25 January (the Feast of the Conversion of St Paul).

249 The mediators who pleaded the king's case with the pope: Countess Matilda, Henry IV's kinswoman; Abbot Hugh I ('the Great') of Cluny, 1049–1109, Henry IV's godfather; Adelaide of Susa, Henry IV's mother-in-law; and Margrave Adalbert Azzo II of Este (d. 1097), father of Duke Welf IV of Bavaria. Cf. Bernold, *Chronicle* 1077, pp. 257–63 (*SC*, pp. 158–63); Lampert, *Annals* 1077, p. 290.

250 At an assembly at Forchheim, 13–14 March 1077.

251 The nature of Henry IV's absolution: Morrison (1962), 121–48; Robinson (1999), pp. 162–4.

seem especially out of place to record certain words of that same pope on this matter. For instance, in one letter sent to all the princes of the German kingdom he said:[252] '*We have heard that some among you have doubts concerning the excommunication that we have placed upon the king and ask whether the excommunication was just*' or unjust. We admonished him that he should do penance for his deeds, but, in truth, '*he took it badly that anyone should reproach him: not only would he not be called to repentance from his crimes, but he was seized by a still greater fury of mind; he did not pause until he had shipwrecked the Christian faith of almost all bishops of Italy and of as many of the Germans as he could, making them deny the obedience due to St Peter and the apostolic see and the honour granted them by our Lord Jesus Christ*.[253] *For these well-known reasons, first, namely, because he would not keep himself from the society of men who had been excommunicated for the sacrilege and crime of simoniacal heresy, and then because he would not even promise, let alone perform, penance for the criminal acts of his own life, we excommunicated him by synodal judgement*.'[254]

Also in another letter after the date of the reconciliation:[255] '*I restored him only to communion*', he says, '*I did not restore him to the kingdom, from which I had deposed him in a Roman synod*.' And a little further on he says, '*the bishops and princes beyond the mountains, hearing that he had not fulfilled what he had promised to me, as though despairing of him, elected Rudolf to the kingship without my counsel*'.

21. The year of the Lord 1077. Rudolf, a native of Swabia, who was completely unconnected with the royal lineage,[256] through the collaboration of Archbishop Siegfried [of Mainz], Bishop Adalbero of Würzburg, Duke Berthold of Carinthia,[257] the aforementioned Otto and several of the other princes,[258] was reluctantly elevated to the kingship

252 Gregory VII, *Epistolae vagantes* 14, pp. 32, 38, 40 (summer 1076). An abridged quotation by Frutolf. The full text also appears in the *Codex Udalrici* (compiled by Udalric of Bamberg, *c.* 1125): cf. *Codex Udalrici* 2, no. 146, ed. Eccard, cols 146–9. Frutolf's source was also the source of the *Codex Udalrici*: Erdmann (1936), 33–4; McCarthy (2011).

253 At the Councils of Worms and Piacenza in 1076.

254 At the Lenten synod of 1076.

255 Record of the Lenten synod of 1080: Gregory VII, *Register* 7.14a, p. 484; trans. Cowdrey (2002), p. 343. Cf. *Codex Udalrici* 2, no. 150, ed. Eccard, cols 152–4.

256 Rudolf was connected to the Salian dynasty through marriage: Cowdrey (1998), p. 169.

257 Berthold I of Zähringen ('the Bearded'), duke of Carinthia 1061–78.

258 Rudolf's election was the work of a small 'deposition faction' of German princes: on the identifiable electors see Robinson (1979), 721 n. 1. The Gregorian chronicler

at Forchheim in the presence of certain legates of the Roman see.[259] He was conducted by them to Mainz and in the middle of Lent, on the twelfth Kalends of April [21 March],[260] he was anointed king by Archbishop Siegfried. On the same day by the worst auspices a riot occurred, in which a great crowd of the common people was cut to pieces by Rudolf's soldiers; whereupon the crowd blazed up in anger against them and, killing many with tremendous blows, it chased others to the confines of the palace where it intended to burn the buildings that belonged to the king himself, except that Archbishop Siegfried offered himself as a hostage to enable the speedy withdrawal of Rudolf.[261] Thus Rudolf and all who had come with him were driven out; also Archbishop Siegfried himself was forced out with great insults and could not enter Mainz again. Thereupon Rudolf assembled a large army from Saxony and besieged Würzburg, which remained faithful to King Henry and despised its bishop, Adalbero, as much as Rudolf.[262] But having already built various machines with which to assault the city, Rudolf withdrew without success in terror of King Henry, who had returned from Italy around the Kalends of July [1 July].[263]

King Henry then led an expedition into Swabia where he fought Hugh,[264] one of the natives, as well as other rebels there with great devastation of the province.[265] Meanwhile, Berthold of Zähringen, the former duke of Carinthia, remained in Limburg, a certain fortress of his that was naturally protected. Seeing that all could be devastated with impunity according to the will of the king, he was seized by sickness – it is said the sickness of the mind that physicians call lunacy – and surviving after that for seven days, uttering many crazed words

---

Berthold of Reichenau portrayed Rudolf's election as the work of the 'whole senate and people': *Chronicle* 1077, pp. 268–9 (*SC*, p. 167).

259 Cardinal deacon Bernard, and Bernard, abbot of St Victor in Marseilles 1064–79. The assembly at Forchheim: Schlesinger (1973), pp. 61–85; Vogel (1983), pp. 41–6; Cowdrey (1998), pp. 167–71; Robinson (1999), pp. 165–70.

260 Actually 26 March 1077.

261 Sigebert of Gembloux, *Chronicle* 1077, p. 364; *Annals of Augsburg* 1077, p. 129. Berthold of Reichenau offers an anti-Henrician account of the riots: Berthold, *Chronicle* 1077, p. 269 (*SC*, p. 168). See Vogel (1983), pp. 53–68.

262 August 1077. Berthold, *Chronicle* 1077, pp. 292–5 (*SC*, pp. 183–5); Bruno, *Saxon war* 94, p. 87. The siege of Würzburg: Höss (1950), 306–7.

263 The king returned from Italy in April.

264 Hugh III, count of Tübingen. Berthold of Reichenau dated the king's attack on Hugh to 1079: Berthold, *Chronicle* 1079, p. 346 (*SC*, pp. 220–1).

265 Berthold, *Chronicle* 1077, pp. 301–2 (*SC*, p. 187).

FRUTOLF OF MICHELSBERG, *CHRONICLE* 117

as if delirious, he ended his life.[266] Archbishop Udo of Trier died in that expedition.[267]

22. The year of the Lord 1078. King Henry opposed Rudolf, who was hastening towards him with a great army, at the Streu.[268] At the beginning of the battle not a few from each side were struck down and, since victory was uncertain, each side fled in its own direction. There Archbishop Werner of Magdeburg[269] was killed in flight by the common people or, as some say, he was hanged; Duke Magnus[270] was robbed; Count Herman,[271] the uncle of the same Magnus, and Bishop Adalbert of Worms were captured and many of the Saxon knights perished ignominiously. On King Henry's side Poppo,[272] a wonderfully strong man, lay dead. The first year of the indiction.

23. The year of the Lord 1079. Again there was a battle between Henry and Rudolf, in the place that is called Flarchheim, in exceedingly bitter winter, where at the first clash the Saxons turned to flee.[273] There Duke Vratislav of Bohemia[274] captured Rudolf's royal lance, which thereafter by the permission of King Henry remained a sign of ducal authority over that people and preceded all festal processions.[275] But when King Henry returned to his own camp he found virtually none of the arms bearers he had left there [alive]: for one of the contingents of the Saxons, deserting the fighting at the first engagement (since it was dark with mist), secretly invaded the king's camp, seized and strangled many of the boys and, carrying off much spoil, fled. The king then dismissed the army and with a few followers turned towards Lotharingia.

266 5 or 6 November 1078. Compare the very different account by Berthold of Reichenau: *Chronicle* 1078, p. 313 (*SC*, pp. 215–16).

267 11 November 1078.

268 The Battle of Mellrichstadt on the River Streu, 7 August. Compare the anti-Henrician accounts by Bruno and Berthold: Bruno, *Saxon war* 96–102, pp. 88–92; Berthold, *Chronicle* 1078, pp. 332–5 (*SC*, pp. 212–13). See Cram (1955), pp. 140–3.

269 Werner, archbishop of Magdeburg 1063–78, the brother of Anno of Cologne and a staunch supporter of the rebel princes.

270 Magnus Billung, duke in Saxony 1073–1106.

271 Count Herman Billung (d. 1086). See Meyer von Knonau (1900), pp. 143–4.

272 Count Poppo of Henneberg: Bruno, *Saxon war* 102, p. 92.

273 The Battle of Flarchheim (27 January 1080): see Vogel (1983), pp. 185–6; Robinson (1999), p. 193. Compare the anti-Henrician accounts of Bruno, *Saxon war* 117, pp. 109–11, and Berthold, *Chronicle* 1080, pp. 324–5 (*SC*, pp. 241–3).

274 Vratislav II, duke of Bohemia 1061–85, king 1085–92.

275 See Schramm (1968), p. 351; Wegener (1959), pp. 118–19.

24. The year of the Lord 1080. *When*[276] *a meeting of thirty of the bishops in addition to a great host of the nobles, not only of Italy but also of Germany, was convened at Brixen in Bavaria by the command of King* Henry,[277] *there was a general consensus against Pope Hildebrand, also known as Gregory VII, whom they affirmed to be a false monk and the author of all the pestiferous madness, but above all an invader of the holy Roman see. Although he was absent,*[278] *they judged that he should be expelled from the apostolic see and, having proposed Archbishop Wibert of Ravenna,*[279] *they elected him* [*as pope*]. *The conclusion of this decretal follows:*

'Since',[280] it is written, '*he has certainly not been elected by God, but has thrust himself forward by fraud and through shameless bribery, in which he subverted the ecclesiastical order, threw the kingdom of the Christian empire into confusion, intended death to the body and soul of the catholic and peaceful king, defended a perjured king,* [sowed] *scandals among brothers, divorce among the married and shook whatever seemed to stand quietly among those living devoutly, we, who have congregated as one at the urging of God, supported by the legates and letters of the nineteen bishops who met together at Mainz on the holy day of Whitsun past,*[281] *judge canonically that the same most impudent Hildebrand, preaching sacrilege and arson, defending perjuries and murders, putting in question the catholic faith concerning the Body and Blood of the Lord (being an old disciple of the heretic Berengar),*[282] *a worshipper of divinations and dreams, a manifest necromancer working with the spirit of the serpent and therefore straying beyond the true faith,*[283] *must be*

276 Quoted from the decree of the Council of Brixen: Henry IV, *Letters* (Appendix C), p. 70 (*IL*, p. 157). Frutolf's citation of this decree contains text not transmitted in its two other surviving sources (the *Codex Udalrici* and the *Hanover letter collection*), suggesting that Frutolf's source may have been closer to the original: McCarthy (2011).

277 The Council of Brixen, 25 June 1080. See Vogel (1983), pp. 209–19; Cowdrey (1998), pp. 201–3; Robinson (1999), pp. 198–201.

278 See n. 245 above.

279 Wibert of Parma, archbishop of Ravenna 1072–1100, antipope 'Clement III', 1084–1100.

280 Decree of the Council of Brixen, ed. Erdmann, *Die Briefe Heinrichs IV.*, pp. 71–2. Quoted with abridgements by Frutolf. Cf. *Codex Udalrici* 2, no. 164, ed. Jaffé, pp. 133–6.

281 Council of Mainz, 31 May 1080: Vogel (1983), pp. 200–9.

282 Berengar of Tours (d. 1088), archdeacon of Angers, dialectician and theologian whose study of the Eucharist led him to deny the doctrine of transsubstantiation. His views were condemned in Gregory VII's Lenten synod of 1079. See Cowdrey (1990), pp. 109–38.

283 Details of the pope's alleged crimes were provided by Hugh Candidus, cardinal priest of S. Clemente, ?1049–85, and cardinal bishop of Palestrina, ?1085–99. The charges have been dismissed as absurd by modern scholars: Goez (1968), 123.

deposed and expelled, and that unless he descends from this seat after hearing this, he will be forever condemned.

These matters were enacted on Thursday, the seventh Kalends of July [25 June], in the third year of the indiction.'

After this Bishop Anselm of Lucca[284] wrote a letter to that same Wibert in which he accused him of apostasy and arrogance, among other things adding:[285] *'That, therefore, I might speak of our blessed father Gregory, as the blessed Cyprian*[286] *wrote concerning Cornelius:*[287] *he was made bishop by the judgement of God and of His anointed; by the testimony of virtually all or, to speak more truly, entirely all of the clergy; by the acclamation of the people who were then present; by the college of venerable priests and good men since no one had been elected before him, since the place of Alexander – that is the place of Peter and the steps to the priestly throne – was free. He was raised up and ordained by the will of God as well as the consensus of all of us. Any other bishop who wishes to become [pope], must of necessity be disqualified; neither can he hold an ecclesiastical office, since he is not upholding the unity of the church. Whosoever he may be, he is greatly given boasting about himself and arrogates too much to himself; he is a layman, a foreigner, he is cast apart and, since after the first it is not possible to be second, whosoever is placed after the first – who ought to be alone – is not second, but nothing.'* This, quite contrary to the foregoing sentences, wrote Bishop Anselm, a man especially learned in letters, of most acute intelligence, of extraordinary eloquence and – which is most important of all – widely known for his fear of God and saintly conduct, to such an extent that he is reported to have distinguished himself by miracles both in life as well as after his death.

After these events King Henry and Rudolf did battle again, near the River Elster.[288] In this battle Rudolf was struck down but, still living, was carried to Merseburg by his followers, where he died soon afterwards and was honourably buried. It is reported, however, that in his last hour and looking at his amputated right hand, he said with grave sighs to the bishops who happened to be there: 'Behold, this is the hand

---

284 Anselm II, bishop of Lucca 1073–86.

285 Anselm II of Lucca, *Liber contra Wibertum*, p. 521. See Märtl (1985), 196–9; Cushing (1998), pp. 133–7.

286 Cyprian, bishop of Carthage (d. 258).

287 Pope Cornelius, 251–3. Cyprian, *Letter* 55 (in support of Cornelius against the antipope Novatian), pp. 629–30.

288 Battle of Hohenmölsen (15 October): see Cram (1955), pp. 145–8, 214; Robinson (1999), pp. 203–4.

with which I swore fealty to my lord Henry by oath; behold, I am now leaving his kingdom and this present life; you who have made me to climb upon his throne, see if you have led me, who followed your advice, on the right path.'[289]

On the side of King Henry in this battle also perished Count Rapoto,[290] who was very devoted to the king.

25. The year of the Lord 1081. King Henry advanced into Italy with an army and,[291] reaching Rome on the vigil of Whitsun,[292] he pitched his camp outside the fortress of St Peter,[293] although he was resisted by Pope Hildebrand and the Romans. Here for two years he was pestered by frequent incursions from the city, though with small detachments he accomplished much that was manly.

The cathedral of Bamberg caught fire on the eve of Easter.[294] The Saxons and Swabians came to a meeting in eastern Franconia and returned to their own provinces, not without great slaughter.[295] There was a battle in eastern Bavaria on the fourth Ides of May [12 May] between Conrad,[296] the brother of the duke of Bohemia, and Margrave Leopold.[297] There was also another between the Swabians and the

---

289 The loss of Rudolf's right hand as a punishment for perjury was a favourite theme of royalist accounts of the battle: *Life of Henry IV* 4, p. 10 (*IL*, p. 111); Wenrich of Trier, *Letter written in the name of Bishop Theoderic of Verdun* 6, p. 294.

290 Rapoto IV, count of Cham, who commanded the Bavarian contingent in the royal army. Cf. Bruno, *Saxon war* 122, p. 116.

291 In March 1081 via the Brenner Pass. See Cowdrey (1998), p. 213; Robinson (1999), p. 211.

292 22 May.

293 Possibly Castel S. Angelo or the whole of the walled Leonine city (fortified by Pope Leo IV, 847–55). According to Bonizo of Sutri, Henry pitched camp on the field of Nero (on the right bank of the Tiber, north of the Leonine city): *To a friend* 9, p. 613; trans. Robinson (2004b), p. 248.

294 Easter Day: 4 April.

295 Frutolf is probably connecting Saxon attacks on Franconian enemies, which began following the expiration of the truce of Kaufungen in mid-June, and a meeting at Ochsenfurt in August at which Herman of Salm was elected anti-king: Bruno, *Saxon war* 130–1, pp. 122–3; Bernold, *Chronicle* 1081 (*SC*, p. 267). See Meyer von Knonau (1900), pp. 415–18; Robinson (1999), pp. 206–9.

296 Margrave Conrad of Moravia (1061–92).

297 Leopold II, margrave of the East March (Austria) 1075–95 (Babenberg family). The Battle of Mailberg, on the Austrian–Moravian boarder, on 12 May 1082 at which Leopold was defeated by Conrad. Leopold rebelled on the eve of Henry IV's 1081 Italian expedition at the instigation of Bishop Altman of Passau. The king responded by depriving Leopold of the East March and conferring it on Duke

Bavarians on the third Ides of August [11 August] by the Danube at Höchstädt[298] where Conrad, the son of Count Palatine Conrad, was killed.[299]

26. The year of the Lord 1082. Herman,[300] a certain very powerful and noble man from *Germania*,[301] was made king by the Saxons and Swabians. Although in his own parts, that is in Lotharingia or *Germania*, no one could equal him in martial prowess or in wealth, once he assumed the name of king his own people as well as outsiders soon began to despise him.

27. The year of the Lord 1083. Herman invaded Franconia with few forces in the manner of an enemy and in the same area something like an army of knights was seen wandering about, traces of which could, nevertheless, not be recognized at all.[302]

King Henry celebrated Easter[303] at Santa Rufina and shortly afterwards headed for Rome, pitching his camp as before to the west of the fortress of St Peter; and the city was captured on the Friday before the octave of Whitsun, the fourth Nones of June [2 June].[304] At this time Pope Hildebrand was shut up in the castle of the Crescentii, which is commonly called the house of Theoderic,[305] waiting for the outcome of this affair. King Henry, however, erected a fort on the Palatine hill[306]

Vratislav II of Bohemia. Cf. Cosmas of Prague, *Chronicle* 1082, trans. Wolverton (2009), pp. 157–9. See also Meyer von Knonau (1900), pp. 462–7.

298 Cf. Bernold, *Chronicle* 1081, p. 428 (*SC*, p. 267). Herman of Salm defeated Henrician forces commanded by Duke Frederick I of Swabia (Hohenstaufen family). See Meyer von Knonau (1900), pp. 419–21.

299 Conrad, leader of the Bavarian contingent in the royal army, son of Conrad of Vohburg (d. 27 March, probably after 1081), count palatine of Bavaria. See Meyer von Knonau (1900), p. 420.

300 Herman, count of Salm (Luxemburg family), anti-king 1081–8. Herman was elected at an assembly at Ochsenfurt at the beginning of August 1081 and was crowned by Archbishop Siegfried of Mainz at Goslar on St Stephen's Day (26 December) that year. See Robinson (1999), pp. 208–10.

301 *Germania*: the classical designation of the Roman provinces west of the Rhine.

302 Apparently a ghostly apparition. For a parallel see the anonymous *Life of Pope Leo IX* 2.21, trans. Robinson (2004b), p. 151.

303 9 April.

304 3 June according to Bernold, *Chronicle* 1083, p. 431 (*SC*, pp. 268–9). Henry captured the Leonine city (Rome on the right bank of the Tiber, including St Peter's).

305 The Castel S. Angelo on the west bank of the Tiber controlling the Ponte S. Angelo.

306 More likely the Palatiolus, a hill to the east of St Peter's: Bernold, *Chronicle* 1083, p. 431 (*SC*, p. 269). See Meyer von Knonau (1900), p. 479 n. 14.

and lost many of those he had placed in its garrison because of the increasing summer heat, to which they were unaccustomed. Many others from his army were also overcome by the same death.³⁰⁷

At the same time emissaries of the Greeks came, bringing many gifts and much in silver and gold as well as vases and silks.³⁰⁸ The Romans, however, gave twenty noble hostages to the king and asked him to fix a day on which the pope and all the senators should come into his presence.³⁰⁹ Setting the day as the Kalends of November [1 November], the king went up to the mountains at the beginning of July and lingered there until the appointed time when he returned to Rome;³¹⁰ but the pope did not come into his presence.³¹¹ Whence the worried Romans *gave their hands*³¹² to the king and unanimously renounced Hildebrand as pope.³¹³ He, secretly fleeing, withdrew to Salerno and remained there until the day of his death.³¹⁴

In the same year³¹⁵ Welf, the former duke of Bavaria, entered the city of Augsburg at daybreak and Bishop Siegfried³¹⁶ barely escaped; he

---

307 It was garrisoned by 300 soldiers under the command of Udalric of Godesheim, one of five royal advisers excommunicated in 1073 and 1075: Bernold, *Chronicle* 1083, p. 431 (*SC*, pp. 269–70). See also Robinson (1999), pp. 225–6.

308 Concluding negotiations that the Byzantine emperor, Alexius I Comnenus, had opened with Henry IV probably in the summer of 1081. In return for Henry's aid against Robert Guiscard, Alexius offered payment and the possibility of a marriage alliance: Robinson (1999), pp. 214–15, 222–3. Henrician chroniclers were greatly impressed by the gifts: *Life of Henry IV* 1, p. 12 (*IL*, p. 105); Benzo of Alba, *Ad Heinricum* 6.4, p. 548.

309 The Romans swore an oath that the pope should hold a synod in November and that, if he failed to do so, they would elect another: Cowdrey (1998), pp. 223–7; Robinson (1999), pp. 224–5.

310 Henry spent the late summer and early autumn campaigning against Countess Matilda of Tuscany: Meyer von Knonau (1900), p. 491.

311 Henry's attempts to influence the November synod failed: Robinson (1999), pp. 226–7.

312 Ezra 10.19. 'They gave their hands': they pledged fidelity. See Ganshof (1964), pp. 26–7.

313 Early in 1084. Gregory's position became untenable when twelve cardinals defected to the king: Beno, *Gesta Romanae aecclesiae*, 1.2, p. 370. See Klewitz (1957), pp. 68–9, 77–9; Hüls (1977), pp. 90, 100–2, 110; Robinson (1990), p. 37.

314 Gregory only withdrew in late summer 1084 with his Norman vassal Robert Guiscard: Robinson (1999), pp. 232–4.

315 Actually in early 1084.

316 Siegfried II, 1077–96, a royal chaplain who had been appointed by Henry IV in 1077.

enthroned [as bishop] a certain Wigold,³¹⁷ a canon of the same place.

1.³¹⁸ 28. The year of the Lord 1084. Henry celebrated Christmas in Rome at St Peter's; about the Kalends of February [1 February] he went over to Campania, taking possession of it and a large part of Apulia.³¹⁹ After this, at the request of the legates of the Romans that he should return peacefully, he returned to Rome and, pitching his camp at the Lateran Gate, he received the surrender of all; and since they themselves entreated him for Wibert of Ravenna – because Hildebrand had fled after they renounced him³²⁰ – he entered [the city] on the Friday before Palm Sunday,³²¹ with large crowds and in great glory leading that same bishop himself. Wibert was consecrated pope the following Sunday by many bishops and, taking the name Clement, was reverently enthroned.³²² By him the king and Queen Bertha were elevated to the imperial dignity on the holy Sunday of Easter.³²³ After this Emperor Henry departed from Italy,³²⁴ besieged the city of Augsburg – which had been taken by the Swabians – and captured it.³²⁵ Archbishop Siegfried of Mainz died and Wezilo succeeded him.³²⁶

The imperial years of Henry IV.

2. 29. The year of the Lord 1085. A synod was held at Mainz in which the emperor participated, where, in the presence of legates from the

317 Wigold, provost of the church of St Maurice in Augsburg, Gregorian anti-bishop 1077–88. His election in 1077 had been set aside by the king. Cf. Berthold, *Chronicle* (second version) 1077, p. 297, and Bernold, *Chronicle* 1084, p. 438 (*SC*, pp. 187, 273). See McCarthy (2004), 141.

318 From this point onwards, Frutolf gives the imperial years of Henry IV (here 1) as well as the regnal years (here 28) at the beginning of each annal. See above, p. 29.

319 Henry invaded the territories of Robert Guiscard at the request of the Byzantine emperor. Cf. Bernold, *Chronicle* 1084, p. 439 (*SC*, p. 274).

320 At this time Gregory VII was actually an effective prisoner in Castel S. Angelo.

321 On St Benedict's Day (21 March), which was the Thursday before Palm Sunday, according to a letter from Henry IV to Bishop Theoderic of Verdun: *Letter* 18, p. 27 (*IL*, p. 166).

322 On 24 March (Palm Sunday). Wibert was consecrated by the diocesan bishops of Ravenna; Bernold, *Chronicle* 1084, pp. 440–1 (*SC*, p. 275): by the bishops of Modena and Arezzo; Bonizo, *To a friend* 9, trans. Robinson (2004b), p. 250: by the bishops of Modena, Bologna and Cervia.

323 31 March.

324 In June 1084.

325 On the night of 6–7 August; *Annals of Augsburg* 1084, pp. 130–1. See Zoepfl (1952), 312–13; Kottje (1978), 149–50; Volkert and Zoepfl (1974), no. 350.

326 Wezilo (Werner), clerk of Halberstadt, archbishop of Mainz 1084–8.

Romans, all bishops who had rebelled against the emperor were judged to be deposed and others were condemned with anathema.[327] There, in addition, by common consent and counsel the Peace of God was established.[328] Not long afterwards replacements were made by the emperor in the dioceses of the deposed bishops; in Adalbero's place Meinhard – a man of admirable conduct who in learning and intelligence as well as eloquence was second to virtually no one and who for his merits ought already to have been a bishop – was chosen as the bishop of the church of Würzburg.[329]

Although Emperor Henry had already been accepted peacefully by the Saxons,[330] a certain Margrave Ekbert,[331] a blood relative of the emperor, who was vigorous and bold in arms as well as being wealthy, stirred up tyranny against the emperor again in Saxony.[332] Once the emperor heard of this he hastened back to Franconia.

In the same year a conference was arranged by the supporters and enemies of the emperor in Thuringia at a place called Berka,[333] and there came together from each side whoever was judged to be the wisest of the nobles, to prove on the authority of the canons which party justice favoured; although the emperor was absent, he nevertheless consented

---

327 At the monastery of St Alban in Mainz during the second week after Easter (27 April–3 May): *Liber de unitate ecclesiae conservanda* 2.19, p. 235; *Annals of Augsburg* 1085, p. 131. Cf. Bernold, *Chronicle* 1085, pp. 452–3 (*SC*, p. 282). See Hauck (1954), pp. 844–6; Cowdrey (1998), pp. 240–1; Robinson (1999), pp. 246–52.

328 Gernhuber (1952), p. 44. On the 'Peace of God' and the related 'Truce of God' movement see Cowdrey (1970), 42–67.

329 Meinhard, *scholasticus* of Bamberg, imperial bishop of Würzburg 1085–8. See Erdmann (1932), 332–431; Erdmann (1938), pp. 16–116; Schieffer (1987), 310–13; Märtl (1991), pp. 331–41. The comment 'and who for his merits ought already to have been a bishop' is not printed in *Chroniken*, p. 98, but will be printed in the new *MGH* edition by Christian Lohmer.

330 *Liber de unitate* 2.28, p. 250. Cf. Bernold, *Chronicle* 1085, p. 456 (*SC*, p. 284). The Saxons may have formally deposed the anti-king, Herman of Salm: Giese (1979), p. 178. See also Robinson (1999), pp. 254–6.

331 Ekbert II (of Brunswick), margrave of Meißen, 1068–90.

332 *Liber de unitate* 2.28, p. 250: 'But shortly after the emperor had dismissed his army, the Saxons and Thuringians reverted to their customary infidelity and after barely two months, forgetting the promises of fealty and peace they had sworn under oath, made war on the emperor and forced him to depart from Saxony.'

333 The conference of Gerstungen-Berka (on opposite banks of the River Werra) on 20 January. Cf. Odo of Ostia, *Encyclical*, pp. 375–80; the 'Saxon report' of the conference in the *Annals of Magdeburg* 1085, pp. 176–7, and the *Annalista Saxo* 1085, pp. 721–2; *Annalium Ratisbonensium maiorum fragmentum* 1085, p. 88; Bernold, *Chronicle* 1085, pp. 447–8 (*SC*, p. 278); *Liber de unitate* 11.18, pp. 234–5. See Robinson (1978a), pp. 105–9; Cowdrey (1998), pp. 235–7; Melve (2007), pp. 509–28.

to this. Therefore, they selected suitably learned and eloquent men, on one side Archbishop Wezilo of Mainz, on the other Archbishop Gebhard of Salzburg, and the disputation began. Gebhard affirmed that the emperor had not been deprived either of the kingdom or of communion [with the church] by an unjust judgement and verdict of the pope, as Wezilo had previously claimed; against this, Wezilo contended that his lord had suffered prejudice no less from the pope than from the princes, for while he was at Canossa making satisfaction and had, moreover, already been received back into communion by the pope, they had raised another king over him. The same [prelate] of Mainz also added that since the emperor had long been driven out of Saxony and since the resources for ruling had already been plundered during the rebellion that was recorded to have occurred before Rudolf[334] he should, according to canon law, neither be accused, judged nor condemned.[335] Gebhard, striving to refute this, asserted that nobody was exempted from divine laws on this account, even if he had in any manner been stripped of his family possessions, still less a king; that Saxony was not merely his property but a kingdom of the Lord who, as Daniel and King Nebuchadnezzar himself testify,[336] gives it to whomsoever He wishes; that even before the loss of Saxony the king had been called to make satisfaction, first by Alexander and then by Hildebrand, but had scorned to do so. Thus in the end each party withdrew, favouring and applauding its own [position].

It should be noted, however, that this very same argument was pursued with such zeal by the enemies of the emperor, that at a council held afterwards in Quedlinburg, where Bishop Odo of Ostia[337] was present as a legate for Pope Hildebrand, they exaggerated it excessively, calling it the heresy of Wezilo and Wezilo himself – which is monstrous to say – an heresiarch, accusing him of teaching against the faith that, while a person is deprived of his goods, he should not be subject to divine laws.[338]

334 The Saxon rebellion of 1073–5.
335 The canonical principle of *exceptio spolii*, taken from the preface of the ninth-century *Pseudo-Isidorian Decretals*, that no bishop should face judicial proceedings when not in full possession of his see and all its property: *Pseudo-Isidorian Decretals*, ed. Hinschius (1863), p. 18. See Fuhrmann (1982), 52–69.
336 See Daniel 1.2, 2.37, 5.18.
337 Odo (of Châtillon), cardinal bishop of Ostia 1080–8, Pope Urban II, 1088–99.
338 The Synod of Quedlinburg on 20 April (Easter Day), held by Odo of Ostia to counter the success of the Henrician *exceptio spolii* argument at Gerstungen-Berka. The synodal protocol in *MGH Constitutiones* 1, pp. 652–3, was quoted extensively in Bernold, *Chronicle* 1085, pp. 448–52 (*SC*, pp. 279–82). Robinson (1989), pp. 183–4, argues that Bernold was the author of the protocol. On the synod see Becker (1964),

Pope Hildebrand, also called Gregory VII, died at Salerno and was buried in the church there.[339] With the assent of the Normans and Matilda, the most powerful woman in the kingdom of Italy, and all those of this sort emulating that sect, Desiderius,[340] a cardinal of the Roman church, abbot of Monte Cassino and a true servant of Christ, replaced him although he resisted greatly with his heart and body. But because he laboured under severe sickness he was exalted to this high dignity reluctantly, or rather as a prisoner; his prayers were answered and after not many days he was taken away from this life.[341] After this Bishop Odo of Ostia[342] was given the same office by the same electors and choosers; after his death a certain Urban was appointed to the same seat by these.[343]

3. 30. The year of the Lord 1086. Emperor Henry devastated Saxony.[344] Würzburg was besieged by the Saxons and Swabians.[345] To liberate the city the emperor gathered a large army of foot-soldiers and knights, and gave battle at Pleichfeld, but retired from there without victory.[346] Soon the city [Würzburg] was captured by his enemies, who introduced Bishop Adalbero, leaving with him a military garrison while each of them [the Saxons and Swabians] returned to their homelands. But shortly afterwards the same city was recaptured by the emperor, Adalbero was expelled with his followers and Meinhard was reinstituted.[347]

---

pp. 71–4; Cowdrey (1998), pp. 238–40; Robinson (1999), pp. 244–5.

339 25 May. He was buried in the cathedral church of St Matthew, which he had consecrated that year.

340 Desiderius, abbot of Monte Cassino 1058–87, cardinal priest of S. Cecilia, Pope Victor III: elected 24 May 1086, consecrated 9 May 1087. On his election see Cowdrey (1983), pp. 177–213.

341 16 September 1087.

342 Elected on 12 March: Bernold, *Chronicle* 1088, p. 470 (*SC*, p. 292). His election: Becker (1964), pp. 91–6; Robinson (1990), p. 62.

343 A mistake. On fol. 182r of Frutolf's autograph (Jena, Thüringer Universitäts- und Landesbibliothek, Boe q. 19) the 1106 continuator corrected the statement as follows: 'After this *the aforementioned* Bishop Odo of Ostia was given the same office by the same electors and choosers, *and changing his name in the Roman fashion was called Urban*.'

344 In January, after the expiration of the Christmastide truce prescribed by the Mainz peace legislation. Cf. Bernold, *Chronicle* 1086, p. 457 (*SC*, p. 284); *Annalium Ratisbonensium maiorum fragmentum* 1085–6, p. 91.

345 From 6 July to 11 August: Bernold, *Chronicle* 1086, p. 459 (*SC*, p. 285).

346 Battle of Pleichfeld (north-east of Würzburg), 11 August. Cf. the eyewitness account of Bernold, *Chronicle* 1086, pp. 458–61 (*SC*, pp. 285–7). See Meyer von Knonau (1903), pp. 125–31; Cram (1955), pp. 148–9, 215; Robinson (1999), pp. 260–2.

347 Adalbero and his garrison were allowed to go free by Henry IV: Robinson (1999), p. 261.

4. 31. The year of the Lord 1087. Giving up the false title of king, Herman returned to his own with the permission of the emperor.[348] After not many days he was killed in the siege of a certain city.[349]

5. 32. The year of the Lord 1088. Empress Bertha died and was buried at Speyer.[350] Bishop Burchard of Halberstadt was killed at Goslar.[351] The city of Augsburg was captured in an attack by the Swabians on Maundy Thursday[352] and was destroyed on Easter Monday,[353] and Siegfried, the bishop of the same city, was held in captivity.[354] Wigold, the invader of the same church, died after not many days.[355] Bishop Meinhard of Würzburg died[356] and he was succeeded by Emehard,[357] although Adalbero was still living. Archbishop Wezilo of Mainz died;[358] he was succeeded by Ruothard.[359]

6. 33. The year of the Lord 1089. Bishop Otto of Regensburg died.[360] In his place the adolescent Gebhard was appointed.[361] The emperor celebrated his marriage at Cologne,[362] taking as his wife the widow of

348 Herman was compelled to retire by the desertion of his Gregorian supporters and the dissolution of Saxon opposition to Henry IV: Robinson (1999), pp. 267–8.

349 28 September 1088. See Meyer von Knonau (1903), pp. 221, 226 and n. 50; Robinson (1999), pp. 268–9.

350 d. 27 December 1087.

351 Burchard II, bishop of Halberstadt 1059–6/7 April 1088. He was killed in a fight between the citizens of Goslar and the vassals and *ministeriales* of Halberstadt. Contemporary sources blame Margrave Ekbert II of Meißen, who had launched a vendetta against the diocese of Halberstadt: *Annalista Saxo* 1088, pp. 724–6; *Liber de unitate* 11.31, 11.35, pp. 257, 261. See Meyer von Knonau (1903), pp. 209–13; Fenske (1977), pp. 116–18, 201.

352 On 13 April by Duke Welf IV of Bavaria.

353 17 April.

354 For two years in Welf IV's castle at Ravensburg. See Meyer von Knonau (1903), pp. 204–5.

355 11 May.

356 20 June.

357 Emehard, bishop of Würzburg 1089–1105; elected: 25 July 1089.

358 6 August. Cf. the account of the deaths of Wezilo and Meinhard (see n. 329 above) by Bernold, *Chronicle* 1088, p. 472 (*SC*, p. 293).

359 Ruothard, archbishop of Mainz 1089–1109; elected: 25 July 1089.

360 Otto, bishop of Regensburg 1061–89 (d. 6 July).

361 Gebhard IV, bishop of Regensburg 1089–1105. It was alleged that Henry IV 'sold Regensburg [to Otto] ... in return for military service': Herrand of Halberstadt, *Letter*, p. 289. Meyer von Knonau (1903), p. 262.

362 Summer 1089. Eupraxia was crowned empress by Archbishop Hartwig of Magde-

the former Margrave Udo,[363] the daughter of the king of the Russians.[364] After this he assembled an expedition and besieged a certain very strongly situated fortress of Margrave Ekbert[365] in Thuringia, called Gleichen. Since on Christmas Eve – the day in question was Sunday – a greater part of the princes had already left on account of the feast day,[366] Ekbert and his followers decided boldly to attack the emperor and compelled him to give way, although he initially resisted bravely.[367] There Bishop Burchard of Lusanne, who that day carried the Holy Lance of the emperor, was killed.[368]

7. 34. The year of the Lord 1090. Emperor Henry again advanced into Italy and stayed there for almost seven years.[369] The aforesaid Ekbert was apprehended by some vassals of the emperor while he was resting in a mill and died an ignominious death.[370] Adalbero of Würzburg, who had already been long expelled from his seat, died in Bavaria and was buried there in his own monastery of Lambach.[371]

8. 35. The year of the Lord 1091. In many regions there were seen utterly unknown small worms flying not far above the ground, that is to say it was possible to touch them by hand or with a rod; they were

---

burg. See Meyer von Knonau (1903), pp. 217, 251–2.

363 Actually of Count Henry of Stade (d. 1087), margrave of the Saxon North March. The Udo mentioned by Frutolf was Henry's father, Count Udo II of Stade and margrave of the North March (d. 1082).

364 Eupraxia (Praxedis)-Adelaide (d. 1109), daughter of Prince Vsevolod of Kiev (1030–93). Vsevolod was the son of Grand Prince Yaroslav 'the Wise', ally of Conrad II: Bresslau (1879), p. 331. On Henry's motives for marrying Eupraxia see von Giesebrecht (1890), p. 628; Robinson (1999), p. 269.

365 See n. 331 above. The siege began on 14 August 1088.

366 Henry had sent a detachment under the command of Archbishop Hartwig of Magdeburg to defend the royal monastery of Quedlinburg (where the emperor's sister, Adelaide, was abbess and his betrothed, Eupraxia, was staying), which had been attacked by Ekbert: Robinson (1999), pp. 270–1.

367 *Annals of Augsburg* 1088, p. 133; *Annals of Disibodenberg* 1089, p. 9; *Liber de unitate* 11.35, p. 262; Bernold, *Chronicle* 1088, 1089, pp. 473–4 (*SC*, p. 294).

368 Burchard, 1056/7–89, chancellor of the Italian kingdom. Archbishop Liemar of Bremen was also captured: Bernold, *Chronicle* 1089, p. 473 (*SC*, p. 294).

369 The emperor's expedition began in March, during Lent. See Robinson (1999), pp. 275–95; Eads (2010), 23–68.

370 On 3 July at a mill on the River Selke. He was killed by vassals of the abbess of Quedlinburg. Cf. Bernold, *Chronicle* 1090, p. 481 (*SC*, p. 299).

371 6 October. Lambach was consecrated on 15 September 1089. See Hallinger (1950), p. 320.

at least equal in girth to flies but in length quite a bit shorter.[372] The swarm appeared so infinite that it seemed to occupy a mile in length and two or three miles in breadth, and its density even blocked sunlight from the earth. Certain people interpreted this monstrous apparition as prefiguring the departure of the expedition to Jerusalem, which happened four years later.[373]

9. 36. The year of the Lord 1092. There was a great pestilence among men as well as livestock.[374]

10. 37. The year of the Lord 1093. Duke Vratislav of Bohemia fell unexpectedly from his horse while hunting and died an instantaneous death.[375] Conrad, the son of the emperor and of Empress Bertha, shamefully rebelled against his father.[376] There was seen a marvel in which something like a torch flew through the air from east to west. There was an eclipse of the sun on the ninth Kalends of October [23 September] at the third hour,[377] and great mortality followed soon afterwards. The first year of the indiction.

11. 38. The year of the Lord 1094. The church was greatly devastated by incredible death, in addition to pestilence, tornadoes and floods of rain, as well as being excessively afflicted by various calamities.[378]

12. 39. The year of the Lord 1095. King Ladislav of Hungary, full of merciful works, finished this life in the Lord.[379] Margrave Leopold[380] and Count Palatine Henry[381] also died.

372 A report unique to Frutolf: Curschmann (1900), p.123.

373 The First Crusade, 1095/6–9.

374 *Annals of Rosenfeld* 1092, p. 101; *Annals of St Alban* 1092, p. 246; Bernold, *Chronicle* 1092, p. 494 (*SC*, p. 308).

375 14 January 1092. See Meyer von Knonau (1903), pp. 25, 163–4, 373.

376 Conrad (1074–1101), duke of Lower Lotharingia 1076–87, king 1087–98. Conrad joined the rebellion of Matilda of Tuscany and her husband Welf V. See Meyer von Knonau (1903), pp. 391–4; Robinson (1999), pp. 287–8.

377 Cf. Bernold, *Chronicle* 1093, p. 505 (*SC*, p. 315). 24 September: *Annals of Augsburg*, p. 134.

378 Cf. *Annals of Augsburg* 1094, p. 134; Bernold, *Chronicle* 1094, pp. 512–13 (*SC*, pp. 319–20). See Curschmann (1900), pp. 123–5; Meyer von Knonau (1903), p. 433.

379 King Ladislaus I ('the Pious'), 1077–95 (d. 29 July). He was canonized by Pope Celestin III in 1192.

380 12 October. See Meyer von Knonau (1903), p. 462.

381 Henry II, count of Laach, count palatine of Lotharingia 1085–95 (d. 12 April). See Meyer von Knonau (1903), pp. 461–2.

13. 40. The year of the Lord 1096. Welf, formerly duke of Bavaria, who had already been repudiated by the emperor some time ago and because of that had lost his duchy, was restored to the emperor's grace and received his duchy back.[382]

An image appeared in the sun on Monday the fifth Nones of March [3 March] at the beginning of Lent. It was reported also that everywhere the world brought forth diverse prodigies. Soon afterwards from nearly all parts of the earth, but chiefly from the western kingdoms, innumerable armed troops of kings, nobles and even common people of both sexes began to travel towards Jerusalem, passionately stirred up by frequent reports about the oppression of the Lord's Sepulchre and the devastation of all the churches, which had been subjected to the power of the ferocious people of the Turks for several years and which had repeatedly been destroyed through unheard-of calamities. To come to their aid, as is reported, a great many set off hurriedly in different groups with different and unreliable leadership.[383]

The first group, estimated at 15,000 and following a certain monk named Peter[384] – who, however, many said afterwards was a hypocrite – travelled peacefully through Lotharingia, and then through Bavaria and Hungary. Many also travelled in boats on the Danube or by foot through Swabia, besides others – about 12,000 – led through Saxony and Bohemia by a certain priest, Folkmar,[385] and a considerable number led through Franconia by the priest Gottschalk.[386] In the cities through which they passed they either completely destroyed the abominable remnants of the Jews as the true inner enemies of the church, or forced them to seek refuge in baptism; but most of them afterwards reverted to their earlier belief, *like dogs* returning *to their vomit*.[387] Whether this was done by the judgement of God, or in what manner it pleased Him, must

---

[382] The reconciliation allowed Henry IV to return to Germany from north-eastern Italy (the march of Verona and duchy of Venice), where he had been confined by the rebellion of his son Conrad and the Welf–Canossa coalition since late 1093: Robinson (1999), pp. 288–90, 295.

[383] Cf. Bernold, *Chronicle* 1096, pp. 527–9 (*SC*, pp. 329–30); Cosmas, *Chronicle* 1096, trans. Wolverton (2009), p. 186.

[384] Peter the Hermit (d. 1115). Cf. *AA* 1.2–7, pp. 2–16. See also Blake and Morris (1985), 79–107; Flori (1999); Costick (2008), pp. 106–10, 126–8.

[385] Folkmar (d. 1096). See *1106 Continuation* 1099, below, pp. 138, 151.

[386] *AA* 1.23, p. 44, identifies him as a Rhinelander.

[387] Proverbs 26.11; 2 Peter 2.22. Cf. the contemporary addition in Bernold of St Blasien's *Chronicle*: *SC*, p. 331; Cosmas, *Chronicle* 1096, trans. Wolverton (2009), p. 180. On the Rhineland pogroms see Riley-Smith (1984), 51–72.

be left to Him. Once these travellers – by then laden down with booty – reached Hungary, they attracted through certain acts of violence, as it seemed, the hatred of the inhabitants; but in reality it was the abundance of their wealth that kindled the avarice of those semi-barbarians. On the orders of King Coloman[388] they were taken prisoner, more by trickery than by force: many were sentenced to death and only a few, deprived of their weapons and effects, are reported to have escaped at great cost. Although a great multitude of both [sexes] was seduced by a certain soldier named Emico,[389] just as the Israelite army was once *deceived* by the *spirit of fornication*,[390] the few of them who entered Hungary were blocked by the garrison at the Wieselburg[391] and *fled* home *when nobody pursued*[392] them.

There was an eclipse of the moon on the sixth Ides of August [8 August], in the fourteenth year of the lunar cycle.[393]

14. 41. The year of the Lord 1097. Returning from Italy,[394] Emperor Henry came to the city of Regensburg in Bavaria, where he stayed for a considerable time and allowed the Jews who had been coerced into baptism the use of their own laws, as it seems. Meanwhile, Duke Godfrey of Lotharingia,[395] a man of most illustrious origin, nature and martial prowess, who the year before had converted virtually all his possessions into money, made the journey through Franconia fortified with no little faith and many knights.[396] He was not frightened by those fleeing from Hungary, but with the permission of Emperor Henry and King Coloman, he traversed Hungary and Bulgaria, made an alliance with the emperor of Constantinople and, supported by his

---

388 Coloman I, 1095–1116.

389 Count Emico of Flonheim (formerly identified as Emico of Leiningen). See Toussaint (1982), pp. 25–8; Murray (1992), 315–22; Möhring (1992), 97–111; Gabriele (2007), pp. 61–82.

390 Hosea 4.12.

391 The border fortress of Mosonmagyaróvár by the River Leitha. Cf. *AA* 1.27–9, pp. 50–8. See *1106 Continuation*, below, pp. 151–2.

392 Proverbs 28.1.

393 The nineteen-year lunar or Metonic cycle, based upon the fact that every nineteen years lunar events occur on the same calendar date again. The cycle was used in the calculation of the date of Easter. See Ware (1992), pp. 268–70.

394 Probably in early May through the Brenner Pass: Robinson (1999), p. 298.

395 Godfrey V (of Bouillon), duke of Lower Lotharingia 1087–96, advocate of the Holy Sepulchre (d. 1100), grandson of Godfrey 'the Bearded' through his mother Ida.

396 That is, he embarked on the First Crusade.

troops, reached Rum,[397] where he joined the armies of Sicily, Greece, the Danes, the Normans and others from overseas, or rather the forces of all Christ-honouring nations. He clashed in numerous battles with the barbarians and, eventually, subjugating Rum, encamped at Antioch.

Emperor Henry held a peace council with the princes at Mainz about the Kalends of December [1 December] and celebrated Christmas at Strasburg. A comet appeared. This same year the summer was most fruitful, but the winter was mild and pestilentious; there were exceedingly heavy floods from deluges and rivers.

15. 42. The year of the Lord 1098. An inquisition was held in Mainz[398] by the emperor concerning the assets of the murdered Jews and among those accused of stealing from them were some of the archbishop's relatives. When the emperor sent for them they did not come into his presence and the bishop, wishing but unable to defend their cause and stirred up with indignation, left the city and took himself to Thuringia with them, as though he could better shelter his own there and, in proximity to rebellion against the emperor, could inflict terror on him and thus avenge the accusation. But there were some who said that the bishop himself had accepted a large part of the stolen money and on that account applied his heart to the defence of the others with such great care. Since the bishop had so foolishly left his seat, however, the emperor took over all the bishopric's revenue as well as the management of its various affairs for his own use and, confiscating the possessions of the fugitives, had the walls torn down; and in this way the bishop, thinking to provide for others by such rash haughtiness, was himself deprived of the many amenities of his surroundings like his predecessor.[399]

Welf, once more duke of Bavaria, reconciled his sons[400] with the emperor when they sought to rebel and succeeded in getting the duchy committed to one of them after him.[401]

397 Rum (*Romania* in Latin): the sultanate of Rum (whose inhabitants referred to themselves as 'Romans'), created by the Seljuks from the southern and eastern parts of the former Byzantine province of Anatolia in the aftermath of the Battle of Manzikert (1071).

398 May 1098.

399 See Robinson (1999), pp. 303–4. His predecessor: Archbishop Siegfried of Mainz (see above, p. 116).

400 Welf V, duke of Bavaria 1101–20; Henry 'the Black', duke of Bavaria 1120–6.

401 At an assembly at Worms: Welf V and Henry 'the Black' had recently imprisoned Anzo, Henry IV's appointee to the bishopric of Brixen. See Meyer von Knonau (1904), pp. 22–3.

Duke Godfrey and the others united to him on the aforementioned journey and quest, *resumed*[402] *their march after having captured Nicaea, with more than 300,000 soldiers. And it was allowed this great multitude to occupy Rum, to drink up the rivers and to devour all the grain in one day; yet however* God *led them* to the necessities of life *in such abundance that one coin was accepted for a ram and hardly twelve for a cow. Moreover, though the princes and kings of the Saracens rose up against* them, *nevertheless by God's will were they easily conquered and crushed.*[403] *Since some were puffed up on account of these happy deeds, God opposed them at Antioch, a city impregnable to human power, where for nine months he detained them in siege and humiliated them, so that all their swollen pride left them.*[404] *Thus were they so humiliated that there were barely 100 good horses left in the army; but God opened the fullness of His blessings and mercy, and led* them *into the city and gave the Turks and all their possessions into* their *hands.*[405] *Taking possession of it as if* they *had done so with their own strength and not suitably glorifying God, who had given it to* them, they *were besieged by such a multitude of Saracens that no one from such a large* crowd *dared to leave the city.*[406] *Moreover, famine in the city so weakened them that they could barely refrain from eating human flesh. It would be tedious to relate the miseries that existed in the city. But God looked down upon His people*[407] *whom He had so long chastised, and consoled them; and to recompense their tribulation as a sign of victory He first bestowed upon them His lance,* with which He was wounded on the cross, *a gift not seen since the days of the apostles.*[408] *Then He so inspired the souls of the men that those who because of sickness or hunger had not the strength to walk were imbued with the power to take up their weapons and to fight bravely* against the enemy.

After they *had triumphed over the enemy, the army, which was wasting away from hunger and weariness at Antioch, principally because of disagreements*

---

402 Quoted by Frutolf with emendations from the letter of Archbishop Daimbert of Pisa, Godfrey of Lower Lotharingia and Raymond of Toulouse to the pope, ed. Hagenmeyer, *Die Kreuzungsbriefe* (1901), pp. 167–74.

403 A reference to the crusaders' success at the siege of Nicaea (May–June 1097) and the Battle of Dorylaeum (1 July 1097).

404 The siege of Antioch, October 1097–June 1098. See France (1994), pp. 197–268.

405 The city was betrayed to Bohemund of Taranto by one of its defenders on the night of 2/3 June 1098: France (1994), pp. 257–67.

406 The second siege of Antioch (4–28 June 1098), during which the crusaders were besieged by Kerbogha al-Mawsili, atabeg of Mosul. See France (1994), pp. 269–96.

407 Ruth 1.6.

408 The finding of the Holy Lance by Peter Bartholomew: 14 June 1098. Cf. *AA* 4.44, p. 316. See Morris (1984), pp. 33–45.

among the princes,[409] *proceeded into Syria, assaulted Barra and Marra,*[410] *cities of the Saracens, and captured the castles in that region. While they were delaying there the famine in the army was so great that the already putrid bodies of the Saracens were eaten by the Christian people. Then by divine command* they entered the interior of Hispania,[411] *and the most bountiful, merciful and victorious hand of the almighty Father was with* them. *Indeed, the cities and fortresses of* that *region through which* they *were proceeding sent legates with many gifts, offering to aid* them *and to hand over their fortified towns. But because the army was not large and everybody* [wished] *to make haste to Jerusalem,* they [the crusaders] *accepted their pledges and made them tributary. Indeed, one of the cities, which was on the coastline, had more men than were in the* Christian *army. And when it was heard at Antioch, Laodicea and Edessa that the hand of the Lord was with* those who had continued on, *many from the army who had remained there followed* them *to Tyre. Thus with the Lord's companionship and co-operation* they *proceeded as far as Jerusalem.*[412] *And when the army had laboured greatly in the siege of that city, especially because of the dearth of water, a council was held and the bishops and princes ordered that all should march around the city with bare feet, in order that He who entered it humbly for men might be moved by their humility to open it to* them *and to exercise judgement upon His enemies.*[413] *Thus placated by this humility, on the eighth day after the humiliation the Lord* delivered *the city to* them, *evidently the same day on which the primitive church was expelled from there, when the festival of the dispersal of the apostles is celebrated.*[414] *If one should seek to learn what happened to the enemy that was found there,* he should know that *in the porch* that is called *Solomon's and in his temple* the victors *rode in the blood of the*

---

409 See France (1994), pp. 297–304.

410 The neighbouring cities of Al-Bara and Ma'arra (Ma'arrat-an-Nu'man). Ma'arra was besieged from 27 November to 11 December 1098 by Raymond of Toulouse and Robert of Flanders, who were joined by Bohemund on 29 November. See France (1994), pp. 311–15.

411 Hagenmeyer, Die Kreuzungsbriefe, pp. 381–2, suggested Isphahan; J. H. and L. L. Hill (*RA*, p. 13) suggested that it might be a vocal corruption of some form of the word 'pagan'. The rendering 'land of the Saracens' is probably more accurate, a suggestion I owe to Professor John France. Raymond of Aguilers uses the term *Hispania* in his account of the siege of Antioch to refer to the land of the Saracens – an analogy to Muslim Spain as seen from his homeland of southern France (*RA* 6, 11, pp. 50, 89). Professor France pointed out to me that the letter of the crusading princes, which is being quoted here, was probably written by Raymond.

412 7 June 1099.

413 The council was held on 6 July and the procession took place on 8 July.

414 15 July. *RA* 18, p. 151.

Saracens up to the knees of their horses.⁴¹⁵ *Then, when they were considering who ought to hold the city, and some moved by love for their country and for the sake of their parents wished to return home, it was announced that the king of Babylon had come to Ascalon with an innumerable multitude of pagans to lead the Franks,*⁴¹⁶ *who were at Jerusalem, into captivity and to assault Antioch, as he himself said; but the Lord had decided otherwise in regard to them* [the Franks]. *Therefore since* they who were at Jerusalem *learned in truth that the army of Babylon was at Ascalon, they went down to meet them, leaving their baggage and sick at Jerusalem with the garrison. When* their *army and the enemy saw each other,* the Christians *evoked the aid of God on their knees, so that He who in other necessities had confirmed* His *Christian law might in the present battle break the strength of the* pagans *and the devil and might extend the kingdom of Christ and of the church from sea to sea. There was no delay; God presented Himself to those who called upon Him and furnished them with such great boldness that those who saw them rushing upon the enemy would have taken them for a herd of deer hastening to quench their thirst in running water.*⁴¹⁷ *It was wonderful, indeed, since there were in* the Christian *army not more then 5,000 horsemen and 15,000 foot-soldiers,* while *in the army of the enemy there were probably 100,000 horsemen and 400,000 foot-soldiers. Then* God *appeared wonderfully to His servants, for before they fought, by their charge alone, He* turned *that multitude in flight and scattered all their weapons, so that if they wished afterwards to attack them, they would not have the weapons in which they hoped.*⁴¹⁸ *Concerning the spoils, there can in truth be no question as to how much was captured, for the treasures of the king of Babylon were captured. They killed more than 100,000 Moors with the sword. Moreover, the Moors' fear was so great that in the city gate 2,000 were crushed; those who perished in the sea are innumerable; many of them also were entangled in thickets. The entire world was certainly fighting for* the Christians, *and had not many* of them *been detained by the spoils of the camp, few of the great multitude of the enemy would have been able to escape from the battle alive. On the day preceding the battle the* [Christian] *army captured many thousands of camels and cattle and sheep. When they advanced to battle – wonderful to tell – the camels formed in many squadrons and the sheep and cattle did likewise. Moreover, those animals accompanied*

---

415 The description refers symbolically to Revelation 14.20; *RA* 18, p. 150; Alphandéry (1929), 154; Tyerman (2006), p. 31.

416 An army from the Fatimid caliphate of Egypt commanded by the vizier al-Afdal. See France (1994), pp. 357–66.

417 See Psalm 41.2.

418 The Battle of Ascalon, 12 August 1099.

them, halted when they halted, advanced when they advanced and charged when they charged. The clouds also protected the Christians *from the heat of the sun and cooled them.*

Thus having celebrated the victory, the army returned to Jerusalem and, leaving Duke Godfrey there, Count Raymond of St Gilles,[419] *Count Robert of Normandy*[420] *and Count Robert of Flanders*[421] *returned to Laodicea. There they found the fleet belonging to the Pisans and Bohemund.*[422] *After the archbishop of Pisa*[423] *had established peace between Bohemund and the others who had disagreed with him, Raymond prepared to return for the sake of God and of his brethren.* A truly great multitude, as mentioned above, sought to return to their homeland; the others who remained have hitherto occupied the country in peace by God's will.

16. 43. The year of the Lord 1099. Emperor Henry celebrated Christmas at Cologne and during Epiphany at Aachen made his younger son King Henry V,[424] renouncing his elder son Conrad, whom he had earlier crowned.[425] After this he travelled to Bavaria and commended this same son whom he had made king to those who were not present earlier, so they might have him as king.[426]

Meanwhile, the Count Palatine Rapoto[427] and his cousin Udalric,[428] who was said to be very wealthy, died.

The emperor spent the feast of the apostles in Bamberg,[429] and with great imploring exhorted the princes of those parts to preserve the Peace faithfully, compelling them under solemn oath to pursue without

---

419 Raymond IV of St Gilles, count of Toulouse, count of Tripoli (d. 1105).

420 Robert II (c. 1054–1134), duke of Normandy 1087–1106.

421 Robert II, count of Flanders (c. 1065–1111).

422 Bohemund I, prince of Tarento and Antioch (d. 1111), son of Robert Guiscard.

423 Daimbert (d. 1105), archbishop of Pisa 1088–99, patriarch of Jerusalem 1099–1102.

424 Henry V (1086–1125). Henry had been elevated to the kingship on 10 May 1098 at Mainz. The Epiphany (6 January) was closely associated with kingship in the middle ages.

425 Conrad (1074–1101), crowned 30 May 1087. The emperor renounced Conrad at Mainz in May 1098: Meyer von Knonau (1904), pp. 26–7.

426 Possibly at Regensburg, where Henry IV celebrated Easter (10 April).

427 Rapoto V, count of Cham and Vohburg, count palatine of Bavaria (d. 14 April) and son of the Count Rapoto who was killed fighting for Henry IV at the Battle of Hohenmölsen in 1080.

428 Count Udalric II of Passau. See Loibl (1997), pp. 157–65.

429 The Feast of Sts Peter and Paul (29 June).

hesitation and to condemn brigands and thieves.[430] He utterly forbade advocates[431] from exploiting the people and the churches under their advocacy. But this law, alas, had little power, since the princes were unwilling to give up their retinues of knights, for by these they gain great benefits for themselves, and soon after the emperor departed they proceeded in the usual manner of old.

Jerusalem was captured by the Christians on Friday the Ides of July [15 July]. In these days Bishop Conrad of Utrecht was killed by his own people.[432] Archbishop Herman of Cologne died.[433] Pope Urban died;[434] he was succeeded by Paschal,[435] though Pope Wibert, also [known as] Clement, was still alive.

The five-thousand-and-sixtieth year since the beginning of the world.[436]

17. 44. The year of the Lord 1100. Emperor Henry celebrated Christmas at Speyer and at Epiphany designated Frederick,[437] a canon of Bamberg, as archbishop of Cologne, although he was still an adolescent. He was consecrated on the feast of St Martin [11 November], a Sunday. Pope Wibert, who was also called Clement, died.[438] The five-thousand-and-sixty-first year since the beginning [of the world].

18. 45. The year of the Lord 1101. Emperor Henry celebrated Christmas at Mainz in the presence of many. Archbishops Egilbert of Trier[439] and Liemar of Bremen died.[440] Count Henry of Limburg rebelled,[441] but upon the besieging and destruction of his castles he came to surrender.

---

430 The Peace of God; see n. 328 above.

431 Secular representatives who transacted secular business on behalf of churchmen (who were prevented by canon law from doing so).

432 Conrad, bishop of Utrecht 1076–99. Cf. Bernold, *Chronicle* 1099, pp. 536–7 (*SC*, p. 335).

433 Herman, archbishop of Cologne 1089–99 (d. 21 November).

434 29 July. See Becker (1964), p. 112.

435 Rainer of Bieda, cardinal priest of S. Clemente, Pope Paschal II, 1099–1118.

436 On Frutolf's calculation of the beginning of the world see above, pp. 25–7.

437 Frederick of Schwarzenburg, archbishop of Cologne 1100–31.

438 8 September in Città Castellana. See Meyer von Knonau (1904), p. 107; Zeise (1982), p. 266.

439 Egilbert, archbishop of Trier 1079–1101 (d. 3 September).

440 Liemar, archbishop of Bremen 1072–1101 (d. 16 March).

441 Count Henry of Limburg 1082–1119, duke of Lower Lotharingia 1101–6 (Luxemburg family). Henry's rebellion stemmed from his being deprived of the office of Lotharingian count palatine: see Robinson (1999), pp. 314–15.

THE *1106 CONTINUATION* OF FRUTOLF'S *CHRONICLE* (1096–1106)

The year of the Lord 1096.[1] *Welf,*[2] *formerly duke of Bavaria, who had already been repudiated by the emperor some time ago and because of that had lost his duchy, was restored to the emperor's grace and received his duchy back.*

An image appeared in the sun on Monday the fifth Nones of March [3 March] *at the beginning of Lent. It was reported also that everywhere the world brought forth diverse prodigies. Soon afterwards from nearly all parts of the earth, but chiefly from the western kingdoms, innumerable armed troops of kings, nobles and even common people of both sexes began to travel towards Jerusalem, passionately stirred up by frequent reports about the oppression of the Lord's Sepulchre and the devastation of all the churches, which had been subjected to the power of the ferocious people of the Turks for several years and which had repeatedly been destroyed through unheard-of calamities. To come to their aid, as is reported, a great many set off hurriedly in different groups with different and unreliable leadership.*[3]

The first group, estimated at 15,000 and following a certain monk named Peter,[4] *travelled peacefully through Lotharingia, and then through Bavaria and Hungary. Many also travelled in boats on the Danube or by foot through Swabia, besides others – about 12,000 – led through Saxony and Bohemia by a certain priest, Folkmar,*[5] *and a considerable number led through Franconia by the priest Gottschalk.*[6] *In the cities through which they passed they either completely destroyed the abominable remnants of the Jews as the true inner enemies of the church, or forced them to seek refuge in baptism; but most of them afterwards reverted to their earlier belief, like dogs returning to their vomit.*[7]

---

1 Frutolf, *Chronicle* 1096, above, pp. 130–1.

2 Welf IV, duke of Bavaria 1070–1101. See above, p. 110 n. 215.

3 Cf. Bernold, *Chronicle* 1096, pp. 527–9 (*SC*, pp. 329–30); Cosmas, *Chronicle* 1096, trans. Wolverton (2009), p. 186.

4 Peter the Hermit (d. 1115). Cf. *AA* 1.2–7, pp. 2–16. See also Blake and Morris (1985), 79–107; Flori (1999); Costick (2008), pp. 106–10, 126–8.

5 Folkmar (d. 1096). See below, p. 151.

6 *AA* 1.23, p. 44, identifies him as a Rhinelander.

7 Proverbs 26.11; 2 Peter 2.22. Cf. the contemporary addition in Bernold of St Blasien's *Chronicle*: *SC*, p. 331; Cosmas, *Chronicle* 1096, trans. Wolverton (2009), p. 186. On the Rhineland pogroms see Riley-Smith (1984), 51–72.

Once these travellers — by then laden down with booty — reached Hungary, they attracted through certain acts of violence, as it seemed, the hatred of the inhabitants; but in reality it was the abundance of their wealth that kindled the avarice of those semi-barbarians. On the orders of King Coloman[8] they were taken prisoner, more by trickery than by force: many were sentenced to death and only a few, deprived of their weapons and effects, are reported to have escaped at great cost.[9] Although a great multitude of both [sexes] was seduced by a certain soldier named Emico,[10] just as the Israelite army was once deceived by the spirit of fornication,[11] the few of them who entered Hungary were blocked by the garrison at the Wieselburg[12] and fled home when nobody pursued[13] them.

There was an eclipse of the moon on the sixth Ides of August [8 August], in the fourteenth year of the lunar cycle.[14]

The year of the Lord 1097.[15] Returning from Italy,[16] Emperor Henry came to the city of Regensburg in Bavaria, where he stayed for a considerable time and allowed the Jews who had been coerced into baptism the use of Jewish rites.[17] *Meanwhile, Duke Godfrey of Lotharingia,[18] a man of most illustrious origin, nature and martial prowess, who the year before had converted virtually all his possessions into money, made the journey through Franconia fortified with no little faith and many knights.[19] He was not frightened by those fleeing from Hungary but, with the permission of Emperor Henry and King Coloman, he traversed Hungary and Bulgaria, made an alliance with*

---

8 Coloman I of Hungary, 1095–1116.

9 See below, p. 151. Cf. *AA* 1.24, pp. 46–8.

10 Count Emico of Flonheim (formerly identified as Emico of Leiningen). See Toussaint (1982), pp. 25–8; Murray (1992), 315–22; Möhring (1992), 97–111. See below, pp. 151–2.

11 Hosea 4.12.

12 The border fortress of Mosonmagyaróvár by the River Leitha. Cf. *AA* 1. 27–9, pp. 50–8. See below, p. 152.

13 Proverbs 28.1.

14 See above, p. 131 n. 393.

15 Frutolf, *Chronicle* 1097, above, pp. 131–2.

16 Probably in early May through the Brenner Pass: Robinson (1999), p. 298.

17 Fol. 183v of Frutolf's autograph (Jena, Thüringer Universitäts- und Landesbibliothek, Bose q. 19) reads 'the use of their own laws, as it seems' (*legibus suis uti, ut fertur*); 'the use of Jewish rites' (*iudaizandi ritum*) has been added above, probably by the 1106 continuator. Cf. Frutolf, *Chronicle* 1097, above, p. 131.

18 Godfrey V (of Bouillon), duke of Lower Lotharingia 1087–96, advocate of the Holy Sepulchre (d. 1100), grandson of Godfrey 'the Bearded' through his mother Ida.

19 That is, he embarked on the First Crusade.

the emperor of Constantinople and, supported by his troops, reached Rum,[20] where he joined the armies of Sicily, Greece, the Danes, the Normans and others from overseas, or rather the forces of all Christ-honouring nations. He clashed in numerous battles with the barbarians and, eventually, occupying Rum, besieged Antioch.

Emperor Henry held a peace council with the princes at Mainz about the Kalends of December [1 December] and celebrated Christmas at Strasburg. A comet appeared. This same year the summer was most fruitful, but the winter was mild and pestilentious; there were exceedingly heavy floods from deluges and rivers.

The year of the Lord 1098.[21] An inquisition was held in Mainz[22] by the emperor concerning the assets of the murdered Jews and among those accused of stealing from them were some of the archbishop's relatives.[23] When the emperor sent for them they did not come into his presence and the bishop, wishing but unable to defend their cause and stirred up with indignation, left the city and took himself to Thuringia with them, as though he could better shelter his own there and, in proximity to rebellion against the emperor, could inflict terror on him and thus avenge the accusation.[24] But there were some who said that the bishop himself had accepted a large part of the stolen money and on that account applied his heart to the defence of the others with such great care.

Welf, once more duke of Bavaria, reconciled his sons with the emperor when they sought to rebel and succeeded in getting the duchy committed to one of them after him.[25]

The year of the Lord 1099.[26] Emperor Henry celebrated Christmas at Cologne and during Epiphany at Aachen made his younger son King Henry V,[27] renouncing his elder son Conrad, whom he had earlier crowned.[28]

20 Rum (*Romania* in Latin): the sultanate of Rum (whose inhabitants referred to themselves as 'Romans'), created by the Seljuks from the southern and eastern parts of the former Byzantine province of Anatolia in the aftermath of the Battle of Manzikert (1071).
21 Frutolf, *Chronicle* 1098, above, p. 132.
22 10 May 1098.
23 Archbishop Ruothard of Mainz, 1089–1109.
24 Meyer von Knonau (1904), pp. 28–30, 161–2; Schiffmann (1931), p. 49; Rassow (1960), p. 257; Fenske (1977), pp. 141–6; Robinson (1999), pp. 303–4.
25 See above, p. 132 n. 401.
26 Frutolf, *Chronicle* 1099, above, p. 136.
27 Henry V (1086–1125). Henry had been elevated to the kingship on 10 May 1098 at Mainz. The Epiphany (6 January) was closely associated with kingship in the middle ages.
28 Conrad (1074–1101), crowned 30 May 1087. The emperor renounced Conrad at

Conrad, however, discovering from his rebellion[29] that he had only very few close supporters in the kingdom, sent one of his father's *ministeriales* who was likewise named Conrad,[30] an exceedingly strong and prudent man, to certain parts of Italy and obtained the name and dignity of king for almost nine years.[31] In this time the odour of his innate character spread throughout the whole Roman world so that no pious or wise man doubted that the salvation of the commonwealth rested on him. He was a thoroughly catholic man who was most obedient to the apostolic see,[32] more dedicated to religion than to power or arms. Although more than well practised in courage and valour, he preferred to pass his time in reading than in games, and through compassion and mercy he was *neighbour to* [33] the poor of every sort, but especially to destitute knights. He disdained none, he was violent to none, he prejudged none; to all persons of whatever condition he was affable. Thus not undeservedly did he prove always to be loved by God and by men. Although he had resolved always to remain celibate, he was compelled by his family to take as his wife the daughter[34] of Duke Roger of Sicily,[35] virtually the most renowned man of our time. With her he led so chaste a marriage that one could hardly believe he had ever known her.[36] As the law prescribes: *You shall not reveal the shame of your father*;[37] and again:

Mainz in May 1098: Meyer von Knonau (1904), pp. 26–7.

29 Conrad rebelled in 1093. See Frutolf, *Chronicle* 1093, above, p. 129.

30 Perhaps the envoy of the same name sent by Conrad to Roger I of Sicily: Robinson (1999), p. 288 n. 72.

31 Conrad was crowned anti-king by the archbishop of Milan: Bernold, *Chronicle* 1093, p. 456 (*SC*, p. 313). See Robinson (1999), pp. 286–8.

32 Conrad's pro-papal sympathies may have been the result of political calculation: Goez (1996), 26–7.

33 Luke 10.36.

34 Maximilla (d. ? after 1138). Conrad was persuaded to marry Maximilla by Pope Urban II and Countess Matilda of Tuscany in an attempt to outmanoeuvre Henry IV. The marriage took place in Pisa in April 1095: Meyer von Knonau (1903), pp. 449–50; Holtzmann (1963), 149–67; Becker (1964), pp. 136–7; Robinson (1999), p. 292.

35 Roger I, count of Sicily (d. 1101). See Houben (2002), pp. 8–24.

36 In the autograph of the *1106 Continuation* (Jena, Thüringer Universitäts- und Landesbibliothek, Bose q. 19, fol. 184v) this sentence was originally followed by: 'Nevertheless, in dove-like loyalty she so detested a second marriage that, after her body had lost such a head, she dedicated the rest of her life to works that bore fruit sixty-fold.' This passage, however, was erased and is not transmitted in later continuations.

37 Leviticus 18.7.

Honour thy father.[38] He never permitted his own ears to give credence to the rumours of his father's habits that were mangling the whole Roman empire or that he himself was the cause of resistance to his father and of his downfall. He always called him his Lord and Caesar, or emperor; any servant who arrived from his father's court – even the lowest – he treated with friendly good will. In addition to being virtuous in mind and habits, he had a most handsome figure and was very tall.

In the same year Duke Godfrey,[39] Count Raymond of St Gilles,[40] Count Robert of Normandy[41] and Count Robert of Flanders,[42] leading great contingents, reached Jerusalem after many difficulties, by then four years after many warriors had voluntarily taken the cross in that campaign for Christ who had been crucified for them. The remainder of the multitude was dispersed in various regions all around, apart from those who stayed with Bohemund at Antioch,[43] those who departed with Baldwin for Edessa,[44] or those who remained at Laodicea or Tyre.

Here my soul burns to add certain details concerning this campaign or expedition, which was ordained not by men but by God, especially to refute the imprudence – or more correctly the impudence – of some who, persevering always in old error, with rash speech presume to criticize the novelty of something so necessary to an ageing and declining world.[45] In the Epicurean fashion, they cherish the broad way of pleasure over the narrow way of divine service.[46] In the utter blindness of their hearts they consider love of the world wisdom, contempt of the world folly (that is, a prison their homeland), *darkness light, evil goodness*[47] and death life – oh, how shameful! By this they are flattered and furnished with such audacity in their depravity that everywhere – but especially

---

38 Exodus 20.12.
39 See n. 18 above.
40 Raymond IV of St Gilles, count of Toulouse, count of Tripoli (d. 1105).
41 Robert II, duke of Normandy (*c.* 1054–1134).
42 Robert II, count of Flanders (*c.* 1065–1111).
43 Bohemund I, prince of Taranto and Antioch (d. 1111), son of Robert Guiscard.
44 Baldwin (of Boulogne), younger brother of Duke Godfrey of Lower Lotharingia, count of Edessa and king of Jerusalem (d. 1118).
45 The sixth age of the world's history (old age) in St Augustine's paradigm of the 'ages of history'; see above, pp. 25–6.
46 See Matthew 7.14.
47 Isaiah 5.20.

in this land – things are reversed, since wisdom is hated by all, every virtue is offensive, religion is despised, humility is crushed, cunning prevails before all, vice wins over love, cruelty over fear and arrogance rules over honour. We, however, *put our trust* only *in God*;[48] we look not with astonishment to the present but to the future, and although reluctant spectators and yet well-wishing admirers, we praise those glorious men of our times who have conquered the kingdoms of the world and who for piety have left wife and children,[49] power and riches, to seek out the hundredth sheep.[50] They put their souls in His hands;[51] with *zeal* they were *zealous for the Lord of hosts*,[52] and with worthy valour they entered into the service of their heavenly king.

In the time of Henry IV, prince of the Romans, and Alexius,[53] prince of Constantinople, according to the prophecy of the Gospel, everywhere *nation* rose *against nation and kingdom against kingdom, and there were great earthquakes in diverse places, and pestilences and famines and terrors from heaven, and great signs*.[54] For since the Gospel trumpet[55] had already proclaimed to all people the arrival of the righteous Judge,[56] the universal church was understood by the whole world to portend these prophesied signs. Jerusalem, in the possession of Saracen dwellers, was already enslaved to Babylon, the seat of which is now the Egyptian kingdom;[57] already in its weakness had it ransomed the Christian religion through daily tribute. Bethlehem, the *house of* the *bread*[58] of angels, had become a stable for a herd of cattle, and for a number of years all of the churches round about had been completely subject to the mockery of the pagans.

48 Philippians 1.14.
49 See Matthew 19.29.
50 Luke 15.4.
51 Luke 23.46.
52 3 Kings 19.10, 19.14.
53 The Byzantine emperor Alexius I Comnenus, 1081–1118.
54 Luke 21.10–11; cf. Matthew 24.7, Mark 18.8.
55 Matthew 24.31.
56 2 Timothy 4.8.
57 'Saracen' and Babylon refer to the Fatimid dynasty and Cairo respectively. The Fatimids were Shiite Muslims and considered heretics by the 'Abbasid caliphs of Baghdad (who were Sunni or orthodox Muslims). The Fatimids rose to power in North Africa during the tenth century, conquering Egypt, Palestine and Syria from the 'Abbasids. See Brett (2004), pp. 675–9.
58 Isidore, *Etymologies* 15.1.23, trans. Barney (2006), p. 302.

Meanwhile, as bad luck would have it, war broke out between the eastern Christians, that is the Greeks and the Armenians;[59] and the Armenians, because they had a smaller kingdom and fewer numbers, allied themselves with neighbouring Persian warriors of great renown and fame, namely the Turks.[60] With their help the strife was resolved according to the satisfaction of the Armenians, who dismissed them to their own land. But the Turks were drawn very much to the Armenians' abundant and fertile lands. After several years they formed a plan and burst forth in great numbers from *the north*,[61] from the land of Gorrizim,[62] which is said to be richer in men than in provisions. They were divided up under four sultans – as they are wont to call their leaders – who were subject to one Persian emperor[63] virtually in the manner of a divine cult. From Armenia they spread out over Cappadocia and the whole of Rum[64] and Syria. First they conquered Nicaea, once the strongest tower of the catholic faith,[65] and slaughtered the Christians they captured. They installed there one of their own, the tyrant Suleyman,[66] with a garrison; and all the country round about as far as the swamp or the bay that is called the Arm of St George[67] they utterly devastated and spared not one Christian soul, neither one church nor monastery nor even one image of the saints.

We have seen in the half-destroyed churches of those parts – and it is still a miserable spectacle – the pictures of our Saviour, His most glorious mother or the many saints with vandalized noses, ears, hands

59 Perhaps a reference to the gains made by Armenian princes during the political turmoil that engulfed the Byzantine empire in the wake of the Battle of Manzikert (1071). See France (1994), p. 154.

60 The Seljuk Turks: see Cahen (1969), pp. 135–76; France (1994), pp. 145–7; Brett (2004), pp. 691–2.

61 Ezekiel 47.17.

62 Possibly Khorezm, a region to the east of the Caspian Sea in modern Turkmenistan and Uzbekistan. The *Gesta Francorum* refers to 'Korasan' as the Turkish homeland: *GF* 9, pp. 49, 52.

63 The caliph of Baghdad (a member of the 'Abbasid dynasty of Sunni or orthodox Muslims). As with the Fatimids of Egypt, the caliph was a figurehead; practical authority rested with various Seljuk potentates. On the complex power structures of the 'Abbasid caliphate see Hillenbrand (2000), pp. 35–40; Tyerman (2006), pp. 126–9.

64 See above n. 20.

65 An allusion to the Council of Nicaea in 325 and the creed named after it.

66 Kilij Arslan, Seljuk sultan of Rum 1092–1107, and son of the Seljuk sultan Suleyman Ibn Kutulmush (d. 1086). Arslan was commonly called Suleyman in western sources: *AA* 1.16, p. 32.

67 The Bosphorus.

or feet that visibly lament the desolation of the churches and show, as it were, the fresh blows of divine justice, which forever watches over them. Before these swords, O noblest Constantinople, neither your king nor his thousand-fold cunning could protect you;[68] neither the innumerable population of your citizens, your many markets nor boundless quantities of gold could ransom you; neither your great levies of Varangians,[69] Turcopoles[70] nor Pechenegs[71] could defend you: only the aforementioned intervening expanse of water could protect you;[72] only the work of your Creator could safeguard you. This fury quickly conquered once-mighty Antioch and, not to delay longer, all of Syria and Palestine pledged obedience at once.[73]

Accordingly, when the *promised land*[74] was subjected [to the Seljuk Turks], Jerusalem, the mother of our salvation and faith, was oppressed by a double yoke of bondage. It was only a very small consolation that its Saracen oppressors – who are a more shameful people than the Turks – would be punished by the same fate. After a sultan had been placed there with a great number of soldiers,[75] they [the Turks] destroyed the monasteries and several other buildings outside the city to repair the city walls, which can still be seen today. The Lord's Sepulchre was left undefiled merely for reasons of profit,[76] while the most famous Temple of the Lord which, I think, is comparable to no other work of human construction, they sacrilegiously appropriated for the pagan religion. It was always held in such respect by them that they never entered without bare and washed feet. Those whom they had allowed to enter for so many years,[77] both in the time of the Saracens and the Turks,

68 Alexius Comnenus's cunning is a theme in western sources: *GF* 2, p. 17. On western-Byzantine relations see Lilie (1993), 1–82; Ní Chléirigh (2010), pp. 161–88.
69 Vikings who settled in Russia and the Ukraine from the ninth century onwards, some of whom fought as mercenaries for Byzantium: Blöndal (1978), pp. 1–14, 122–66.
70 Imperial auxiliary cavalry, probably originally ethnic Turks: Savvides (1993), pp. 122–36.
71 A nomadic Turkish people who settled in modern-day Serbia during the eleventh century: Golden (1990), pp. 270–5.
72 St George as protector: see Frutolf, *Chronicle* 1001, above, p. 86.
73 Fatimid authority in Palestine and Syria disintegrated in the face of Seljuk attack during the 1060s and 1070s.
74 Hebrews 11.9.
75 Jerusalem was captured from the Fatimids by the Seljuk emir Atsiz bin Uwaq in 1071/3: Gil (1992), pp. 410–11.
76 That is, as a pilgrimage site for Christians.
77 Presumably Christian pilgrims.

were not even allowed to enter the atrium, because they judged them on the whole to be too impure.

As the situation demanded, the victors sometimes toiled in war and other times indulged themselves in games or pleasures, for they had been transplanted from dry gravel to a land of great fruitfulness; what torment, what crucifixion and what misery in all respects the remaining Christians endured in their slavery is hardly believable for someone who has not experienced it for himself. Yet from the frequent messages and letters that we have seen, it is easy to learn of the church of Jerusalem crying out mournfully for the universal church to protect her. Even the aforementioned emperor of Constantinople, Alexius, sent not a few letters to Pope Urban[78] [II] concerning these barbarian depredations, which had already flooded the greater part of his realm. In these letters he lamented not having sufficient forces to defend the eastern churches and implored the pope, if it were possible, to call upon the West – which was already entirely committed to Christianity – to aid him, promising for his part to supply everything that was necessary for waging war on land or at sea.[79]

Thus alarmed, the pope and the whole Roman church held a general council on the borders of Spain or, as some say, in Paris.[80] There the pope himself, after a very laborious journey, explained in a most eloquent manner to the innumerable crowds of people that had come there as well as to the envoys of various kingdoms everything that had been reported and much more.[81]

Soon thousands broke down in tears and in various languages lifted up their lamentation to heaven. At this the most excellent teacher offered remission of their sins to all[82] if they renounced everything that they

---

78 Pope Urban II, 1088–99.

79 Cf. Bernold of St Blasien, *Chronicle* 1095, p. 520 (*SC*, p. 324), who reported that 'a legation from the emperor of Constantinople' arrived at the Synod of Piacenza in 1095 and 'humbly implored the lord pope and all Christ's faithful people to give him some help against the pagans in defence of holy Church, which the pagans had already almost destroyed in that region, having seized that territory up to the walls of the city of Constantinople'.

80 The Council of Clermont, 27 November 1095. See Somerville (1974), 55–90.

81 Accounts of Urban's speech at Clermont: *FC* 1.3, pp. 130–8; Robert of Rheims, *Historia Hierosolymitana*, pp. 727–9; *GF* 1, pp. 1–2; Balderic of Dol, *Historia Ierosolimitana*, pp. 12–15; Guibert of Nogent, *Historia quae dicitur gesta Dei per Francos*, pp. 137–40. For English translations see Peters (ed.), *The First Crusade*, pp. 25–37.

82 The extant decrees of the Council of Clermont show that the spiritual reward offered was more cautious. See Decree of the Council of Clermont 2 [8], ed. Somerville (1972), p. 74: 'whoever sets out to free the church of God in Jerusalem purely out of

owned, if they wholeheartedly took up the cross like Christ and brought aid to their imperilled fellow Christians. By a solemn promise the hearts of all were lifted up and about 100,000 men were called at once for the army of Christ from Aquitaine and Normandy, England, Scotland and Ireland, Brittany, Galicia, Gascony, France, Flanders and Lotharingia, as well as from other Christian peoples, whose names I no longer remember.

This army of true cross-bearers displayed the sign of the cross on its garments as a reminder of self-mortification,[83] believing that by this, just as with the vision revealed to Constantine the Great,[84] it would triumph over the enemies of the cross of Christ.

Thus, through wonderful and inestimable divine dispensation, all these members of Christ, so different in language, tribe and nation, were suddenly joined and cemented together as one body through their love of Christ. While all were under the sole kingship of Christ, the different peoples were managed by their own leaders: Godfrey of Lotharingia and his brothers Baldwin and Eustace, Robert of Flanders, Robert of Normandy, Count Raymond of St Gilles, Hugh,[85] the brother of King Philip of France,[86] and other warriors of similar energy, nobility and strength. The aforementioned pope placed Bishop Adhemar,[87] a venerable man of holiness and wisdom, over all of these and granted him the right to exercise on his behalf the power of binding and loosing that had been transmitted by St Peter to the Roman see in perpetuity.[88] He bestowed the apostolic blessing upon the army marked with the sign of the heavenly host and then, once the time for its departure had been agreed by all, he returned to Italy together with a substantial number of troops from the army.

Once the various messengers had returned to their own lands this report soon spread hither and thither, exciting the whole world.

---

devotion and not for the acquisition of honour or wealth, may reckon that journey as a substitute for every penance'. The chroniclers of the crusade almost universally took the spiritual reward to mean remission of sins. See Robinson (1990), pp. 343–8.
83 See Constable (2008), pp. 45–91.
84 Constantine I (272–337). The vision of Constantine: his dream on the eve of the Battle of the Milvian Bridge (28 October 312), in which he was instructed to paint the Greek letters Chi-Rho (for Christ) on the shields and banners of his army.
85 Hugh of Vermandois (1053–1101).
86 Philip I of France (1052–1108), king 1060.
87 Bishop Adhemar of Le Puy (d. 1 August 1098).
88 The 'Petrine commission': see Matthew 16.18–19.

Moreover – marvellous to relate – it flew over the boundary of the ocean with its habitual speed, and even the sea itself overflowed with fleets from the islands for the army of the heavenly king. For, as we have learned reliably, such unknown peoples poured forth from the ocean, whose customs and demeanours I cannot describe and whose language neither those who dwell by the coast nor even sailors recognized, as well as others who survived on nothing save bread and water, and yet more whose every utensil was of silver instead of iron. From here and everywhere the number of those who subscribed increased daily and, as we have said, the whole world was enflamed by this expedition, was shaken or, rather, was seen to be transformed.

The West Franks were easily persuaded to leave their farms, since for several years France had been greatly afflicted by civil strife, famine and death. Finally a plague, which began near the church of St Gertrude in Nivelles, terrified them to the point of despairing for life. It was always of this type: touched by an invisible fire, some part of the body burned so long with painful or, rather, incomparable and incurable torment that the person lost either his life in anguish or in anguish the afflicted limb. To this day some bear witness to this affliction by their maimed hands and feet.

The common people and other persons from the remaining nations admitted that, besides the apostolic edict, they had been summoned to go to the promised land by certain prophets recently arisen among them or by signs in the heavens and by revelations.[89] Others were compelled to take such vows by all kinds of personal disadvantages. In fact many of them were burdened on the journey with wives and children and all their domestic goods.

The Franconians, Saxons, Thuringians, Bavarians and Swabians, however, only faintly *sounded the trumpet call*,[90] mainly because of the schism between kingdom and priesthood, which from the time of Pope Alexander [II] to the present day has, alas, made us as hated and offensive to the Romans as the Romans are to us. Thus it was that almost all of the German people were, at the beginning of the expedition, ignorant of the reasons for it. They mocked the many legions of horsemen, the troops of infantry, the crowds of country people and the women and children who passed through their land as if they were deranged by

---

89 On apocalypticism and the crusade see Rubenstein (2004), pp. 53–69, more generally Rubenstein (2011).

90 Judges 3.27; 2 Kings 2.28.

unheard-of stupidity, since they were leaving the certainties of the land of their birth for the uncertainties of vain delusions, since they longed for a promised land that offered no certainty but danger and since they renounced their own possessions to covet those of others. But however much more arrogant our people are than others, by divine mercy the anger of the Germans was eventually inclined to the message of this proclamation when they were fully informed of the matter from the passing crowds.

Moreover, *signs* that were seen by many *in the sun*,[91] which have already been described,[92] as well as omens that appeared both in the sky and on the earth, stirred up many who had previously been indifferent about this expedition. While we consider it most useful to include an account of some of them, to describe all would be most tedious. For instance, around the Nones of October [7 October] we saw a comet standing still in the southern half of the sky,[93] the aura of which extended in the manner of a slanting sword. Three years after that we observed on the sixth Kalends of March [24 February] another star in the east which, after long being stationary, changed its position by leaping about. We also saw blood-coloured clouds rising from both the west and the east, which met in the middle of the sky, while again about midnight fiery spectacles rose up from the north and many flares were seen flying through the air, as many witnesses have attested for us.

One day not many years before, about the ninth hour,[94] a certain priest of honourable life named Suigger observed in the sky two knights charging at each other and fighting for a considerable time. One of them, who carried a great cross with which he was seen to pierce the other, proved to be the victor. At the same time the priest G.,[95] who now together with us in the monastic life has paid to Christ the offering of a *sheep* for the *firstling of the ass*,[96] was walking in the forest around midday with two companions and saw a sword of extraordinary length carried high into the air by a whirlwind – it was unknown whence it came – and, until the vision sped into the heavens, he discerned the clashing with his ears and the metal with his eyes.

91 Luke 21.25. See also Acts 2.19–20.
92 See above, p. 138.
93 In 1097. Cf. Sigebert of Gembloux, *Chronicle* 1097, p. 367: 'A comet appeared in the west for the whole of the first week of October.'
94 The ninth hour after sunrise, approximately 3 p.m.
95 None of the surviving manuscripts identify this priest.
96 Exodus 34.20.

Some who were guarding horses in the fields reported that they had seen the appearance of a city in the sky and had observed various troops from different parts, both cavalry and infantry, hastening their march towards it. Some also revealed that the sign of the cross had been divinely stamped on their foreheads, their garments or on other parts of their bodies and they believed that by these marks they had been called for the army of the Lord. Others likewise were compelled by some sudden change of heart or by some dream to sell all their property and possessions and to sew the sign of penance on their garments.[97] And to all the people who rushed into the churches in crowds beyond belief, swords along with staves and purses were distributed with priestly blessing according to a new rite.

What shall I recall of the woman who in these times who had been pregnant for two whole years finally to bring forth a son from her womb who could speak? Of a child with two sets of limbs and another with two heads or of some lambs that were also born with two heads?[98] Or of foals that possessed great teeth – which we usually call horses' teeth and which nature only grants to three-year-old horses – at their birth?

While through these and similar signs the whole of creation roused up the army of the Creator, the watchful enemy, who takes occasion while others *sleep* to *sow his tares among the good seed*,[99] *raised up false prophets*[100] and mixed *false brethren*[101] and dishonourable members of the female sex among the army of the Lord under the *appearance*[102] of religion. In this way the flock of Christ was defiled to such an extent – not only through hypocrisy and lies but also through heinous filth – that as in the prophecy of the Good Shepherd *even the elect* were *led astray*.[103] At that time was concocted the fable concerning Charles the Great,[104] who

---

97 The sign of the cross, the customary sign of penitent pilgrims along with the staff and purse.

98 Prodigies as a portent of future events: Isidore, *Etymologies* 11.3.3–4, trans. Barney (2006), pp. 243–4.

99 Matthew 13.25.

100 Matthew 24.24.

101 Galatians 2.4; 2 Corinthians 11.26.

102 2 Timothy 3.5.

103 Matthew 24.24.

104 Charles the Great (d. 814), king of the Franks 768, emperor 800. The significance of legends concerning Charles the Great: Rubenstein (2008), p. 63; Latowsky (2013), pp. 122–3.

was alleged to have been revived from the dead for this purpose, and about another – whom I do not know – who lived again, as well as the silly tale about the goose who is supposed to have led her mistress[105] and many others of that sort.

Although the individual seducer will be *known by his fruit*,[106] as *wolves* can be recognized *in sheeps' clothing*,[107] one should especially ask those of these who still survive from which harbour they were going to pursue their vow without a ship to cross the sea, in which battles and places was their small force put to flight by the many pagans, which of their fortresses there did they capture, by which part of the walls of Jerusalem did they finally pitch their camp and so forth. Since they have no response they ought of necessity to repent, as much for the offerings of the faithful that they have accepted through hypocrisy as for the slaughter on account of the rapacity of the crowds they seduced, but principally for their own apostasy.

Now, as has been said, a mob followed Folkmar through Bohemia until at Nitra, a Hungarian city,[108] a riot took place in which some were captured and others perished by the sword, while the very few who survived are wont to testify that the sign of the cross appeared in the heavens above them and delivered them from imminent death. Then Gottschalk, not a true servant of God but a false one, entered Hungary with his followers after pillaging eastern Bavaria. Next, under an astonishing spectacle of false religion, he fortified a certain citadel and placed a garrison there,[109] and began with the rest of his rabble to ravage the surrounding part of Hungary. This town was evidently recaptured by the natives without delay and, great numbers of the band having been butchered or taken prisoner, the rest of his *flock* was *dispersed*.[110] He himself, *a hireling, not a shepherd*,[111] shamelessly fled.

In those days, there appeared a certain soldier named Emico,[112] count of the lands around the Rhine, who was long notorious for his exceedingly

---

105 Cf. *AA* 1.30, p. 58.
106 Matthew 7.16.
107 Matthew 7.15.
108 In western Slovakia, in the valley of the River Nitra.
109 Probably the monastery of Pannonhalma (founded in 996 to aid the Christianization of Hungary): see *AA* 1.24, pp. 46–8.
110 Matthew 26.31.
111 John 10.12.
112 See n. 10 above.

tyrannical lifestyle. Called by divine revelation to this manner of religion like another Saul as he maintained, he usurped for himself the leadership of almost 12,000 cross-bearers who, being led through the cities of the Rhine, the Main and also the Danube, either entirely destroyed the execrable race of the Jews wherever they found them (being indeed in this matter zealously devoted to Christianity) or forced them into the bosom of the church. When they reached the borders of Hungary, with their forces already augmented by great numbers of both sexes, they were prevented by well-fortified garrisons from entering that kingdom, which is surrounded partly by swamps and partly by woods. For a rumour had already reached the ears of King Coloman that, to the minds of the Germans, there was no difference between killing pagans and killing Hungarians. And so for six weeks they besieged the fortress of the Wieselburg[113] and suffered many hardships there. Yet at the same time they were in the throes of a most foolish internal quarrel over which one of them should be king of Hungary.

Thus while toiling in the final assault – with the walls already breached, the townspeople already fleeing and the Hungarian army already setting fire to its own town – through the wonderful command of Almighty God, the victorious army of pilgrims fled. And they left behind them all their equipment, for no one carried anything back except his wretched life. And thus the men of our race, doubtless with zeal for God, *though not through knowledge of God*,[114] began to persecute other Christians while yet in the army that Christ had provided for freeing Christians.[115] They were kept from fraternal bloodshed only by divine mercy and the Hungarians were also freed. This is the reason why some of the more simple-minded brethren, ignorant of the matter and too hasty in their judgement, were scandalized and concluded that the whole expedition was vain and foolish.

Nevertheless, we see by these means the *chaff*[116] shaken from the *threshing-floor* of the Lord by the *winnowing-fan* and discern the grains of *wheat* that endure because of their natural solidity and weight,[117] namely Godfrey and the others mentioned above, the true leaders of the army of the Lord, each with his own people. Their camps were

113 See above, p. 139. Cf. the broadly similar account in *AA* 1.28–9, pp. 52–8.
114 Romans 10.2.
115 *AA* 1.29, pp. 56–8, attributed the failure to the army's excessive impurities and massacres of the Jews.
116 Matthew 3.12.
117 Matthew 3.12.

more *beautiful* to behold *than the array of all the stars*;[118] by the example of their humility and love as true disciples of Christ they met with peace and good will from all princes and peoples through whose lands they passed; after they had journeyed with various difficulties through Bulgaria, they reached the towers of Constantinople.[119]

In Jerusalem we read a little book,[120] which from this moment follows the whole history most diligently and concludes the many hardships that the people of God suffered for three years with the joyous victory of the capture of Jerusalem. Therefore, we shall note henceforth only a few of many things: namely that Emperor Alexius befriended all of those heroes with utterly feigned kindness and afterwards with an extorted oath restrained them from turning against his kingdom with their power,[121] although it is evident that the first contingents should all have been killed by trickery while they were waiting there for the arrival of the others had not Godfrey watched over the Lord's flock with care and caution.[122] This strife was borne witness to in the suburbs, which he then destroyed, and on the bridge, which he assaulted.[123] What more? For a period of almost two months the army in Byzantium daily received new arrivals, so that it was estimated to contain 300,000 fighting men, apart from the incredible multitude of ordinary people, children and women.[124] On the other hand the contingents who followed Peter [the Hermit], transported long before [across the Bosphorus] by the order of Alexius,[125] had already become a laughing-stock to the pagans.[126]

Breaking camp, they [the princes] reached Nicaea, captured it by storm and handed it over it to the emperor's forces (the aforementioned prince

---

118 Wisdom 7.29.

119 23 December 1096. Godfrey's journey to Constantinople: *AA* 2.1–10, pp. 60–76.

120 Hagenmeyer (1890), p. 1, identified this as the *Gesta Francorum*. This identification is no longer accepted: Schmale-Ott (1971), 421 n. 36; France (1998a), p. 41; France (1998b), pp. 29–42.

121 Tyerman (2006), pp. 118–22.

122 An allusion to 1 Peter 5.2.

123 Cf. *AA* 2.12–13, pp. 78–9.

124 The size of the crusading army: France (1994), pp. 122–42.

125 Alexius had established Peter's contingent at Kibotos on the Gulf of Nicomedia, separated from Constantinople by the Sea of Marmora.

126 Peter's forces were destroyed by Kilij Arslan about 21 October 1096. *AA* 1.15–22, pp. 28–44, attributed the events that led to their defeat to a breakdown in discipline during their stay at Kibotos. See Tyerman (2006), pp. 98–9.

Suleyman had fled).[127] They did so because they had sworn an oath to return to their former rule each of the cities that had been taken from Alexius's empire if they captured them, and not to doubt that he in turn would support them with royal weapons and supplies in equal measure. From there they travelled through the kingdom of Constantine,[128] in all respects a most rich country, until they reached the sea at Rugia.[129] In such a way, as a letter brought by Count Robert[130] shows, Christ led his army to such abundant provisions *that a ram sold for one coin*[131] *and an ox for a shekel.*

Moreover, it says, *though the princes and kings of the Saracens rose up against us, nevertheless by God's will were they easily conquered and crushed.*[132] *Since some were puffed up on account of these happy deeds, God opposed* them *at Antioch, a city impregnable to human power, where for nine months he detained* them *in siege and humiliated* them, *so that all* their *swollen pride left* them.[133] *Thus were they so humiliated that there were barely 100 good horses in the army; but God opened the fullness of his blessings and mercy, and led* them *into the city and gave the Turks and all their possessions into* their hands.[134] *Taking possession of it as if they had done so with their own strength and not suitably glorifying God, who had given it to* them, *they were besieged by so many Saracens that no one from such a large* crowd *dared to leave the city.*[135] *Moreover, famine in the city so weakened them that they could hardly refrain from eating human flesh. It would be tedious to relate the miseries that existed in the city. But God looked down upon His people*[136] *whom He had so long chastised and consoled them* and *to recompense their tribulation, as a sign of victory He first bestowed upon them His lance,* with which he was

127 The siege of Nicaea: 6 May–19 June 1097. Kilij Arslan ('Suleyman'), who had been attempting to gain control of the city of Melitene, returned to relieve Nicaea but was defeated by the crusaders on 16 May: France (1994), pp. 160–2.

128 The Armenian ruler Constantine of Gargar (d. *c.* 1117), who ruled over part of Cilicia.

129 The area of Rugia (Ruj) – the most probable identification of *Ruscia* – to the east of the River Orontes. Cf. *GF* 4, pp. 26–7; *RA* 11, p. 99. See Dussand (1927), pp. 163–7.

130 Count Robert of Flanders.

131 Daimbert of Pisa and the crusading princes, *Letter* to the pope, ed. Hagenmeyer, *Die Kreuzungsbriefe,* pp. 169–74. Cf. Frutolf, *Chronicle* 1098, pp. 133–6.

132 A reference to crusader successes at the siege of Nicaea and the Battle of Dorylaeum (1 July 1097).

133 The siege of Antioch, October 1097–June 1098. See France (1994), pp. 197–268.

134 Antioch was betrayed to Bohemund of Taranto by one of its defenders on the night of 2–3 June. See France (1994), pp. 257–67.

135 The second siege of Antioch (4–28 June 1098), during which the crusaders were besieged by Kerbogha al-Mawsili, atabeg of Mosul. See France (1994), pp. 269–96.

136 Ruth 1.6.

wounded on the cross, *a gift not seen since the days of the apostles.*[137] *Then He so inspired the hearts of the men that those who from sickness or hunger had not the strength to walk were imbued with the power to take up their weapons and to fight bravely* against the enemy.

After they *had triumphed over the enemy, the army, which was wasting away from hunger and weariness at Antioch, principally because of disagreements among the princes,*[138] *proceeded into Syria, assaulted the Saracen cities Barra and Marra,*[139] *and captured the castles in that region. While they were delaying there the famine in the army was so great that the putrid bodies of the Saracens were now eaten by the Christian people. Then by divine* command *they entered the interior of Hispania,*[140] *and the most bountiful, merciful and victorious hand of the almighty Father was with* them. *Indeed, the cities and fortresses of that region through which they were proceeding sent legates with many gifts and offered to aid* them *and to hand over their fortified towns. But because the army was not large and everybody* [wished] *to make haste to Jerusalem, accepting their pledges they* [the crusaders] *made them tributary; indeed, one of the many cities, which was on the coastline, had more men than were in the* Christian *army. And when it was heard at Antioch, Laodicea and Edessa that the hand of the Lord was with* them, *many from the army who had remained there followed* them *to Tyre. Thus with the Lord's companionship and co-operation they proceeded as far as Jerusalem.*[141] *And when they had laboured in the siege, especially because of the dearth of water, a council was held and the bishops and princes ordered that all should march around the city with bare feet, in order that He who entered it humbly for men might be moved by their humility to open it to* them *and to exercise judgement upon His enemies.*[142] *Thus placated by this humility, on the eighth day after their humiliation the Lord* delivered *the city to* them, *evidently the same day on which the primitive church was expelled from there, when the festival of the dispersal of the apostles is celebrated.*[143]

---

137 The finding of the Holy Lance by Peter Bartholomew: 14 June 1098. Cf. *AA* 4.44, p. 316. See Morris (1984), pp. 33–45.

138 See France (1994), pp. 297–304.

139 The neighbouring cities of Al-Bara and Ma'arra (Ma'arrat-an-Nu'man). Ma'arra was besieged from 27 November to 11 December by Raymond of Toulouse and Robert of Flanders, who were joined by Bohemund on 29 November. See France (1994), pp. 311–15.

140 The *dictator* of the original letter, most likely Raymond of Aguilers, probably used *Hispania* figuratively to refer to the 'land of the Saracens'. See above, p. 134 n. 411.

141 7 June 1099.

142 The council was held on 6 July and the procession took place on 8 July.

143 15 July. *RA* 18, p. 151.

Meanwhile, it seems wrong to conceal that when the army was delayed with the siege of Antioch, panic gripped all the peoples of the East. Messengers and spies hurried from all parts of the world, some for peace and others to prosecute war. Even the Babylonian king[144] sent legations to the assembled princes, which promised, among other things, that their lord would be their brother and friend with all the Saracens if, after the victory against Antioch, they expelled the Turks from Jerusalem;[145] for, as we have already written, Judah with Jerusalem and all of Palestine had been taken from the Saracens by the Turks.[146] On that account, after they had received assurances of security, many of the choicest knights were sent to Babylon. Their strength, height, deportment and gait, but especially their nobility, so astonished the barbarians that they acknowledged the Franks – as they are used to calling all the peoples of the West – to be more like gods than men and assured them that it was no wonder that such warriors should desire to subdue the whole world to themselves. At length, the king of Babylon held a council and besieged Jerusalem. He displayed these legates to give the impression that he was allied with the Franks, to whose swords he threatened to deliver the residents if the city was not handed over to him. With such trickery the barbarian king took the city, not because he was feared but because the Franks were feared; and sending away all the Turks he made every attempt to secure it with machines and soldiers against the advance of the Christians.[147] So it was that in one year Jerusalem was twice captured: first by the Saracens and then by the Franks.

If one should seek to learn what happened to the *enemy that was found there*, he should know that *in the porch that is called Solomon's and in his temple* the *victors rode in the blood of the Saracens up to the knees of their horses*.[148] Then, when they were considering who ought to hold the city, and some moved by love for their country and for the sake of their parents wished to return home, it was announced that the king of Babylon had come to Ascalon

---

144 The Fatimid caliph of Egypt, Ahmad al-Musta'li (d. 1101). In reality Fatimid power was controlled by the vizier al-Afdal (1066–1121), who designated al-Musta'li in 1094. See Brett (2004), p. 706.

145 Cf. *RA* 7, 17, pp. 58, 109–10. On the negotiations see Köhler (1991), pp. 56–69; France (1994), pp. 251–3, 325–6.

146 See above, p. 145.

147 Jerusalem was captured from the Ortoqid dynasty (vassals of the Seljuk Turks) by Fatimid forces under the command of the Egyptian vizier al-Afdal in August 1098. See Hillenbrand (2000), p. 44.

148 Cf. Revelation 14.20. *RA* 18, p. 50; Alphandéry (1929), 154; Tyerman (2006), p. 31.

with an innumerable multitude of pagans to lead the Franks,[149] who were at Jerusalem, into captivity and to assault Antioch, as he himself said; but the Lord had decided otherwise in regard to them [the Franks]. Therefore, since they who were at Jerusalem *learned in truth that the army of Babylon was at Ascalon*, they *went down to meet them, leaving* their *baggage and sick at Jerusalem with the garrison. When* their *army saw* the innumerable number of *the enemy*, the Christians *evoked the aid of God on their knees, so that He* who had always been present in all other necessities *might in the present battle break the strength of the pagans and the devil and might extend the kingdom of Christ and of the church from sea to sea. There was no delay; God presented Himself to those who called upon Him and furnished them with such great boldness that those who saw them rushing upon the enemy would have taken them for a herd of deer hastening to quench their thirst in running water.*[150] *It was wonderful, indeed, since there were in* the Christian *army not more then 5,000 horsemen and 15,000 foot-soldiers,* while *in the army of the enemy there were probably 100,000 horsemen and 400,000 foot-soldiers. Then* God *appeared wonderfully to His servants, for before* they *fought, by* their *charge alone,* He turned *that multitude in flight and scattered all their weapons, so that if they wished afterwards to attack them, they would not have the weapons in which they hoped.*[151] *Concerning the spoils, there can in truth be no question as to how much was captured, for the treasures of the king of Babylon were captured. They killed more than 100,000 Moors with the sword. Moreover, the Moors' fear was so great that in the city gate 2,000 were crushed; those who perished in the sea are innumerable; many of them also were entangled in thickets. The entire world was certainly fighting for* the Christians, *and had not many* of them *been detained by the spoils of the camp, few of the great multitude of the enemy would have been able to escape from the battle alive. On the day preceding the battle the* [Christian] *army captured many thousands of camels and cattle and sheep. When they advanced to battle – wonderful to tell – the camels formed in many squadrons and the sheep and cattle did likewise. Moreover, those animals accompanied them, halted when they halted, advanced when they advanced and charged when they charged. The clouds* also *protected* the Christians *from the heat of the sun and cooled them.*

Thus having celebrated the victory, the army returned to Jerusalem and, leaving Duke Godfrey there, Count Raymond of St Gilles, Count Robert of Normandy and Count Robert of Flanders returned to Laodicea. There they

---

149 An army commanded by the Fatimid vizier al-Afdal. France (1994), pp. 357–66.
150 See Psalm 41.2.
151 The Battle of Ascalon, 12 August 1099.

found the fleet belonging to the Pisans and Bohemund. After the archbishop of Pisa[152] *had established peace between Bohemund and the others who had disagreed with him, Raymond prepared to return for the sake of God and of his brethren. A*[153] *truly great multitude, as mentioned above, sought to return to their homeland; the others who remained have hitherto occupied the country in peace by God's will.*

The magnanimous duke,[154] whose equal in piety can scarcely be found, began to undertake great things for the Lord despite his limited resources. He pursued whatever remnants of the heathen were left, established garrisons at appropriate places and repaired Jaffa, which had long been destroyed, and its port, which had long been abandoned.[155] He repaired the ruined churches as far as he was able, while elsewhere he brought together monastic communities and conferred many gifts with the utmost devotion on the monasteries and the hospital that had always been in Jerusalem. He made a most firm peace with the people of Ascalon and Damascus for the sake of trade.[156] He honoured the knights of our people before all warriors and proved their fierceness with great skill to the French knights, while he soothed the envy that dwells in a certain natural manner between the two peoples by his innate skill in both languages.

In this year *Bishop Conrad of Utrecht was killed by his own people.*[157] *Bishop Herman of Cologne died* and was succeeded by Frederick.[158] *The Count Palatine Rapoto and his cousin* Count Udalric,[159] *who was said to be very wealthy, died.* While the emperor was holding a council with the princes in Regensburg the sudden death of those two magnates, of lesser men and of others occurred;[160] throughout the countryside and in the cities

---

152 Daimbert (d. 1105), archbishop of Pisa 1088–99, patriarch of Jerusalem 1099–1102. Hamilton (1980), pp. 14–17, 53–7; Murray (2000), pp. 81–93.

153 Frutolf, *Chronicle* 1098, above, p. 136.

154 Godfrey of Lower Lotharingia.

155 Cf. *AA* 7.13, p. 502, and the Damascus chronicler Ibn al-Qalanisi, *Chronicle*, p. 51.

156 Cf. *AA* 7.18, p. 510, who records that Godfrey led an expedition against Damascus. See also Nicholson (1940), p. 108 n. 5, who suggests the peace was a result of that expedition.

157 Frutolf, *Chronicle* 1099, above, p. 137. Conrad, bishop of Utrecht 1076–99.

158 Archbishop of Cologne, 1089–99 (d. 21 November); Archbishop Frederick of Cologne, 1100–31.

159 Rapoto V, count of Cham and Vohburg, count palatine of Bavaria (d. 14 April); Count Udalric II of Passau. See Loibl (1997), pp. 157–65.

160 At Easter (10 April). See Robinson (1999), p. 305.

also not a few of the common people died. Unexpected famines also occurred in many places.

Pope Urban died.¹⁶¹ On account of the unrest in the church, which – alas! – continues still, he called together many councils and promulgated many decrees. Among these he called together 200 fathers in the city of Piacenza¹⁶² and declared that, like his predecessor, he had excommunicated Emperor Henry, especially because the emperor's wife Queen Adelaide,¹⁶³ who was also present, testified many abominable things against him in the hearing of the whole synod.¹⁶⁴ But before departing this life, instructed by the Holy Spirit he designated Cardinal Rainer of San Clemente,¹⁶⁵ an abbot of holy conversation and good repute and a noble Roman,¹⁶⁶ to be elected to the apostolic lordship. This was additionally indicated by other revelations and, although he resisted, the whole Roman church consecrated him as its shepherd, naming him Paschal.

The year of the Lord 1100. Under Duke Godfrey, the defender of the church of Jerusalem, a vast meeting took place in Jerusalem of all those in the East who were Christian, but especially of the pilgrims who had settled in Antioch, Syria, Edessa or Palestine, so that on the feast of Christmas not only were many bishops consecrated¹⁶⁷ for the surrounding areas but the mystical prophecies were changed into visible events: *Arise, be enlightened, O Jerusalem!*¹⁶⁸ and *Rejoice with Jerusalem, and be glad with her, all you that love her!*¹⁶⁹ and so forth.

After that, with the heat of summer the air over Palestine was tainted

161 29 July.
162 The Council of Piacenza (1 March 1095): Bernold of St Blasien, *Chronicle* 1095, pp. 518–22 (*SC*, pp. 323–6). See Somerville (2011).
163 Eupraxia (Praxedis)-Adelaide (d. 1109), daughter of Prince Vsevolod of Kiev (1030–93). She married Henry IV in summer 1089.
164 Cf. Bernold, *Chronicle* 1094, 1095, pp. 512, 519 (*SC*, pp. 319, 324). See Becker (1964), pp. 132–3; Goez (1996), 31–2; Robinson (1999), pp. 290–1.
165 Rainer of Bieda, cardinal priest of S. Clemente, Pope Paschal II, 1099–1118 (elected 13 August; enthroned 14 August). See Servatius (1979), pp. 33–41.
166 Actually from Bieda near Forlì in the archdiocese of Ravenna.
167 Perhaps a reference to the consecration of Benedict of Edessa, Roger of Tarsus, Bartholomew of Mamistra and Bernard of Antioch by the new patriarch of Jerusalem, Daimbert of Pisa, at the request of Bohemund and Baldwin of Edessa. Cf. Ralph of Caen, *Gesta Tancredi* 140, p. 704; *Historia belli sacri* 135, p. 226. See Hamilton (1980), p. 16.
168 Isaiah 60.1.
169 Isaiah 66.10.

with the stench of dead bodies. Some maintain that the barbarians had spoiled the springs with poison and the reservoirs with the putrid fluids of the dead, whence there arose a pestilence which killed many of our people who fought under foreign skies.[170] Among these the whole catholic church tearfully laments Godfrey, snatched away much too soon, who provided for the people of God with paternal zeal and cherished them with maternal tenderness. For only one year he led the people of God; overcome by a prolonged sickness, he ended this present life in Christ on the fifteenth Kalends of August [18 July], *full of faith*[171] and good works.[172] Besides all the virtues he possessed in abundance, he so united both the natives and his fellow pilgrims by his gentleness that it was hard to tell whether the Franks lamented more than the Greeks or Syrians.[173] His tomb, built of Parian stone, stands in the narthex of the church of Golgotha in front of the Mount of Calvary.[174]

At that time Count Baldwin had settled at the renowned city of Edessa, or more correctly in the region and area of Armenia. He acquired lordship over that people on the death of their aged and most Christian ruler who,[175] having called Baldwin from Antioch to fight for him, adopted him as his son and heir after he had fought many successful battles.[176] From ancient times this great city had always been assailed by the pagans but had never fallen to them, for it was protected by walls stronger than the works of men, a river that roars through the city, its natural location and its wealth of people and produce. It is not within the bounds of this work or of time to relate how with few forces the aforesaid man scattered a great multitude of barbarians. Sometimes he was victorious in defeat, since having departed from the army he led another to the siege of Antioch and afterward he subtly escaped

---

170 See Edgington (2010), p. 194.

171 Acts 6.5. See also James 2.17.

172 Cf. *AA* 7.18–21, pp. 510–16.

173 Cf. *Ibid.* 7.21, p. 516.

174 The tomb was destroyed by fire in 1808. A seventeenth-century cutaway drawing is extant: Vicenzo Favi, *Relatione del viaggio di Gerusalemme*, MS London, British Library, Add. 33566, fol. 90r; reproduced in Hallam (1989), p. 107.

175 Thoros (d. 1098).

176 Baldwin reached Edessa on 20 February 1098 and by 8 March controlled the city. The eyewitness account of Matthew of Edessa claims that Baldwin intrigued with disaffected citizens: *Chronicle*, p. 37. *AA* 3.21, p. 170, also describes the adoption; *FC* 1.14, p. 210, claims that Thoros wished in the event of his death that Baldwin should 'possess the city and all his land as a permanent inheritance just as if he were his son'. See also Amouroux-Mourad (1988), pp. 57–91.

the trickery of a certain Turk named Balduk,[177] who had falsely joined him in order to capture and kill him. Whoever wishes to write down everything will have to abandon the task on account of time rather than material.[178] Having heard of the death of his brother, he entrusted the city and its people to his kinsman Baldwin the Younger[179] and travelled to Jerusalem with about 300 men.[180] He outwitted, fought and defeated thousands of pagans who lay in ambush for him and, laden with booty, he entered Jerusalem in triumph.[181] Beseeched and extolled by all, he consented to their petitions that he should be their prince. Not long afterwards he bowed his head over the tomb of the Lord and submitted himself to His personal service. After that, so that even greater fear of the Christians would be instilled in the pagans, he received royal benediction and was crowned by the legate of the apostolic see on Whitsunday.[182] Then he vanquished the coastal cities of Arsuf and Caesarea,[183] killing the Saracens that were there, and enlarged his kingdom at the expense of the king of Babylon.

Archbishop Wibert of Ravenna,[184] who had been placed over Hildebrand-Gregory and was called Pope Clement, died.[185] He was undoubtedly a man full of intelligence and eloquence, and most distinctly eminent in nobility and person. Yet neither in Rome nor in Ravenna did any good come of it and since he ascended against one living pope[186] (albeit coerced as they say) and outlived three who succeeded each

---

177 Balduk, emir of Samosata. Cf. *AA* 3.21–5, 5.22, pp. 170–80, 364.

178 An example of the rhetorical color of epistolary brevity (*epistolaris brevitas*), whereby attention is drawn to the incompleteness of a given account. See Arbusow (1963), pp. 97, 100–1; McCarthy (2002), 199.

179 Baldwin of Bourcq (d. 1131), count of Edessa (1100), king of Jerusalem (1118). See Murray (2000), pp. 185–6.

180 *AA* 7.31, p. 530, says 400 cavalry and 1,000 infantry. Cf. the eyewitness account of *FC* 2.1–5, pp. 352–84.

181 In November. Cf. *AA* 7.32–6, pp. 530–40.

182 He was crowned on Christmas Day 1100 by Patriarch Daimbert of Jerusalem in Bethlehem: *FC* 2.6, pp. 384–5; Fink (1969), pp. 381–2. Ekkehard of Aura omitted the incorrect date when reworking this material in his *Hierosolimita*.

183 Arsuf surrendered on 29 April 1101, Caesarea on 17 May 1101. *FC* 2.8–9, pp. 397–404; *AA* 7.54–5, pp. 562–4.

184 Wibert of Parma, archbishop of Ravenna 1072–1100, antpope 'Clement III', 1084–1100.

185 8 September in Città Castellana. See Meyer von Knonau (1904), p. 107; Zeise (1982), p. 266.

186 Gregory VII, 1073–85.

other,[187] he was exiled from each seat, Rome and Ravenna, and would have preferred – as we learned from his own mouth – never to have accepted the apostolic title.

The year of the Lord 1101. Nine years after leaving his father's palace the young King Conrad,[188] who in administering Italian matters had always relied upon the advice of Matilda[189] (that great, most noble and, as some say, religious woman who was related to him by blood and close association), as well as upon the lord pope and other God-fearing persons, was cut off by premature death and departed this transitory kingdom for the kingdom that is eternal, full of faith and having made a good confession.[190] Some say that he was killed with poison. There are those who testify that they saw the sign of the cross appear suddenly on the arms of his lifeless body and that his funeral rites were hallowed by certain miracles.

A member of our house saw a fire in the likeness of a great city flying from the west to the east. An incredibly numerous swarm of tiny insects, which because of their similarity to soldiers' tents are called pavilions,[191] flew for three whole days from the borders of Saxony to Bavaria.

Soon afterwards there followed a very large expedition, which was almost comparable in numbers to the former one.[192] After hearing stories of how matters in Jerusalem had prospered beyond expectation, the remainder of people throughout the entire West, but especially those who before had resisted taking the vow out of fear, want of faith, poverty or feebleness, prepared anew.[193] First, 50,000 people were marked [with the sign of the cross] by the bishops of Milan,[194] Pavia[195] and the others of Lombardy. Then, from the various German provinces and finally from Aquitaine (led by William of Poitiers[196]) came, in addition to the common folk, 30,000 wearing coats of mail. The people

---

187 Gregory VII, Victor III and Urban II.
188 See above, pp. 141–2.
189 Matilda, margravine of Tuscany (1046–1115).
190 Conrad died on 27 July in Florence.
191 Cf. Isidore, *Etymologies* 15.10.1, trans. Barney (2006), p. 313.
192 The crusade of 1101. Cate (1969), pp. 343–67; Riley-Smith (1986), pp. 120–34; Mulinder (1996).
193 Cf. *AA* 8.1, p. 568; Orderic Vitalis, *Ecclesiastical history* 5, pp. 268, 280, 322.
194 Archbishop Anselm IV of Milan, 1097–1101.
195 William, bishop of Pavia 1069–1100/2.
196 Duke William IX of Aquitaine (1071–1126).

of Lombardy passed through Carinthia with the permission of Duke Henry,[197] and after they had left Hungary behind them they wintered in the cities of Bulgaria, where their numbers began to dwindle. When they finally arrived in Constantinople they were transported to the other side [of the Bosphorus][198] – the usual kindness with which the accursed Alexius was wont to hurry pilgrims – and immediately exposed to the arrows of the pagans.[199] Once the Turks had perceived the incompetence of the Lombards they threshed them like straw,[200] so that the German army,[201] which followed the same route and arrived at the metropolis in early June, was unable to learn what had happened to those who had gone before it; for no survivors returning from Rum could be tracked down. Of course from our crossing into Bulgaria – or from its first city to the seat of Alexius – his envoys of peace continually hastened to meet us; yet, however, sometimes preceding us or accompanying us, they vanished again like embers. His soldiers, which are called Pechenegs,[202] sometimes sought to inflict losses upon our army from the rear, sometimes to attack the flanks, sometimes with skirmishes to bear upon us directly from the front and at other times to raid our camp by night. For twenty days they were always close to us and worried us until, enjoying a rest at the aforementioned place, we were joined by the contingents of Duke Welf, the army of William and other groups that arrived daily; and within fifteen days we had grown to number 100,000. From the many members of each contingent Alexius received the princes and, according to his habit, called them his sons. Similarly, having accepted their hands[203] and confirming this with an oath, as with the earlier expedition, he distributed gifts. For the poor, however, he distributed alms outside the city and ordered the establish-

197 Henry III (of Eppenstein), duke of Carinthia 1090–1122.
198 They were transported to Nicomedia after Easter (21 April) according to *AA* 8.5, p. 592. *AA* 8.3, p. 588, blamed indiscipline in the Lombard army for worsening relations with Alexius Comnenus: 'they provoked the emperor himself to hatred and anger by many injuries, as they had done all along'. See Riley-Smith (1986), pp. 129–30.
199 *AA* 8.8, 8.14, 8.16, 8.38, pp. 596, 604, 608, 628: the effectiveness of Turkish archery against the crusaders.
200 From late June, culminating at Merzifon in early August. A series of disastrous engagements is described in *AA* 8.7–21, pp. 594–614. See Cate (1969), pp. 354–58; Mulinder (1996), pp. 153–81.
201 Led by Duke Welf of Bavaria. *AA* 8.6, p. 592, mentions a smaller German army led by Conrad, the 'constable' of Henry IV, which joined the Lombards.
202 See n. 71 above.
203 They pledged fidelity. See Ganshof (1964), pp. 26–7.

ment of a market. In order to minimize suspicion only very few persons were permitted to enter any city, camp or fortification in the whole empire, and then only for a price and secretly. For this reason when William and his army had been forbidden to pass through the middle of Adrianople,[204] which leads to the royal highway, the Aquitanians, swelling with their inborn pride, raised the war cry, set the suburbs on fire and attacked the city. While they were fiercely pursuing this attack the army of Pechenegs which, as I have already said, always watched their progress on the emperor's orders, attacked them from the rear. Grappling with them the Aquitanians felled many but [also] lost many until again they moved forward along the hated road.[205] Therefore, the whole contingent decided to take the route through Rum, and everyone bought what he needed for the march through the desert. As much forced as willingly we were transported across the inlet that is called the Arm of St George[206] while we waited with great suspense to know the outcome of the princes' daily meetings and their discussions with the emperor.[207] Then suddenly the rumour arose that the hated emperor favoured the Turks more than the Christians and, having reconnoitred our position, had incited them against us through frequent messengers. 'This is', it was heard, 'the faithless Alexius who with the help of a few Swabian mercenaries expelled his lord Michael[208] and usurped his empire, only to exile his partners in crime and murder them; and now he says that he will let the Franks fight with the Turks so that they might tear each other apart like dogs.' When someone attempted to collect ships together, he heard that the emperor had laid ambushes at sea for the pilgrims and had already sunk many of their ships through this outrage. On that account, all spoke evil of him and anathematized him, and in their own languages all called him not emperor but traitor. It is incredible to remember and horrible to recall for those who experienced it, how great was the consternation in our – that is, German – contingent, which was the smallest of all, at seeing father separated from son, brother from brother and friend from dearly beloved friend in life as if they would be separated by death. One entrusted himself to the land, the other to the sea; yet others, having paid their passage, spent only one or two nights aboard ship before rushing back to the

204 Modern Edirne in Turkey, near the Greek and Bulgarian borders.
205 Cf. *AA* 8.34–5, pp. 624–6.
206 The Bosphorus.
207 *AA* 8.37, p. 628.
208 Actually Nicophorus III Botaniates, 1078–81.

shore laden with belongings and incurring great financial loss. They redeemed horses at a greater price than that for which they had recently sold them in order to escape death and to prevent the hastening of violent destruction. We too were vexed long and hard by the same indecision and at last, along with those who dared to trust in the sea, with our wretchedness steered by divine mercy, we reached the port of Jaffa after six weeks – praise for everything to Jesus Christ!

Hereafter the main army, which had accepted 300 Turcopoles[209] from the emperor so that the contingents might be guided along the proper path, turned towards Nicomedia. Then, turning aside to Rum, it moved north against the land of Gorrizim, the homeland of the Turks.[210] The perjured Alexius had devastated the regions of Rum that were around the public road,[211] just as before he had not dared to send his promised aid to our men while they besieged Antioch,[212] for he was suspicious of Franks and Turks alike. Moreover, this army wanted to make as great a name for itself among the heathens as the former one had, but as the outcome of things proved, this did not please divine providence. For a few days before, as mentioned earlier, the same pagans had sharpened their previously blunt swords on the still-warm blood of the Lombards, and thenceforth an animated and infinite multitude of their warriors dared to oppose [the crusaders]. Not more than 4,000 Turks, all of whom had been hand-picked, with very fast horses and exceedingly skilled in the exercise of arms, missiles and arrows, approached more by scouting than in an open attack to test their luck and the strength of the unknown army. At first they harried the vanguard of the army in the manner of brigands, after which they either took prisoners or withdrew. Then riding ahead by side roads they destroyed the forage by fire or other efforts. Sometimes, when the army advanced through rushes or sedge-plots,[213] they tormented it throughout the day with fire or smoke; other times they caused the wells and the pools to run dry, infested safe places with arrows and disturbed everything during the nights by breaking into one or other part of the camp. For all that, they never made a direct attack and never fought an open battle in the manner of warriors, but withdrew before resistance and fled when pursued only to

209 See n. 70 above.
210 *AA* 8.37–8, p. 628, does not mention the diversion from the main road through Anatolia and states that the army proceeded south towards Heraclea.
211 *AA* 8.38, p. 628, blames the Turks for the devastation.
212 During the First Crusade: see n. 133 above.
213 Cf. *AA* 8.38, p. 628.

turn and follow again when their pursuers turned back. If we tried with the pen to describe in full those miseries, which were more miserable than all miseries, we would exceed both ability and measure: we record that so many of the nobles perished there in a shameful manner, so many of the rich through poverty and so many of the brave for want of a sword, since accompanying servants could not help their lords, sufficient money could not even help the rich and the brave were not allowed to fight. The areas in which the machinations of the treacherous Alexius had imprisoned the people of God were narrow, impassable and uninhabitable, known to the enemy but unknown to us. Why should I continue? Thus exposed to arrows like a target for almost twenty days, thus daily counted as *sheep for the slaughter*,[214] eventually, taking extreme measures, they spent the nights in the wooded ravines and tried hard to quicken their slow but certain death. All, except for the very few who had taken advantage of whatever opportunity of flight [presented itself], met their final, drawn-out fate.[215] We do not believe that more than a thousand survived from the innumerable people of God – alas! alas! We saw them afterwards with hardly anything clinging to their bones at Rhodes, Paphos and other ports, or even occasionally at Jaffa. Among them Count Bernard[216] and Count Henry of Regensburg[217] died in Jerusalem, while Duke Welf died on the return journey and was buried at Paphos. During the interminable history of their tortures, which the nature of this brief work does not permit me to relate here, we can report that from our people Archbishop Thiemo of Salzburg[218] was captured, Margravine N.[219] was butchered and two canons named Bruno,[220] noble men, died from hunger and thirst. Among the Latin princes they say that William, Raymond and Stephen[221] survived, as well as others.

While these things were happening, the Christians in Judea were not spared but were daily subjected to brigandage from the inhabitants of Ascalon or Damascus, or to war from those of Babylon. After the

214 Romans 8.36.
215 Cf. *AA* 8.39, p. 630.
216 Unidentified.
217 Son of Burgrave Henry II of Regensburg.
218 Thiemo, abbot of St Peter, Salzburg; archbishop of Salzburg 1090–1101. Thiemo's martyrdom after his capture is recorded in three *Passiones, RHC Occ.* 5, pp. 199–223.
219 Identified as Ida of Cham, widow of Margrave Leopold II of Austria, in *Chroniken*, p. 171 n. 59. The *Historia Welforum Weingartensis*, p. 462, claims that she was seized by a Saracen prince to whom she bore a son, Zengi. See Cate (1969), p. 362.
220 Unidentified.
221 Stephen, count of Blois (*c*. 1045–1102).

Kalends of May [1 May] the Babylonian army pitched its camp not far from Ramla. King Baldwin directed an attack against it, having encouraged his own not to submit before so numerous an enemy since only a few days before, through the will of God, they had with few forces taken much of the treasure of Arabia. 'Through their damnation', he said, 'will we live or else die in the attempt. O honest soldiers, this is the battle that we have long desired, for which we turned our backs upon our homeland, our parents and peace. It is honourable to fight for the inheritance of Christ against the invaders of the Holy Land and foreign thieves; to vanquish such kind is by no means certain and to die is glorious. Their homeland puts them to flight, exile from our homeland furnishes us victory. Let us prove their reproach that the Franks do not fear death, or rather that Christian pilgrims wish either to be victorious in Christ or to die for Christ!' After having said much of this kind, with the spirits of his own men being raised by the marvellous will of Almighty God, the enormous multitude of the Saracens fell back at the advance of little more than one of our legions, so that they did not even dare to fight but, after having spent several days in the same position, withdrew shamefully and without success. Again, around the Kalends of September [1 September], which was of course the time the Christians – whom we have already described – were rumoured to be approaching, the kingdom of Babylon was terrified. Having taken counsel to plan and decide our destruction – that is the destruction of all those who were then to be found in Judea or its surrounding country – they sent letters to Damascus, Tripoli, Gibel and other barbarian cities encouraging them to form a mutual alliance against the Christians. Consequently, an army of 40,000 soldiers left Babylon intending to occupy Jaffa and not long afterwards encamped at Ascalon, evidently reinforced by its allies. Baldwin, however, did not ignore matters and called together his men from everywhere – that is from Jerusalem, Nicopolis, Mount Tabor, Hebron, Caesarea and Arsuf – to Jaffa, where a not insignificant crowd of pilgrims was staying.

During those days we saw death run such riot among the people – which we only scarcely avoided ourselves – that day by day up to 300 dead bodies could be counted being carried out of Jerusalem. Within a few days Jaffa was covered by a huge field of graves. Finally, at about the third hour one day,[222] with the king preceded by the wood of the Lord's cross (which had long lain hidden in the earth until a certain Syrian of Duke Godfrey's had found it the previous year), the entire population of

[222] 9 a.m.

Jaffa gathered together outside the city. At the king's command a certain Arnold,[223] an honourable and well-educated clerk, from the midst of the congregation began: '*Blessed is the nation whose God is the Lord: the people whom He has chosen.*[224] You, O most beloved brothers, are that blessed people, that holy people; you are that people of *Christ's inheritance,*[225] the *purchased people,*[226] who have *left all things*[227] – homeland, parents and possessions – to bear the cross daily after Christ; you have handed over your bodies unto suffering for Christ. You seemed to fight, but Christ of His own will has deemed it worthy to cleanse the place of His sanctification with your blood and with the costly deaths of your brothers and comrades.[228] He wanted through your devoted service to liberate Jerusalem, the city of His rest,[229] which for so many years had been held captive by a foul people. "*This*", says God, "*is my resting place for ever and ever, here will I dwell, for I have chosen it.*"[230] Against this hope, which has been imparted to us by divine promise, behold! by God's will the day before yesterday letters of the pagans were obtained from captured messengers. They contained a diabolical prophecy: we are to be exterminated this year by their attacks. Jerusalem is to be utterly destroyed and – which of all evils is most horrible to say – the very rock of the glorious tomb of the Lord is to be destroyed chip by chip, brought by camels to the sea and then sunk in some utterly remote part of the ocean where it can never again be discovered by Christians. See, therefore, ye Christians what must be done! Consider carefully what end this great audacity has in store!' Although he wished to say more, a loud clamour then interrupted him and, as if from one mouth, the voice of each unanimously resounded: 'The matter', they said, 'is decided. Our counsel is brief and quite succinct: we can either struggle bravely for Christ, Christ's laws and our holy [places] or die ignominiously. It either lies before us to die gloriously and live eternally or remains for us to submit most shamefully and by this short and shameful life to secure everlasting death. But neither in this time nor in eternity will

223 Arnulf of Choques, patriarch of Jerusalem in 1099 and 1112–18. Hamilton (1980), pp. 12–16, 56–8, 61–4.
224 Psalm 32.12.
225 See Romans 8.17.
226 1 Peter 2.9.
227 Luke 5.11.
228 Alluding to Revelation 7.14–17 and other apocalyptic themes in the same biblical book.
229 See Psalm 131.14.
230 *Ibid.*

anyone be permitted to live who does not fight against such profane and such blasphemous pagan audacity!' At once they confessed their sins unanimously and humbly before the cross of our redemption, and after the pronouncement of absolution by the papal legate, who happened to be there, they accepted the blessing and returned eagerly to the camp invoking the help of the Lord. Thereupon in the early morning about 7,000 foot-soldiers and 1,000 knights were mustered,[231] who offered themselves with great joy for this great peril.[232] When they sighted the barbarians' camp – wonderful to relate – they were seized with such fervent faith that each one of them did not doubt that he could overthrow such a great number of legions by himself. Thus it happened that the first cohort, charging almost a mile in disorder and pouring into the enemy without caution, was attacked from the side and immediately utterly wiped out. His heart enraged at this, Baldwin broke into so fierce a cavalry attack that, although assured of victory by the responses of their idols and more violent in their resistance than before, they [the Egyptians] melted away before him like wax before the face of a fire. The venerable Abbot Gerard,[233] who at that time always carried the cross of the Lord beside the king, told me that he had never seen snow or rain of such density as the missiles that then flew towards the king. Yet after they had seen the precious wood [of the cross], none of the enemy trusted in his missiles or weapons, but each sought protection in flight. After victory had been given by God, for whom it is no different to *save many or to save few*,[234] while the camp and spoils of the heathens were being plundered, there arrived a messenger sent from Jaffa who announced that the city was being besieged from land and sea. Then, laden down with spoils and setting the rest on fire, they [Baldwin's men] hurried as quickly as possible to our help, for although the gates had been barricaded from the inside we were surrounded from the land by many horsemen and from the sea by forty-two war galleys. Although we had begun that day to observe the feast of the Mother of God with sadness after so many enemy attacks and such misery from scarcity and pestilence,[235] we ended it with great jubilation. The next day thirty

---

231 *FC* 2.11, p. 409, says 260 knights and 900 foot-soldiers.

232 The First Battle of Ramla (6–7 September 1101). Cf. the first-hand account of *FC* 2.11–13, pp. 407–20; also *AA* 7.64–70, pp. 576–84. See Brett (1995), pp. 17–37.

233 Abbot Gerard of Schaffhausen, treasurer of the Holy Sepulchre: cf. *AA* 7.66, p. 578; *FC* 2.11, pp. 409, 411.

234 1 Kings 14.6.

235 The Nativity of the Blessed Virgin Mary, 8 September.

ships brought us abundant grain and victuals, along with about 12,000 pilgrim brothers. When the enemy's fleet sought to attack them God's marvellous power forced them back through the strength of the Holy Cross – which, since no human assistance could be rendered from the city, had been raised on high against them by order of the king – so that no effort or feat of oarsmanship could move more than one of so many [enemy] ships from their place, at which both the pagan and Christian peoples were very much amazed.

We should not pass over in silence what we know to have happened there in the same year, which the venerable priest Herman, who was then dwelling on the Mount of Olives, reported to us in these words: 'On Holy Saturday',[236] he said, 'when baptism had already been performed following the ancient mercy of the Lord's paraclete, we were waiting in great reverence for the light from heaven[237] to appear as we devoted ourselves to the customary prayers at vespers. But because of our sins the desired heavenly gift, which even the Christians before us were accustomed to receive in the sight of the gentiles, was in every way frustrated and we passed the night of the resurrection of the Lord without any festive church service in nothing but sadness and mourning. Early the next morning, however, we processed barefoot and with litanies from the Sepulchre of the Lord to the Temple of the Lord, in which place – the Mount of Moria in the *threshing-floor of Areuna*[238] – we read that David was answered when in great need[239] and Solomon was promised that all who prayed there with devout hearts would be answered.[240] Soon, after prayers and flowing tears that Christ might not forsake us and make His name to be blasphemed *among the gentiles*,[241] before we had left that renowned atrium, behold! we heard a worthy noise: the resounding of high-pitched praises coming towards us from those who had remained behind. Entering the aforementioned church we were filled with immense joy as we saw two lamps that were lit from heaven. What more? Beginning from the office of baptism, where the day before we had stopped, we completed with joyful devotion the whole service incumbent on us – which God had long withheld – to the end of the

---

236 20 April 1101.
237 The Fire of Easter. Cf. Caffaro of Genoa, *Annales Ianuenses*, pp. 8–9, who witnessed it in 1101, and *AA* 12.33, p. 880, who describes its occurrence in 1119.
238 2 Kings 24.16.
239 See 2 Kings 24.16–25.
240 See 3 Kings 8.28–30, 9.1–5.
241 Romans 2.24.

Mass. Once we had departed, other lamps were divinely lit during the Mass of the Syrians, who always sing together in the same manner after we leave. Truly, before vespers and during the praises of vespers, more than sixteen of these lights were visible. Thus it was that few can be found in Jerusalem, whether Christian or pagan, who will swear to not having seen Christ's very evident power.'

The year of the Lord 1102. Holding an assembly with the princes,[242] Emperor Henry promised that he would go to Rome and there convene a general council around the Kalends of February [1 February], so that the discussion of his case and that of the lord pope according to canon law might confirm the catholic unity of the royal and spiritual power, which for so many years had remained sundered. It is clear, however, that he neither came in accordance with this resolution nor sent word proclaiming his submission to the apostolic dignity. Neither is it a secret that he sought, if he could, to set another pope over the Lord Paschal, but without success.[243]

After that a general council of all the bishops of Apulia, Calabria, Sicily, Tuscany and the whole of Italy, as well as representatives of very many of the fathers from north of the Alps, was held in Rome in the middle of Lent where,[244] apart from reverently confirming the decrees of the ancient Fathers in the accustomed manner, the oft-mentioned schism of our times was declared to be among the chief heresies and was condemned with perpetual anathema together with its authors and followers through subscription to the following decree:

'I anathematize all heresies and especially that which disturbs the state of the church at present, which teaches and affirms that excommunication is to be held in contempt and that the strictures of the church are to be spurned. Moreover, I promise obedience to the Lord Paschal, the pontiff of the apostolic see, and to his successors, as Christ and the church witness, affirming what the holy and universal church affirms and condemning what it condemns.'[245]

There, furthermore, about Maundy Thursday[246] and among an innumerable crowd of different peoples in the church of the Lateran, we heard from his own mouth the sentence that the same Pope Paschal

---

242 At Mainz.
243 See Meyer von Knonau (1904), pp. 102–3; Robinson (1999), p. 309.
244 The Lateran synod of 1102, held around mid-March. Blumenthal (1978b), pp. 11–23.
245 On this oath see Gottlob (1936), pp. 49–51; Blumenthal (1978b), pp. 21–2.
246 3 April.

promulgated against Henry the emperor and patrician of the Romans;[247] for after we had embarked upon the waves of the sea at Jaffa on the eighth Kalends of October [24 September 1101], we arrived in Rome during Holy Week[248] through the grace of Christ. 'Since', the pope said, 'he [Henry IV] has *cut the garment of Christ*,[249] that is, he has devastated the church by rapine and fire and has not ceased to defile it by extravagance, perjuries and murders, he has been excommunicated and condemned because of his disobedience, first by Pope Gregory of blessed memory and then by my predecessor the most holy man Urban.[250] We also in our most recent synod,[251] by the judgement of the whole church, placed him under perpetual interdict. This is according to the will of us all and pertains especially to those from beyond the mountains, so that they may keep themselves from his iniquity.'

Archbishop Hartwig of Magdeburg died.[252] He was a most praiseworthy man who was extremely popular and who with great toil increased the income of the church over which he presided. He was also an indefatigable mediator for the repairing of the oft-mentioned schism between the two parties. Bishop Rupert of Bamberg[253] died and Emperor Henry replaced him with his chancellor Otto,[254] believed to be a very religious man. Aribo,[255] already of great age, a noble prince from Carinthia and sometime count palatine in Bavaria, was gathered to the Lord.

Baldwin and those who were with him at Jerusalem fought a battle against an infinite multitude of Saracens in which, because they acted imprudently, our men were surrounded by great numbers of archers.[256]

---

247 Patrician of the Romans: originally the Byzantine emperor's representative in Rome, the title was also held by Henry III and Henry IV. See Martin (1994), 257–95; Robinson (2004b), pp. 56–8.

248 30 March–5 April.

249 See John 19.23, 24.

250 Gregory VII excommunicated Henry in 1076, 1080 and 1081. Urban II excommunicated him in a letter to Bishop Gebhard of Constance of 18 April 1089 (*JL* 5393) and probably again at the Council of Piacenza in 1095: Bernold, *Chronicle* 1089, 1095, pp. 475, 520–1 (*SC*, pp. 295, 325).

251 The Lateran council of 1102 held in the middle of Lent: above, p. 171.

252 Hartwig of Spanheim, archbishop of Magdeburg 1079–1102 (d. 17 June).

253 Rupert, bishop of Bamberg 1078–1102 (d. 11 June).

254 Otto, bishop of Bamberg 1102–39.

255 Aribo II (d. 18 March 1102), count palatine of Bavaria 1041–55, count of Haigermoos *c.* 1070–1102. See Mayer von Knonau (1904), p. 163 n. 18; Bosl (1972), pp. 1121–46.

256 The Second Battle of Ramla, *c.* 17 May 1102. *FC* 2.18, pp. 436–40; *AA* 9.1–6,

Since they had already dwindled to a few they were compelled to retreat inside the walls of the city of Ramla, which was in that area; it is said that the king and three knights escaped. Since several of them [Baldwin's men] were seen on the battlements of the fortress, however, the barbarians demolished the entire wall in a short time and, having captured or killed all that they found, they sent those prisoners along with messengers of their victory to Babylon. In the mean time, however, while the messengers of their king were returning, they [the Egyptians] pitched their camp, untroubled, in an open field as if they were already masters of the land that they had acquired by the sword. But that victory was not granted to them without retribution, since it was not through their ability but through divine disposition that they won (because God wishes not to dwell on earth any more but in paradise). Thus on the third day Baldwin arrived with a large army, which he ought to have awaited before, and he smashed them in such pieces that they neither enjoyed nor profited from their victory.[257] This new army was brought from Tripoli by Raymond, who he had recently conquered [the city],[258] and from Antioch by Tancred,[259] whose uncle Bohemund had been captured in a ruse by the Turks two years before[260] and had left him his principality of Antioch.

The year of the Lord 1103. Emperor Henry, celebrating Christmas at Mainz, announced publicly through Bishop Emehard[261] that he intended to leave the direction of the kingdom to his son King Henry and visit the Sepulchre of the Lord. By this he gained great applause from the people, the princes, the clergy and the entire kingdom, and by his vow he stirred up many people from different parts of the realm to prepare to accompany him on this journey.[262]

---

pp. 638–44. An excellent synthesis of the different primary-source reports is provided by Mulinder (1996), pp. 252–69.

257 The Battle of Jaffa (4 July 1102), at which King Baldwin, having gathered many reinforcements, defeated the Fatimid army. See Mulinder (1996), pp. 265–9.

258 Raymond began to blockade Tripoli in 1103, but the city only fell in 1109, four years after his death in 1105: Fink (1969), pp. 396–8.

259 Tancred (c. 1075–1112), prince of Galilee, regent of Antioch and Edessa, grandson of Robert Guiscard.

260 At the Battle of Melitene (August 1100) by the Danishmendid ruler Malik Ghazi.

261 Emehard, bishop of Würzburg 1089–1105.

262 Robinson (1990), pp. 419–20, suggests that Henry saw the crusade as a means of achieving a *rapprochement* with the papacy.

Conrad,[263] the son of Duke Otto,[264] one of the great princes, to whom nobody in the whole human world was superior in dignity, who was quite remarkable in birth, in letters and knowledge, in strength as well as in wealth, and who with politeness and eloquence was amiable and affable to all good people, was, as he travelled by night, attacked and done away with through the conspiracy of a certain wretched man. This left the nobles of the kingdom with both great grief and suspicion, since the lowest could presume to commit such great crimes against the highest. Three years before, indeed, Henry the Fat,[265] the elder brother of this same Conrad, was prosecuting judicial business in the Frisian March of which he was in charge; at a time when he expected obedience he was surrounded in an ambush by some common Frisians for whom his dominion was a great yoke. When he realized his position and fled to the sea, he was wounded by sailors and then strangled. The death of such a man, who ruled over the whole of Saxony as second after the king,[266] was felt deeply by the whole German kingdom; and this sorrow was now, as we have said, doubled by the murder of his brother.

Margrave Henry,[267] the most powerful man of his times in Saxony, died.

The year of the Lord 1104. Emperor Henry celebrated Christmas at Regensburg. While he tarried there for some time, and the Bavarian princes had already begun to murmur that the Saxons and Franconians received more friendly and honourable treatment from the emperor than the natives, the emperor began little by little to become more hostile to Count Sigehard,[268] who expressed the strongest suspicion about these things, especially because he had brought with him a larger force of knights than all the other princes who were then present and seemed to have armed himself so as to resist any evil that might befall him at court.

A few days after this, when the count felt more secure and had permitted his troops to withdraw, a furious riot was sparked against him by the conspiracy both of the citizens of Regensburg and of *ministeriales*[269]

---

263 Conrad of Beichlingen (d. 1103). See Meyer von Knonau (1904), p. 184.
264 Otto I, count of Northeim, duke of Bavaria 1061–70 (d. 1083).
265 Count Henry 'the Fat' of Northeim (d. 1101), margrave of Frisia 1099–1101.
266 Henry of Northeim enjoyed viceregal status in Saxony: Robinson (1999), p. 273.
267 Count Henry I of Eilenburg (d. 1103), margrave of the Lower Lausitz and Meißen. He had married Gertrude of Brunswick, the widow of Henry 'the Fat'.
268 Count Sigehard of Burghausen (d. 1104). See Robinson (1999), pp. 321–2.
269 Unfree knights bound to the service of a greater lord. See Arnold (1985).

from many regions, which nothing – not even the intervention of the emperor's son – could assuage. From the third hour of the day until the ninth[270] he was besieged in his lodgings until finally the door was broken down and he, having already made his confession and taken the viaticum of the Lord's sacrament, lay dead from having his head cut off.[271] We must refrain from reporting more of this crime, especially since vengeance and the other evils flowing from it are still before our eyes and what the end of it may be we cannot know.

Apart from these things the country everywhere was quiet, there was peace and fertility, and also the quality of the air and bodily health were encouragingly favourable. Some returning from Jerusalem decorated with palms announced that Acre, which is also called Accaron, had been captured by our people.[272] Others besides these related to us many auspicious things about the state of the church of Jerusalem, which gave us great joy.

Count Boto, known as 'the Strong',[273] the full brother of that Aribo whom we mentioned above,[274] already *full of days*,[275] died not far from Regensburg and was honourably buried at the monastery of Theres, which he had lavishly enriched with his own resources and estates. These two brothers, that is Aribo and Boto, were descended from the Bavarian people's most ancient nobility through their father's bloodline. They were descendants of that famous Aribo who was gored while hunting a bison,[276] as the popular songs proclaim, and the sons of Count Palatine Hartwig,[277] whose full brother was Sigehard[278] who begat the Sigehard killed in Regensburg.[279] On their mother's side they stemmed from the eminent Saxon tribe of the Immidinger, which was

---

270 Approximately 9 a.m. and 3 p.m.

271 5 February 1094. Cf. the uncorroborated report of the *Annals of Rosenfeld* 1104, p. 102: the killers were 'the king's knights'. See also Arnold (1985), pp. 35, 95, 102, 226.

272 The siege and capture of Acre (1104). Cf. *AA* 9.27–9, pp. 670–4.

273 Count Boto of Pottenstein. See Egger (1897), 414–15.

274 See n. 255 above.

275 Genesis 25.8.

276 Probably Margrave Aribo (d. 909), who commanded the Danube frontier from the area south of Passau to the River Raab. On the Aribones see Egger (1897), 385–525; Diepolder (1964), 74–119; Störmer (1977), 929–30.

277 Hartwig II (d. 1027), count palatine of Bavaria.

278 Hartwig's brother was actually Count Frederick I of Tengling (d. 1071). This mistake was corrected in Ekkehard's *Chronicle*, but not in the *1125 Continuation*.

279 See n. 268 above.

closely related to the celebrated lineage of the Ottonians. The same Immid is remembered in these words in the *History of the Saxons*: 'There was',[280] it says, 'a beautiful, most noble and singularly prudent *queen*, namely Matilda,[281] the mother of Otto the Great[282] and *the daughter of Theoderic, whose brothers were Widukind, Immid and Reginbern. Reginbern was the same person who fought against the Danes – who had been devastating Saxony for a long time – and vanquished them, freeing the fatherland from their incursions until this day. And they were of the lineage of the great duke Widukind,*[283] *who waged a powerful war against Charles the Great for almost thirty years.*' From the seed of these most excellent princes, as we have said, the noble Friderun,[284] the mother of Aribo and Boto, was begat by Reting[285] the son of Boto, whose father Reting was the son of another Boto. Immediately after the death of Hartwig, Friderun took the widow's veil, for Aribo was but a small child and she was posthumously pregnant with Boto. That both made considerable progress in letters, in arms and in their duties we know; nevertheless, virtually the whole population of Germany and Italy testifies that just as Boto was taller and more elegant in body, so too he was more outstanding and renowned in matters of war. The Hungarians found him to be of such size that they truly believed one of the giants of old was among them.[286] A great deal more about him could be reported, would it not interfere with the plan of this brief work.

Bishop John of Speyer,[287] struck with an ulcer around his genitals – about which certain remarkable slanders were spreading – died after a long illness and was buried in his city. The adolescent Conrad,[288] the son of Margravine Beatrice,[289] having spurned the study of letters – in which he had been taught from the very beginning – for the profession of arms, *perished by the sword* since, in Christ's prophecy, *he had taken up*

280 Widukind of Corvey, *Deeds of the Saxons* 1.31, p. 44.
281 Matilda (*c.* 896–968), wife of King Henry I (*c.* 875–936).
282 Otto I 'the Great' (d. 973), king 936, emperor 962.
283 Widukind (d. 807), a Westphalian nobleman who led resistance to Charles the Great's conquest of Saxony. See Schneidmüller (1999), 74–6.
284 Friderun, wife of Count Palatine Hartwig II.
285 Retting II (d. before 994), Bavarian count.
286 A possible reference to Boto's role in the Hungarian war of 1060.
287 John I (d. 26 October), bishop of Speyer 1090–1104. He was a prominent royal adviser during the last years of Henry IV's rule: Robinson (1999), p. 365.
288 Known only from this report.
289 Beatrice of Schweinfurt (d. *c.* 1104), widow of Count Henry II of Hildrizhausen.

the sword.²⁹⁰ Not long after this that same Beatrice died and was buried in the castle of Schweinfurt beside her father Duke Otto.²⁹¹

Around the summer solstice the sky was transformed into a tempest and in the countryside surrounding Würzburg there fell among hailstones slabs of ice so large that even if they were divided in four parts they could not be carried by as many men. In the bishop's palace in Speyer blood was seen *flowing from bread* and prodigious edible lentils were discovered, which were interpreted as a portent of *civil*, or rather internal, *war* according to the ancient pattern of Roman history.²⁹²

The year of the Lord 1105. While Emperor Henry was celebrating Christmas at Mainz, his son Henry, the fifth king of that name, raised a rebellion against his father in Bavaria through the machinations of Margrave Diepold,²⁹³ Count Berengar²⁹⁴ and Count Otto,²⁹⁵ a noble man related to him through his mother's lineage; on their counsel and advice he had abandoned his father's side a few days previously. First condemning the aforementioned heresy, he promised due obedience to the pontiff of the apostolic see and then, allying himself with the princes of Bavaria as well as several of the nobles from Swabia and East Francia, he turned towards Saxony. He was honourably received by them and, celebrating Easter in Quedlinburg,²⁹⁶ he was soon master of all the Saxon cities and honoured with royal dignity by all the most powerful men. Moreover, through the advice and service of Bishops Ruothard of Mainz²⁹⁷ and Gebhard of Constance²⁹⁸ (who was the representative of the lord Pope Paschal), he [Henry V] reconciled all of Saxony to communion with the Roman church.²⁹⁹ He declared a general council of

---

290 Matthew 26.52.

291 Duke Otto III of Swabia, 1048–57. See above, p. 99 n. 124.

292 Cf. Orosius, *History against the pagans* 5.18. The continuator may have been influenced here by the version of this passage quoted by Frutolf in the year 659 from the founding of Rome: *Chronicle, MGH SS* 6, p. 87.

293 Diepold III of Cham-Vohburg, margrave of the Bavarian Nordgau 1099–1146.

294 Berengar I, count of Sulzbach 1099–1125.

295 Count Otto of Kastl-Habsberg (d. *c.* 1125). Otto was the great-grandnephew of Adelaide of Turin, the maternal grandmother of Henry V. See Robinson (1999), p. 324.

296 9 April.

297 See n. 23 above.

298 Gebhard of Zähringen, bishop of Constance 1084–1110 (the third son of Berthold of Zähringen, duke of Carinthia).

299 See Robinson (1999), pp. 325–7.

the bishops and clergy for the fourth Kalends of June [29 May][300] at the royal estate that is called Nordhausen, where the perverted discipline of the church's institutions was to be dealt with. As regards the urgent matters of this council, the decrees of the Fathers were first re-read, the things that could be improved by those present were corrected and certain things, which seemed more serious, were deferred to the attention of the pope. Simoniacal heresy was condemned according to the customs of the Fathers and the fornication of nicholaitism was abjured by all who were there. By virtue of apostolic authority the aforementioned bishops declared that, following Roman custom, the fast of the month of March was to be observed in the first week of Lent and the fast of the month of June in the week of Whitsun; and the Peace of God was confirmed. Those who had been consecrated by false bishops were promised that on the next fast day they would be reconciled [to the church] by catholic consecration. We see in these things, which we cannot pass over in silence, how King Henry, both by his great humility and authority, excited in all no little hope by his good character.

Although he wished to be present at the meeting of the servants of God only by request – for along with the bishops and clerks a vast multitude of abbots and monks had flocked there thirsting for unity in the church – finally, with humble demeanour and standing in a raised place, he renewed all his statutes and laws reasonably according to the decision of the princes. But if something unreasonable was asked of him, he rejected it by responding marvellously with prudence beyond his years and with the magnanimity of his ancestors. In all these things he maintained for himself in a marvellous fashion the modesty of a youth and showed appropriate respect for the priests of Christ. With this, his own tears welled up so that the king of heaven and the whole heavenly host might testify that it was not out of lust for power that he had usurped his father's authority, that he did not long to depose his lord and father from the Roman empire but, rather, that he had always shown compassion for his sins of defiance and disobedience. If only his father would submit to St Peter and his successors according to Christian law, he promised to cede him the kingdom and submit to him like a servant. Hearing this the whole multitude rejoiced and wept at once, and began to offer prayers for the conversion of the father and the prosperity of the son, crying out in a great voice '*Lord, have mercy upon us*'.[301] At

300 In reality, 21 May.
301 *Kyrie eleison*, from the Ordinary of the Mass.

the same time Bishops Udo of Hildesheim,[302] Henry of Paderborn[303] and Frederick of Halberstadt[304] prostrated themselves at the feet of the metropolitan and, standing before the king, promised their obedience to the pope with the whole assembled church as witness. Nevertheless, their offences were reserved for the judgement of the pope and they were suspended from office.

These things having been duly ordered, the king celebrated Whitsun[305] in Merseburg and Henry,[306] who had long been designated as archbishop of the church of Magdeburg but had been driven out by followers of the emperor, was consecrated. Not long afterwards the king led an expedition against Mainz to restore its expelled bishop;[307] his father was waiting for him within the walls with a not inconsiderable band of knights and several princes (who were, nonetheless, not entirely loyal to him). Since, however, he [Henry V] was denied entry into the city by the current of the Rhine and the lack of boats, each forbade – both son and father having sworn oaths – the consideration of a parricidal war. Nevertheless, many messages were sent back and forth by boat and the leading men of the kingdom held many common councils among themselves, with the father promising a division of the kingdom and the confirmation of hereditary succession and the son demanding nothing less than submission to the pope and the accomplishment of unity in the church. Abandoning such inaction, he [Henry V] came to Würzburg where he expelled a certain Erlung[308] – whom the emperor had long ago designated as bishop after the death of Emehard[309] – and had Rupert,[310] the provost of that church who had already been elected by the clergy and people, enthroned by the aforementioned Archbishop Ruothard. Thus that church was returned to communion with the papacy and, having accepted surety from the citizens, he [Henry V] dismissed the Saxons and with the Bavarians turned to besiege the castle of Nuremberg. After two or more months he successfully captured it,

302 Udo of Gleichen, bishop of Hildesheim 1079–1114.
303 Henry of Werl, bishop of Paderborn 1084–1127.
304 Frederick, bishop of Halberstadt, before 1102–6.
305 29 May.
306 Henry, archbishop of Magdeburg 1102–6/7.
307 In the last week of June.
308 Erlung, bishop of Würzburg 1105/6–21. See *Anonymous imperial chronicle* 1105, 1106, below, pp. 197–8, 200, 207; Ekkehard, *Chronicle* 1106, below, p. 234.
309 Emehard, bishop of Würzburg 1089–1105; elected: 25 July 1089.
310 Rupert, (Gregorian) bishop of Würzburg 1105–6. See Wendehorst (1962), pp. 124–7.

dissolved the army and carried on to Regensburg.[311] Following in his footsteps, his father put Rupert to flight and reinstalled Erlung; then he devastated everything that belonged to his son's supporters and eventually, with the help of the treacherous citizens of Regensburg, drove his son from the city. Staying there, he made a certain youth named Udalric[312] bishop of that very seat, gathered an army from all about, advanced and cruelly devastated Diepold's march,[313] above all with [the help of] the Bohemian people.[314] The knights and their lord the king did not delay any longer, but rallied all together to repay the imperial forces from the rear with fire and plundering, and afterwards sought out battle with 10,000 chosen warriors divided into five legions. Now the camps were pitched against each other – an exceedingly horrible spectacle! – and for three whole days from one bank of the River Regen flew the standard of the emperor and from the other the standard of [his son] the king. Duels were frequently sought out on the river bed, during one of which Count Hartwig[315] from the party of the emperor was killed; not a few from each side were consumed by the unpredictable lot of Mars. Yet on the day before the impending battle the princes who appeared to be the foremost and most powerful from each army, having held mutual peace talks and protracted discussions among themselves on the causes of the current war, at length concluded unanimously – guided by the Spirit of God no doubt – that little justice or reward would come from being part of such a harsh and dangerous undertaking. Consequently, they decided that they should at all costs vow to show consideration to their brothers, that is the Christian people on both sides or, rather, to desist from parricidal war. Since already, as we have said, *bloodthirsty Mars*[316] had begun to gnash his teeth through the arrayed battle-lines on each side, the young king, whose *bowels were moved upon*[317] his father, mournfully cried out: 'My fellow warriors', he said, 'I give you the greatest thanks for your good will towards me and I shall not refuse to pay back each of you in equal

311 Nuremberg surrendered in September. See Brühl (1968), pp. 134 and n. 83, 141 n. 112, 158.

312 Udalric, bishop of Regensburg 1105 (otherwise unknown).

313 See n. 293 above.

314 Henry IV was reinforced by the forces of Margrave Leopold III of Austria and Duke Borivoi of Bohemia. Cf. *Annals of Hildesheim* 1105, p. 53; *Life of Henry IV* 9, p. 32. See Meyer von Knonau (1904), pp. 235–7, 239.

315 Count Hartwig of Bogen (d. 1105).

316 Statius, *Thebaid* 8.231.

317 3 Kings 3.26: that is, he was deeply agitated on account of his father.

measure if the situation require it. But let no one wish or believe that he will be my ally if he should boast that he has killed my father and lord or at any time has been minded to kill him. As heir and successor to the emperor I might indeed hold a kingdom subject to me by Christian laws, if it pleases the ruler of all things; I do not wish to be called a parricide or something similar. If my father obediently submits himself to the yoke of the pope, I shall be satisfied at once with whatever he will grant me in his goodness. Until then you should know that I am not fighting against my father, but fighting on behalf of my father's kingdom.' With evening approaching that day, the king's forces yielded their position and declared that they wanted to prove their reverence to the imperial majesty.

The emperor, however, while organizing his camp in certainty of the following day's battle, heard from the duke of Bohemia[318] and Margrave Leopold[319] that, contrary to his hopes, the princes would neither fight nor wished to fight. Distraught, he implored and entreated them to help him but they would not. Informed then by secret messengers from his son that his own had secretly conspired against him, he sneaked away from the camp with very few men and thus through divine providence, by the salvation of one the blood of many – which would undoubtedly have been shed – was saved. As soon as the absence of the emperor became known throughout the camp, each person hastened to return home, especially because the darkness of the night furnished security by hiding his departure. Although the king could have had the satisfaction of destroying his enemies at will, he decided to spare rather than pursue them and because of the failure of the earlier alliance he secured the city [Regensburg] to himself on much more severe terms. After the abdication of Udalric he enthroned Hartwig,[320] a thoroughly upright, catholic and noble man. He also won over to himself certain bishops and princes from his father's army who had been found within the walls and soon afterwards, returning to Franconia, he gave the treacherous citizens of Würzburg the same cup to drink. Meanwhile, the aforementioned Erlung, who had usurped the title of bishop of that place, with his hope frustrated, relinquished the seat to Rupert and gave himself up to the king; and from then on he was equally esteemed as one of his chaplains.

318 Borivoi II, duke of Bohemia 1100–7, 1117–20.
319 Leopold III (1073/5–1136), margrave of Austria 1095–1136. Leopold's sister, Gerberga, married Borivoi.
320 Hartwig, bishop of Regensburg 1105–26.

In the mean time, the king heard that his father had been discovered with Wiprecht,[321] a certain most illustrious and prudent man who ruled over those parts in which the Sorbs live, and permitted him [his father] – for he had begged this himself through messengers – to be conducted to the Rhine. So as not to be harassed there by any of them, he [Henry V] moved swiftly from Würzburg and soon travelled over to Speyer, not without danger from the aforementioned river. Shortly afterwards he took possession of the city and of his father's treasury, which he found there, and gave to the people of Speyer as their bishop Abbot Gebhard of Hirsau,[322] a wise and noble man, famed for his saintly way of life and loved by all wise people for the excellence of his sound morals. In these days also Archbishop Ruothard, who had been fleeing rabid tyranny for eight years in Thuringia, was led by an escort of the catholic princes and restored to his throne, to the great joy of the nobles of Mainz.[323] He reconciled its people and church to the apostolic church and was honoured by all not only as a father of great age, but even as if he had been raised from the dead.

Having settled matters around the Rhine, King Henry turned to Burgundy;[324] but having been called back by the messengers of his followers, he forestalled with extraordinary speed the machinations that his father had undertaken with the help of Count Siegfried.[325] For the emperor had hastened to Mainz to try to impede the discussions of the assembly that had been convened by all the king's princes to deal with the present business and which was expected to take place at Christmas. The king met with him at Bingen about the Ides of December [13 December] and, face to face in the wrong order, but necessarily switched, the son reminded the father of the sentence of excommunication as well as other insolent acts he had committed against the commonwealth, and promised due obedience once he deigned to come to his senses. The elder put off these and other such matters to the hearing of the princes and the decision of the senate at the forthcoming assembly, and they parted peacefully, each going with his followers to the oft-mentioned metropolitan city. Meanwhile, when the son's followers observed the

---

321 Count Wiprecht II of Groitzsch (d. 1124). See Robinson (1999), p. 332.
322 Gebhard, bishop of Speyer 1105–7 (enthroned 1 November).
323 See Meyer von Knonau (1904), pp. 252–3.
324 *Chroniken*, p. 199 n. 64, suggests Lotharingia and Alsace in reality.
325 Siegfried of Ballenstedt (d. 1113), count palatine of Lotharingia. See Robinson (1999), p. 333.

father attempting through secret messengers to lead some people in ways not consistent with this agreement and peace, it was obvious to them that the father should await the assembly of the princes separately with his followers in an absolutely secure fortress,³²⁶ especially since the bishops of Mainz and Speyer, as well as others who were there, protested in public that it was not possible for him to have contact with their recently reconciled churches.³²⁷ These things being arranged, and guards also so that nothing unexpected should happen through him or to him,³²⁸ the king was summoned and hastened to the public assembly of the princes at Mainz. But the stupidity of the common people spread the rumour all about that the son had captured the father by treachery and had sent him into captivity.

In this year King Baldwin blockaded Ascalon from the sea with an immensely large fleet and from the land with a not insubstantial army, and made it tributary to him after a long siege.³²⁹ A few months afterwards 50,000 Saracens attacked unexpectedly,³³⁰ but divine power so extended before him and his mere 4,000 soldiers that they captured an emir who was reckoned to be second after the king of Babylon and killed another in the remaining crowd.³³¹ The clemency of Christ prospered His pilgrims at Antioch, Syria, Palestine and throughout the whole of Asia, and with their service eradicated the filthiness of the barbarians that was everywhere about. He revealed the long-concealed toxic madness and treachery of the hateful and thus far secret persecutor of His church, Alexius, who won over to himself the Turks (to whom no hope or only slim hopes of reigning in the East remained) and – O most shameful outrage! – restored Nicaea, which as we have already described was once a tower of our faith³³² and had been purchased shortly before with the blood of many Christians, to the sons of the

---

326 Böckelheim on the River Nahe.

327 Since Henry IV was excommunicated.

328 Bishop Gebhard of Speyer oversaw his guard. Cf. Henry IV, *Letters* 37, 39, pp. 48–9, 54–5 (*IL*, pp. 184–9, 190–5).

329 The continuator is probably confusing Ascalon with Acre, which Baldwin captured with the help of Genoese and Pisan ships in 1104. *FC* 2.25, pp. 462–4; *AA* 9.27–9, pp. 672–4.

330 The Third Battle of Ramla (27 August 1105). *FC* 2.32, pp. 495–501; *AA* 9.48–50, pp. 704–10.

331 *AA* 9.50, p. 710, identifies two captured emirs – those of Acre and Arsuf – as well as the emir of Ascalon, who was killed.

332 See above, p. 144.

tyrant Suleyman.[333] He [Alexius] set up guards to prohibit the travelling of pilgrims by land or sea and by frequent messengers roused up the king of Babylon against us. The Antiochenes captured the ships that had been sent against them and to confound Alexius they cut off the noses and thumbs of all [the sailors], loaded one of the skiffs with them and sent these savouries to the same king, the murderer of many thousands. Bohemund also was set free by divine providence after three years of imprisonment and came to Italy by ship,[334] where he organized the building of a fleet and travelled as far as the kingdoms of Spain so that through whatever alliances he might gather together the largest possible army against the aforementioned tyrant.

Duke Frederick died.[335] He was a prudent man, quite illustrious because of his habits and nobility, but most illustrious for his marriage to the emperor's daughter Adelaide,[336] a woman of unique and famous reputation, and for the wonderful natural abilities of the offspring that adorned that marriage.[337] The day before Christmas Eve there was seen in the west so great a fire in the middle of a star that one would have believed it to be the light of the sun had it been in the east.

The year of the Lord 1106. At the instigation of the younger Henry a council of the whole German kingdom was held in Mainz at Christmas, the size of which had not been seen for many years. Participants report that fifty-two princes or more were present and that only the Saxon duke named Magnus,[338] impeded by his great age, was noted as absent. The legates of the apostolic see, namely the bishops of Albano[339] and Constance,[340] arrived there and proclaimed to the whole multitude the

---

333 Nicaea remained in Byzantine hands until 1330. For German rumours that Alexius Comnenus had returned cities to the Turks see Bernold, *Chronicle* 1098, p. 535 (*SC*, p. 334): 'For he [Alexius] was not afraid ... to give back to the pagans those cities that our men had seized from the hands of the pagans.' See also Neocleous (2010), 255.

334 Bohemund was released in 1103 and journeyed back to Europe in 1104/5.

335 Frederick I (of Büren), duke of Swabia 1079–1105 (Hohenstaufen family).

336 Actually Agnes (1072/3–1124), the third child of Henry IV and Bertha of Turin. Adelaide (1070–1085/6) was their first child.

337 Their children included Duke Frederick II of Swabia (1090–1147) and King Conrad III (1093–1152; king 1138).

338 Magnus Billung, duke in Saxony 1073–1106.

339 Cardinal Bishop Richard of Albano, 1101–15. Other sources imply that Richard of Albano was not at Mainz: *Annals of Hildesheim* 1105, p. 55 and *Historia Hirsaugiensis monasterii* 6, p. 258, which records that he installed Bruno as the new abbot of Hirsau on 26 December. See Jakobs (1961), pp. 33 n. 22, 220–1.

340 Bishop Gebhard of Constance; see n. 298 above.

sentence of excommunication against the elder Henry, the so-called emperor, which so many successive popes had promulgated both orally and in writing. Moreover, they confirmed by the authority of Christ and St Peter that the entire church spread throughout the whole world had already been separated from communion with him for many years. Wherefore, when he [Henry IV] himself was tempted to leave the castle where he was staying to go to Mainz, the princes, in order to avoid an uprising of the common crowd (for they were accustomed to favour the party of the father more than that of the son), hastened to meet him at Ingelheim and, surrounding him, finally led him back to the general council to confess his guilt and promise satisfaction.[341] Since the legates could not restore him to communion or impose penance without the judgement of a general synod and apostolic advice, he assented to the advice of his own party as well as that of the council and gave the *regalia* or imperial insignia – namely the cross and lance, the sceptre, orb and crown – into the hands of his son, praying for his prosperity and commending him to the foremost princes with many tears; and he promised from then on for the sake of his soul to heed the decrees of the great high priest and the whole church.[342] This done, Henry, the fifth of that name, was elected to the kingship for the second time, first by his father and then by all of the German princes.[343] He was also confirmed in a catholic manner through the imposition of hands by the apostolic legates and, having accepted oaths from both the bishops and the laity according to the custom of the country,[344] he began to rule in the eighty-eighth place since Augustus, in the fiftieth year of his father, in the one-thousand-eight-hundred-and-fifty-seventh year since the founding of the city, in the five-thousand-and-fifty-eighth year since the beginning of the world and, as it is called, in the eleven-hundred-and-sixth year since the Incarnation of the Lord.

After the many and long-standing defilements of the churches in this kingdom had been related in the presence of the king and all the princes and bishops from the whole of Germany as well as the clergy and people and the legates of the Roman see, and after all had unanimously promised their eradication, it pleased both the king and the leading men to send to the holy Mother Church of Rome so many and such legates

---

341 31 December 1105. Henry IV's forced abdication actually took place at Ingelheim and not Mainz. See Robinson (1999), pp. 336–7.

342 Cf. Henry IV, *Letters* 37, 39, pp. 49–50, 56–7.

343 On 5 January 1106 in Mainz: *Annals of Hildesheim* 1106, p. 55.

344 From Ruothard of Mainz: *Annals of Hildesheim* 1106, p. 56.

from these parts as were appropriate to give a proper account of the allegations, to investigate what was doubtful intelligently and to consult wisely on all things for the benefit of the church. For this work men full of the *spirit of wisdom*[345] were chosen, not unworthy of respect either before God or the world because of their dignity, birth, sophistication and wealth: Bruno of Trier from Lotharingia,[346] Henry of Magdeburg from Saxony,[347] Otto of Bamberg from Franconia,[348] Eberhard of Eichstätt from Bavaria,[349] Gebhard of Constance from Swabia and [the bishop] of Chur from Burgundy,[350] as well as even noble laymen from the side of the king. Among other things they received the command that should it be possible, that they should secure the presence of the lord pope from across the Alps.

---

345 Deuteronomy 34.9; Sirach 15.5.

346 Bruno of Laufen, archbishop of Trier 1101–24.

347 See n. 306 above.

348 See n. 254 above.

349 Bishop Eberhard of Eichstätt, 1099–1112.

350 Bishop Wido of Chur, 1095–1122.

THE *ANONYMOUS IMPERIAL CHRONICLE* (1096–1114)

HERE BEGINS THE PROLOGUE
TO THE FOLLOWING CHRONICLE

How happy that state, attests Cicero, which is ruled by the wise or whose rulers strive for wisdom, without which, it is plain, courage degenerates into mere foolhardiness.[1] We, therefore, ought more zealously to render thanks to God than other peoples, since the storms that hitherto shook us have abated and a prince of great wisdom and strength has appeared to govern the Roman empire with enterprise, in whom by the grace of God the whole world, both Roman and German, rejoices in complete applause – namely Henry,[2] the fifth king and fourth emperor [of that name],[3] a man of many virtues, ferocious in war, pious and gentle in peace. Since he, like the gleaming morning star, has arrayed himself with the splendour of wisdom and has perfumed all with the sweetness of his good odour, he deigned to order our insignificant selves to compile for him a chronicle from the times of Charles the Great[4] until his own time, preserving therein *the truth of history*.[5] When we declined to undertake this task because of our inexperience,[6] he nevertheless compelled us by his authority and benevolence to execute it in some fashion.

Wherefore, most serene emperor, on account of the charity you bestowed you have here an excerpted chronicle that is not unworthy – I do not say for the eyes of an emperor – but at least for the lowliest readers of your court, if only for the authority of the ancient chroniclers and not of ourselves. Since the whole intention of this book is to serve the honour both of the Roman empire and the German kingdom, the union of which began with Charles of the Franks, we consider it

1 In fact an allusion to Boethius, *Consolation of philosophy* 1, prose 4.
2 Henry V (1086–1125).
3 King Henry I of Germany, 919–36 was never crowned emperor.
4 Charles the Great (d. 814), king of the Franks 768, emperor 800.
5 Maurus Servius Honoratus, *Commentary on Aenead* 9.745.
6 Self-deprecation: a standard feature of the *captatio benevolentiae*, a greeting used in letters and treatises designed to secure the good will of the recipient.

necessary to repeat the lofty origins of such a most noble people, which was found suitable to beget the lords of Roman power.⁷ Thus the story is traced from the most ancient generations of their nobility until the same Charles. How he took control of the weakened commonwealth and then how the Roman empire was excellently governed by a succession of kings from that people until this time is set out with appropriate brevity, the narrations of other chronicles having been excluded. The first book, therefore, discourses of the time from the origin of the Franks to the kings of that people. The second book briefly covers the reigns, deeds and years of all the successors to the empire of Charles the Great. The third book, however, sets out the deeds and undertakings of this fifth Henry – may he never have an end or at least may his end come after many years, well favoured by God and in serene old age!

BOOK 2, 1096–1105

*The year of the Lord 1096.*⁸ *Welf,*⁹ *formerly duke of Bavaria, who had already for some time been repudiated by the emperor and because of that had lost his duchy, was restored to the emperor's grace and received his duchy back.*

An image appeared in the sun on Monday the fifth Nones of March [3 March] *at the beginning of Lent. It was reported also that everywhere the world brought forth diverse prodigies. There was an eclipse of the moon on the sixth Ides of August* [8 August] *in the fourteenth year of the lunar cycle.*¹⁰ *Soon afterwards from nearly all parts of the earth, but chiefly from the western kingdoms, innumerable armed troops of kings, nobles and even common people of both sexes began to travel towards Jerusalem, passionately stirred up by frequent reports of the oppression of the Lord's Sepulchre and the devastation of all the churches, which had been subjected to the power of the ferocious people of the Turks for several years and which had repeatedly been destroyed through unheard-of calamities. To come to their aid, as is reported, a great many set off hurriedly in different groups with different and unreliable leadership.* We refrain from reporting more about this journey since it demands so great a treatment and we already have enough other elegant accounts of it.

7 A reference to the first book of the *Anonymous imperial chronicle* (not translated here), which is entitled 'Concerning the origins of the Franks'.
8 Frutolf, *Chronicle* 1096, above, pp. 130–1.
9 Welf IV, duke of Bavaria 1070–1101. See above, p. 110 n. 215.
10 See above, p. 131 n. 393.

The year of the Lord 1097.[11] *Returning from Italy, Emperor Henry*[12] *came to the city of Regensburg in Bavaria, where he stayed for a considerable time and allowed the Jews who had been coerced into baptism* the use of Jewish rites.[13]

Emperor Henry held a peace council with the princes at Mainz about the Kalends of December [1 December]. A comet appeared. This same year the summer was most fruitful, but the winter was mild and pestilentious; there were exceedingly heavy floods from deluges and rivers.

The year of the Lord 1098. When the emperor inquired into [14]*the assets of the murdered Jews* at Mainz,[15] and when both the bishop[16] and his relations were accused [of stealing] their money, the outraged bishop took himself to Thuringia with his followers. Then Henry took over all the bishopric's revenue for his own use and, confiscating the possessions of the fugitives, had the walls [of Mainz] torn down.

Welf, once more duke of Bavaria, reconciled his sons with the emperor when they sought to rebel and succeeded in getting the duchy committed to one of them after him.[17]

The year of the Lord 1099.[18] *Emperor Henry celebrated Christmas at Cologne and during Epiphany at Aachen made his younger son Henry king.*

In the same year Our Lord Jesus Christ opened Jerusalem, the city of His rest,[19] to His faithful, and *eradicating* the *filthiness*[20] of the pagans through the greatness of His power, He mercifully restored there the free exercise of Christian worship.[21]

Bishop Conrad of Utrecht[22] *was killed by his own people. Bishop Herman of Cologne died and was succeeded by Frederick.*[23] The Count Palatine Rapoto

11 Frutolf, *Chronicle* 1097, above, pp. 131–2.
12 Henry IV (1050–1106), king 1056, emperor 1084.
13 Following the alternative wording of the *1106 Continuation*. See above, p. 139 n.17.
14 Frutolf, *Chronicle* 1098, above, p. 132.
15 10 May 1098.
16 Archbishop Ruothard of Mainz, 1089–1109.
17 At an imperial council at Worms: Störmer (1991), p. 517; Robinson (1999), p. 297.
18 *1106 Continuation* 1099, above, p. 140.
19 See Psalm 131.14.
20 Cf. *1106 Continuation* 1105, above, p. 183.
21 The capture of Jerusalem by the First Crusade: 15 July 1099.
22 *1106 Continuation* 1099, above, pp. 158–9. Conrad, bishop of Utrecht 1076–99.
23 Archbishop Herman of Cologne, 1089–99 (d. 21 November); Archbishop Frederick of Cologne, 1100–31.

and his cousin Count Udalric, who was said to be very wealthy, died.[24] *While the emperor was holding a council with the princes in Regensburg the sudden deaths of those two magnates, of lesser men and of others occurred; throughout the countryside and in the cities also not a few of the common people died. Unexpected famines also broke out in many places.*

Pope Urban died.[25] *On account of the unrest in the church, he convened many councils and promulgated many decrees. But before departing this life, instructed by the Holy Spirit he designated Cardinal Rainer of San Clemente,*[26] *an abbot of holy conversation and good repute and a noble Roman, to be elected to the apostolic lordship. This was additionally indicated by other revelations and, although he resisted, the whole Roman church consecrated him as its shepherd, naming him Paschal.*

The year of the Lord 1100.[27] *Under Duke Godfrey,*[28] *the defender of the church of Jerusalem, a vast assembly took place in Jerusalem of all those in the East who were Christian, but especially of the pilgrims who had settled in Antioch, Syria, Edessa or Palestine, so that on the feast of Christmas not only were many bishops consecrated for the surrounding areas, but the mystical prophecies were changed into visible events:*[29] *Arise, be enlightened, O Jerusalem!*[30] *and Rejoice with Jerusalem, and be glad with her, all you that love her!,*[31] *and so forth.*

After that, with the heat of summer the air over Palestine was tainted with the stench of dead bodies. Some maintain that the barbarians had spoiled the springs with poison and the reservoirs with the putrid fluids of the dead, whence there arose a pestilence that killed many of ours that fought under foreign skies. Among them the whole catholic church tearfully laments Godfrey, snatched away much too soon, who provided for the people of God with paternal zeal and cherished them with maternal tenderness. For only one year he led the people of God; overcome by a prolonged sickness he ended this present life in Christ on the fifteenth Kalends of August [18 July], *full of faith*[32] *and good*

24 Rapoto V, count of Cham and Vohburg, count palatine of Bavaria (d. 14 April); Count Udalric II of Passau. See Loibl (1997), pp. 157–65.

25 Pope Urban II, 1088–99 (d. 29 July).

26 Rainer of Bieda, cardinal priest of S. Clemente, Pope Paschal II, 1099–1118 (elected 13 August; enthroned 14 August).

27 *1106 Continuation* 1100, above, pp. 159–61.

28 Godfrey V (of Bouillon), duke of Lower Lotharingia 1087–96, advocate of the Holy Sepulchre (d. 1100).

29 The 'mystical prophecies': the prophecies of Isaiah.

30 Isaiah 60.1.

31 Isaiah 66.10.

32 Acts 6.5. See also James 2.17.

works. His tomb, built of Parian stone, stands in the narthex of the church of Golgotha in front of the Mount of Calvary.

His brother Baldwin[33] succeeded him, *receiving royal benediction and coronation from the legate of the apostolic see;*[34] and from then onwards the duty of the Lord's warfare was prosecuted indefatigably by no *braver knight nor more pious guardian.*[35]

Archbishop Wibert of Ravenna, who had been placed over Hildebrand-Gregory and was called Pope Clement, died.[36] *He was undoubtedly a man full of intelligence and eloquence, and most distinctly eminent in nobility and person; yet neither in Rome nor in Ravenna did any good come of it and since he ascended against one living pope (albeit coerced as they say) and outlived three who succeeded each other, he was exiled from each seat, Rome and Ravenna, and would have preferred – as we learned from his own mouth – never to have accepted the apostolic title.*

The year of the Lord 1101.[37] *Nine years after leaving his father's palace the young King Conrad,*[38] *who in administering Italian matters had always relied upon the advice of Matilda (that great, most noble and, as some say, religious woman who was related to him by blood and close association),*[39] *as well as upon the lord pope and other God-fearing persons, was cut off by premature death and departed this transitory kingdom for the kingdom that is eternal, full of faith and having made a good confession.*[40] *Some say that he was killed with poison. There are those who testify that they saw the sign of the cross appear suddenly on the arms of his lifeless body and that his funeral rites were hallowed by certain miracles. Not unjustly. In this time,*[41] of course, *the odour of his innate character spread throughout the whole Roman world*

---

33 Baldwin (of Boulogne), younger brother of Godfrey, count of Edessa and king of Jerusalem (d. 1118).

34 Baldwin was crowned on Christmas Day 1100 by Daimbert (d. 1105), archbishop of Pisa 1088–99 and patriarch of Jerusalem 1099–1102.

35 A paraphrase of Sallust, *Bellum Catilinae* 60.4.

36 *1106 Continuation* 1100, above, pp. 161–2. Wibert of Parma, archbishop of Ravenna 1072–1100, antipope 'Clement III', 1084–1100 (d. 8 September in Città Castellana). See Meyer von Knonau (1904), p. 107; Zeise (1982), p. 266.

37 *1106 Continuation* 1101, above, p. 162.

38 Conrad (1074–1101), the fourth child and eldest surviving son of Henry IV. He was crowned king of the Germans on 30 May 1087, but was renounced by his father at Mainz in May 1098.

39 Matilda, margravine of Tuscany (1046–1115).

40 On 27 July in Florence.

41 *1106 Continuation* 1099, above, pp. 141–2.

so that no pious or wise man doubted that the salvation of the commonwealth rested on him. He was a thoroughly catholic man who was most obedient to the apostolic see and more dedicated to religion than to power or arms. Although more than well practised in courage and valour, he preferred to pass his time in reading than in games, and through compassion and mercy he was neighbour to[42] *the poor of every sort, but especially to destitute knights. He disdained none, he was violent to none, he prejudged none; to all persons of whatever condition he was affable. Thus not undeservedly was he always loved by God and by men.* According *as the law prescribes: 'Honour thy father'.*[43] *He never permitted his own ears to give credence to the rumours of his father's habits that were mangling* a great many *or that he himself was the cause of resistance to his father and of his downfall. He always called him his Lord and Caesar, or emperor; any servant who arrived from his father's court – even the lowest – he treated with friendly good will. In addition to being virtuous in mind and habits, he had a most handsome figure and was very tall.*

[44]*A member of our house saw a fire in the likeness of a great city flying from the west to the east. A swarm of incredibly numerous tiny insects, which because of their similarity to soldiers' tents are called pavilions,*[45] *flew for three whole days from the borders of Saxony to Bavaria.*

Soon after there followed a very large expedition, which was almost comparable in numbers to the former one.[46] *After hearing stories of how matters in Jerusalem had prospered beyond expectation, the remainder of people throughout the entire West, but especially those who before had resisted taking the vow out of fear, want of faith, poverty or feebleness, prepared anew.* We have many other writings concerning the outcome of this matter.

The year of the Lord 1102.[47] *Holding an assembly with the princes,*[48] *Emperor Henry* began to discuss *going to Rome, if he could, around the Kalends of February* [1 February], *so that the discussion of his case and that of the lord pope according to canon law might confirm the catholic unity of the royal and spiritual power. While he was hindered by other business, however, a general council of all the bishops of Apulia, Calabria, Sicily, Tuscany and the*

---

42 Luke 10.36.
43 Exodus 20.12.
44 *1106 Continuation* 1101, above, p. 162.
45 Isidore, *Etymologies* 15.10.1, trans. Barney (2006), p. 313.
46 The crusade of 1101. See Cate (1969), pp. 343–67; Riley-Smith (1986), pp. 120–34; Mulinder (1996).
47 *1106 Continuation* 1102, above, pp. 171–2.
48 At Mainz.

whole of Italy, as well as representatives of very many of the fathers from north of the Alps, was held in Rome in the middle of Lent where,[49] *apart from reverently confirming the decrees of the ancient Fathers in the accustomed manner, the oft-mentioned schism of our times was reckoned among the chief heresies and was condemned with perpetual anathema together with its authors and followers through subscription to the following decree:*

'*I anathematize all heresies and especially that one which disturbs the state of the church at present, which teaches and affirms that excommunication is to be held in contempt and that the strictures of the church are to be spurned*', and so forth.

Bishop Rupert of Bamberg[50] *died. Emperor Henry replaced him with his chancellor Otto,*[51] *a very religious man* in all things and, in particular, most *faithful* to his lord the emperor above all and before all *until death,*[52] even through great danger. *Archbishop Hartwig of Magdeburg died.*[53]

The year of the Lord 1103.[54] While *Emperor Henry* was *celebrating Christmas at Mainz* and discussing necessary matters relating to the state of the kingdom with the princes, suddenly and by chance a rumour spread that the emperor *intended to leave the direction of the kingdom to his son King Henry and visit the Sepulchre of the Lord* in order to make satisfaction to Christ for his sins. Thus with *great approbation* many *prepared* themselves *to accompany him.*

Conrad, the son of Duke Otto,[55] *one of the great princes, to whom nobody in the whole human world was superior in dignity, who was quite remarkable in birth, in letters and knowledge, in strength as well as in wealth, and who with politeness and eloquence was amiable and affable to all good people, was, as he travelled by night, attacked and done away with through the conspiracy of a certain wretched man.* This left the nobles of the kingdom with both great grief and suspicion, since the lowest could presume to commit such great crimes against the highest. Three years earlier, indeed, Henry the Fat,[56] the elder brother of that same Conrad, was prosecuting judicial business in the Frisian

49 The Lateran synod of 1102. See Blumenthal (1978b), pp. 11–22.
50 Rupert, bishop of Bamberg 1078–1102 (d. 11 June).
51 Otto, bishop of Bamberg 1102–39.
52 Apocalypse 2.10.
53 Hartwig of Spanheim, archbishop of Magdeburg 1079–1102 (d. 17 June).
54 *1106 Continuation* 1103, above, pp. 173–4.
55 Conrad of Beichlingen (d. 1103); Otto I, count of Northeim, duke of Bavaria 1061–70 (d. 1083).
56 Count Henry 'the Fat' of Northeim (d. 1101), margrave of Frisia 1099–1101.

March of which he was in charge; at a time when he expected obedience he was surrounded in an ambush by some common Frisians for whom his dominion was a great yoke. When he realized his position and fled to the sea, he was wounded by sailors and then strangled. The death of such a man, who ruled over the whole of Saxony as second after the king, was felt deeply by the whole German kingdom; and this sorrow was now, as we have said, doubled by the murder of his brother.

Margrave Henry of Eilenburg,[57] the most powerful man of his times in Saxony, died.

The year of the Lord 1104.[58] Emperor Henry celebrated Christmas at Regensburg. While he tarried there for some time, and the Bavarian princes had already begun to murmur that the Saxons and Franconians received more friendly and honourable treatment from the emperor than the natives, the emperor began little by little to become more hostile to Count Sigehard,[59] who expressed the strongest suspicion about these things, but especially because he had brought with him a larger force of knights than all the other princes who were then present and seemed to have armed himself so as to resist any evil that might befall him at court.

A few days after this, when the count felt more secure and had permitted his troops to withdraw, a furious riot was sparked against him by the conspiracy both of the citizens of Regensburg and of ministeriales[60] from many regions, which nothing – not even the intervention of the emperor's son – could assuage. From the third hour of the day until the ninth[61] he was besieged in his lodgings until finally the door was broken down and he, having already made his confession and taken the viaticum of the Lord's sacrament, lay dead from having his head cut off.

The adolescent Conrad,[62] the son of Margravine Beatrice,[63] having spurned the study of letters – in which he had been taught from the very beginning – for the profession of arms, perished by the sword since, in Christ's prophecy, he had taken up the sword.[64] Not long after this that same Beatrice died.

57 Count Henry I of Eilenburg (d. 1103), margrave of the Lower Lausitz and Meißen.
58 *1106 Continuation* 1104, above, pp. 174–5.
59 Count Sigehard of Burghausen (d. 1104).
60 Unfree knights bound to the service of a greater lord. See Arnold (1985), pp. 23–52.
61 Approximately 9 a.m. until 3 p.m.
62 *1106 Continuation* 1104, above, pp. 176–7. Conrad's identity is otherwise unknown.
63 Beatrice of Schweinfurt (d. *c.* 1104), widow of Count Henry II of Hildrizhausen.
64 See Matthew 26.52.

In the bishop's palace in Speyer blood was seen flowing from bread and prodigious edible lentils were discovered, which were interpreted as a portent of civil, or rather internal, war according to the ancient pattern of Roman history.[65]
The year of the Lord 1105. The young King Henry, endowed with innate magnanimity, began to foresee in his father's many troubles, circumspect though his father was, and in his father's frequent physical ailments the *fluctuations of fortune*[66] and the mutability of the world. Guarding against the possibility that his father's sudden death would leave him not yet fully provided with friends and knights and with no special reputation in matters of war, thereby giving rise to scruples about his kingship, and so, not content in his father's palace or with this shared – though by all accounts most august – co-existence, he took himself to Bavaria where he drew to himself and made allies of those princes who were in some way connected to his mother's lineage[67] and began *to take counsel for the commonwealth*[68] as the king and the son of a king. *First*, with a pledge of *due obedience*[69] he was united to the see of Rome by Bishop Gebhard of Constance,[70] who was then [71]*the representative of Pope Paschal*, and then, having drawn to himself many of the Bavarians as well as several of the nobles from Swabia and Franconia, he turned towards Saxony. He was honourably received by them and, celebrating Easter in Quedlinburg,*[72] he was soon master of all the Saxon cities and honoured with royal dignity by all the most powerful men.* There are some who say that this discord was planned by the efforts of the emperor himself – whose foresight virtually no one could equal – so that by this simulated strife the part of the kingdom that had defected from the emperor would be drawn by artifice into an alliance with the son: then would his adversaries lack any opportunity or the resources to set up another and truly hostile head [of the kingdom]. We believe that all these things undoubtedly happened through divine dispensation and, with God's assent, we approve of the matter because of its good fruit.

---

65 Cf. Orosius, *History against the pagans* 5.18. See above, p. 177 n. 292.

66 Cicero, *De divinatione* 2.6.15.

67 Particularly Count Otto of Kastl-Habsberg (d. *c.* 1125), the great-grandnephew of Adelaide of Turin, Henry V's maternal grandmother. See Robinson (1999), p. 324.

68 Cicero, *De provinciis consularibus* 30.

69 *1106 Continuation* 1105, above, p. 177.

70 Gebhard of Zähringen, bishop of Constance 1084–1110.

71 *1106 Continuation* 1105, above, p. 177.

72 9 April.

Instructed by letters from the lord Pope Paschal as well as [73]*the advice and service of Bishops Ruothard of Mainz and Gebhard of Constance*, he [Henry V] *reconciled all of Saxony to communion with the Roman church.*[74] *He declared a general council of the bishops and clergy for the fourth Kalends of June* [29 May][75] *at the royal estate that is called Nordhausen, where the perverted discipline of the church's institutions was to be dealt with. As regards the urgent matters of this council, the decrees of the Fathers were first re-read, the things that could be improved by those present were corrected and certain things that seemed more serious were deferred to the attention of the pope. Simoniacal heresy was condemned according to the customs of the Fathers and the* abomination *of nicholaitism was abjured by all who were there. By virtue of apostolic authority the aforementioned bishops declared that, following Roman custom, the fast of the month of March was to be observed in the first week of Lent and the fast of the month of June in the week of Whitsun; and the Peace of God was confirmed. We see in these things, which we cannot pass over in silence, how King Henry* [Henry V], *by his great humility and authority, excited in all no little hope by his good character.*

Although he wished to be present at the meeting of the servants of God only by request – along with the bishops and clerks a vast multitude of abbots and monks had flocked there thirsting for unity in the church – yet finally, with humble demeanour and standing in a raised place, he renewed all his statutes and laws reasonably according to the decision of the princes. But if something unreasonable was asked of him, he rejected it by responding marvellously with prudence beyond his years and with the magnanimity of his ancestors. In all these things he maintained for himself in a marvellous fashion the modesty of a youth and showed appropriate respect for the priests of Christ. With this, his own tears welled up so that the king of heaven and the whole heavenly host might testify that it was not out of lust for power that he had usurped his father's rule, that he did not long to depose his lord and father from the Roman empire but, rather, that he had always shown compassion for his father's sins of defiance and disobedience. If only his father would submit to St Peter and his successors according to Christian law, he promised to cede him the kingdom and submit to him like a servant. Hearing this the whole multitude rejoiced and wept at once, and began to offer prayers for the conversion of the father and the prosperity of the son, crying out in a great voice 'Lord, have mercy upon us'.[76]

---

73 *1106 Continuation* 1105, above, pp. 177–9.

74 See Robinson (1999), pp. 325–7.

75 In reality 21 May.

76 *Kyrie eleison*, from the Ordinary of the Mass.

At the same time Bishops Udo of Hildesheim,[77] *Henry of Paderborn*[78] *and Frederick of Halberstadt*[79] *prostrated themselves at the feet of the metropolitan and, standing before the king, promised their obedience to the pope with the whole assembled church as witness. Nevertheless, their offences were reserved for the judgement of the pope and they were suspended from office.*

These things having been duly ordered, the king celebrated Whitsun[80] *in Merseburg and Henry,*[81] *who had long been designated as archbishop of the church of Magdeburg but had been driven out by followers of the emperor, was consecrated. Not long afterwards the king led an expedition against Mainz to restore its expelled bishop;*[82] *his father was waiting for him within the walls with a not inconsiderable band of knights and several princes (who were, nevertheless, not entirely loyal to him). Since, however, he [Henry V] was denied entry into the city by the current of the Rhine and the lack of boats, each forbade – both son and father having sworn oaths – the consideration of a parricidal war. Nevertheless, many messages were sent back and forth by boat and the leading men of the kingdom held many common councils among themselves, with the father promising a division of the kingdom and the confirmation of hereditary succession and the son demanding nothing less than submission to the pope and the accomplishment of unity in the church.*

Leaving there in the middle of the night he [Henry V] came to Würzburg and pitched his camp outside the city. Bishop Emehard,[83] after his death in the same year, was succeeded by Erlung,[84] a canon of the church of Bamberg, who was most diligently educated and instructed above all in the liberal disciplines by the distinguished scholar Meinhard,[85] his uncle and sometime bishop of that same seat; and Erlung, because of the good odour of his reputation, was taken from the cathedral of Bamberg and into the palace where for some years he strenuously discharged the office of chancellor, and then obtained the bishopric with the consent of

77 Udo of Gleichen, bishop of Hildesheim 1079–1114.
78 Henry of Werl, bishop of Paderborn 1084–1127.
79 Frederick, bishop of Halberstadt, before 1102–6.
80 29 May.
81 Henry, archbishop of Magdeburg, 1102–6/7.
82 In the last week of June.
83 Emehard, bishop of Würzburg 1089–1105 (elected 25 July 1089).
84 Erlung, (imperial) bishop of Würzburg 1105/6–21. Cf. *1106 Continuation* 1105, above, p. 179.
85 Meinhard, *scholasticus* of Bamberg, imperial bishop of Würzburg 1085–8. Cf. Frutolf, *Chronicle* 1085, above, p. 124. On Meinhard see Erdmann (1932), 332–431; Erdmann (1938), pp. 16–116; Schieffer (1987), 310–13; Märtl (1991), pp. 331–41.

the people and clergy. Believing that perseverance is the virtue of good works, he preferred – since he had not yet been consecrated – to cede the position than to appear in the least unfaithful to the emperor, whom he had thus far served tirelessly and sincerely. Erlung having ceded it, the king [Henry V] had Rupert,[86] the provost of that same church, [87]*enthroned by the aforementioned Archbishop Ruothard. Thus that church was returned to communion with the papacy and, having accepted surety from the citizens, he* [Henry V] *dismissed the Saxons and with the Bavarians turned to besiege the castle of Nuremberg. After two or more months he successfully captured it, dissolved the army and carried on to Regensburg.*[88] *Following in his footsteps, his father put Rupert to flight and reinstalled Erlung; then he devastated everything that belonged to his son's supporters and eventually, with the help of the treacherous citizens of Regensburg, drove his son from the city. Staying there, he made a certain youth named Udalric*[89] *bishop of that very seat;* for Gebhard,[90] who had miserably occupied the position of shepherd of that place for sixteen years, was that same year butchered by one of his own knights, whom he had very intolerably injured, and died in double shame. Therefore, [91]*gathering an army from all about,* Caesar *advanced and cruelly devastated Diepold's march,*[92] *above all with* [the help of] *the Bohemian people.*[93] *The knights of the king and their lord did not delay any longer, but rallied all together to repay the imperial forces from the rear with fire and plundering, and afterwards sought out battle with 10,000 chosen warriors divided into five legions. Now the camps were pitched against each other – an exceedingly horrible spectacle! – and for three whole days from one bank of the River Regen flew the standard of the emperor and from the other the standard of the king. Duels were frequently sought out on the river bed,* during which *not a few from each side were consumed by the unpredictable lot of Mars. Yet on the day before the impending battle the princes who appeared to be the foremost and most powerful in each army, having held*

86 Rupert, (Gregorian) bishop of Würzburg 1105–6. See Wendehorst (1962), pp. 124–7.
87 *1106 Continuation* 1105, above, pp. 179–80.
88 Nuremberg surrendered in September. See Brühl (1968), pp. 134 and n. 83, 141 n. 112, 158.
89 Udalric, bishop of Regensburg 1105 (otherwise unknown).
90 Gebhard IV, bishop of Regensburg 1089–1105. Cf. Frutolf, *Chronicle* 1089, above, p. 127, claimed that Gebhard was below the canonical age when appointed.
91 *1106 Continuation* 1105, above, pp. 180–1.
92 The Bavarian Nordgau of Margrave Diepold III of Cham-Vohburg, 1099–1146.
93 Henry IV was reinforced by the forces of Margrave Leopold III of Austria and Duke Borivoi of Bohemia. Cf. *Annals of Hildesheim* 1105, p. 53; *Life of Henry IV* 9, p. 32. See Meyer von Knonau (1904), pp. 285–7, 289.

mutual peace talks and protracted discussions among themselves on the causes of the current war, at length concluded unanimously – guided by the Spirit of God no doubt – that little justice or little reward would come from being part of such a cruel and dangerous undertaking. Consequently, they decided that they should at all costs vow to show consideration to their brothers, that is the Christian people on both sides or, rather, desist from parricidal war. Since already, as we have said, bloodthirsty Mars[94] *had begun to gnash his teeth through the battle-lines arrayed on each side, the young king, whose bowels were moved upon*[95] *his father, mournfully cried out: 'My fellow warriors'*, he said, *'I give you the greatest thanks for your good will towards me and I shall not refuse to pay back each of you in equal measure should the situation require it. But let no one wish or believe that he will be my ally if he should boast that he has killed my father and lord or at any time has been minded to kill him. As heir* to my forefathers *and successor to the emperor I might indeed hold a kingdom subject to me by Christian laws, if it pleases the ruler of all things; I do not wish to be called a parricide or something similar. If my father obediently submits himself to the yoke of the pope,* which is the most important thing, *I shall be satisfied at once with whatever he will grant me in his goodness. Until then you should know that I am not fighting against my father, but fighting for my father's kingdom.'* Among other things *on that day, with evening approaching the king's forces* returned to their camp, while *the emperor,* who was preparing his own as if *in certainty of the following day's battle, heard that the princes would neither fight nor wished to fight* nor [believed there] to be any lawfulness in it.

Informed[96] *then by secret messengers from his son that his own had secretly conspired against him, he* [Henry IV] *sneaked away from the camp with very few men and thus through divine providence, by the salvation of one the blood of many – which would undoubtedly have been shed – was saved. As soon as the absence of the emperor became known throughout the camp, each person hastened to return home, especially because the darkness of the night furnished security by hiding his departure. Although the king could have had the satisfaction of destroying his enemies at will, he decided to spare rather than pursue them and because of the failure of the earlier alliance he secured the city* [Regensburg] *to himself on much more severe terms. After the abdication of Udalric he enthroned Hartwig,*[97] *a thoroughly upright, catholic and noble man. He also won over to himself certain bishops and princes from his father's*

94 Statius, *Thebaid* 8.231.
95 3 Kings 3.26: that is, he was deeply agitated on account of his father.
96 *1106 Continuation* 1105, above, pp. 181–2.
97 Hartwig, bishop of Regensburg 1105–26.

army and soon afterwards, returning to Franconia, he gave the treacherous citizens of Würzburg the same cup to drink.

Meanwhile, the aforementioned Erlung, who had accepted that bishopric from the emperor, considering the *wheel of fortune*[98] with displeasure like a prudent and discreet man, *gave himself up to the king,* who reinstated Rupert, *and from then* was treated with great and special honour *as one of his chaplains,* since he had already for a long time been very notable. After this the king travelled to Speyer and made Abbot Gebhard of Hirsau its bishop.[99] He also reinstated Ruothard, who had been expelled from his *throne for eight years,* to the *nobles of Mainz* and *thereby reconciled that people and clergy* to *apostolic* communion.

Then *turning*[100] *to Burgundy*[101] *he was called back by messengers from his followers,* thereby *forestalling* the *machinations* of a certain deceitful *Count Siegfried,*[102] since it is said that, along with the emperor, he was attempting to *impede the discussions of the assembly that had been convened to deal with the present business by all the princes* of the kingdom. He *encountered* his father *at Bingen about the Ides of December* [13 December] and *face to face in the wrong order, but necessarily switched, the son reminded the father* of those things requiring emendation and *promised due obedience if he would not deny them to God. The elder put off these and other such matters to the hearing of the princes and the decision of the senate at the forthcoming assembly, and they parted peacefully, each going with his followers to the oft-mentioned metropolitan city. Meanwhile, when the son's followers observed the father attempting through secret messengers to lead some people in ways inconsistent with this agreement and peace, it was obvious to them that the father should await the assembly of the princes separately with his followers in an absolutely secure fortress.*[103] *These things being arranged and guards*[104] *also, so that nothing unexpected could happen through him or to him, the king was summoned and hastened to the public assembly of the princes at Mainz. But the stupidity of the common people spread the rumour all about that the son had captured the father by treachery and had sent him into captivity.*

98 Cicero, *In Pisonem* 10.
99 Gebhard, bishop of Speyer 1105–7 (enthroned 1 November).
100 *1106 Continuation* 1105, above, pp. 182–3.
101 *Chroniken*, p. 199 n. 64 suggests Lotharingia and Alsace in reality.
102 Siegfried of Ballenstedt (d. 1113), count palatine of Lotharingia. See Robinson (1999), p. 333.
103 Böckelheim on the River Nahe.
104 Bishop Gebhard of Speyer oversaw his guard. Cf. Henry IV, *Letters* 37, 39, pp. 48–9, 54–5.

The[105] *day before Christmas Eve there was seen in the west so great a fire in the middle of a star that one would have believed it to be the light of the sun had it been in the east. Duke Frederick,*[106] *a prudent man who was quite illustrious because of his habits and nobility, but was most illustrious for his marriage to the emperor's daughter Agnes,*[107] *a woman of unique and celebrated reputation, and for the wonderful and natural abilities of the offspring that adorned that marriage, died.* His duchy was taken over by his eldest son Frederick,[108] still a boy, who was treated with great honour and love as befitted him by his uncle the king.

HERE ENDS THE SECOND BOOK.

HERE BEGINS THE THIRD BOOK.

The year of the Incarnation of the Lord 1106. [109]*At the instigation of the younger Henry a council of the whole German kingdom was held in Mainz at Christmas, the size of which had not been seen for many years. Participants report that fifty-two princes or more were present and that only the Saxon duke named Magnus,*[110] *impeded by his great age, was noted as absent. The legates of the apostolic see, namely the bishops of Albano*[111] *and Constance, arrived there and* announced, *both orally and in writing, the decree* of the apostolic pastor, which accused the lord emperor of many transgressions. *Wherefore, when he* [Henry IV] *himself was tempted to leave the castle where he was staying to go to Mainz, the princes, in order to avoid an uprising of the common crowd (for they were accustomed to favour the party of the father more than that of the son), hastened to meet him at Ingelheim and, surrounding him, finally led him back to the general council to promise satisfaction.*[112] Since the legates could not absolve him *or impose penance without the judgement of a general synod and apostolic advice, he assented to the advice of his own party as well as that of the council and gave the regalia or imperial insignia – namely the cross and lance, the sceptre, orb and crown – into the hands of his son, praying for his prosperity and commending him to the foremost princes*

---

105 *1106 Continuation* 1105, above, p. 184.

106 Frederick I (of Büren), duke of Swabia 1079–1105 (Hohenstaufen family).

107 Agnes (1072/3–1124), the third child of Henry IV and Bertha of Turin.

108 Duke Frederick II of Swabia (1090–1147).

109 *1106 Continuation* 1106, above, pp. 184–6.

110 Magnus Billung, duke in Saxony 1073–1106.

111 Cardinal Bishop Richard of Albano, 1101–15. Other sources imply that Richard of Albano was not at Mainz: see Jakobs (1961), pp. 33 n. 22, 220–1.

112 31 December 1105. See Robinson (1999), pp. 336–7.

with many tears; and he promised from then on for the sake of his soul to heed the decrees of the great high priest and the whole church.[113] *This done, Henry, the fifth of that name, was elected to the kingship for the second time, first by his father and then by all of the German princes.*[114] *He was also confirmed in a catholic manner through the imposition of hands by the apostolic legates and,*[115] *having accepted oaths from both the bishops and the laity according to the custom of the country, he began to rule in the eighty-eighth place since Augustus, in the fiftieth year of his father, in the one-thousand-eight-hundred-and-fifty-seventh year since the founding of the city, in the five-thousand-and-fifty-eighth year since the beginning of the world and, as it is called, in the eleven-hundred-and-sixth year since the Incarnation of the Lord.*

After the many and long-standing defilements of the churches in this kingdom had been related in the presence of the king and all the princes and bishops from the whole of Germany as well as the clergy and people and the legates of the Roman see, and after all had unanimously promised their eradication, it pleased both the king and the leading men to send to the holy Mother Church of Rome so many and such legates from these parts as were appropriate to give a proper account of the allegations, to investigate what was doubtful intelligently and to consult on all things wisely for the benefit of the church. For this work men full of the spirit of wisdom[116] *were chosen, not unworthy of respect either before God or the world because of their dignity, birth, sophistication and wealth:* Archbishops *Bruno of Trier from Lotharingia*[117] *and Henry of Magdeburg from Saxony, Otto of Bamberg from Franconia and Eberhard of Eichstätt*[118] *from Bavaria,* each designated bishop, *Gebhard of Constance from Swabia,* as well as *several* other bishops and *even* many noble laymen from the side of the king.[119] *Among other things, they received the* particular *command, if it were possible,* to entreat *the lord pope to come across the Alps.*

Thus without doubt, thus by the most profound mercy of our God with such a morning star rising upon us, the light of the church – which had been obscured for many years – began to shine. And, to summarize many things briefly, through the taking over of the commonwealth and

---

113 Cf. Henry IV, *Letters* 37, 39, pp. 49–50, 56–7.

114 On 5 January 1106 in Mainz: *Annals of Hildesheim* 1106, p. 55.

115 From Ruothard of Mainz: *Annals of Hildesheim* 1106, p. 56.

116 Deuteronomy 34.9; Sirach 15.5.

117 Bruno of Laufen, archbishop of Trier 1101–24.

118 Bishop Eberhard of Eichstätt, 1099–1112.

119 Cf. the description of the emissaries in the *Translatio S. Modoaldi* 11, pp. 295–6, which identifies the Saxon Count Herman of Reinhausen.

the defending of the Roman seat by Henry – this exquisite flower of the world – the vile scandals of schisms that were everywhere round about were eliminated, the rent garment of Christ was mended and through the choosing of the good fish for the ship of the church the bad fish were thrown out of Peter's net.

After this, when the aforementioned nobles came from their own parts to spend the night[120] in the valley of the Trent at the city of the same name, that is Trent, a certain youth named Adalbert,[121] who was distinguished by the possession of a certain county in those parts, rushed upon those unarmed pilgrims early in the morning with armed citizens. He plundered them, captured them and held them in custody, claiming that this had been demanded of him by messengers of his lord the emperor. But Jesus, *who is always close to those who call upon Him*[122] and especially *to those whose hearts are troubled*,[123] suddenly sent Duke Welf of Bavaria[124] upon these most stupid captors of such great men. Like a shining sword drawn from His scabbard, he came on the third day with strong forces and broke open the barricaded enclosure. He forced the citizens to accept Gebhard,[125] a man praised by all, who had been made bishop of the church of Trent by Henry our king, although they had conspired never to have him. He so terrified Adalbert and his wicked accomplices that they brought out the princes whom they had captured, returned the castle to the new bishop and, moreover, with bare feet begged mercy of those they had afflicted.

Then also from the first week of Lent – during the middle of which we had endured these things – we saw a comet of immense brightness for two weeks. Returning poorer rather than richer, with everyone having lost something, we learned from inauspicious reports that Henry our king was enduring some misfortune from several seditious rebellions against him in Alsace. In Lotharingia also Duke Henry and Bishop Otbert of Liège[126] were arming themselves against the king, and Cologne, Jülich and Bonn – which is also called Verona – as well as

---

120 3/4 March.
121 Count either of Eppan (Appiano) or of Tyrol. See Meyer von Knonau (1904), p. 295 n. 28.
122 See Psalm 144.18.
123 Psalm 33.19.
124 Welf V, duke of Bavaria 1101–20.
125 Bishop Gebhard of Trent, 1106–20.
126 Count Henry of Limburg, 1082–1119, duke of Lower Lotharingia 1101–6 (Luxemburg family); Bishop Otbert of Liège, 1092–1116.

several towns on either side of the Rhine, were preparing themselves to resist him.[127]

But strengthened by divine confidence, King Henry turned to Liège as if to humble the lands of his enemies by holding his Easter[128] court there. Nevertheless, although he celebrated Palm Sunday with full joy in Cologne, which had been yielded by his enemies, once his forces had moved on he felt again the *wheel of fortune*[129] spin to his disadvantage. This matter was without doubt rashly handled[130] since, blazing with youthful impetuosity, he attempted to hold the planned assembly against the will of his enemies and with insufficient forces. He sent 300 men to guard the bridge over the River Maas, which had been constructed at the place called Visé, for all the other crossings on the river had been destroyed by his enemies. While the king was celebrating Maundy Thursday at the palace of Aachen, Duke Henry attacked the royal forces at the bridge; and though the king's knights steadfastly resisted the great feats of horsemanship – for those people employ them more than others – he [Duke Henry] surrounded them on the plain with much greater numbers, overwhelmed them, scattered them and captured them, while some even fell into the river and were devoured by it.[131] You may observe here the most strong Maccabees battling for catholic peace who, after the slaughter of many by an apostate people, commended their souls with great faith and happiness to Christ who had suffered for them and consoled each other that by dying in such a manner they would acquire forgiveness of their former sins on this day of indulgence. Through these *vagaries of fortune*,[132] or rather through the disposition of the divine judge, the minds of the schismatics began to swell with pride but, nevertheless, the hope of the orthodox did not fade. Then during the Easter festivities, which were being celebrated at Bonn because of events, the king deprived Duke Henry of his duchy (since by the judgement of the princes he was guilty of contumacy and an enemy of the commonwealth) and, having accepted oaths from the princes, announced and prepared for a general expedition against Lotharingia.

127 See Robinson (1999), p. 338.
128 25 March.
129 Cicero, *In Pisonem* 10.
130 An echo of Sallust, *Bellum catilinae* 42.
131 Cf. the account of the *Life of Henry IV* 12, pp. 38–9 (*IL*, pp. 131–2). See Robinson (1999), p. 339.
132 Ammianus Marcellinus, *Res gestae* 31.19.13.

About the middle of June after that he [Henry V] besieged Cologne with 20,000 fighting men. But since it possessed ramparts and bulwarks along with many soldiers and excellent defence mechanisms of every kind, he was detained there for three or four weeks in almost *futile effort*,[133] excepting the youths, who are wont to be *impatient of delay*,[134] skirmishing in front of the walls and fleeing from or killing each other in a cruel game. There, indeed, Count Dietrich,[135] who was most faithful to the king, was overwhelmed with sickness and went the way of all flesh. He was a man of most noble Saxon lineage, fervently dedicated as much to all manner of religion as to the defence of catholicism and was also well instructed in letters.

Then at the time when the king's father was delaying at Liège – for the people of Liège adhered faithfully to him with long-standing good will – messengers and letters were frequently sent back and forth. During this time there spread the unexpected news that the emperor was ill and that he had died in his camp after languishing briefly. Those who were present report that he ended his life[136] after making a good confession and not without great courage. After he had disposed of all his possessions and had sent envoys both to the pope and to his son the king, he received viaticum and died, like one falling asleep. He governed the Roman empire for fifty years, sometimes dutifully taking care of those Romans who were well disposed towards him and sometimes resisting, as was necessary, the ungrateful who attempted to humble the royal power in Germany. He was vigorous and warlike, accustomed to give everyone his due according to age and circumstances, and he could hardly bear to be ignorant of anything. Like his father, he wished to have clerks at his side, particularly those who were learned. He treated them honourably and spent his time amicably among them, sometimes in singing psalms, sometimes in reading or conversation or in discussion of the scriptures or the liberal arts. We could also prove from the evidence of very many witnesses that no one in our times seemed more fitted for the office of emperor by birth, intelligence, courage and boldness, and also by stature and bodily grace. Of all the churches in his kingdom he most cherished that of Speyer, adorning it with royal and magnificent works as well as with benefices. He now rests there beside his ancestors, having been honourably buried in the presence of his son

133 Lucan, *Pharsalia* 2.663.
134 *Ibid.* 4.424.
135 Count Dietrich III of Kaltenburg (d. 1106). See Meyer von Knonau (1904), p. 310.
136 7 August. Cf. *Life of Henry IV* 13, p. 43 (*IL*, p. 136).

and all the princes of the kingdom.[137]

After this, in the fourth week of the month of October, a general council was held in the province of Lombardy, on the River Po at the place that is called Guastalla,[138] where all things were presided over by Pope Paschal II in the presence of a vast multitude of clerics as well as laymen who were performing the legations of different kingdoms and churches; also present were legates from the lord king.[139] As the canons fairly dictate, many *hostile tares*[140] were rooted out and many seedlings of genuine stock were planted more deeply;[141] structures built *upon sand*[142] were destroyed and *fortified* bulwarks[143] were raised up for the protection of the churches. On the same Sunday, the twelfth Kalends of November [21 October], certain bishops were consecrated by him.[144] It would take long to relate how that indefatigable, *prudent and faithful steward* of the great Father of the *family*[145] amply refreshed his fellow servants each day with the wheat of the word of God, deposed pseudo-bishops,[146] established catholic ones, granted the pallium[147] to archbishops and privileges to monasteries,[148] instructed those shepherds of Christ's sheep who were in his presence with sweet addresses and those who were absent through letters of fatherly guidance, brought certain formerly amputated members of the church back to its body and even maimed certain members that seemed incurable with the severance of

---

137 Henry IV was eventually buried at the cathedral in Speyer on 7 August 1111. See Robinson (1999), pp. 343–4.
138 The Council of Guastalla, *c.* 22 October 1106. See Blumenthal (1978b), pp. 36–73.
139 On the participants see Blumenthal (1978b), pp. 38–42.
140 Matthew 13.28–9.
141 See Matthew 13.2–8.
142 Matthew 7.26.
143 See Song of Songs 8.9.
144 Including Archbishop Conrad of Salzburg and Bishop Gebhard of Trent: Ekkehard, *Chronicle* 1106, below, p. 233.
145 Luke 12.42.
146 Those who had been invested by Henry IV and who refused to be reconciled to the papacy.
147 The pallium: the metropolitan's ceremonial garment of office. From the middle of the eleventh century the papacy had insisted that new metropolitans come to Rome in person to collect the pallium. Archbishop Bruno of Trier, who had been invested by Henry IV, had assumed his duties without receiving the pallium. At Guastalla he was deposed but reinstated and granted the pallium: *Gesta Treverorum*, p. 192. See von Hacke (1898), p. 131; Benson (1968), pp. 169–73; Blumenthal (1978b), p. 72.
148 Cf. *JL* 6093, 6095–7.

anathema.¹⁴⁹ Concerning the arrangements made during the time of schism, about which many questions were raised, he promulgated a decree that with the discretion of a mother skilfully healed the innermost parts of the body.¹⁵⁰

With these and such things and the joyful splendour of divine light having risen upon the church like the dawn, *since* at last without doubt *the time of His mercy had come*,¹⁵¹ each honoured with the apostolic blessing returned to his own parts. But we who had crossed the Alps were especially joyful, above all because we were certain that the journey of the lord pope had been so planned that he would follow as soon as possible and celebrate the birthday of the Lord in Mainz together with Henry our new king and all the princes.

In this year Duke Magnus of Saxony died,¹⁵² and in his place Lothar¹⁵³ was raised up. Margrave Udo of Saxony also died.¹⁵⁴ Bishop Rupert of Würzburg died on the journey while travelling to the council [of Guastalla]. After his death, lord Erlung was fervently sought by both the clergy and people of Würzburg as a true shepherd.¹⁵⁵ Although he had formerly obtained [the bishopric] unjustly, he was offered it again by God's just judgement; and being permitted both by the king and the pope through legates of the Roman see, he was received with great expectation and incredible joy by the whole city and many people, and enthroned with great honour.

The year of the Lord 1107. King Henry celebrated Christmas at Regensburg in the presence of legates from the lord Pope Paschal, whose arrival he had for some time been awaiting at Augsburg, the chief city of Swabia and the other southern parts [of Germany]. The

149 The *Annals of Paderborn* 1106, p. 116, describe a less congenial synod: 'There many Italian bishops were condemned and some were excommunicated. The Patriarch of Aquileia was excommunicated; Frederick of Halberstadt was deprived of episcopal rank having been accused by the canons of his church. Widelo of Minden received a similar sentence. [The bishops of] Liège and Cambrai were excommunicated.' The annalist's account of the fate of Bishop Otbert of Liège, however, does not mention that he was restored on the strength of a delegation that reached Guastalla shortly after the synod. Cf. *JL* 6099. See Blumenthal (1978b), pp. 72–3.

150 For the text of the decree see *MGH Constitutiones* 1, p. 565; Ekkehard, *Chronicle* 1106, below, pp. 233–4.

151 Psalm 101.14.

152 23 August.

153 Lothar of Supplinburg, duke of Saxony 1106–37, king (Lothar III) 1125–37.

154 Count Udo III of Stade, margrave of the Saxon North March (d. 2 June).

155 See John 10.12.

pope, however, declined [to come] on the advice of his own counsellors and, as it were, because of the recklessness of the Germans, but especially because of a certain seditious rebellion that had occurred while he was staying in Verona, in addition to the suggestion of certain persons that it would not be easy for our people to accept that decree which forbade acceptance of any ecclesiastical investiture from the hands of the laity and also because of the ardent heart of a youthful king, which was not yet used to the yoke of the Lord[156] in all respects. Hearing this and much of its kind, I say, the *man of God*[157] considered and, since the passes to the German lands were not yet open to him, announced his departure with regret. With Spanish legates he started for France through Burgundy and by his presence greatly amplified the joy of Christmas at Cluny. Moving on from there he was received with immense honour by all churches in that territory as a true disciple of Christ and vicar of the apostles. He was treated with due reverence and he was listened to as none other than a lawgiver sent from heaven. Thus for several months as a *faithful and wise steward*[158] he bore daily the anxiety of the whole church and at last, about the Ascension of the Lord [23 May], he held a great council at Troyes[159] where, among many things, he corrected what required correction according to the times and necessity, and promulgated judgement according to the decrees of his predecessors on the free election of bishops and on restraining the presumptuousness of the laity in ecclesiastical matters.[160]

But King Henry, who was travelling from the borders of Saxony, celebrated Easter at Mainz [14 April] and presented himself in the vicinity of this same council – he was not present – with several of the bishops and nobles.[161] When he had taken counsel with them he sent honourable legates to the pope,[162] through whom he wished to inform

---

156 See Matthew 11.29–30.

157 Judges 13.6. A frequently used *epithaton ornans* for religious figures. See the *Life of Leo IX*, trans. Robinson (2004b) for example.

158 Luke 12.42.

159 The Council of Troyes (23 May 1107). See Blumenthal (1978b), pp. 74–101.

160 For the canons of the council see Blumenthal (1978b), pp. 90–6, which provides a fuller record than that of *MGH Constitutiones* 1, pp. 566–7.

161 At Verdun.

162 Henry V's ambassadors, led by Archbishop Bruno of Trier, met the pope at Châlons-sur-Marne. The *Annals of Paderborn* 1107, p. 117, and Abbot Suger of St Denis, *Vita Ludovici*, pp. 56–60 (written thirty years later), place the meeting at Châlons-sur-Marne before the Council of Troyes. Luchaire (1890) suggested 3–13 May for the meeting at Châlons.

both the pope and the whole synod that the power of constituting bishops had been given to Emperor Charles [the Great] by apostolic privileges.¹⁶³ Since Henry could not permit this question to be decided in a foreign kingdom, in as much as he had already begun [the process of] obtaining the Roman sceptre,¹⁶⁴ he was granted a deferral so that he might come to Rome within the next year and discuss the same matter in a general council. Then the lord pope punished several of our bishops – those who did not attend that same council – with suspension from their office, although not long afterwards they gave satisfactory assurances and he mercifully absolved them.¹⁶⁵ Again he lamented greatly that the humility he sought could not be found in German hearts and that he could by no means visit us as he had planned; so he decided to return to the lands of Italy with his retinue. When he returned there after a delay, he was received with such joy by the Roman clergy and people as if he had been revived from the dead.¹⁶⁶

Meanwhile, the king returned to the eastern parts [of Germany] and held a council in Regensburg with the Bavarians,¹⁶⁷ at which he announced a campaign against Robert of Flanders.¹⁶⁸ Starting around October, he entered the land of the rebels and, not without great losses to his own army, devastated it for more than a month until the matter was postponed to the next court by the exchange of messengers and the quarrel ended.

The year of the Lord 1108. King Henry celebrated Christmas at Mainz¹⁶⁹ and received the aforementioned Robert back into his grace.¹⁷⁰

At this time enmity broke out between King Coloman¹⁷¹ of Hungary

---

163 Cf. the spurious privilege of Pope Hadrian I, *MGH Constitutiones* 1, no. 446, pp. 659–60.

164 That is, he wished to be crowned emperor.

165 Paschal made sweeping suspensions among the German episcopacy, including the archbishops of Cologne (with his suffragans) and Mainz (with all but two of his suffragans). Cf. *Annals of Paderborn* 1107, p. 118. See Blumenthal (1978b), pp. 99–101.

166 In late August 1107.

167 The planned council in Regensburg did not take place: Meyer von Knonau (1907), p. 66.

168 Robert II, count of Flanders (*c.* 1065–1111).

169 Other sources say Aachen: see Meyer von Knonau (1907), p. 73 n. 60.

170 Henry and Robert were reconciled at Cambrai in November 1107. See Meyer von Knonau (1907), pp. 68–9.

171 Coloman I of Hungary, 1095–1116.

and his brother named Almus[172] because each of them insisted that he was more deserving of the royal dignity according to the law of that people. Almus lost his possessions and his duchy, which had given him prestige among the Hungarians and, as befits the brother of a king, the second place after the king. He went to King Henry and, complaining before the entire senate of his misfortune, not unlike Atherbal the brother of Hiempsal,[173] he managed to persuade the magnificent Roman empire to compassion and to procure its protection. These complaints, as well as the fact that the same Coloman had invaded the borders of our kingdom at the coastal areas, caused King Henry to lead an army against Hungary; but since his adversaries had prepared in many ways, especially by barricading all the river fords, after a sorry and pointless siege of the fortress of Pressburg[174] he returned home *empty-handed*.[175]

The year of the Lord 1109. King Henry celebrated Christmas at Mainz and shortly afterwards held a council with the foremost nobles in Frankfurt, at which he delivered Count Palatine Siegfried[176] into the custody of the bishop of Würzburg because he had concocted a plan to kill the king and overturn the kingdom. This was revealed by Henry,[177] the former duke of Lotharingia, who was received back into the king's grace.[178] There the king also deposed Abbot Godfrey of Fulda[179] and replaced him with Wolfhelm[180] from the same congregation. After this he led an army against the Poles,[181] a distant people, and after he had laboured hard there for a long time he collected the long-denied tribute owed by that country. Archbishop Ruothard of Mainz died.[182]

The year of the Lord 1110. While King Henry was celebrating Christmas at Bamberg he was unexpectedly disturbed by the inauspicious news

172 Almus (d. 1127). See Engel (2001), pp. 34–5.
173 Sallust, *Bellum Iugurthinum* 13–14.
174 Modern Bratislava. Cf. Cosmas of Prague, *Chronicle* 3.22, 3.25, trans. Wolverton (2009), pp. 208, 213.
175 Sallust, *Bellum Iugurthinum* 58.7.
176 See n. 102 above.
177 See n. 126 above.
178 See Meyer von Knonau (1907), p. 92.
179 Godfrey, abbot 1096–1109.
180 Wolfhelm, abbot 1109–14.
181 In the second half of August in response to Polish attacks on Henry's ally Duke Svatopluk of Bohemia. Cosmas, *Chronicle* 3.27, trans. Wolverton (2009), p. 214, records that they entered Poland in September. See Meyer von Knonau (1907), pp. 96–8.
182 On 2 May.

that Werner[183] had occupied Prague, the capital city of Bohemia, with an army and had usurped ducal authority over that people for himself against the will of the king. Then with raging spirit he sent ahead his most faithful princes with a strong force;[184] with marvellous and quick success they captured the city along with the enemies discovered within, and returned triumphantly to the king, who was cautiously following.

At the Epiphany of the Lord, [King Henry] held a council of the princes at Regensburg and unfolded his mind's plans to them, namely that he wished to make himself known in the territories beyond the Alps, in order to secure imperial benediction from the great pontiff in the city of Rome, which is the *capital of the world*,[185] to bring the extensive Italian provinces into fellowship with the German kingdom through fraternal peace with ancient justice and laws and, in addition, to demonstrate his readiness to do all things necessary for the defence of the church according to the will of the apostolic father. All now directed their eager minds to the pious vow of the provident consul who undoubtedly loved his country, and no one was believed to be a man who sought to evade participation in such a manly business. Accordingly, after those who were there had fully committed themselves to this matter by a voluntary oath, the king did not cease to arrange for this expedition quickly and urgently among the several German provinces; and though the advent of an inauspicious comet that remained visible for almost six months terrified the minds of some, the king, giving everywhere inestimable sums of money with munificent liberality, ordered the departure of the army from all places about August. Some crossed the Alps with him through the Great St Bernard Pass and others via the valley of the Trent. But the king, who in foresight was second to none among the kings of the world, knowing that the Roman republic was formerly accustomed to being governed not so much by arms as by wisdom, provided himself with the necessary protection not only of armed men but also of educated men, so that he would be ready to respond to all the matters demanded of him.

---

183 Possibly a mistaken reference to Wiprecht III of Groitzsch (d. 1116), the son of Count Wiprecht II of Groitzsch (see n. 221 below). Wiprecht III aided Borivoi, who seized Prague on Christmas Eve 1109, in response to the succession of his brother Vladislav to the duchy of Bohemia after the murder of Duke Svatopluk on 21 September 1109. Cf. Cosmas, *Chronicle* 3.27–31, trans. Wolverton (2009), pp. 214–21.

184 Margrave Diepold III of Cham-Vohburg and Count Berengar I of Sulzbach according to Cosmas, *Chronicle* 3.32, trans. Wolverton (2009), p. 221. See above, p. 177 nn. 293, 294.

185 Lucan, *Pharsalia* 2.136, 2.655.

Among these the most illustrious was a certain Irishman named David, formerly head of the school at Würzburg, who had been promoted by the king to be one of his chaplains because of the probity of his character and his expertise in all of the liberal arts. On the king's request he wrote about the history and all the events of this expedition in three books in so simple a style that it hardly differs from the common speech, considering in this even what the intellect of lay readers or others less learned could grasp.[186]

Thus as it is related by that same historian, the king and his contingent overcame the rugged mountains with difficulty and arrived happy and unharmed at Ivrea,[187] while the other army, having captured certain castles, joined up happily with the king (who had stormed Novarra) at Roncaglia as planned. He stayed there for a few days and then successfully crossed the Po and pitched camp at Piacenza, where he received many gifts and [promises of] complete fidelity from the citizens. Remaining in this region for three weeks, he moved on to Parma, where he conferred upon Countess Matilda,[188] who had submitted to him through messengers, his grace and her own privileges. After this, afflicted by an exceedingly severe winter, he crossed Monte Bardone[189] at great cost to the army for the deplorable loss of equipment and horses. For seven weeks they suffered the incessant deluge of great rains upon them according to the habit of that climate and at last, sorely afflicted, they reached Florence immediately before the feast of the birth of the Lord.

The year of the Lord 1111. Once King Henry had dealt with matters in Lombardy and Tuscany, he celebrated the joy of the birth of the Lord at Florence, to the immense delight of his followers and with such marvellous splendour and honour as the citizens of that country had never yet seen. Then he set out for Arezzo, where he was received favourably by the clergy but treacherously by the citizens, whose

186 William of Malmesbury, *Deeds of the English kings* 5 (420), p. 764, identifies this David as the later bishop of Bangor: 'But that expedition to Rome, accompanied by such great exertion of heart and bodily discomfort, had been described by David the Irishman, bishop of Bangor, though he inclines more to favour the king than is fitting for an historian [my translation].' In what follows (420–6, pp. 764–70), William shows that he had read David's account of the expedition.

187 The *Annals of Paderborn* 1110, p. 125, state that Henry departed 'around the Assumption of St Mary' (15 August), while the *Chronicle of St Peter at Erfurt* 1110, p. 159, states that he entered Lombardy 'around the Nativity of St Mary' (8 September). Other sources claim that the expedition was 30,000 strong: see Meyer von Knonau (1907), p. 129 n. 40.

188 See n. 39 above. See Meyer von Knonau (1907), p. 132.

189 A pass in the Apennines, south-west of Parma.

insolence he afterwards completely and abundantly crushed, for he utterly demolished their city along with the towers they had prepared to resist him, and at the request of the clergy he returned to the church all the privileges that those citizens had taken from her by force.[190] From there he advanced to Acquapendente where he found the legates he had recently sent to the pope from Arezzo bearing good news. He then sent other messengers along with those of the Romans (who had hastened to that place to submit to him)[191] and gradually proceeded to Sutri. Meeting there[192] with the pope's legates[193] and the royal messengers[194] [he was informed that] the pope was ready to crown him and to grant him every royal honour and wish if he would concede the freedom of the church, prohibit lay investiture and likewise receive back from the church all duchies, marches, counties, advocacies, monies, tolls and other *regalia* that it possessed.[195] The king gave his assent, but only on this condition: that not withstanding the strong and genuine reasons for this change, it ought to be confirmed by the agreement of a council of the whole church and the assent of the princes of the kingdom – something thought hardly to be possible, if at all.[196] After this meeting, with the legates having been dismissed and hostages given by both sides,[197] the king cheerfully hastened to the City, where the lord pope and all the clergy, or rather the whole of Rome, prepared to meet him.

It would take too long to relate what happened after that: how he was received with immense honour and led in the ancient Roman manner

---

190 *MGH DD H. V* no. 62 (19 January 1111), in which Henry V confirmed the privileges granted by Henry IV in 1081 (*MGH DD H. IV* 2 no. 335, pp. 439–41). See Meyer von Knonau (1907), p. 138.

191 The letter he sent to Rome with these messengers: *MGH Constitutiones* 1 no. 82, p. 134.

192 On 9 February.

193 Led by Cardinal Peter Pierleoni (d. 1138), subsequently antipope 'Anacletus II', 1130–8.

194 Named in *MGH Constitutiones* 1, no. 84, p. 138: Henry's chancellor Adalbert, archbishop-elect of Mainz, Count Frederick of Arnsberg, Count Herman of Winzenburg, Count Palatine Godfrey of Calw and Henry's steward Folkmar. See Meyer von Knonau (1907), p. 140.

195 The agreement of S. Maria in Turri (a small church in the complex of St Peter's), reached between the royal and papal representatives on 4 February, five days before the subsequent meeting at Sutri. Cf. *MGH Constitutiones* 1, nos 83–6, pp. 137–9. See Blumenthal (1978b), p. 9; Robinson (1990), pp. 424–5.

196 Cf. *MGH Constitutiones* 1, nos 87–8, pp. 139–40.

197 Cf. *Chronicle of Monte Cassino* 4.35, p. 501.

through the Silver Gate[198] to the ancient wheel[199] and there, having read the privileges publicly, how the princes were in a boundless tumult because of the spoliation of the church and the removal of their benefices; what immense danger there was; how there were such varied disputes that the whole day was spent there;[200] and, afterwards, how the apostolic father was taken into custody by the bishops and others faithful to the king until the emperor had been consecrated peacefully in church, just as the patriarch Jacob said to the angel, *I will not let thee go except thou bless me.*[201]

These things were done on Quinquagesima Sunday.[202] The Romans gathered throughout the night and early in the morning attacked the army of the king from all sides so that the fight had already lasted some time when the king himself ran to the aid of his army.[203] He did this with great energy; until the close of day as a *most strong soldier and excellent leader*,[204] he helped his own to victory through the grace of God and, after inflicting great slaughter, he put the enemy to ignominious flight.

Withdrawing from Rome after three days, he took the lord pope with him and treated him as honourably as possible. Responding to matters in the area as the situation demanded and pacifying all his adversaries, he celebrated the approaching Easter[205] in his camp, not far from the City. Here the long-standing dispute between him and the pope, between the kingship and the priesthood was settled. After the octave of Easter, to the great joy of the Roman people, or rather the inestimable delight of the whole church and army, before confession to St Peter, before accepting the title Augustus and the empire from Christ, and before being anointed and hallowed according to the rites of unction and being crowned with the most sublime pomp,[206] he received in person from

---

198 The *Porta argentaria*, the principal gate of the old basilica of St Peter, adorned with 975 pounds of silver by Pope Honorius I, 625–38: *Liber pontificalis* 1, p. 323.

199 The *rota porphyretica* or 'coronation wheel' on which emperors stood for coronation.

200 Cf. the contradictory accounts of Henry V's Encyclical, *MGH Constitutiones* 1, p. 151 and Paschal II's register, *MGH Constitutiones* 1, pp. 147–50. See also Blumenthal (1978b), pp. 13–15.

201 Genesis 32.26. Cf. William, *Deeds of the English kings* 5 (420), p. 764.

202 12 February. Quinquagesima Sunday: the Sunday fifty days before Easter Day, that is, the Sunday before Ash Wednesday.

203 Cf. *Chronicle of Monte Cassino* 4.39, pp. 505–6.

204 A paraphrase of Sallust, *Bellum Catilinae* 60.4.

205 2 April.

206 On 13 April.

the hand of the pope and witnessed by the church standing there the privilege of ecclesiastical investiture according as it had pleased the predecessors of both and had been accustomed to continue, the absolute immutability of which the pope then confirmed on pain of anathema.[207] Thus finally on that day *glory* was returned *to God in the highest, and on earth peace to men of good will,*[208] as it may be said, since this long-standing and thus-far incorrigible scandal and schism in the kingdom of Christ was removed.

Not long afterwards, Henry distributed so many gifts of such great size and kind with munificent imperial liberality to his spiritual father the pope, each of the cardinal bishops and the greater and lesser clergy, that they seemed almost incredible to those who were not there. After the pope and all [with him] had prayed for his prosperity and, bound to him with great affection, had escorted him for a considerable while, he joyfully returned through Lombardy[209] to the Alps and thence to Germany.[210]

After his return what seemed to need correction was polished to a shine, not only by the king himself but also by the bishops who had accompanied him according to what the high pontiff had conceded and enjoined to each, and faults were *purged clean.*[211] Thus as Christ looked down on the earth from His holy heaven, everywhere devotion and the Christian religion began to increase and there too were prosperity, abundant crops and new joy.

Holding court at Mainz,[212] the king invested his chancellor Adalbert,[213] who had already been elected to that very seat, with the staff and ring.

The year of the Lord 1112. Count Siegfried,[214] who had been sufficiently afflicted by his long imprisonment, was reconciled to the king and released through the counsel and petition of the princes.[215] The king

---

207 The Treaty of Ponte Mammolo (11 April), *MGH Constitutiones* 1, nos 91–6, pp. 142–5. See Robinson (1990), p. 429.

208 Luke 2.14.

209 Henry's diplomas show that he returned through Morengo, Verona and the vicinity of Lake Garda: *MGH DD H. V,* nos 73–80.

210 He was in Bavaria by 24 June, when he issued a privilege for the church of Passau: *MGH DD H. V,* no. 84.

211 Isaiah 1.25.

212 On 15 August.

213 Archbishop Adalbert I of Mainz, 1109/11–37. See Büttner (1973), p. 396.

214 See n. 102 above.

215 At Goslar, shortly before Christmas 1111. See Meyer von Knonau (1907), p. 219.

began to treat him so kindly that he even sponsored the baptism of his son and promised to forget past injuries.[216]

At that time the aforementioned Adalbert, who had been designated archbishop of Mainz, who was second to the king in all matters and without whose advice the king would do nothing, was accused of conspiring against the emperor with several of the princes – which hardly anyone could believe.[217] When the matter became known the king had him taken into custody.[218]

The year of the Lord 1113. Emperor Henry celebrated Christmas at Erfurt. Duke Lothar,[219] the aforementioned Siegfried, Margrave Rudolf,[220] Wipert the Elder,[221] Count Palatine Frederick[222] and Count Ludwig[223] started a rebellion against the emperor.[224] He led an army against them without delay and did not cease to attack them with fire and the destruction of their fortifications until Siegfried was killed by his faithful followers,[225] Lothar and Rudolf were reconciled,[226] and Frederick and Wipert the Elder were justly captured and held in

---

216 That is, he became godfather to Siegfried's son.
217 In December 1112 Henry V published a letter to the princes accusing Adalbert of usurping royal privileges and fomenting treachery: *MGH DD H. V*, no. 110. Cf. Helmold of Bosau, *Chronicle*, p. 81; trans. Tschan (1966), p. 135. See Mayer von Knonau (1907), pp. 259–63; Weinfurter (1999), pp. 174–5; Stroll (2004), pp. 211–14.
218 Adalbert was imprisoned until 1115. See Ekkehard, *Chronicle* 1115, below, p. 247.
219 See n. 153 above.
220 Count Rudolf I of Stade (d. 1124), margrave of the Saxon North March 1106–14.
221 Count Wiprecht II of Groitzsch (d. 1124). See n. 183 above.
222 Frederick I of Sommerschenburg (d. 1120), count palatine of Saxony.
223 Count Ludwig II of Thuringia (d. 1123).
224 A reference to the second of two conflicts between Henry V and the Saxon princes in 1112. In spring Lothar of Supplinburg and Rudolf of Stade rebelled over the imprisonment of Count Frederick of Stade. Cf. *Annals of Paderborn* 1112, p. 125: 'Duke Lothar and Margrave Rudolf quarrelled with the emperor. On this account the emperor was furious and each was condemned by the judgement of the princes.' They were deposed, but submitted and were reinstated at Salzwedel in June. The second conflict, which involved a larger number of princes, was sparked by the claims of Count Palatine Siegfried to the inheritance of his kinsman Count Udalric of Weimar, who had died without an heir and whose possessions had been appropriated by the king. Cf. Ekkehard, *Chronicle* 1112, below, pp. 243–4. See Meyer von Knonau (1907), pp. 251–8.
225 9 March. Siegfried died of wounds inflicted at Warmstädt (near Quedlinburg) when the rebels were defeated by a royal army under the command of Count Hoier of Mansfeld. Cf. Ekkehard, *Chronicle* 1113, below, p. 244. See Meyer von Knonau (1907), pp. 271–2.
226 Lothar submitted and was reconciled at an assembly in Mainz at Epiphany 1114.

custody; and thus fortune, or rather the grace of Christ, brought things to an end.

In the same year the emperor, unwilling that any discord should arise in his kingdom, led an expedition against a certain Rainald of Mousson, who had opposed him and devastated the possessions of his bishoprics.[227] He besieged the castle of Bar and, although Rainald defended it manfully, he captured him and many nobles of that country, and burned that castle to the ground.

The year of the Lord 1114. Emperor Henry celebrated Christmas in Bamberg and arranged for his wedding at Mainz at the coming Epiphany;[228] for three years before he had been betrothed to Matilda,[229] the daughter of Henry, king of the English.[230] She was a virgin of noble manners, charming and beautiful of face, and was held in distinction and glory in the Roman empire as well as in the English kingdom. Her forbears on both sides came from a long line of magnificent nobility and royal stock; the mark of future goodness radiated abundantly in her words and deeds to such an extent that all wished her to be the mother of the heir to the Roman empire. Such a multitude of archbishops, bishops, dukes, counts, abbots and provosts as well as the most erudite clerics assembled for this wedding that no old man of the times could remember or in any way testify to having seen or even heard of such a multitude of so many of the nobles coming together in one place. At this wedding there were assembled five archbishops, thirty bishops and five dukes, among whom the duke of Bohemia[231] was the high cupbearer. The number of counts, abbots and provosts could not be guessed by anyone present, be he ever so wise. No chronicler of the emperor could describe in writing the gifts that many kings and innumerable nobles sent to the lord emperor on the occasion of his wedding, or those that the emperor distributed to the innumerable multitude of jesters and play-actors as well as to many different types of people – to such an extent that none of his chamberlains could keep track of who received and who gave.[232]

---

227 Count Rainald of Bar and Mousson (d. 1149). Rainald was involved in a conflict with Bishop Richard of Verdun: Stroll (2004), pp. 207–9.

228 The wedding took place on 7 January.

229 Matilda (d. 1167). See Chibnall (1993).

230 Henry I (1068/9–1135), king of England 1100, duke of Normandy 1106. See Hollister (2001).

231 Vladislav I, duke of Bohemia 1109–17, 1120–5.

232 In the manuscript the remainder of this annal has been copied by a different hand

In the same year as this wedding the princes swore to undertake an expedition against the Frisians in the second week after Whitsun.[233] The Frisians had refused to give the subjection they owed to the lord emperor and to pay the lawful tribute that is due every year. Swollen with insolence and trusting in their fortified places, they disdained to submit to any lord or to follow the orders of anyone, even if he were very powerful. But when the army began to advance against them, the archbishop of Cologne[234] and certain other princes impeded its march. With his citizens and many knights as well as with help from various counts he began fiercely to resist his lord the emperor and to harass his followers day and night. Therefore, with the counsel and consent of his princes the emperor returned to Mainz *empty-handed*,[235] frustrated in his and his followers' effort. But he who had devised this rebellion against the emperor had no pretext of which they could accuse him other than that one of the king's *ministeriales* had exercised his lordship too ferociously in his lands.

---

and is probably a subsequent addition.
233 17 May.
234 Archbishop Frederick I; see n. 23 above; Meyer von Knonau (1907), pp. 298–301.
235 Sallust, *Bellum Iugurthinum* 58.7.

EKKEHARD OF AURA, *CHRONICLE*, BOOK 5 (1106–16)

To Erkembert, the *faithful and prudent steward*[1] of the house of Christ, and his handsome flock who under such a fine shepherd keep watch over Christ's martyrs Stephen and Vitus,[2] brother Ekkehard and the other poor of St Laurence, though oppressed by great burdens, send what *unfeigned charity*[3] they can. For lo, while we left our own burden in the middle of the road, since your authority imposed this large responsibility upon us, we have – thanks be to God and praise to Christ! – persevered to the end. Only because of charity – since nothing is impossible when God is present[4] – can we justly believe that, with His hand always outstretched, our insignificant person could do so much. See how we have hurried through and abbreviated the narrations of various chroniclers from the beginning of the world and supplied with our own pen the deeds of our times, hoping – albeit not without danger to our own reputation – that the wish of your command be satisfied. Consequently, to remedy boredom this work is divided into five books. The first finishes with the founding of the city of Rome, the second with the birth of Christ, the third with the emperorship of Charles[5] and the fourth with one who is still alive and is called Emperor Henry V.[6] It did not seem incongruous to inscribe the fifth book with his name; at the advice of one of our scribes we have decided to finish with that book. At the end of the work we have also added a little book, which we call *Hierosolimita* and which we do not doubt, O venerable father, will be a special alleviation of the pilgrimage that God has now inspired in you.[7] But the one thing for which we long with all our hearts and for which we ask above all as compensation for our work, is that this present volume may

---

1 Luke 12.42.
2 St Stephen the Protomartyr (see Acts 6.8–7.59). St Vitus (d. 303), martyred during the persecutions of Diocletian and Maximian.
3 2 Corinthians 6.6.
4 An allusion to the antiphon *Ubi caritas et amor Deus ibi est* ('Where there is charity and love, there God is'); see also 1 John 4.8.
5 Charles the Great (d. 814), king of the Franks 768, emperor 800.
6 Henry V (1086–1125), king 1098, emperor 1111.
7 Erkembert went on pilgrimage to Jerusalem in 1117: *Annals of Hildesheim* 1117, p. 64.

perpetually pay the debt of our service to the monastery of Corvey and, renewing the old friendship that we established under our most beloved father Marcward[8] of blessed memory, that it may stand out in future as a monument to the poor of St Laurence in the library of St Vitus. To this end, because of your great and not-unmerited reverence, we are sending Amel, the prior of our congregation, with the fervent affection of our love. He is of one mind with us but, nonetheless, is deeply devoted to you and will, since you intend to follow the footsteps of Christ, make our heartfelt farewell to you in person on our behalf. As a well-known mediator between our two congregations and as a suitable witness he is authorized to confirm by mouth our desire for confraternity and, if anything has been neglected in these letters, to answer both on our behalf and yours. We pray unceasingly and with one spirit for your well-being here and your eternal life.

HERE BEGINS THE PROLOGUE[9]

In your golden times – O my king may you live for ever! – I, Ekkehard, so insignificant a little man, restored after years of misery, having excerpted the trifling works of different chroniclers and being carried on a voyage[10] from the beginning to the end of time through the manifold threats of Charybdis and Scylla,[11] have finally reached the port of your glorious reign, which delights me beyond every human degree. And so – not unreasonably I believe – I am denying the prize of freedom to my pen, which desires it exceedingly as it is already worn out. Rather, I submit most devotedly that it will henceforward serve your praises with more and more vigour as long as it is guided by these fingers. Why not? For you, O lord of nations, are the ruler finally and with difficulty obtained from the Father of Life by the many tears of those sitting in sadness; and, therefore, not without just cause does every catholic and orthodox member of the church follow you with all good will; raising himself up from the dust, with indescribable delight he wishes you joy of the whole Roman world from sea to sea or, rather, *from the rising up*

---

8 Abbot Marcward of Corvey, 1081–1107.
9 Berlin, Preußischer Kulturbesitz, Staatsbibliothek zu Berlin, MS lat. fol. 295, fol. 99v. This heading and the heading at the end of this prologue (n. 17 below) are not printed in *Chroniken*, pp. 206–9. See above, pp. 68–9.
10 A literary work as a sea voyage: Jerome, *Letters* 1.2, CSEL 54, pp. 1–2.
11 Two sea monsters in Greek mythology, situated on opposite sides of the Strait of Messina. Ovid, *Metamorphoses* 8; Augustine, *Meditations* 24 (PL 40.0919). More likely Isidore, *Etymologies* 13.18.3–6 and 14.6.32.

of the sun until the going down of the same.[12] In you all sound and wise hearts observe the *raising up of a just branch to David*;[13] but especially the servants of God, everywhere bursting from their hiding places take you for *a light shining in darkness*;[14] they tell of God's prophecies in relation to you and testify that the *time of mercy has already come*;[15] it is confidently believed that it is the fruit of their service to Christ the king to hear that which is just and holy from your innate character. May your times be blessed and prolonged more gloriously than those of your magnificent forbears, your grandfather and mother, if you prepare a dwelling place[16] in your most august heart for the Spirit who day and night asks and invokes the prayers of all those pleasing to God on your behalf.

HERE ENDS THE PROLOGUE

HERE BEGINS THE FIFTH BOOK[17]

The year of the Lord 1106. [18]*At the instigation of the younger Henry,*[19] *a council of the whole German kingdom was held in Mainz at Christmas, the size of which had not been seen for many years. Participants report that fifty-two princes or more were present and that only the Saxon duke named Magnus,*[20] *impeded by his great age, was noted as absent. The legates of the apostolic see, namely the bishops of Albano*[21] *and Constance,*[22] *arrived there and proclaimed to the whole multitude the sentence of excommunication against the elder Henry,*[23] *the so-called emperor, which so many successive popes had promulgated both orally and in writing. Moreover, they confirmed by the authority of Christ and St Peter that the entire church spread throughout*

---

12 Psalm 112.3.

13 Jeremiah 23.5.

14 See Psalm 111.4; John 1.5.

15 See Psalm 101.14.

16 See John 14.23.

17 Berlin, Preußischer Kulturbesitz, Staatsbibliothek zu Berlin, MS lat. fol. 295, fol. 99v. See n. 9 above.

18 *1106 Continuation* 1106, above, pp. 184–6; *Anonymous imperial chronicle* 1106, above, pp. 201–2.

19 Henry V.

20 Magnus Billung, duke in Saxony 1073–1106.

21 Cardinal Bishop Richard of Albano, 1101–15. Other sources imply that Richard was not at Mainz: see Jakobs (1961), pp. 33 n. 22, 220–1.

22 Gebhard of Zähringen, bishop of Constance 1084–1110.

23 Henry IV of Germany (1050–1106).

the whole world had already been separated from communion with him for many years. Wherefore, when he [Henry IV] himself was tempted to leave the castle where he was staying to go to Mainz, the princes, in order to avoid an uprising of the common crowd (for they were accustomed to favour the party of the father more than that of the son), hastened to meet him at Ingelheim and, surrounding him, finally led him back to the general council to confess his guilt and promise satisfaction.[24] *Since the legates could not restore him to communion or impose penance without the judgement of a general synod and apostolic advice, he assented to the advice of his own party as well as that of the council and gave the regalia or imperial insignia – namely the cross and lance, the sceptre, orb and crown – into the hands of his son, praying for his prosperity and commending him to the foremost princes with many tears; and he promised from then on for the sake of his soul to heed the decrees of the great high priest and the whole church.*[25] *This done, Henry, the fifth of that name, was elected to the kingship for the second time, first by his father and then by all of the German princes.*[26] *He was also confirmed in a catholic manner through the imposition of hands by the apostolic legates and,*[27] *having accepted oaths from both the bishops and the laity according to the custom of the country, he began to rule in the* eighty-second *place since Augustus, in the fiftieth year of his father, in the* one-thousand-eight-hundred-and-fifty-eighth *year since the founding of the city, in the* five-thousand-and-fifty-eighth *year since the beginning of the world and, as it is called, in the* eleven-hundred-and-sixth *year since the Incarnation of the Lord.*

After the many and long-standing defilements of the churches in this kingdom had been related in the presence of the king and all the princes and bishops from the whole of Germany as well as the clergy and people and the legates of the Roman see, and after all had unanimously promised their eradication, it pleased both the king and the leading men to send to the holy Mother Church of Rome so many and such legates from these parts as were appropriate to give a proper account of the allegations, to investigate what was doubtful intelligently and to consult wisely on all things for the benefit of the church. For this work men full of the spirit of wisdom[28] *were chosen, not unworthy of respect either before God or the world because of their dignity, birth, sophistication*

---

24 31 December 1105. See Robinson (1999), pp. 336–7.
25 Cf. Henry IV, *Letters* 37, 39, pp. 49–50, 56–7.
26 On 5 January 1106 at Mainz: *Annals of Hildesheim* 1106, p. 55.
27 From Archbishop Ruothard of Mainz: *Annals of Hildesheim* 1106, p. 56.
28 Deuteronomy 34.9; Sirach 15.5.

and wealth:[29] *Archbishops Bruno of Trier from Lotharingia*[30] *and Henry of Magdeburg from Saxony,*[31] *Otto of Bamberg from Franconia*[32] *and Eberhard of Eichstätt from Bavaria,*[33] *each designated bishop, Gebhard of Constance from Swabia, as well as several other bishops and even many noble laymen from the side of the king.*[34] *Among other things, they received the particular command, if it were possible, to entreat the lord pope to come across the Alps.*

Thus without doubt the light of orthodoxy, which for so many years had been obscured, began to shine in our land. The heresy of Wibert,[35] or of Henry, was made public and debated, judged and convicted, stank and was spat out, was condemned and anathematized; the heretics abdicated or fled, catholic men were placed on the bishops' thrones and some were consecrated on that feast day. So suddenly did zeal for divine law boil over that the dead bodies of pseudo-bishops were even removed from their churches and however many had been ordained by them were suspended from their offices pending a general hearing. The Roman church, whose *horn* had already been divinely *exalted*[36] to *strike fear*[37] into all members of the schismatics, even scattered the bones of their leader – namely Wibert who had been called pope – from his grave, which had been in the possession of the church of Ravenna for six years,[38] and decided to annul all his decrees, which were in truth not those of a true apostolic priest, but of an apostate invader.

In the meantime Werner,[39] one of the king's *ministeriales*, who controlled the march that is in the area of Ancona, all but resuscitated this same heresy by collecting troops from every part of Italy, corrupting many of the Romans with much money while the lord pope was staying on the borders of Benevento, and by imposing a certain pseudo-abbot of Farfa

---

29 *Anonymous imperial chronicle* 1106, above, p. 202.

30 Bruno of Laufen, archbishop of Trier 1101–24.

31 Archbishop Henry of Magdeburg, 1102–6/7.

32 Bishop Otto of Bamberg, 1102–39.

33 Bishop Eberhard of Eichstätt, 1099–1112.

34 Cf. the description of the emissaries in the *Translatio S. Modoaldi* 11, pp. 295–6, which identifies the Saxon Count Herman of Reinhausen.

35 Wibert of Parma, archbishop of Ravenna 1072–1100, antipope 'Clement III', 1084–1100.

36 See Psalm 88.18.

37 See 2 Maccabees 12.22.

38 'Clement III' was buried in Città Castellana, approximately 50 km north of Rome.

39 Werner, duke of Spoleto and margrave of Ancona 1093/4–1119. On Henry IV's use of *ministeriales* in government see Robinson (1999), p. 357.

upon the throne of St Peter – what sacrilege! This pope he wished the emperor to call Silvester.[40] After a short time, however, he was driven out in shame by the catholics, as he deserved, and as a reward for his madness he bore the loss of his evil and ill-gotten gains apart from the forfeiture of his faith, which his miserable blind heart did not grieve.

[41]*After this, when the aforementioned nobles came from their own parts to spend the night*[42] *in the valley of the Trent at the city of the same name, that is Trent, a certain youth named Adalbert,*[43] *who was distinguished by the possession of a certain county in those parts, rushed upon those unarmed pilgrims early in the morning with armed citizens. He plundered them, captured them and held them in custody, claiming that this had been demanded of him by messengers of his lord,* namely Henry the ex-*emperor.* For with his customary skill, Henry had, as far as he could, secretly flooded every city and province of the kingdom with all kinds of entreating letters and messengers:[44] he lamented the violence done to him by the princes, or rather that he had been expelled from the empire by his only son; he warned of the confusion in the empire that would follow his misfortune and that every single father should fear the same fate. For this reason none of the passes to Italy was open to the emissaries. Only Bishop Gebhard of Constance, who journeyed with his followers through the secret Alpine passes of Countess Matilda[45] – undoubtedly another Deborah[46] – was present at the threshold of the apostles. The other magnates who, as we have said, had been taken prisoner by this exceedingly stupid captor, were treated dishonourably except for Bishop Otto of Bamberg, whom that same Adalbert, because he was Otto's knight, thought to spare. Through Otto's mediation Bishop Bruno of Trier and Count Wibert[47] were released on condition that they meet with the ex-emperor to conclude a peace with him and then return to report what he commanded

40 Maginulf, archpriest of S. Angelo, 'Silvester IV', 1105–11.
41 *Anonymous imperial chronicle* 1106, above, p. 203.
42 3/4 March.
43 Either count of Eppan (Appiano) or of Tyrol. See Meyer von Knonau (1904), p. 295 n. 28.
44 Henry IV, *Letters* 40, 41, pp. 58–64 (*IL*, pp. 195–200). See Robinson (1999), pp. 341–3.
45 Countess Matilda of Tuscany (1046–1115).
46 Judges 4–5: the heroine Deborah who freed Israel from King Jabin of Canaan. The parallel was frequently applied by Gregorian writers: Ranger of Lucca, *Vita metrica Anselmi,* p. 1232; Donizo of Canossa, *Life of Matilda* 2.8, p. 394; Paul of Bernried, *Life of Pope Gregory VII* 59, p. 506, trans. Robinson (2004b), p. 303.
47 Identified by Schmale-Ott as Count Wiprecht II (Wibert) of Groitzsch (d. 1124): *Chroniken,* p. 277 n. 17.

regarding the others. [48]*But Jesus, who is always close to* all *those who call upon Him*[49] *and especially to those whose hearts are troubled,*[50] *suddenly sent Duke Welf of Bavaria*[51] *upon these rebels; like a sword drawn from His scabbard, he came on the third day with strong forces and broke open the barricaded confines. He forced the citizens to accept Gebhard,*[52] an esteemed man, who had been made the new bishop *of the church of Trent by* the catholic king, although they had conspired never to have him. He so terrified Adalbert and his wicked accomplices that they brought out the princes whom they had captured, returned the castle to the new bishop and, moreover, with bare feet begged mercy of those they had afflicted.

Then also from the first week of Lent – during the middle of which we had endured these things – we saw a comet of immense brightness [lasting] until the Passion of the Lord. Returning poorer rather than richer, with every one having lost something, we learned from inauspicious reports that Henry our king was enduring some misfortune from several seditious rebellions against him in Alsace. For the king's father had attracted to himself not insignificant support against his son, that is from the bishop of Liège,[53] Duke Henry of Lotharingia,[54] Cologne, Jülich and Bonn – which is also called Verona – as well as other towns* of those parts; and all of these threatened the wavering catholic religion in some measure.

But[55] *strengthened by divine confidence* and no less enlivened by his innate magnanimity, *King Henry turned to Liège as if to humble the lands of his enemies by holding his Easter*[56] *court there. Nevertheless, although he celebrated Palm Sunday with full joy in Cologne, which had been yielded by his enemies, once his forces had moved on he felt again the wheel of fortune*[57] *revolve to his disadvantage, since the matter was without doubt rashly handled. For when he became aware of the machinations of his father – ever a warrior*

---

48 *Anonymous imperial chronicle* 1106, above, pp. 203–4.
49 See Psalm 144.18.
50 Psalm 33.19.
51 Duke Welf V of Bavaria, 1101–20.
52 Bishop Gebhard of Trent, 1106–20.
53 Bishop Otbert of Liège, 1092–1116.
54 Count Henry of Limburg, 1082–1119, duke of Lower Lotharingia 1101–6 (Luxemburg family).
55 *Anonymous imperial chronicle* 1106, above, p. 204.
56 25 March.
57 Cicero, *In Pisonem* 10.

*from his youth*⁵⁸ – who had sufficient resources to hire and equip troops to defend the city where the assembly was to be held, as we wrote, *he* [Henry V], *blazing with youthful impetuosity and consumed with rage, hastened to meet him with only a small force.* On account of this, *he sent 300 men to guard the bridge over the River Maas, which had been constructed at the place called Visé, for all the other crossings on the river had been destroyed by his enemies. While the king was celebrating Maundy Thursday at the palace of Aachen,* Duke Henry and the imperial forces *attacked the royal forces at the bridge; and though the king's knights steadfastly resisted the great feats of horsemanship – for those people employ them more than others – he* [Duke Henry] *surrounded them on the plain with much greater numbers, overwhelmed them, scattered them and captured them, while some even fell into the river and were devoured by it.*⁵⁹ *You may observe here the most strong Maccabees battling for catholic peace who, after the slaughter of many by an apostate people, with great faith and happiness commended their souls to Christ who had suffered for them and consoled each other that by dying in such a manner they would acquire forgiveness of their former sins on this day of indulgence. Through these vagaries of fortune*⁶⁰ *or rather through the disposition of the divine judge, the minds of the* heretics *began to swell with pride but, nevertheless, the hope of the orthodox did not fade. Then during the Easter festivities, which were being celebrated at Bonn because of events, the king deprived Duke Henry of his duchy (since by the judgement of the princes he was guilty of contumacy and an enemy of the commonwealth) and, having accepted oaths from the princes, announced and prepared for a general expedition against Lotharingia.* While he then turned south, his father returned to Cologne and, expelling the bishop, fortified the city mightily with *ramparts*⁶¹ *and bulwarks and excellent defence mechanisms of every kind*, and then took himself to Liège.

Consequently, *about the middle of June* King Henry *besieged Cologne with* a very large army of *20,000; but since it possessed* a great number of defences *of every kind, he was detained there for three or four weeks in almost futile effort,*⁶² *excepting the youths, who are wont to be impatient of delay,*⁶³

---

58 1 Kings 17.33. The reference is to Goliath (and David, by implication, signifies Henry V).

59 Compare the account of the *Life of Henry IV* 12, pp. 38–9 (*IL*, pp. 131–2). See Robinson (1999), p. 339.

60 Ammianus Marcellinus, *Res gestae* 31.19.13.

61 *Anonymous imperial chronicle* 1106, above, p. 205.

62 Lucan, *Pharsalia* 2.663.

63 *Ibid.* 4.424.

skirmishing in front of the walls, fleeing from or killing each other in a cruel game. There, indeed, Count Dietrich,[64] *who was most faithful to the king, was overwhelmed with sickness and went the way of all flesh. He was a man of most noble Saxon lineage, fervently dedicated as much to all manner of religion as to the defence of catholicism and was also well instructed in letters.*

Meanwhile, messengers of the father sent from Liège presented themselves before King Henry carrying letters for him and for the princes of the kingdom, an example of which I do not think it out of place to insert here to attest to the manifold evasions of this man, who had up to this point his whole life long got the better of all who resisted him through feigned submission.

Henry,[65] *by the grace of God august emperor of the Romans, to the bishops, dukes, margraves, counts and other princes of the kingdom, sends his grace and love to those worthy to receive it. I lament before Almighty God and my Lady, holy Mary*[66] *and blessed Peter our patron, prince of the apostles, and before all you princes, how unjustly and inhumanely and cruelly we have been treated, having trusted in that loyalty which we ought not to have been obliged to doubt; and how the honour of the kingship as well as its estates and everything we had has been plundered from us against divine and human law to the disgrace and reproach of the kingdom, so that absolutely nothing save only our own life has been left untouched. When almost all of you were there, the greater part of you seemed aggrieved and sad but – but alas! – your sadness brought us nothing but the satisfaction of our enemies' odious desires towards us. And although, on the advice and request of our son who had previously promised us loyalty and security for our life and dignity, we endeavoured to go to Mainz faithfully and eagerly to meet the Roman legates and the princes so that we might conduct ourselves according to their plan – as much for the state of the church and the honour of the kingdom as for the salvation of our own soul – because he had no respect for this desire and our obedience, he took us captive contrary to his promise of loyalty and has brought us almost to the brink of death; thus we dared not entrust ourselves to him lest he treat us as before with the injuries and indignities of which he is capable. Wherefore, we ask you many times and entreat you strenuously that you should strive diligently for the fear of God, the honour of the kingdom and your honesty, for as by your hands injury was done to us, so by you can we regain justice. We are also prepared, on your advice and the advice of others who do not hate us as well as that of*

---

64 Count Dietrich III of Kaltenburg (d. 1106). See Meyer von Knonau (1904), p. 310.
65 Henry IV, *Letter* 41, pp. 61–3, with abridgements.
66 Henry IV's devotion to the Blessed Virgin: Robinson (1999), pp. 203, 258, 285, 352–3.

devout men, freely to make amends if we have in any way offended our son or anyone else in the kingdom. Moreover, as we were ready to obey the lord pope in the presence of his legates and all of you, so are we now prepared to show him all due reverence and the sincere obedience and devotion of our heart in his presence, and to regulate, as far as is within us, the situation of the church and the honour of the kingdom as much according to your counsel as to that of our spiritual father, Abbot Hugh of Cluny,[67] and other devout men. Since, therefore, we are prepared to do all these things, we ask and strenuously entreat you, for God, for the honour of the kingdom and for your own honour urgently to admonish our son – for according to the aforementioned agreement he had no remaining complaint against us – henceforth to desist from persecuting us and our followers, and to permit us to live quietly and peacefully so that the aforementioned [process] may be accomplished honestly and in tranquillity. But if he is unwilling, we ask you by the authority of the Roman church to which we have committed ourselves and the honour of the kingdom, not to descend upon us or our followers; for it is manifest that all this began, not out of zeal for divine law nor out of love for the Roman church, but out of a lust for royal power which unjustly deprived his father [of the kingdom]. In regard to which, should your appeal or any other intervention not prove useful in the present matter, we shall appeal to the Roman pontiff and the holy universal Roman see and church.

After this and another shorter letter – not unlike the former in sense and intention but nevertheless specifically directed at the son[68] – had been read in the presence of them all, King Henry, on the advice of the princes, decided to send a legation to his father, [the purpose of] which was first made known in public by Archbishop Henry of Magdeburg, who by doing so strengthened the spirits of the people very much. It went as follows:[69]

'After the inveterate schism in the Roman empire for about the last forty years, which has seen the obliteration of virtually all laws both divine and human – to say nothing of all types of death, sacrilege, perjury, robbery and arson – this kingdom of ours has been reduced not only to a wilderness but even to apostasy from the catholic faith, if not to very paganism. Divine mercy, considering at last His church and us, the sons of that same bride of Christ, has converted us with equanimity to unity of faith; and the incorrigible leader of that schism, namely Henry who

---

67 Hugh I ('the Great'), abbot of Cluny 1049–1109, godfather of Henry IV.
68 Henry IV, *Letter* 40, pp. 58–60 (*IL*, pp. 195–7).
69 See Erdmann (1939), 228.

is called our emperor, we have renounced out of zeal for God and obedience to the apostolic faith, and have elected ourselves a catholic king born of his very same seed. Seeing that the beginning of this reign was the end of his own, he himself [Henry IV], so to speak, even voluntarily commended him [Henry V] (though all too reluctantly as his letters reveal), returned the *regalia*, tearfully committed the care of his son and the kingdom to our fidelity and for the rest promised, moreover, to desire no longer the pomp of royalty but rather to care for the salvation of his soul. But, lo and behold, now he tries to restore himself with his former evasions and complains throughout the whole world that he has been prejudged. The swords of the French,[70] English, Danes and other peoples on our borders he intends to thrust into our hearts because of the injuries inflicted upon him and he begs to have justice restored to him. He also readily promises to follow our advice, but in reality he is attempting with his usual tricks to scatter the *camp of the Lord*,[71] to disarm the Christian army and, as is obvious, he is preparing himself like a wild beast to *devour* again *the vineyard* [72] of the Lord that had only lately begun to bloom, and, evidently, with those *foxes* who are the pestilential men that follow him, to *demolish*[73] and by the sacrilegious priests of Baal to return to recurring anathema, or rather – and this is abominable – to crucify Christ, who has risen again in His church, in the hearts of all. Wherefore, it pleases both the king and all the princes of the kingdom, or rather the whole orthodox army, that the elder one – to avoid giving him any just complaint against us – should have whatever security he chooses, whatever place he prefers to put his case before this present senate and people so that he may receive justice and render justice in order that all causes of conflict – as if conflict had decided anything yet – from the beginning of the schism may be in all respects discussed. Thus justice will answer both to the son and the father, and the status of the church and kingdom, which is divided by these controversies, will be decided, not as he [Henry IV] proposes after a long truce, but immediately.'

An embassy composed of especially wise and prudent persons, namely the priests Albuin and Richwin[74] as well as certain laymen known for

---

70 Henry IV had written to the French king about his treatment: *Letter* 39, pp. 52–8 (*IL*, pp. 190–5).
71 See Genesis 32.2.
72 See Isaiah 3.14.
73 See Song of Songs 2.15.
74 Unidentified.

their piety, was sent by the king and the princes, or indeed by the whole army, to the oft-mentioned ex-emperor, but could hardly obtain permission to speak in his presence. It is horrible to recall what great danger their lives were in for six days because they in no way wished to mix with that *gathering of evildoers*,[75] how indignantly they were treated and how, finally, they were freed by a mob who stormed the place where they were being held and were led back to the camp outside Cologne without an escort. As to the main point of the elder's response, they reported that for the present arms should be laid down and that a general assembly should be summoned for the future to discuss this conflict.

It was heard, meanwhile, that the ex-emperor Henry and the ex-duke Henry[76] were gathering an army from every direction and were in every way ready to tempt fortune once more. Thus the whole army of the king, or rather of Christ, resolved finally to end matters with the sword, lest – as was certain – the emperor's citizens should come to his aid against them.[77] They broke siege and moved into Lotharingia,[78] laying waste to the fortifications and other goods of the rebels along their way and sending messengers to the elder Henry for a second time. They gave him the choice either of hastening to Aachen and ratifying the aforementioned pact with his son for the sake of peace or of expecting imminent and certain war. After these messengers had been taken into custody, he [Henry IV] began – albeit secretly – to prepare himself in every way to resist. But these messengers, who were released after a few days, were followed by the unexpected news – and nothing more acceptable could have been brought into this camp – of the death of Emperor Henry.[79] It is miserable to relate how a man of such an exalted name, such status and such spirit, who had dominated the world for so long while professing Christianity, was himself not even mourned piously or compassionately like any dead pauper, as any Christian at all deserves, but how the hearts and mouths of all true Christians everywhere were filled with boundless joy at the rumour of his death. Israel did not resound the praises of the Lord louder when Pharaoh was

---

75 Psalm 63.3.
76 Duke Henry of Lower Lotharingia; see n. 54 above.
77 Henry IV consistently enjoyed the support of German cities, particularly those in the Rhineland.
78 Cf. *Annals of Paderborn* 1106, p. 114. See Meyer von Knonau (1904), pp. 307–11; Robinson (1999), p. 342.
79 7 August 1106.

drowned,[80] neither did Rome applaud the triumphant Octavian nor any other emperor more gloriously! For the *bridle that was in the jaws of the people*[81] had been turned for them into *a song as in the night of sanctified solemnity.*[82] Therefore, since the *oppressor* at last had *come to nothing and the tribute had ceased,*[83] soon all who had once adhered to that prince merely for the sake of gain and handed over their souls out of venality surrendered themselves both to the king and the catholic communion. Bishop Otbert of Liège and other co-bishops were received back into communion with penance on condition that the body of the excommunicate, which Otbert had buried the previous day in his church, should be exhumed and deposited in non-consecrated ground without any burial rites or obsequies, as sanctioned by the archbishops and bishops who were there – for he who lives out of communion with the church cannot enjoy communion even in death. These things being done,[84] shortly afterwards his corpse was, with the approval of the king, brought to the city of Speyer in a stone sarcophagus and remained unburied outside the church for several years.[85]

This was the end, this was the downfall, this was the ultimate fate of Henry who was called the fourth Roman emperor of that name by his own, but suitably called by catholics – that is by all those preserving fealty and obedience to St Peter and his successors according to Christian law – archpirate and heresiarch, as well as apostate and persecutor of souls more than bodies. Not content with natural and ordinary wickedness, he was disgraced for thinking up and executing new and for ages unheard-of and therefore all the more incredible [crimes]. If someone wishes to write who shares the opinion of those who judge that both the good and the evil deeds of the emperor are worthy of record, then we shall step back, above all because we do not doubt that it is better to commit some things to oblivion than to memory. *We*[86] *could prove from the evidence of very many witnesses that no one in our times seemed more fitted for the office of emperor by birth, intelligence, courage and boldness and* even *by stature and bodily grace,* if only the vile man had not

80 See Exodus 15.4.
81 Isaiah 30.28.
82 Isaiah 30.29.
83 Isaiah 14.4.
84 Henry IV's body was exhumed on 15 August.
85 The body was eventually buried at the cathedral in Speyer on 7 August 1111: Robinson (1999), pp. 343–4.
86 Cf. *Anonymous imperial chronicle* 1106, above, p. 205.

degenerated and surrendered in the battle with vice. Although there are still not a few left, and in high positions, who are guilty of assisting the actions of this man, there is one thing that we wish to suggest, albeit with great temerity: that the example of his condemnation may be a remedy, so that they turn and pursue not the perverse flower of honour but attend to the seed; for it is preferable to struggle to eradicate weeds than to pluck in the future the fruit of eternal death.[87] Moreover, it is as exceedingly foolish to believe that a sword wound will heal completely as to wish to *serve God* and *mammon*[88] at the same time, and a monstrosity similar to the arrogant loftiness of the pharisees to climb by sacrilegious payment, as they say, and usurp the dignity of apostolic humility, or to hope for the fruits of hierarchy from the seeds of apostasy. But this will suffice. Thanks be to God who, although late, nevertheless granted an utterly magnificent victory to His church, since that same Galilean who once defeated Julian[89] has turned the *fiftieth year* of the exactions of Nebuchadnezzar into a year of *jubilee*.[90] If there are indeed some zealots who, for the posterity of the church, cannot ignore the day of Henry's death like the day Aman[91] perished, know that it was the seventh Ides of August [7 August], namely the day on which he first attacked his mother the church on the Unstrut[92] and sent innumerable souls to the underworld, that same day of Mars on which he accustomed himself to perpetrating all his arts by pagan auspices.

[93]*After this, in the fourth week of the month of October, a general council was held in the province of Lombardy, on the River Po at the place that is named* Guastalla,[94] *where all things were presided over by Pope Paschal II in the presence of a vast multitude of clerics as well as laymen who had come together from* the churches *of different kingdoms; also present were legates*

---

87 See Matthew 15.13.

88 Matthew 6.24.

89 Julian 'the Apostate' (d. 363), Roman emperor 355. A reference to the reputed dying words of Julian: 'You have defeated me, Galilean, you have defeated me.' Cf. Frutolf, *Chronicle* 364, *MGH SS* 6, p. 114.

90 Leviticus 25.10–11. The parallel was apposite since 1106 was the fiftieth year of Henry IV's kingship.

91 Aman, servant of King Ahasuerus and persecutor of the Jews: see Esther 7.10.

92 Ekkehard has confused the Battle of Homburg on the River Unstrut (9 June 1075) with the Battle of Mellrichstadt (7 August 1078). See Frutolf, *Chronicle* 1075, 1078, above, pp. 113, 117.

93 See *Anonymous imperial chronicle* 1106, above, pp. 206–7.

94 The Synod of Guastalla, c. 22 October 1106. See Blumenthal (1978b), pp. 36–73.

from the lord king, Henry.[95] *As the canons fairly dictate, many hostile tares*[96] *were rooted out,* many *structures built upon sand*[97] *were destroyed, and many seedlings of genuine stock were* planted *more deeply and watered,*[98] and many *fortified bulwarks*[99] *were raised up for the protection of the churches.* On the same Sunday, which was the twelfth Kalends of November [21 October], Conrad of Salzburg[100] and Gebhard of Trent[101] were *consecrated bishop. It would take long to relate how that indefatigable, prudent and faithful steward of the great Father of the family*[102] *amply refreshed his fellow servants each day with the wheat of the word of God, deposed pseudo-bishops,*[103] *established catholic ones, granted the pallium*[104] *to archbishops and privileges to monasteries,*[105] *instructed those shepherds of Christ's sheep in his presence with sweet addresses and those absent through letters of fatherly guidance, brought certain formerly amputated members of the church back into its body and even maimed certain members that seemed incurable with the severance of anathema. Concerning the arrangements made during the time of schism, about which many questions were raised, he promulgated a decree that with the discretion of a mother skilfully healed the innermost parts of the body* in these words:

Already[106] *for many years the breadth of the German kingdom has been separated from unity with the apostolic see. This schism has undoubtedly become so dangerous that – and it is with sadness that we say so – hardly any catholic priests or clerics are to be found in the whole breadth of the land. Since so many sons have fallen in this slaughter, necessity requires Christian peace so that the maternal bosom of the church may be opened for them. Consequently, since our Fathers have instructed us in their example and writings, which they*

---

95 On the participants see *ibid.*, pp. 38–42.
96 See Matthew 13.28–9.
97 Matthew 7.26.
98 1 Corinthians 3.8.
99 See Song of Songs 8.9.
100 Archbishop Conrad of Salzburg, 1106–47.
101 See n. 52 above.
102 Luke 12.42.
103 Those who had been invested by Henry IV and who refused to be reconciled to the papacy.
104 The pallium: the ceremonial garment of office of an archbishop, or metropolitan. See above, p. 206 n. 147.
105 *JL* 6093, 6095–7.
106 Record of the Synod of Guastalla, *MGH Constitutiones* 1, p. 565.

undertook in the various times of the Novatians,[107] *Donatists*[108] *and other heresies in their turn, we accept the episcopal offices of the existing bishops of the kingdom ordained during the schism, unless they are proven invaders or simonists or criminals. The same we ordain for clerics of any rank who are recommended by their life and learning.*

With[109] *these and such things and the joyful splendour of divine light having risen upon the church like the dawn, since at last without doubt the time of His mercy had come,*[110] *each honoured with the apostolic blessing returned to his own parts. But we who had crossed the Alps were especially joyful above all because we were certain that the journey of the lord pope had been so planned that he would follow as soon as possible and celebrate the birthday of the Lord in Mainz together with our new king and all the princes.*

In this year Duke Magnus of Saxony died[111] *and in his place Lothar*[112] *was raised up. Margrave Udo of Saxony also died.*[113] *Bishop Rupert of Würzburg died on the journey while travelling to the council* [*of Guastalla*]. *After his death, lord Erlung, who had previously been driven out, was especially sought by both the clergy and people of Würzburg, and being permitted both by the king and the pope through legates of the Roman see, he was received with great expectation and incredible joy by the whole city and many people and enthroned with great honour.*

The year of the Lord 1107.[114] *King Henry celebrated Christmas at Regensburg in the presence of legates from the lord Pope Paschal, whose arrival he had for some time been awaiting at Augsburg, the chief city of Swabia and the other southern parts* [*of Germany*]. *The pope, however, declined* [*to come*] *on the advice of his own counsellors and, as it were, because of the recklessness of the Germans, but especially because of a certain seditious rebellion that had occurred while he was staying in Verona, in addition to the suggestion of certain persons that it would not be easy for our people to accept that decree which forbade any ecclesiastical investiture from the hands of the laity and also because of the ardent heart of a youthful king, which was not yet used to the*

---

107 Supporters of Novatian, antipope 251–8.

108 Adherents of Donatus (d. 355) and the heresy named after him.

109 *Anonymous imperial chronicle* 1106, above, p. 207.

110 Psalm 101.14.

111 23 August.

112 Lothar of Supplinburg, duke of Saxony 1106–37, king (Lothar III) 1125–37.

113 Count Udo III of Stade, margrave of the Saxon North March (d. 2 June).

114 See *Anonymous imperial chronicle* 1107, above, pp. 207–9.

yoke of the Lord[115] *in all respects. Hearing this and much of its kind, I say, the man of God*[116] *considered and, since the passes to the German lands were not yet open to him, announced his departure with regret. With Spanish legates he started for France through Burgundy and by his presence greatly amplified the joy of Christmas at Cluny. Moving on from there he was received with immense honour by all churches in that territory as a true disciple of Christ and vicar of the apostles. He was treated with due reverence and he was listened to as none other than a lawgiver sent from heaven. Thus for several months as a faithful and wise steward*[117] *he bore daily the anxiety of the whole church and at last, about the Ascension of the Lord* [23 May], *he held a great council at Troyes where,*[118] *among many things, he corrected what required correction according to the times and necessity, and promulgated judgement according to the decrees of his predecessors on the free election of bishops and on restraining the presumptuousness of the laity in ecclesiastical matters.*[119]

But King Henry, who was travelling from the borders of Saxony, celebrated Easter at Mainz [14 April] *and presented himself in the vicinity of this same council – he was not present – with several of the bishops and nobles.*[120] *When he had taken counsel with them he sent honourable legates to the pope,*[121] *through whom he wished to inform both the pope and the whole synod that the power of constituting bishops had been given to Emperor Charles* [the Great] *by apostolic privileges.*[122] *Since Henry could not permit this question to be decided in a foreign kingdom, in as much as he had already begun* [the process of] *obtaining the Roman sceptre, he was granted a deferral so that he might come to Rome within the next year and discuss the same matter in a general council. Then the lord pope punished several of our bishops – those who did not attend that same council – with suspension from their office, although not long afterwards they gave satisfactory assurances and he mercifully absolved them.*[123] *Again he lamented greatly that the humility he sought could not be found in German hearts and that he could by no means visit us as he had planned; so he*

115 See Matthew 11.29–30.

116 Judges 13.6.

117 Luke 12.42.

118 The Council of Troyes (23 May 1107). See Blumenthal (1978b), pp. 74–101.

119 For the canons of the council see *ibid.*, pp. 90–6, which provides a fuller record than that of *MGH Constitutiones* 1, pp. 566–7.

120 At Verdun.

121 See above, p. 208 n. 162.

122 Cf. the spurious privilege of Pope Hadrian I, *MGH Constitutiones* 1, no. 446, pp. 659–60.

123 See above, p. 209 n. 165.

decided to return to the lands of Italy with his retinue. When he returned there after a delay, he was received with such joy by the Roman clergy and people, as if he had been revived from the dead.[124]

Meanwhile, the king returned to the eastern parts [of Germany] and held a council in Regensburg with the Bavarians,[125] at which he announced a campaign against Robert of Flanders.[126] Starting around October, he entered the land of the rebels and, not without great losses to his own army, he devastated it for more than a month until the matter was postponed to the next court by the exchange of messengers and the quarrel ended.

The year of the Lord 1108.[127] King Henry celebrated Christmas at Mainz[128] and received the aforementioned Robert back into his grace.[129]

At this time enmity broke out between King Coloman[130] of Hungary and his brother named Almus[131] because each of them insisted that he was more deserving of the royal dignity according to the law of that people. Almus lost his possessions and his duchy, which had given him prestige among the Hungarians and, as befits the brother of a king, the second place after the king. He went to King Henry and, complaining before the entire senate of his misfortune, not unlike Atherbal the brother of Hiempsal,[132] he managed to persuade the magnificent Roman empire to compassion and to procure its protection. These complaints, as well as the fact that the same Coloman had invaded the borders of our kingdom at the coastal areas, caused King Henry to lead an expedition against Hungary; but faced by many different types of adversity, especially by the barricading of all the river fords, after a sorry and pointless siege of the fortress of Pressburg[133] he returned home empty-handed.[134]

The year of the Lord 1109.[135] King Henry celebrated Christmas at Mainz

---

124 In late August 1107.
125 The planned council in Regensburg did not take place: Meyer von Knonau (1907), p. 66.
126 Robert II, count of Flanders (c. 1065–1111).
127 See *Anonymous imperial chronicle* 1108, above, pp. 209–10.
128 Other sources say Aachen: see Meyer von Knonau (1907), p. 73 n. 60.
129 At Cambrai in November 1107. See *ibid.*, pp. 68–9.
130 Coloman I of Hungary, 1095–1116.
131 Almus (d. 1127). See Engel (2001), pp. 34–5.
132 Sallust, *Bellum Iugurthinum* 13–14.
133 Modern Bratislava. Cf. Cosmas of Prague, *Chronicle* 3.22, 3.25, trans. Wolverton (2009), pp. 208, 213.
134 Sallust, *Bellum Iugurthinum* 58.7.
135 *Anonymous imperial chronicle* 1109, above, p. 210.

and shortly afterwards held a council with the foremost nobles in Frankfurt, at which he delivered Count Palatine Siegfried[136] into the custody of the bishop of Würzburg because he had concocted a plan to kill the king and overturn his kingdom. This was revealed by Henry,[137] the former duke of Lotharingia, who was received back into the king's grace.[138] There the king also deposed Abbot Godfrey[139] of Fulda and replaced him with Wolfhelm[140] from the same congregation. After this he led an army against the Poles,[141] a distant people, and after he had laboured hard there for a long time he collected the debt of the long-denied tribute of that country. Archbishop Ruothard of Mainz died.[142]

The year of the Lord 1110.[143] While King Henry was celebrating Christmas at Bamberg he was unexpectedly disturbed by the inauspicious news that <>[144] had occupied Prague, the capital city of Bohemia, with an army and had usurped ducal authority over that people for himself against the will of the king. Then with raging spirit he sent ahead his most faithful princes with a strong force,[145] who with marvellous and quick success captured the city along with the enemies discovered within, and returned triumphantly to the king, who was following cautiously.

At the Epiphany of the Lord, Henry held a council of the princes at Regensburg and unfolded his mind's plans to them, namely that he wished to make himself known in the territories beyond the Alps, in order to secure imperial benediction from the great pontiff in the city of Rome, which is the capital of the world,[146] to bring the extensive Italian provinces into fellowship with the German kingdom through fraternal peace with ancient justice and laws and, in addition, to demonstrate his readiness to do all things necessary for the defence of the church according to the will of the apostolic father. All directed now their eager minds to the pious vow of the provident consul who undoubtedly loved his country, and no one was believed to be a man who sought to evade participation in such a manly business. Accordingly, when those who were

136 See above, p. 200 n. 102.
137 See above, p. 203 n. 126.
138 See Meyer von Knonau (1907), p. 92.
139 Godfrey, abbot of Fulda 1096–1109.
140 Wolfhelm, abbot of Fulda 1109–14.
141 See above, p. 210 n. 181.
142 On 2 May.
143 *Anonymous imperial chronicle* 1110, above, pp. 210–12.
144 The *Anonymous imperial chronicle* transmits the name Werner here: see above, p. 211 n. 183.
145 See above, p. 211 n. 184.
146 Lucan, *Pharsalia* 2.136, 2.655.

there had fully committed themselves to this matter by a voluntary oath, the king did not cease to arrange for this expedition quickly and urgently among the several German provinces; and though the advent of an inauspicious comet that remained visible for almost six months terrified the minds of some, the king, giving everywhere inestimable sums of money with munificent liberality, ordered the departure of the army from all places about August. Some crossed the Alps with him through the Great St Bernard Pass and others via the valley of the Trent. But the king, who in providence was second to none among the kings of the world, knowing that the Roman republic was formerly accustomed to being governed not so much by arms as by wisdom, provided himself with the necessary protection not only of armed men, but also of educated men, so that he would be ready to reply to all the matters demanded of him.

Thus, having overcome with difficulty the rugged mountains, the king and his contingent arrived happy and unharmed at Ivrea, while the other army, having previously captured certain castles, joined up happily with the king (who had stormed Novara) at Roncaglia as planned. He stayed there for a few days and then successfully crossed the Po and pitched camp at Piacenza, where he received many gifts and [promises of] complete fidelity from the citizens. Remaining in this region for three weeks, he moved on to Parma, where he conferred upon Countess Matilda,[147] *who had submitted to him through messengers, his grace and her own privileges. After this, afflicted by an exceedingly severe winter, he crossed Monte Bardone*[148] *at great cost to the army for the deplorable loss of equipment and horses. For seven weeks they suffered the incessant deluge of great rains upon them according to the habit of that climate and at last, sorely afflicted, they reached Florence immediately before the feast of the birth of the Lord.*

The year of the Lord 1111.[149] *Once King Henry had dealt with matters in Lombardy and Tuscany, he celebrated the joy of the birth of the Lord at Florence, to the immense delight of his followers and with such marvellous splendour and honour as the citizens of that country had never yet seen. Then he set out for Arezzo, where he was received favourably by the clergy, but treacherously by the citizens, whose insolence he afterwards completely and abundantly crushed, for he utterly demolished their city with its towers, which they had prepared to resist him, and at the request of the clergy he returned to the church all the privileges that those citizens had taken from her by force.*[150]

---

147 See n. 45 above. See Meyer von Knonau (1907), p. 132.
148 A pass in the Apennines, south-west of Parma.
149 *Anonymous imperial chronicle* 1111, above, pp. 212–15.
150 See above, p. 213 n. 190.

From there he advanced to Acquapendente where he found the legates, which he had recently sent to the pope from Arezzo, bearing good news. He then sent other messengers with those of the Romans (who had hastened to that place to submit to him)[151] and gradually proceeded to Sutri. Meeting there[152] with the pope's legates[153] and the royal messengers[154] [he was informed that] the pope was ready to crown him and to grant him every royal honour and wish if he would concede the freedom of the church, prohibit lay investiture and likewise receive back from the church all duchies, marches, counties, advocacies, monies, tolls and other regalia that it possessed.[155] The king gave his assent, but only on this condition: that not withstanding the strong and genuine reasons for this change, it ought to be confirmed by the agreement of a council of the whole church and the assent of the princes of the kingdom – something thought hardly to be possible, if at all.[156] After this meeting, with the legates having been dismissed and hostages given by both sides,[157] the king cheerfully hastened to the City, where the lord pope and all the clergy, or rather the whole of Rome, prepared to meet him.

It would take too long to relate what happened after that: how he was received with immense honour and led in the ancient Roman manner through the Silver Gate[158] to the ancient wheel[159] and there, having read the privileges publicly, how the princes were in a boundless tumult because of the spoliation of the church and the removal of their benefices; what immense danger there was; how there were such varied disputes that the whole day was spent there;[160] and, afterwards, how the apostolic father was taken into custody by the bishops and others faithful to the king until the emperor had been consecrated peacefully in church, just as the patriarch Jacob said to the angel, I will not let thee go except thou bless me.[161]

151 The letter he sent to Rome with these messengers: *MGH Constitutiones* 1 no. 82, p. 134.

152 On 9 February.

153 Led by Cardinal Peter Pierleoni (d. 1138), subsequently antipope 'Anacletus II', 1130–8.

154 See above, p. 213 n. 194.

155 See above, p 213 n. 195. *MGH Constitutiones* 1, nos 83–6, pp. 137–9. Blumenthal (1977), p. 9; Robinson (1990), pp. 424–5.

156 Cf. *MGH Constitutiones* 1, nos 87–8, pp. 139–40.

157 Cf. *Chronicle of Monte Cassino* 4.35, *MGH SS* 34, p. 501.

158 The *Porta argentaria*, the principal gate of the old basilica of St Peter, adorned with 975 pounds of silver by Pope Honorius I, 625–38: *Liber pontificalis* 1, p. 323.

159 The *rota porphyretica* or 'coronation wheel' on which emperors stood for coronation.

160 See above, p. 214 n. 200.

161 Genesis 32.26.

These things were done on Quinquagesima Sunday.[162] *The Romans gathered throughout the night and early in the morning attacked the army of the king from all sides so that the fight had already lasted some time when the king himself ran to the aid of his army. He did this with great energy; until the close of day as a most strong soldier and excellent leader,*[163] *he helped his own to victory through the grace of God and, after inflicting great slaughter, he put the enemy to ignominious flight.*

Withdrawing from Rome after three days, he took the lord pope with him and treated him as honourably as possible. Responding to matters in the area as the situation demanded and pacifying all his adversaries, he celebrated the approaching Easter[164] *in his camp, not far from the City. Here the long-standing dispute between him and the pope, between the kingship and the priesthood was settled. After the octave of Easter, to the great joy of the Roman people, or rather the inestimable delight of the whole church and army, before confession to St Peter, before accepting the title Augustus and the empire from Christ, and before being anointed and hallowed according to the rites of unction and being crowned with the most sublime pomp*[165] *– as those who were there affirm for us, although others think quite differently about it – he was also given*[166] *in person from the hand of the pope and witnessed by the church standing there the privilege of ecclesiastical investiture according as it had pleased the predecessors of both and had been accustomed to continue, the absolute immutability of which the pope then confirmed on pain of anathema.*[167] *Thus finally on that day glory was returned to God in the highest, and on earth peace to men of good will,*[168] *as it may be said, since this long-standing and thus-far incorrigible scandal and schism in the kingdom of Christ was removed.*

Not long afterwards, Henry distributed so many gifts of such great size and kind with munificent imperial liberality to his spiritual father the pope, each of

162 12 February. Quinquagesima Sunday: see above, p. 214 n. 202.
163 A paraphrase of Sallust, *Bellum Catilinae* 60.4.
164 2 April.
165 On 13 April.
166 This comment appears only in Berlin, Preußischer Kulturbesitz, MS lat. fol. 295, fol. 108r (and its copy Paris, Bibliothèque nationale, MS lat. 4889a, fol. 95r). It is not possible to know whether it represents Ekkehard's reflexion on the passage or an addition by the scribe. The Berlin manuscript also transmits a *nota bene* mark along the side of this passage and, in the text scribe's hand, the following comment: 'a fictitious account of the conflict' (*dictantis fictam dissensionem*). Compare the criticisms of William of Malmesbury, *Deeds of the English kings* 5.420–6, pp. 762–71.
167 The Treaty of Ponte Mammolo (11 April), *MGH Constitutiones* 1, nos 91–6, pp. 142–5. See Robinson (1990), p. 429.
168 Luke 2.14.

the cardinal bishops and the greater and lesser clergy, that they seemed almost incredible to those who were not there. After the pope and all ⌈with him⌉ had prayed for his prosperity and, bound to him with great affection, had escorted him for a considerable while, he joyfully returned through Lombardy to the Alps and thence to Germany.[169]

After his return what seemed to need correction was polished to a shine, not only by the king himself but also by the bishops who had accompanied him according to what the high pontiff had conceded and enjoined to each, and faults were purged clean.[170] *Thus as Christ looked down on the earth from His holy heaven, everywhere devotion and the Christian religion began to increase and there too were prosperity, abundant crops and new joy.*

In the month of August, therefore, Emperor Henry along with many bishops and abbots as well as a considerable number of the princes met together at Speyer, and with their assent and co-operation he celebrated the anniversary of his father's death very magnificently. Although his father had been refused the communion of burial and prayer for five years in total, he was buried in the church next to his ancestors with apostolic authority by those same priests who in Rome in the presence of the pope had given testimony to his penance and by which testimony it was conceded; and the obsequies were such as no emperor ever had.[171]

Holding court at Mainz,[172] *the king invested his chancellor Adalbert,*[173] *who had already been elected to that very seat, with the staff and ring.*

The year of the Lord 1112.[174] *Count Siegfried,*[175] *who had been sufficiently afflicted by his long imprisonment, was reconciled to the king and released through the counsel and petition of the princes.*[176] *The king began to treat him so kindly that he even sponsored the baptism of his son*[177] *and promised to forget past injuries.*

During this time the lord pope had to endure many injustices from the Roman church. He was accused of having elevated King Henry,

169 See above, p. 215 n. 210.
170 Isaiah 1.25.
171 On 7 August. Cf. *Annals of Paderborn* 1111, p. 125. See above, pp. 70–1. See Meyer von Knonau (1907), pp. 206–9; Heidrich (1991), pp. 215–16; Robinson (1999), p. 344.
172 On 15 August.
173 Archbishop Adalbert of Mainz, 1109/11–37.
174 *Anonymous imperial chronicle* 1112, above, pp. 215–16.
175 See above, p. 200 n. 102.
176 At Goslar, shortly before Christmas 1111. See Meyer von Knonau (1907), p. 219.
177 That is, he became godfather to Siegfried's son.

the tyrannical devastator of the commonwealth and destroyer of the churches, to the imperial dignity and also of having conceded to him a sacrilegious privilege, contrary to all the principles of the church's teaching. Therefore, compelled by the council, [178]*which took place on the fifteenth Kalends of April* [18 March] *in the basilica of Constantine at the Lateran*,[179] *he* [the pope] *made a profession of his catholic faith in front of everyone on the last day of the council, so that no one should doubt his faith, saying:* 'I embrace the holy scriptures of the Old and New Testament, the Law written by Moses and by the holy prophets. I embrace the four gospels, the seven canonical epistles, [the letters] of the glorious doctor St Paul the apostle, the holy canons of the apostles, the four universal councils like the four gospels – Nicaea, Ephesus, Constantinople and Chalcedon[180] – and the Council of Antioch,[181] and the decrees of the holy Fathers the Roman popes and especially the decrees of my lords Pope Gregory VII[182] and Pope Urban[183] of blessed memory. What they have approved I approve, what they have upheld I uphold, what they have confirmed I confirm, what they have condemned I condemn, what they have rejected I reject, what they have enjoined I enjoin, what they have prohibited I prohibit; in all these things, through all and for ever will I persevere.'

This having been completed, Bishop Gerard of Angoulême, legate in Aquitaine, arose and with the joint assent of the lord Pope Paschal and the whole council read the following text before all: 'That privilege, which is not a privilege, but which should in truth be called a depravity,[184] extorted by violence by King Henry from Pope Paschal for the freeing of the church prisoners, all we gathered in this holy council condemn with canonical censure and with ecclesiastical authority through the judgement of the Holy Spirit, and declare it to be utterly void and excommunicate it so that it may have no authority or efficacy; and it is condemned for the reason that in this privilege *is contained* [the injunction] that [a person] canonically elected is not to be consecrated by anyone unless he has first been invested by the king, which is contrary to the Holy Spirit and canonical principles.' *This document having been read,* all *acclaimed* 'So be

---

178 Quoted from the acts of the Lateran council, *MGH Constitutiones* 1, pp. 571–2. William of Malmesbury was also well informed about the council: *Deeds of the English kings* 5.427–9, pp. 770–5.

179 The Lateran council of 1112: see McKeon (1966), 3–12; Blumenthal (1978a), 82–98; Servatius (1979), pp. 309–20; Robinson (1990), pp. 128–30.

180 The four ecumenical councils: Nicaea (325), Constantinople (381), Ephesus (431) and Chalcedon (451).

181 The Council of Antioch of 341. See Blumenthal (1978b), pp. 119, 162.

182 Pope Gregory VII, 1073–85.

183 Pope Urban II, 1088–99.

184 In Latin *pravilegium*: a pun on the Latin word for privilege (*privilegium*).

it! So be it!' Archbishop John,[185] the patriarch of Venice, Archbishop Sennes of Capua[186] and about one hundred other bishops subscribed.

On this occasion the archbishop of Vienne[187] and his accomplices tried to sow a new schism in our land by attempting to extend the sword of anathema against the emperor, but since his attempt obviously lacked any papal authority, and consequently any church authority, he could do little in the meantime.[188] Nevertheless, the evil of jealousy started everywhere to crawl out of the seeds of this dissension, so much so that some thought to act against the commonwealth, in their agitation seizing on this issue as the shield for their intentions. In addition, [189]*the aforementioned Adalbert, who had been designated archbishop of Mainz, who was second to the king in all matters and without whose advice the king would do nothing, was accused of conspiring against the emperor with several of the princes — which hardly anyone could believe.*[190] When the matter became known the king had him taken into custody.[191]

At this time one of the Saxon princes named Udalric,[192] once the son-in-law of Count Ludwig,[193] died — although [Ludwig] hated him because he had repudiated his daughter. The aforementioned Siegfried[194] claimed his possessions by hereditary right,[195] but the lord emperor attempted to place them under the legal protection of the kingdom. This matter provided the kindling for recurring disorder. For this same count exaggerated his earlier miseries even further and filled almost

185 Patriarch John IV of Grado, 1112–29 (the metropolitan of Venice).
186 Archbishop Sennes of Capua, 1097–1116.
187 Archbishop Guido of Vienne, 1088–111, Pope Calixtus II, 1119–24.
188 Guido excommunicated Henry V at a synod in Vienne on 16 September 1112. Cf. Abbot Suger of St Denis, *Vita Ludovici* 10, p. 68: 'turning to the German kingdom, [Guido] stirred up the princes ... against him [Henry]'. See Servatius (1979), pp. 320–4; Robinson (1999), pp. 429–30; Schilling (1998), pp. 368–73; Stroll (2004), pp. 46–9.
189 *Anonymous imperial chronicle* 1112, above, p. 216.
190 In December 1112 Henry V published a letter addressed to the princes accusing Adalbert of usurping royal privileges and fomenting treachery: *MGH DD H. V*, no. 110. Cf. Helmold of Bosau, *Chronicle*, p. 81; trans. Tschan (1966), p. 135. See Meyer von Knonau (1907), pp. 259–63; Weinfurter (1999), pp. 174–5; Stroll (2004), pp. 211–14.
191 Adalbert was imprisoned until 1115. See below, 1115, p. 247.
192 Count Udalric of Weimar (d. 13 May 1112).
193 Count Ludwig II of Thuringia (d. 1123).
194 See above, p. 200 n. 102.
195 Siegfried was a kinsman of Udalric and claimed his inheritance since Udalric died without heir.

the whole of Saxony, his homeland, with such complaints that Duke Lothar, Margrave Rudolf,[196] Count Palatine Frederick,[197] Wipert[198] and Ludwig, as well as several others, withdrew their obedience from the emperor. Not to mention that the bishop of Halberstadt[199] as well as Gertrude,[200] one of the most powerful widows in Saxony, likewise cried out that they had suffered violence from the emperor's unjust invasion of their own private estates. These and similar tares of scandal stirred up a continuous murmuring in the recently pacified realm.

The year of the Lord 1113.[201] *Emperor Henry celebrated Christmas at Erfurt.* As the aforementioned Saxon princes did not appear at court there, the emperor was moved with excessive indignation and commanded that their goods be pillaged and their property devastated with fire, even on the feast day; and not much later he utterly destroyed the extremely well-fortified castle of the Hornburg after a long siege. Then, leaving his followers as a garrison, he weakened those who despised him by ambushes and skirmishes. In the course of this the oft-mentioned Count Palatine Siegfried – a most noble man who in his times was second to none in probity – died,[202] while Wipert was captured and Ludwig was compelled to surrender. And so things became quiet, if only for a short while.

After that a certain Rainald,[203] a count in the province of Burgundy and reputedly a blood relation of the emperor, raised up tyranny against the commonwealth by his insolent and juvenile actions.[204] When the august Henry advanced upon him with strong forces, however, he lost his fortress of Mousson upon which he greatly relied and was himself captured; thus the quarrel was quickly settled and he was sent into captivity.

196 Count Rudolf I of Stade (d. 1124), margrave of the Saxon North March 1106–14.
197 Frederick I of Sommerschenburg (d. 1120), count palatine of Saxony.
198 Count Wiprecht II of Groitzsch (d. 1124).
199 Bishop Reinhard of Halberstadt, 1107–23.
200 Gertrude of Brunswick (d. 1117), widow of Count Henry 'the Fat' of Northeim (d. 1101), margrave of Frisia, and Count Henry of Eilenburg (d. 1103), margrave of Meißen and Lausitz; mother-in-law of Lothar of Supplinburg.
201 *Anonymous imperial chronicle* 1113, above, p. 216.
202 9 March. Siegfried died of wounds inflicted at Warmstädt (near Quedlinburg) when the rebels were defeated by a royal army under the command of Count Hoier of Mansfeld. See Meyer von Knonau (1907), pp. 216.
203 Count Rainald of Bar and Mousson (d. 1149).
204 Rainald was involved in a conflict with Bishop Richard of Verdun: Stroll (2004), pp. 207–9.

The year of the Lord 1114. The lord emperor celebrated Christmas with the greatest magnificence and with a great multitude of the princes at Bamberg – not unreservedly, however, because he had some distrust of the man of God, Otto,[205] who was bishop there and who had refused to come to court because of certain scandals that had arisen in the kingdom.[206] Otto, however, not sparing transitory things for peace in the church, gloriously overcame the animosity of the king with unceasing gifts. After an assembly at Mainz had been announced, the emperor arranged for his magnificent wedding after the Epiphany of the Lord,[207] from which he wished hardly any, or rather none, of the magnates to be absent. With their advice and agreement, the daughter of the king of England,[208] who was named Matilda[209] and who had long been his betrothed, was lawfully joined to him and made consort of the kingdom.

With great enthusiasm the emperor then launched a naval expedition against some of those who lived on the islands in the marshy areas beyond Frisia. As he journeyed there, he found Cologne in rebellion against him as well as many from beyond the Rhine and Westphalia who agreed with them, among whom were the well-known Archbishop Frederick of Cologne,[210] Duke Godfrey,[211] Henry the former duke[212] and Frederick of Arnsberg.[213] He delayed his departure for he was eager to extend his hand against his present enemies: he besieged Cologne, a city in truth marvellously fortified, but, not prevailing against it, he devastated the region around it and at last, after the army had been disbanded, he proclaimed another expedition against the same rebels. [This army] gathered around the Kalends of October [1 October] and attacked the possessions of Frederick. When the emperor had completely wasted them, he built a strong castle in the middle of Frederick's lands,[214]

---

205 See n. 32 above.

206 Meyer von Knonau (1907), p. 282, suggested that Otto had expressed reservations about Henry V's treatment of Archbishop Adalbert of Mainz.

207 On 7 January.

208 Henry I (1068/9–1135), king of England 1100, duke of Normandy 1106. See Hollister (2001).

209 Matilda (d. 1167). See Chibnall (1993).

210 Frederick of Schwarzenburg, archbishop of Cologne 1100–31.

211 Godfrey I of Leuven (d. 1139), duke of Lower Lotharingia 1106–29.

212 See n. 54 above. Henry of Limburg had been deposed as duke of Lower Lotharingia on the death of Henry IV, whom he had supported against Henry V in 1105–6.

213 Count Frederick of Arnsberg (d. 1124).

214 Frederick of Arnsberg is probably intended here: Meyer von Knonau (1907), p. 306.

which he furnished with knights, arms and other supplies, and with the approach of winter he laid down his arms.

The year of the Lord 1115. The emperor, perceiving clearly that Saxony had defected from him, came as well armed as he was angry and set up a not insignificant camp, both with those he had brought with him and with volunteers he found there. The Saxons, however, recognizing that they faced danger gathered their forces from different places: not to fight against their lord out of audacity but to defend themselves out of necessity, as they declared to the emperor through messengers. While for several days each side threatened the other but refrained [from attacking], a certain strong man named Hoier[215] – who among many other warlike deeds had, a short time before, won great fame for himself in the king's palace by killing the Count Palatine Siegfried – took a select group of youths who like himself had become impatient with the delay, and evidently launched an audacious attack on the Saxons with his compatriots. Fighting with the ferocity of a lion and burning with lust for glory, he paid for it with his own life and the fall of many who were with him.[216] Bishop Reinhard of Halberstadt took part in this fight and even reputedly directed it; for a short time before he had suffered not insignificant injuries from the emperor. Evidently, he preached the great consolation of justice to his own and even prohibited the fallen on the emperor's side from burial in communion [with the church]. Thus the lord emperor turned back to the Rhine not a little embittered, while the resolve of the Saxons to resist him was strengthened more and more. At this the Saxons called through messengers upon a certain Roman cardinal named Theoderic[217] who had been performing a legation in Hungary; he announced the acts of the aforementioned council[218] and excommunicated the emperor,[219] while the archbishop of Magdeburg[220] and other bishops of the church received reconciliation.[221] Thus again schism in the kingdom was everywhere reborn afresh and both parties again undertook hostilities against each other.

215 Count Hoier of Mansfeld (d. 1115).
216 The Battle of Welfesholz in south-eastern Saxony (11 February). Cf. Helmold of Bosau, *Chronicle* 1.40, pp. 81–2; trans. Tschan (1966), p. 136.
217 Theoderic, cardinal priest of S. Grisogono (d. 1115).
218 The Lateran council of 1112.
219 In a synod at Goslar on 1 September. Cardinal Bishop Conrad of Palestrina had independently excommunicated Henry V in 1115, also without papal sanction. See Robinson (1990), p. 430.
220 Archbishop Adelgoz of Magdeburg, 1106/7–19.
221 See Meyer von Knonau (1907), pp. 330–1.

Meanwhile, messengers direct from Italy announced the death of the renowned Matilda[222] and invited the emperor to take possession of her vast estates and lands by hereditary right. Without doubt nobody in our times was as rich or as famous as she and nobody from the laity could be found who was more distinguished in virtue or piety.

On the advice of his friends, or rather compelled by the complaints of the whole kingdom, the emperor called a general council for the Kalends of November [1 November] in Mainz, where he promised a free hearing for all, satisfaction for the charges against him and correction for his extraordinary, or juvenile, acts according to the advice of the senate. While he himself was present at the appointed time in Mainz and waiting in vain for the appointed council (for excepting a few of the bishops none of the princes had come), the citizens of Mainz, thinking this a suitable time and armed with mail-coats and weapons, suddenly surrounded the palace. Others stormed into the hall full of rage, assembling into bands and wedge-formations, all in uproar, all clamouring and offering to the courtiers a terrifying spectacle. What more? There can be no doubt that, unless the emperor had given hostages promptly and promised speedily to do all that they imposed on him, he and perhaps all that were in the palace would immediately have been killed and destroyed most cruelly. Having barely calmed the irate fury of the knights and people, Caesar withdrew from the city and three days later, in accordance with what had been agreed, returned Adalbert (who had been held in close confinement for three years and was virtually *skin and bones*[223]) to his [archiepiscopal] throne. Not long afterwards Adalbert submitted by messengers and letters to Theoderic, the legate of the apostolic see, whom he asked to meet him and many other bishops at Cologne, where the commands of the pope, which Theoderic was delivering, could be received by all and he himself could seek consecration, which had been delayed for so long, by such great authority. This meeting took place shortly before the feast of Christmas – not without the emperor's indignation, for his consent to this consecration was not entirely voluntary.

The year of the Lord 1116. The emperor celebrated the birth of the Lord at Speyer with few bishops and princes, and what was happening at Cologne in the mean time affected him gravely. Indeed he heard that many had gathered there, not only archbishops but also other bishops and the magnates of the kingdom, principally to pass a sentence of excommunication against him, although the cardinal on whose authority

---

222 Matilda of Tuscany (d. 24 July). Matilda was a kinswoman of Henry V.
223 Perhaps an allusion to Lamentations 4.8.

these [proceedings] had been initiated had already died on his journey and was borne there for burial rather than to hold a council.[224] The bishop of Würzburg,[225] who had been sent there by the emperor, won an audience and communion only after having been reconciled. When he returned having completed his mission, he now refused to have communion with him who had sent him, although compelled under threat to his life he celebrated Mass in the presence of the king. Then he departed secretly, *sorrowful unto death*,[226] and was reconciled again to the former communion with many tears; and thenceforward he forfeited Caesar's confidence and grace.

Enraged by this commotion the emperor conferred the duchy of Franconia – which according to ancient royal custom had been granted to the bishopric of Würzburg – on Conrad,[227] the son of his sister.[228] Then in order to avoid the outcry of the princes he went to Italy with the queen and his whole household,[229] and in the region of the Po attended to the business of the kingdom and sent suppliant legates to the pope in order to settle the matter that had once again begun to disturb the royal and ecclesiastical powers. The abbot of Cluny[230] held the leadership of the legation, a relative of the pope[231] as they say, who with many initiatives strove diligently to be a faithful and tireless mediator in order to resolve the dispute between the two sides peacefully.

In the same year, the eighteenth since the ordination of the lord Pope Paschal II, on the second Nones of March [6 March], at Rome, in the Lateran, in the church of the Holy Saviour which is called [the basilica] of Constantine, a synod of universal council was held at which bishops, abbots, catholic dukes and counts came together from diverse kingdoms and provinces as well as many legates from all provinces.[232] On the first

---

224 Theoderic died at Schwelm on his way to Cologne. See Meyer von Knonau (1907), p. 343.
225 Erlung, bishop of Würzburg 1105/6–21.
226 See Mark 14.34.
227 Conrad of Staufen (d. 1152), King Conrad III (1138). See Arnold (1997), pp. 65–6. Adam of Bremen also comments on the bishop of Würzburg's exercising of ducal authority in Franconia: *History of the archbishops of Hamburg-Bremen* 3.46, p. 188; trans. Tschan (2002), p. 152.
228 Agnes (1072/3–1143).
229 Henry went to pursue his claims to Matilda of Tuscany's inheritance.
230 Abbot Pontius of Cluny, 1109–22/6. On Pontius see Cowdrey (1978), 178–298.
231 Actually a kinsman of Pope Calixtus II.
232 The Lateran synod of 6–11 March 1116. See Servatius (1979), pp. 330–2.

day, which was the Monday of the third week of Lent, the conflict between the Milanese bishops Grosulan[233] and Jordan[234] was investigated, for one appeared to be an invader and the other to have deserted his church.[235] The lord pope referred this case to the counsel of the cardinal bishops for discussion. The following day there was much discussion of this case but little was decided. On Wednesday the bishop of Lucca[236] accused the Pisans of invading territory under the jurisdiction of his church. While the [bishop] of Pisa was defending his own against this, there ensued between both parties – to the applause of people on each side – a long legal debate. Thereupon one of the bishops rose from the middle of the council and began thus: 'Our lord and father the pope ought to remember for what purpose the holy gathering of this general council has been invited to come together here under all manner of threats at sea and on land. Here, in topsy-turvy order it is not spiritual or church business that is dealt with but secular business. The first thing to be sought, since this was the principal reason for meeting, as is evident and well known, is what the pope thinks and what ought to be preached in his churches upon returning home.' Then the pope explained the reason for the council and the intentions of his heart with these words: 'After the Lord had done what He wished with His servant and the people of Rome had *delivered* me *into the hands* [237] of the king, I daily saw everywhere rapine, arson, slaughter and adultery. I longed to avert this and other sorts of evil from the church and people of God, and what I have done *for the liberation of the people of God* [238] I have done.[239] Indeed I did it as a man since I am *dust and ashes*.[240] I admit that I acted wrongly, but I ask all of you *to pray for me to God* [241] and to be lenient with me. As for that evil document[242] which was written in the camp and which on

---

233 Peter Grosulan (d. 1117), archbishop of Milan 1102–12/16. Grosulan was expelled by the Milanese in 1112. See Masnovo (1922), 1–28; Cazzani (1955), pp. 133–9.

234 Jordan of Clivio, archbishop of Milan 1112/16–20.

235 See Meyer von Knonau (1907), pp. 351–2.

236 Unidentified.

237 See 1 Kings 14.12.

238 Judith 12.8.

239 A parallel to the plight of Pilate in John 19.22.

240 Genesis 18.27.

241 From the *Confiteor*.

242 The Treaty of Ponte Mammolo (11 April 1111), granting the right of investiture to Henry V. See n. 167 above.

account of his [Henry V's] depravity is called a perversity,[243] I condemn it with perpetual anathema so that it may not be remembered fondly by anyone, and I ask you all to do the same!' Then from all resounded 'So be it! So be it!' Whereupon Bishop Bruno of Segni[244] cried out still louder: 'We give thanks to Almighty God that we have heard the lord Pope Paschal, who is presiding over this council, condemn with his own mouth that perversity, which contains depravity and heresy.' At this someone mockingly added: 'If that privilege contained heresy, he who produced it is a heretic.' But John of Gaeta[245] replied with agitation to [the bishop of] Segni: 'Do you call the Roman pontiff a heretic here in this council before our ears? The document that the lord pope drew up was, admittedly, bad; but it was not heretical.' And another added: 'No indeed, I say that it ought not even to be called bad since, if it is good to free the people of God, what the lord pope did was good. For it is good to free the people of God by the authority of the gospels, in which we are instructed *to lay down* our *lives* for our brothers.'[246] The patience of the lord pope was exasperated by the horrible accusation of heresy and, commanding silence with his hand, he calmed the clamouring and *murmuring*[247] dissent in the following way: 'My brothers and lords, listen! This church has never entertained heresy;[248] rather, here have all heresies been thrown into confusion. Here the Arian heresy,[249] which flourished for almost three-hundred years, was annihilated. From this seat the heresies of Eutyches[250] and Sabellius[251] were crushed, Photinus[252]

243 See n. 184 above.
244 Bruno, bishop of Segni 1079–1123. See North (2000), pp. 199–220; Robinson (2004b), pp. 88–92.
245 John of Gaeta (d. 1119), cardinal deacon of S. Maria in Cosmedin, papal chancellor, Pope Gelasius II, 1118–19.
246 See John 15.13.
247 See *Rule of St Benedict* 5.
248 Cf. Gregory VII, *Dictatus papae* 22, *Register* 2.55a, p. 207; trans. Cowdrey (2002), p. 150: 'The Roman church has never erred nor, as scripture testifies, will she ever err'.
249 The heresy of Arius (*c.* 259–*c.* 336), priest of Alexandria, which taught that Christ was not of the same nature as the Father and thus not divine. His teaching was condemned at the Council of Nicaea (325).
250 The Christological heresy derived from the teaching of Eutyches of Constantinople (*c.* 380–456), which was condemned at the Council of Chalcedon (451).
251 A non-Trinitarian heresy derived from the teaching of the third-century theologian Sabellius, which taught that the persons of the Godhead were different modes of God and not distinct persons within the Godhead.
252 Photinus (d. 376), bishop of Sirmium (in Pannonia). Among other things, the Photinian heresy taught that the Son did not exist with the Father before the Incarnation.

and other heretics were destroyed. For this church the Son of God prayed in His passion when He said: '*I have prayed for you, Peter, that your faith fail not.*'²⁵³ On Thursday the pope did not sit in council because he was prevented by a variety of business, especially that of the king, which was brought by the abbot of Cluny, John of Gaeta, Peter Pierleoni,²⁵⁴ the prefect of the city and other supporters of that party. On Friday the pope turned his attention to the greatest concern of all the churches and with John of Gaeta, Peter Pierleoni and the other followers of the king *withstanding* the aforementioned Conrad of Palestrina – who had frequently desired the pronouncement of the sentence of excommunication – *to his face*,²⁵⁵ the pope calmed the *murmuring* ²⁵⁶ with his hand and these words: 'In the time of the martyrs the primitive church flourished in the sight of God and not in that of men. Thereafter kings, Roman emperors and princes – like Constantine and the other faithful – were converted to the faith and, like good sons, adorned their mother the church by conferring estates, allods, secular honours and dignities as well as royal rights and insignia upon the church of God; and so the church began to flourish more in the sight of men than in the sight of God. Our mother and mistress the church may, therefore, hold the things conferred on her by kings and princes; she may dispense and assign to her sons as she understands and wishes.' Wishing to obliterate the depraved privilege of investiture, which seemed to have been conceded in the camp, the pope repeated the sentence of Pope Gregory VII,²⁵⁷ anathematizing again the investiture of ecclesiastical matters by lay hands and excommunicating both donor and recipient. The lord Cardinal Conrad of Palestrina, however, presented his case to the pope and argued in his presence against the disturbers of the present business: 'My lord and father, if it pleases your majesty, if I am truly your legate and if what I have done satisfies you as being correct, proclaim it with your mouth and in the hearing of this present and holy council corroborate my legation with your authority, so that all may know *that you have sent me.*'²⁵⁸ To this the pope responded: 'You were truly sent as a legate

---

253 Luke 22.32.
254 See n. 153 above.
255 Galatians 2.11.
256 See *Rule of St Benedict* 5.
257 The decree against lay investiture of 1080, *Register* 7.14a, pp. 480–1; trans. Cowdrey (2002), p. 340.
258 John 11.42.

from our side,[259] and whatsoever you and our other brothers the cardinal bishops, the legates of God and of the apostles Peter and Paul have done, approved and confirmed by our authority and the authority of this see, I also approve and confirm; and whatsoever you have condemned, I condemn.' Continuing, the lord of Palestrina then added that while in Jerusalem on a legation for this see he had heard how King Henry, after [swearing] an oath and [exchanging] hostages and the kiss [of peace] in the very church of St Peter, had taken the lord pope captive and treated him indignantly. Hearing how the more important members of the church, namely the cardinals, had been despoiled, carried off violently and badly treated, how the Roman nobles had been killed and captured, and how the people had been slaughtered, he [Conrad] groaned in anguish and because of these outrages, with the counsel of the church of Jerusalem and animated with zeal for God, he had declared the sentence of excommunication against the king, repeating and confirming it in five councils in Greece, Hungary, Saxony, Lotharingia and France[260] with the advice of these aforementioned churches, praying at length that as the lord pope had confirmed his legation, so too the fathers and bishops of the present council would assent harmoniously. The legates and letters of the lord [archbishop] of Vienne[261] asked for the same thing. When the assent of such a varied and different multitude was requested in that manner and way, the sounder part did not contradict this true and open reasoning; a few muttered below their voices and the bishops and abbots in no way protested. Finally on Saturday the controversy between the Milanese bishops was ended by the following decision. As Pope Paschal pointed out, the translation of bishops ought to take place for two reasons: necessity or utility. But what had seemed useful in the translation of Grosulan turned out to be harmful to souls and bodies. He returned Grosulan to the place from which he had been translated[262] and gave Jordan to the Milanese. To those who had visited the threshold of the

---

259 In Latin *legatus ex latere*, which from the thirteenth century definitively meant a papal plenipotentiary sent from the curia on an important mission. On the less formalized meaning of the *legatus ex latere* in the early twelfth century see Robinson (1990), pp. 147–64.

260 *Chroniken*, p. 323 n. 21, identifies the five synods as Beauvais (6 December 1114), Rheims (28 March 1115), Cologne (19 April 1115), Châlons-sur-Marne (12 July 1115) and a meeting in Saxony, which took place between those of Cologne and Châlons. The Latin, however, implies that the five synods took place in the regions mentioned by Conrad. See Hiestand (1972), pp. 149–51.

261 See n. 187 above.

262 The bishopric of Savona.

apostles because of the council and for the cure of their souls, and who wished to perform penance for serious [sins], he granted a penance of forty days and with the apostolic blessing joyfully dismissed the six-day council.

The German kingdom, which for a decade or a little more had been harmoniously peaceful, was divided by this and such things, and since the king was absent each and everyone did, not what was right, but what seemed to please himself. First of all, each side incessantly gathered together to devastate the fields of the other and began to despoil the farmers; and this scourge prevailed especially in the bishopric of Würzburg because of Conrad, the brother of Duke Frederick.[263] After this, since the occasion was ripe, brigands sprouted forth everywhere. They showed no regard for time or person but, as they say, pillaged and stole secretly, attacked, killed and left their victims with nothing at all. It would take long to relate the machinations of the bishop of Mainz against the followers of the king and their deceitful operations against him, to describe the seditions of many city-dwellers or to report how some cities were orphaned from their bishop by this pestilence; to describe the fortifications erected in unusual places, the many castles that were destroyed in turn, how regions were devastated through pillaging and arson, how the knights of each side committed skirmishes and mutual killings, how the poor and pilgrims were oppressed and captured in a barbaric way by Christian against Christian; much of this sort could be committed to writing. Since neither the Peace of God nor the other sacraments were preserved by firm agreements, each and every condition and age of person except alone those professed in the church (who had almost nothing remaining save their miserable souls) – all these others, I say – raged at this time like wild beasts. Everywhere the fields were devastated, the villages were depopulated, a great number of towns and regions were virtually reduced to desolation and a daily deficiency in the supply of clerics to churches caused an evident cessation of clerical ministry in certain churches. And – O, overflowing *cup*[264] of the wrath of God! – the wealthiest, most famous and principal monastery in the whole of Germany – Fulda – was reduced to virtually nothing for want of necessary provisions.

263 Duke Frederick II of Swabia (1090–1147).
264 See Apocalypse 16.19.

EKKEHARD OF AURA, *HIEROSOLIMITA*

IN THE NAME OF CHRIST, HERE BEGINS THE LITTLE BOOK THAT IS CALLED *HIEROSOLIMITA*, CONCERNING THE OPPRESSION, LIBERATION AND RESTORATION OF THE HOLY CHURCH OF JERUSALEM.[265]

[266]*My soul burns to add certain details concerning* the *campaign or expedition to Jerusalem from virtually all parts of the world, but especially from the western kingdoms, which* in our times *was ordained not by men but by God,* so that by this, O venerable shepherd,[267] your injunction and that of all the sheep of Sts Stephen and Vitus[268] who tremble under your staff will be satisfied. I do not believe it fair to those to whom I owe everything,[269] that in harkening to our ancestors – that is, in arranging the memorable accounts of different chronicles from the beginning of time until our own rotten times to the best of my knowledge and ability – I should omit those details of lesser importance that you esteem, since that would altogether be like making a burnt-offering to the Lord of a head without a tail. Your injunction also impels me in the same way entirely [270]*to refute the imprudence – or more correctly the impudence – of some who, persevering always in old error and with rash speech, presume to criticize the novelty of something so necessary to an ageing and declining world. In the Epicurean fashion, they cherish the broad way of pleasure over the narrow way of divine service.*[271] In the utter blindness of their hearts they consider love of the world wisdom, contempt of the world folly (that is, a prison their homeland), darkness light, evil goodness,[272] death

---

265 This heading is present only in Berlin, Preußischer Kulturbesitz, Staatsbibliothek zu Berlin, MS lat. fol. 295, fol. 121v (and its thirteenth-century copy Paris, Bibliothèque nationale, MS lat. 4889a, fol. 102r).

266 *1106 Continuation* 1099, above, p. 142.

267 Abbot Erkembert of Corvey.

268 The monastery of Corvey, dedicated to Sts Stephen and Vitus. See n. 2 above.

269 The community at Corvey.

270 *1106 Continuation* 1099, above, pp. 142–3.

271 See Matthew 7.14.

272 Isaiah 5.20.

life – oh, how shameful! By this they are flattered and furnished with such audacity in their depravity that everywhere – but especially in this land – things are reversed, since wisdom is hated by all, every virtue is offensive, religion is despised, humility is crushed, cunning prevails before all, vice wins over love, cruelty over fear and arrogance rules over honour. We, however, put our trust only in God;[273] *we look not with astonishment to the present but to the future, and although reluctant spectators and yet well-wishing admirers, we praise those glorious men of our times who have conquered the kingdoms of the world and who for piety have left wife and children,*[274] *power and riches, to seek out the hundredth sheep.*[275] *They put their souls in His hands;*[276] *with zeal they were zealous for the Lord of Hosts,*[277] *and with worthy valour they entered into the service of their heavenly king,* [278]*passionately stirred up by frequent reports of the oppression of the Lord's Sepulchre and the devastation of all the churches, which had been subjected to the power of the ferocious people of the Turks for several years and which had gradually been obliterated through unheard-of calamities. To come to their aid, as is reported, a great many set off hurriedly in different groups with different and unreliable leadership. The first group, estimated at 15,000 and following a certain monk named Peter,*[279] *travelled peacefully through Germany, and then through Bavaria and Hungary.* But let us return to other matters.

In the time of Henry IV, prince of the Romans ... Thus having celebrated the victory, the army returned to Jerusalem and, leaving Duke Godfrey there, Count Raymond of St Gilles, Count Robert of Normandy and Count Robert of Flanders returned to Laodicea. There they found the fleet belonging to the Pisans and Bohemund.[280] A not insignificant multitude, apart from those who had moved to Antioch with Bohemund, gone to Edessa with Baldwin, remained in Tyre or dispersed into the various regions round about, congregated in that same place. *Once the archbishop of Pisa had established concord among those who had* long been *disagreeing,*[281] a great multitude sought to return home. Duke Godfrey, as has been said, took charge of the people who remained in Jerusalem. Thus the same

273 Philippians 1.14.
274 See Matthew 19.29.
275 Luke 15.4.
276 Luke 23.46.
277 3 Kings 19.10, 19.14.
278 *1106 Continuation* 1096, above, p. 138.
279 Peter the Hermit (d. 1115). See above, p. 138 n. 4.
280 *1106 Continuation* 1099, above, pp. 143–58.
281 *Ibid.*, above, p. 158.

magnanimous duke, whose equal in piety can scarcely be found ... by his innate skill in both languages.[282]

The year of the Lord 1100. Under Duke Godfrey, the defender of the church of Jerusalem ... and enlarged his kingdom at the expense of the king of Babylon.[283]

The following year, which was the year of the Lord 1101, *a member of our house saw a fire in the likeness of a great city ... who will swear to not having seen Christ's very evident power.*[284]

Five years afterwards, *King Baldwin blockaded Ascalon from the sea ... against the aforementioned tyrant.*[285]

The day before Christmas Eve there was seen in the west so great a fire in the middle of a star that one would have believed it to be the light of the sun had it been in the east.[286]

In these times [287] *some returning from Jerusalem decorated with palms announced that Acre, which is also called Accaron, had been captured by our people.*[288] *Others besides these related to us many auspicious things about the state of the church of Jerusalem, which gave us great joy.* Among other things, they recalled that King Baldwin[289] had taken the daughter[290] of Duke Roger of Sicily,[291] the widow of King Conrad,[292] and this had brought him a great fleet of Sicilians and Normans that was sufficient to besiege Ascalon – which was once more very dangerous to the Christians – closely from the sea. The king himself besieged it from the land with his own forces and made it tributary.[293]

---

282 *Ibid.*

283 *Ibid.* 1100, above, pp. 159–61.

284 *Ibid.* 1101, above, pp. 162–71.

285 *Ibid.* 1105, above, pp. 183–4.

286 *Ibid.*, above, p. 184.

287 *Ibid.* 1104, above, p. 175.

288 In 1104. *FC* 2.25, pp. 462–4; *AA* 9.27–9, pp. 672–4.

289 Baldwin (of Boulogne), king of Jerusalem 1100–18.

290 Baldwin actually married Adelaide (d. 1118), the widow of Count Roger I of Sicily, in 1113.

291 Roger I, count of Sicily (d. 1101).

292 Conrad (1074–1101), son of Henry IV; king 1087, deposed 1098.

293 Perhaps a confused reference to Acre, which was captured with the aid of a Genoese and Pisan fleet in 1104. Although Baldwin attempted to capture Ascalon by conspiracy in 1111, the port remained in Egyptian hands until 1153. See Fink (1969), p. 387.

Not long afterwards – once the Lord, who had *hid His face a little while*,[294] looked again on Sion because He had once *chosen it for his dwelling* [295] – the seeds of this joy deservedly began to spread over all the earth. Faithful souls far and wide, who are the true *daughters of Jerusalem*,[296] were impregnated with longing for *good fruit* [297] and even long-forgotten prophecies were repeated in different versions everywhere by hearts, tongues and voices. 'Behold!', they say, 'it is in our time that *the ends of the world have come*;[298] *the Lord* has had regard for *Sion and He shall be seen in His glory. He has had regard to the prayer of the humble, and He has not [despised their petition]*',[299] and so forth. '*Have mercy on Jerusalem, the city which He has sanctified, the city of His rest.*[300] *Rejoice and be glad,* all *that love her,*'[301] and more. Although these and a thousand similar prognostications refer in the anagogical sense[302] to *that which is above, our mother Jerusalem*,[303] in the literal sense they encourage the weaker *members* who have drunk from the aforementioned *breasts of consolation*,[304] to hand themselves over to danger and even to hasten to perform it because of the joy of partaking in such thoughts. We know, for example, of a man who admits to having heard the canticle *I was glad*[305] with its alleluia in a vision and to having joined with the singing voices; and because of this he became so passionate about that same pilgrimage that his spirit could find no rest until, after many physical tribulations, he arrived in person to worship *where* the Lord's *feet stood.*[306] It is not to be wondered at, but worthy of veneration, that after sweeping away the scandals of heathen hearts – which are *harder than stones*[307] – from the path of the

---

294 Isaiah 54.8.
295 Psalm 131.13.
296 Isaiah 37.22; Zephaniah 3.14.
297 Matthew 7.17.
298 1 Corinthians 10.11. On apocalypticism and crusade in general see Rubenstein (2011).
299 Psalm 101.17–18.
300 Ecclesiasticus (Sirach) 36.15.
301 Isaiah 66.10.
302 The final sense of the four senses of scriptural interpretation, which deals with how the literal sense of scripture pertains to heavenly destiny and the last things (eschatology).
303 See Galatians 4.26.
304 Isaiah 66.11.
305 Psalm 121.
306 Psalm 131.7.
307 Gregory I, *Sermon* 10 (for Epiphany).

Lord, the catholic church unanimously seeks afresh the path of penance to the fount of its origin, to the earliest cradle of its institutions[308] and to the special house of true bread,[309] which once comprised its precious members who had not only been killed on the same path, but who had been exposed to every sort of mockery from the pagans, like *sheep for the slaughter.*[310] From these followers of Christ the few who remain testify, which is miserable to record, that among the idolaters *not* even *the pace of a foot,*[311] however much less food and lodgings, was a comfort. Who could write satisfactorily about the unheard-of and innumerable torments they suffered for the extortion of money in order that they might have a most bitter death for a reward and life as their cross?

But to return to our times (*that* indeed *we speak what we know and we testify what we have seen*),[312] those *running in the race,*[313] however *straight the road,*[314] do not lack the *prize*[315] of martyrdom to absolve their sins – for example, in *perils from bandits, in perils from rivers, in perils on the sea, in the wilderness, in hunger and thirst,*[316] in heat and disease, and in a thousand other afflictions on the pilgrimage, scarcely believable to the inexperienced. The many decapitated corpses of Christ's cross-bearers that lie strewn on the road give credibility to our words; they were attacked by the brigandage of the heathens, prostrated to the east like a cross and perceived to have *drunk the chalice*[317] of Christ – for whose sake they were on pilgrimage – while they prayed. On this account, those entangled in the bonds of pleasure should necessarily cease to reproach those carrying the cross after Christ, however much *compelled* like *Simon,*[318] because His followers chose this path although it is not (strictly speaking) prescribed for sin by divine law; because they do not aspire to the harsh ways of the Lord, they prove themselves incorrigible by these detractions which they argue with venomous tongues.

308 Jerusalem.
309 Bethlehem: the 'house of bread'. Isidore, *Etymologies* 15.1.23, trans. Barney (2006), p. 302.
310 Psalm 43.22; Isaiah 53.7; Romans 8.36.
311 Acts 7.5.
312 John 3.11.
313 1 Corinthians 9.24.
314 See Isaiah 10.4.
315 1 Corinthians 9.24.
316 See 2 Corinthians 11.26–7.
317 See Matthew 20.22, 23.
318 Simon the Cyrenian: Matthew 27.32.

Why should we believe them [the crusaders] to be anything other than true martyrs to *whom the world is crucified and* they *to the world*?[319] They mark themselves with the cross for so many torments and from many only a few return, decorated with palms like victors over death. Those that dwell in that same promised land lack no [opportunity for] daily martyrdom: namely, voluntary exile, absence of parents, lack of resources, raids, brigandage, continual fear, the treacherousness of the barbarians, and endless warfare with the kingdoms of the Persians and Babylonians.[320] In the face of this the *daughter of Sion* – undoubtedly the church of Jerusalem – daily *shaking herself from the dust,*[321] does not cease to sing *a new song*[322] *to its beloved,*[323] *who has done wonderful things*[324] for her: '*According to the multitude of my sorrows in my heart*', they say, '*thy comforts have given joy to my soul.*'[325] For with such armies the holy places are cleansed of the inveterate filth of the pagans, the ruined churches restored, bishoprics and monasteries set up in their former places in the land, cities and castles fortified, and once desolate ports and markets made joyful with thronging crowds; thus farmers, winemakers and herdsmen are permitted their business again, and – which excels all benefits of the time – the holy fire offers annually on the [feast of the] Resurrection of Christ a spiritual gift for the good of humanity.[326] There came also into our hands – we believe it has already been spread over all the world – a copy of a certain letter addressed to this church, and through it to all churches, which the angel Gabriel is said to have brought on behalf of our Saviour; although it threatens sinners with many terrors, yet it does not deny the convert the customary consolation of divine mercy.

Since the *glory* of Jerusalem has *risen*[327] because of the multitude of the Lord's mercies towards it,[328] every *tribe*[329] on the earth ought to recall

319 Galatians 6.14.
320 The Turks and the Egyptians.
321 Isaiah 52.2.
322 Psalm 97.1.
323 Isaiah 5.1.
324 Psalm 97.2.
325 Psalm 93.19.
326 The Fire of Easter: see *1106 Continuation* 1101, above, pp. 170–1.
327 Isaiah 60.1.
328 See Isaiah 63.7.
329 Psalm 121.4.

that *salvation* for the world once came from *Mount Sion*.[330] Those who formerly *mourned for her*[331] with filial affection now rejoice like a first-time mother and are satisfied *with the breasts of her consolations.*[332] *Going up thither,*[333] *from the rising and the setting of the sun, from the north and from the sea,*[334] they doubtless confess in every way the name of our Lord Jesus Christ, who – it may be said without prejudice to faith – sanctified that same place more than the earthly paradise itself by His incarnation, miracles, passion, resurrection and ascension, and whose name and mercy be praised and glorified for ever and ever. Amen!

---

330 Joel 2.32; see also Isaiah 59.20.
331 Isaiah 66.10.
332 Isaiah 66.11.
333 Psalm 121.4.
334 Psalm 106.3.

THE *1125 CONTINUATION* OF FRUTOLF'S *CHRONICLE* (1117–1125)

The year of the Lord 1117. For a long time all the kingdoms of the nations round about remained satisfied with their borders and their possessions, and bloody swords and murderous implements were concealed in the scabbard of concord, and likewise the universal Mother Church – whose members had been utterly exhausted by many persecutions, heresies and schisms – was again straightened by the true life of Jesus with much gratitude for the ministry of the divine commandments. It was only German fury – ignorant, alas, of how to put aside its obstinacy and by no means willing to remember that *they who love thy law have much peace,*[1] or rather that it is possible to reach the eternal *vision of peace*[2] through peaceful prosperity in this present [life] – only our people of the whole world, I say, who persisted in increasing perversity and obstinate incorrigibility, in perjury and *lying, overflowing* in other things lamented by the voice of the prophet; and *blood touched blood*[3] no less than once when the similar cry of Sodom and Gomorrah reached unto the ear of the Lord of Hosts.[4] Wherefore, during the feast of Christmas, on the third Nones of January [3 January] around the time of vespers,[5] on account of this great contempt for divine authority, *the earth shook and trembled*[6] to such an extent at the evident *wrath* and fury of the Lord that no one can be found on earth who admits ever to have experienced such an earthquake.[7] Many buildings collapsed and they also say that certain cities in Italy were destroyed. On the third Kalends of February [30 January] a very terrible thunderstorm with great whirlwinds was heard and at the same time lightning was frequently seen.

1 Psalm 118.165.
2 Ezekiel 13.16.
3 Hosea 4.2.
4 See Genesis 18.20.
5 Vespers: the second-last of the daily offices, sung sometime between 4 p.m. and 6 p.m.
6 Psalm 17.8.
7 Also recorded in other sources: Anselm of Gembloux, *Chronicle* 1117, p. 376 (a continuation of the chronicle of Sigebert of Gembloux); *Actuarium Laudunense* 1118, p. 445 (which gives the date as 9 January 1118).

Liège, a city of Lotharingia, is quite famous for its patron St Lambert the Martyr,[8] who was once bishop there, but is chiefly renowned above all other cities for the study of letters. On the eve of the Lord's Ascension[9] the entire clergy from its ten churches had assembled in the Mother Church to sing vespers together, as was their custom. Just when they had ended the first psalm, a most serene sky suddenly turned into a storm and at once cast forth such terrible thunder and lightning with sulphurous flames that no one who was there doubted that the hour of the Last Judgement had come, and two clerics and one illustrious knight were swept away from within the sacred buildings.[10] Two weeks afterwards, in the neighbourhood of this same diocese there broke forth from a certain hill, on which no water except rain had ever been seen, an enormous river which washed away a considerable portion of the city and with the utmost loss to the people of Liège flooded their borders as far as Maastricht.[11] On the thirteenth Kalends of March [17 February] we saw around the time of vespers fiery or bloody clouds looming from the north; they extended across the middle of the firmament and instilled not insignificant terror in the world. For, as we later learned, in every city or region the same radiance appeared to be so near that it seemed to threaten the end of all things.

King Henry, whose heart was deeply wounded by these and other such calamities, did not cease to send legations [promising] satisfaction to the apostolic seat, although he himself was struggling with many problems in Italy. With these [legations], however, he accomplished little. For although the lord pope had refrained from chaining him with the fetters of anathema because of the promise – albeit coerced – given to the king,[12] he refused to dissolve without their advice the

---

8 St Lambert (d. *c.* 701).

9 2 May.

10 Cf. *Annals of St James in Liège* 1117, p. 640: 'Moreover, frequent deluges and mighty winds destroyed many houses and killed those who dwelled in them.'

11 *Traiectum*: probably a reference to Maastricht on the River Mosel (*Traiectum ad Mosam*), rather than Utrecht on the River Rhine (*Traiectum ad Rhenum*). On the flood see *Poetic chronicle of the canons of Liège*, p. 417:'The flood spread over the land / on the day which is the seventh [Ides] of June [7 June]. / We feared the destruction of the city / on account of the sins of the whole community. / It shattered bridges and buildings, / our little river and what is called Liège / is submerged seven-fold or more.' See Curschmann (1900), pp. 130–1.

12 A reference to the oath that Paschal II took at Ponte Mammolo, in which he promised never to excommunicate Henry V. See Ekkehard, *Chronicle* 1111, above, p. 240. Cf. William of Malmesbury, *Deeds of the English kings* 5.421, p. 764.

excommunication that the better members of the church had enjoined on him;[13] but he conceded to both sides the right to a hearing in a synod. Indeed, the pope affirmed that he was daily entreated in this matter by letters from across the Alps, especially from the archbishop of Mainz.[14] On this account there was no end to the raving strife everywhere initiated by both sides, especially in the territories across the Rhine, where in the city of Mainz itself many were killed and the best lands were constantly devastated.[15]

Count Emico was killed by knights of Duke Frederick.[16]

The year of the Lord 1118. The lord Pope Paschal II, purified by a long sickness, ended his present life in the Lord.[17] In his place John of Gaeta,[18] a prudent and venerable man who had always worked irreproachably with that same pope on behalf of the Roman church, was elected and with the unanimous consent of all catholics was duly consecrated.

During a campaign against the Arabs,[19] King Baldwin of Jerusalem felt his life being taken by a sickness which, although mild, had vexed him for a long time.[20] He designated the other Baldwin of Edessa[21] in his place as king and gave himself to Christ the Lord, for whom he had already fought so many battles, with his soul full of faith and

---

13 Henry had been excommunicated by Archbishop Guido of Vienne (1112) and the papal legates Cardinal Bishop Conrad of Palestrina (1115) and Theoderic, cardinal priest of S. Grisogono (1115). See Robinson (1990), pp. 429–30.

14 Archbishop Adalbert of Mainz, 1109/11–37.

15 In fighting between Duke Frederick of Swabia and the archbishop of Mainz. See Meyer von Knonau (1909), pp. 44–6.

16 Count Emico (d. 1117), possibly an ancestor of the counts of Leiningen and probably the commander of Adalbert's Franconian troops, was killed in the fighting with Duke Frederick. Cf. *Annals of Paderborn* 1117, p. 261: 'Duke Frederick of Alsace fought fiercely with the people of Mainz; there Count Emico was killed.' See Meyer von Knonau (1909), p. 46 n. 27; Toussaint (1982), pp. 28–9.

17 21 January 1118.

18 John of Gaeta, monk of Monte Cassino, cardinal deacon of S. Maria in Cosmedin, papal chancellor, Pope Gelasius II, 1118–19 (consecrated 24 January).

19 Against the city of al-Farama, about 20 km east of the modern Suez canal. The campaign took place 'towards the end of the month of March': *FC* 2.64, pp. 609–10; trans. Ryan (1973), p. 221.

20 Cf. *Ibid.*; *AA* 12.23, pp. 858–60: the editor suggests (p. 860 n. 52) that Baldwin was afflicted with chronic sepsis, originating in a severe wound inflicted in 1103.

21 His nephew Baldwin of Bourcq (d. 1131), count of Edessa (1100), king of Jerusalem (1118). See Murray (2000), pp. 185–6.

having made a good confession.²² On Palm Sunday²³ he was received on Calvary next to his brother²⁴ in a tomb similar to his brother's²⁵ with great mourning among the different peoples.

Early in the morning of Easter Day,²⁶ the southern part of the sky opened and such a powerful light shone forth that the light of the moon, which until then had been seen very clearly, was outshone by an inestimable brightness and for more than an hour – as we have confirmed from many witnesses – everything was much brighter than any sun. In the same place there appeared in the same opening a large cross on which gold and various precious stones could clearly be distinguished.

Emperor Henry, who had been delayed in the region of Padua, hurried to Rome upon hearing about the death of Pope Paschal and although at first he assented to the election of lord John, who was called Gelasius II, he afterwards withdrew himself from his communion. Not without the support of some of the Romans, he imposed a certain Burdinus²⁷ from Spain upon the apostolic seat, thereby cruelly reviving the schism that it had been hoped had perished. After this shameless seizure of the Roman seat, Gelasius and the cardinals who were with him as well as other catholics who could, condemned the emperor and his idol at Capua, as the letters from him that circulated everywhere testify.²⁸ From here Gelasius travelled to Burgundy through Campania and held a synod in Vienne.

The year of the Lord 1119. The lord Pope Gelasius II convened a synod at Vienne²⁹ and, a few days after it had ended, finished his present life in the Lord at the monastery of Cluny, where, as befitted, he was honourably buried.³⁰ Lord Milo,³¹ the archbishop of Vienne, himself described how he succeeded in his place in the following manner in a letter to

---

22 2 April.

23 7 April.

24 Godfrey V (of Bouillon), duke of Lower Lotharingia 1087–96, advocate of the Holy Sepulchre (d. 1100).

25 See above, p. 160.

26 14 April.

27 Archbishop Maurice of Braga, antipope 'Gregory VIII', 1118–21. See Erdmann (1927), 205–61; Robinson (1990), pp. 431–2; Stroll (2004), pp. 53–7.

28 *JL* 6642.

29 1 January 1119. Schilling (1998), p. 391.

30 29 January.

31 Archbishop Guido of Vienne, Pope Calixtus II, 1119–24.

Archbishop Adalbert of Mainz: '*As our lord Gelasius of happy memory was leaving Vienne, he enjoined me to hurry into his presence as soon as he had reached Cluny. When, a few days later, I was hastening to fulfil this wish, his death was announced to me on the journey. To comfort the brothers who had come with the same lord, as is right, I proceeded to Cluny in great sorrow. While I was thinking hard about consolation for them, they imposed upon me this most heavy and entirely overwhelming burden. For although I was reluctant and resisted in my heart, the cardinal bishops with a hundred of the Roman clergy and laity who met together the day after I arrived* [32] *unanimously elevated me to be pontiff of the Roman church* [with the name] *Calixtus'.*[33]

At this time Conrad of Palestrina,[34] who had thus far been performing a legation for Gelasius, held a synod at Cologne with the Germans where the excommunication of the emperor was made manifest in every possible way.[35] For the same reason he announced another synod at Fritzlar and there, as before, he reconfirmed the excommunication.[36] Hearing these things, the emperor raged with anger – more particularly since the princes in consensus had proposed holding a general council not long afterwards at Würzburg where,[37] if present, he would have to explain himself to the gathering and, if absent, would be deposed from the kingdom. Leaving his troops with the queen in Italy, he appeared very unexpectedly in Germany. Since the excess of his anger in no way permitted him to keep his hand from injustice to his rivals, soon the fury of attacks, depredations and arson – which it had been hoped were dormant – was stirred up following the example of the universal ruler. For at this time, without doubt, all provinces were continually disturbed by such persistent devastation that not even oaths professed for the preservation of divine peace were kept.[38] On this account Henry was compelled by embassies from all the priests and nobles of the kingdom to assent to a general council at Tribur, where he

32 2 February 1119.

33 JL 6682; *PL* 163.1093AB. See also Falco of Benevento, *Chronicle* 1119, p. 180, who relates that Conrad of Palestrina declined the papacy for himself and advised the dying Gelasius II to send for Guido of Vienne. On the election see Robinson (1990), pp. 63–5; Schilling (1998), pp. 391–403; Stroll (2004), pp. 58–64.

34 Conrad (Cuno), cardinal bishop of Palestrina *c.* 1108–22.

35 The synod actually took place on 19 May 1118.

36 28 July 1118. This report omits the suspension of Bishop Otto of Bamberg for non-attendance at the synod: Meyer von Knonau (1909), pp. 80–1.

37 In August 1118.

38 Oaths sworn to uphold the Peace and Truce of God. See Hoffmann (1964); Cowdrey (1970), 42–67.

promised to make satisfaction for everything of which he was accused according to the advice of the senate. When this council was held in the region of the Rhine,[39] the emperor agreed with the counsel of both his adversaries and his friends that anybody in the entire kingdom who had been despoiled should have his goods returned to him and that in the interim he in his authority would receive all the revenues of the kings of old. In addition, peace was commended to all in all provinces, but what little effect this had is proved by events themselves. Also present were legates both of the Romans and of [the archbishop of] Vienne, or rather the messengers of different churches confirming the election of lord Calixtus.[40] Since all our bishops preserved complete obedience to him, a synod on the feast of St Luke[41] was agreed, in which the king promised to participate personally and to be reconciled to the universal church. The bishop of Châlons[42] and the abbot of Cluny[43] managed to meet him [Henry V] at Strasburg,[44] after much persuasion.

If anybody wishes to know more about the acts of that same council he will find it elegantly explained in a letter written by a certain *scholasticus* named Hesso:[45] that is, how the king agreed to the making of a concordat between the royal and priestly powers;[46] and, moreover, how although he was in the vicinity he was not even present at that council where on the thirteenth Kalends of November [19 October] the aforementioned Pope Calixtus II, surrounded by 426 fathers, presided in the presence of an innumerable multitude of the clergy and people; how he was granted an interview by the pope's legates[47] and, finally, how he sought a new

---

39 On 24 June 1119 near Mainz. Meyer von Knonau (1909), pp. 102–4; Minninger (1978), p. 178.
40 Implying that Henry had tacitly abandoned the antipope 'Gregory VIII'. Büttner (1973), p. 401.
41 18 October. The synod was to be held at Rheims.
42 William of Champeaux (d. 1122), scholar, teacher of Peter Abelard, bishop of Châlons-sur-Marne 1113–22.
43 Abbot Pontius of Cluny, 1109–22/6.
44 In late September 1119.
45 Hesso of Strasburg, *Narrative of the Council of Rheims*, pp. 21–8. Hesso's account, which may have been commissioned by Bishop William, displays strong bias against Henry V: Robinson (1990), pp. 435–6; Stroll (2004), p. 367. The *Codex Udalrici*, compiled by Udalric of Bamberg *c*. 1125, contains a copy of Hesso's *Narrative*: *Codex Udalrici* 2, no. 303, ed. Jaffé, pp. 353–65. The other surviving narrative account of the negotiations is Orderic Vitalis, *Ecclesiastical history* 12.21, pp. 262–6. See also p. xix, where the editor notes that Orderic is an unreliable commentator on German history.
46 On the basis of the negotiations with Bishop William and Abbot Pontius in Strasburg.
47 Cardinal Bishop Lambert of Ostia and Gregory, cardinal deacon of S. Angelo.

delay for holding a general council with the princes on the question of ecclesiastical investiture, which he was compelled to give up with such difficulty. Finally, however, as no agreement was reached between the pope and the king,[48] the pope confirmed the synodal decrees of his predecessors and added several new ones that were necessitated by the situation.[49] Thus after almost twelve days the council was properly ended[50] in the fellowship of the Holy Spirit and the pope permitted all to return home with joy, confirmed by apostolic benediction. He also returned to Italy not long afterwards – it is incredible to remember the great excitement and immense pomp with which he was received in Christ's place, not only by all of Rome but also in every province through which he travelled. From this time both he (who was already the true pope) and the whole flock of Christ who followed him began day by day to flourish, while the whole party of Burdinus,[51] whom some are accustomed to call an idol, weakened over time and ceased to work against the church. Yet the commotion that had broken out in the kingdom – oh, what a calamity! – was in no way quelled.

In this year Archbishop Adelgoz of Magdeburg, a young man acceptable to God and all good men, ended his present life in the Lord through premature death.[52] After a canonical election he was succeeded by the canon Rugger.[53]

The year of the Lord 1120. The emperor un-imperially celebrated the birth of the Lord at Worms. Afterwards, on the instigation of Frederick of Arnsberg,[54] he came to Saxony; but because the bishops of that region abstained from communion with him, he returned to Franconia where he was welcomed by some but detested by most. Meanwhile, even the Lord Himself abhorred the tearing of His *seamless tunic*[55] and among other

---

48 Calixtus travelled to Mouzon in the Ardennes during a break in the proceedings at Rheims (22–26 October) to meet Henry; the papal party broke off the negotiations after Henry twice postponed the ratification of the treaty on account of revisions that had been made to the agreement worked out at Strasburg by the papal side. See Chodorow (1971), 613–40; Robinson (1990), p. 435; Schilling (1998), pp. 416–26; Stroll (2004), pp. 369–74.

49 Calixtus prohibited lay investiture and excommunicated Henry V and 'Gregory VIII': Hesso, *Narrative*, p. 22. See Robinson (1990), pp. 132–3.

50 On 30 October.

51 'Gregory VIII'.

52 12 June.

53 Archbishop Rugger of Magdeburg, 1119–25.

54 Count Frederick of Arnsberg (d. 1124).

55 John 19.23.

things – for the scourges of the whole earth were fighting for Him – in the diocese of Trier in the month of June there was roused up a storm that poured out ice of astonishing size, which destroyed buildings and brought other dangers. In Saxony also and especially in the diocese of Halberstadt, He scourged everything with dreadful hail that destroyed not only the crops of nine villages in that territory but also the animals in the fields and an innumerable number of birds. Prompted by these afflictions, the Saxons began to hold frequent meetings to establish concord, to reconcile their differences, to afford each other assistance, to banish robbers and, bypassing the person of the emperor, they began unanimously to arm themselves against anybody who attempted to invade their lands. Among other things they surrounded certain knights of the emperor, who had been devastating Thuringia, in the castle of Wachsenburg[56] with several detachments and finally expelled them, for they were afflicted with want. Thus for a short while the Saxons instituted a most joyful peace in their own areas, although elsewhere war raged as usual. Encouraged by letters and legations from the pope, they canonically elected shepherds to vacant bishoprics. With the help of the bishop of Mainz who was there at that time avoiding the king's wrath, these were consecrated fittingly and in ecclesiastical freedom.

At this time Count Palatine Frederick, who had recently dissociated himself from the rest and bound himself faithfully to the king, died.[57] He was already advanced in age and – as was evidently revealed to a certain servant of God, as people affirm – was carried down to the place of punishment. Theoger[58] of happy memory, the first abbot of the monastery of St George, who had afterwards been consecrated by the apostolic legate as bishop of Metz, was gathered to the Lord and buried in the church of Cluny where he was presiding, having had many injuries inflicted upon him by the king's followers.[59] He was an extremely learned man and most constant in holy conduct until his last hour.[60]

There is in Saxony a certain pair of fortifications not far from one

---

56 South-west of Erfurt.

57 Frederick of Sommerschenburg, count palatine of Saxony. See above, p. 244 n. 197.

58 Theoger (*c.* 1050–1120), monk of Hirsau, prior of Reichenbach (1082), abbot of St Georgen in the Black Forest (1088), bishop of Metz (1118). See McCarthy (2009), pp. 34–7.

59 Theoger was unable to establish himself in Metz and took refuge in Cluny. Cf. Wolfger of Prüfening, *Vita Theogeri*, p. 479: '[Theoger] remained there four months, passing all his time in holy contemplation and prayer'.

60 His scholarly reputation: McCarthy (2009), pp. 34–5. A learned music treatise by Theoger has survived: *Musica*, ed. and trans. Lochner (1995).

another, the names of which I no longer remember. At about midnight there appeared to the watchmen of both castles, not in imagination but in reality, the figure of a man coming from the wall of one castle and proceeding to the other across the breadth of the intervening meadow, whose entire body was in the form of a torch or flaming as a burning mass, and who disappeared close to the opposite castle. This vision appeared not once, but two or three times in a similar fashion.

The year of the Lord 1121. Lord Theoderic[61] succeeded Burchard the Red[62] (who had recently died on a legation from Emperor Henry to Constantinople[63]) by ecclesiastical election to the cathedral of Münster. Having been treated shamefully by his own, he brought his complaint of injustice to the Saxon princes,[64] and since he was a man of illustrious birth who stood out for his renowned virtue,[65] Duke Lothar gathered together an army to regain his seat, even against the will of the king.[66] But it so happened according to the *hidden judgement of God*[67] that when the citizens beheld with terror the ranks of the enemy and each struggled on his own in the face of imminent danger, certain houses caught fire because of rashness and gradually, as the flames got the upper hand, even the great basilica, which was the seat of that church, was burned to the ground. Thus the citizens obtained a miserable victory and drove away the bishop again, although it took much money to restore the church. Some think the cause to have been not so much a military one as that the offering of the former bishop Burchard, who had amassed much in that place from iniquity, was obviously not pleasing to God.

Meanwhile it was heard – and, moreover, confirmed by messengers who had come from Rome – that the fortress of Sutri, where the pseudo-pope Burdinus[68] resided in enslavement to his miserable office, had been captured and destroyed by the zeal of a Roman army.[69] After much

61 Bishop Theoderic II of Münster, 1118–27.
62 Bishop Burchard of Münster, 1097–1118; Italian chancellor 1111. See Hechelmann (1866), 281–332.
63 19 March 1118. Meyer von Knonau (1909), p. 86: Burchard followed Henry to Italy and from there was sent to Constantinople.
64 Theoderic had been driven out of Münster by Henry V in 1119. Meyer von Knonau (1909), pp. 144–5, 166.
65 He was the brother of Count Herman of Winzenburg.
66 2 February.
67 Augustine, *Ennarationes in psalmos* 9.1.
68 See n. 27 above.
69 The campaign, which took place shortly after Easter, was led by John of Crema, cardinal priest of S. Grisogono.

insult and ridicule by the crowd, he was only with difficulty snatched away from its hand by the pope and sent into exile to do penance.[70] There are some who assert that he was done such a disgraceful act that we think it unworthy to commit to writing.[71]

Consequently, on the advice of his followers Emperor Henry undertook to humble the rebellious citizens of Mainz.[72] First, he blockaded the passage of boats in every way, then through ambushes and fortified garrisons all around he prevented the holding of markets or trading or the bringing into the city of any provisions whatsoever, before finally announcing everywhere a general campaign to besiege the city. Hearing this, Bishop Adalbert and the whole of Saxony – where he was staying – were roused up and since Adalbert had a while before accepted [the power of] apostolic legation from the pope, by this authority he called together a great throng of the bishops and princes of that province for the good of Mother Church. There this eloquent man holding primacy in the many and varied regions north of the Alps finally moved all who profess obedience to the catholic church to defend the chief city of all Germany.[73] There also came the bishops of Speyer[74] and Worms[75] who, if they could otherwise offer no effective resistance [to Henry V] since they had been expelled from their sees and were wandering in exile, yet professed obedience to the pope. Those same princes, who with *zeal were zealous for the Lord God of Hosts*,[76] decided that these bishops should be restored to their proper places. Finally, around the summer solstice, when because of the destruction the year's crops were already very precious, for your sake, O noble Mainz, two armies with different purposes – one from Alsace and the other from Saxony – sought your proud walls of venerable dignity, one threatening to destroy them and the other to defend them, while you lamented saying '*the sons of my*

70 'Gregory VIII' was sent in succession to the castle of Passarano, the monastery of La Cava near Salerno and the castle of Ianula near Monte Cassino: Stroll (2004), p. 331.
71 The hostile account of Cardinal Boso's *Life of Calixtus II* in the *Liber pontificalis* relates that the antipope's captors dressed him up as a horned monster: *Liber pontificalis* 2, p. 377. Suger, *Vita Ludovici*, p. 204, records that he was made to don a bloody goatskin and forced to ride a camel along the Via Cassia while sitting backwards. See Mellinkoff (1973), 155; Schreiner (1989), pp. 151–202; Stroll (2004), pp. 330–3.
72 See Meyer von Knonau (1909), p. 170.
73 This is the sole surviving author to report these events; the location of the council is unknown.
74 Bishop Bruno of Speyer, 1107–23.
75 Bishop Burchard II of Worms, 1120–49.
76 3 Kings 19.14.

mother have fought against me!',⁷⁷ to which Christ answered 'Behold, these are *gathered together* again *to come to you!'*⁷⁸ Meanwhile, all churches held fasts, prayers and litanies, and there was no *daughter of Sion*⁷⁹ who did not share in as great a danger as her mother. At this the Lord *had regard to the prayer of the humble and did not despise their petition*⁸⁰ but, having sent his *perfect spirit*,⁸¹ the *spirit of counsel*,⁸² the spirit of peace, among the princes of both sides, when each army had already encamped a short distance from the other so that they could position their battle-lines to be directed against one another, there were sent from each side some of the most wise and religious nobles who began to negotiate with honour for fraternal concord. What more? The spirit of Jesus, who was fighting for His precious blood's sake and for the sons of His bride,⁸³ prevailed over the spirit of pride and malice to such an extent that the minds of all, which had been joined together in unanimous assent to the divine will, by their counsel, persuasion and entreaties so appeased the anger of the king in everything that he decreed that the present business should be concluded not by his judgement but by the judgement of the princes of both parties. Then with everyone giving thanks to the ruler of all things, twelve nobles whose hearts possessed the *fear of God*⁸⁴ were designated from each side for their God-fearing minds to settle the inveterate discord between kingship and priesthood, and nobody opposed it. To decide this an assembly of all the princes of the kingdom was proclaimed for Würzburg at Michaelmas,⁸⁵ and each with his own hand in the other's hand confirmed this agreement as if under oath, and left in peace and joy.

After almost three months had elapsed, Emperor Henry came as agreed to the city of Würzburg with an enormous entourage. The Saxon princes, for their part, together with the bishop of Mainz and others, pitched their camp by the river that is called the Wern, one day's journey from the king. After three days – once both sides had given security through messengers – they met with the king in the

77 Song of Songs 1.5.
78 Isaiah 49.18.
79 See Isaiah 1.8.
80 Psalm 101.18.
81 Psalm 50.14.
82 Isaiah 11.2.
83 That is, the church.
84 Ecclesiasticus 23.37.
85 29 September.

appointed place. He received them peacefully outside the walls (because of the very large crowd of people on both sides) and daily for seven whole days they met together as one in council where they never ceased to discuss the current schism between the kingdom and the priesthood in an expert manner. Although there were several who *hated peace*[86] and who tried to plant new stumbling blocks among the old,[87] no one was able to resist divine intent and arrangement since so many of the heads of the commonwealth had gathered together. At last Emperor Henry, not forgetting his solemn promise, conceded that all questions under discussion were not to be decided according to his wishes or by the contention of any of his own followers, but in all matters according to the advice of the senate. Since it would take too long to record the many things that were bravely decided there, it will suffice well enough to write down the main decisions of that same meeting here:[88] a most firm and universal peace was legally imposed upon all upon pain of death; the *regalia* or fiscal assets were to go to the kingdom, the ecclesiastical assets to the churches, to the dispossessed their lands, to heirs their inheritances and every person of whatever condition was granted his own justice. It was also confirmed by unanimous oath that robbers and thieves were to be pursued according to imperial edict or punished according to the laws that had been set up of old, and it was decreed that whatever scandals and whatsoever disturbances might grow up in the kingdoms of Germany from the seed of the enemy were to be in every way eradicated. But concerning the excommunication, from which virtually every scandal sprouted, nothing was decided except unanimously and in the fear of God to defer to the pope's hearing, choosing at present legates who would report all of this in Rome so that in a general council called by apostolic authority the Holy Spirit should decide what humans could not. Once these things had been reverently arranged for the honour and benefit of the kingdom, Lord Otto, the bishop of Bamberg, Duke Henry[89] and Count Berengar[90] were chosen to convey all this at a meeting in Regensburg on the Kalends of November [1 November] to the princes of Bavaria, who

---

86 Psalm 119.7.

87 Stroll (2004), p. 223, following Waas (1957), p. 75, suggests Archbishop Adalbert of Mainz; Weinfurter (1999), p. 178, concludes the opposite.

88 Cf. *DD H. V*, no. 230; also *MGH Constitutiones* 1, 158 n. 106.

89 Henry 'the Black' (d. 1126), duke of Bavaria 1120–6; the younger brother of Duke Welf V of Bavaria (d. 1120).

90 Count Berengar of Sulzbach: see above, p. 177 n. 294.

were not at the aforementioned assembly since they happened to be occupied with other business of state; and they judged and confirmed that they were willing in everything.

The year of the Lord 1122. Bishop Erlung of Würzburg, who had been vexed by the disease of elephantiasis for four years, died on Holy Innocents Day[91] and, prevented by schism,[92] was buried not in his city but in the monastery of Münsterschwarzach. Considering the vacant position, the lord emperor came there and on the advice of his own people raised up through episcopal investiture a certain youth named Gebhard[93] who, although well born, had because of his eagerness for the schools not yet received any advancement in the church.[94] Yet no small part of the clergy and people – and, as they say, the healthier part – firmly rejected this and canonically elected another named Rugger,[95] a deacon of the same church who had been brought up there and was a canon.[96] On this account no small dissension arose, to the extent that those who favoured the latter were compelled to leave all they possessed in the city in order to escape the displeasure of the emperor. Likewise Duke Frederick[97] and his brother Conrad,[98] who had assented to this election in vain, also withdrew from their uncle and lord in indignation. Not long afterwards, however, the metropolitan of Mainz as well as several of the Saxon princes held a council by the River Werra and by the authority of the same Archbishop Adalbert and other legates of the pope who had recently come from Rome,[99] confirmed the episcopal election and investiture of the aforementioned Rugger against the will of the king.

At about the same time the bishop of Speyer and the abbot of Fulda,[100] having carried out a legation for the whole kingdom to the apostolic

91 28 December.
92 See Ekkehard, *Chronicle* 1116, above, pp. 248, 253.
93 Count Gebhard of Henneberg. He resigned in 1125 according to the *Annals of Würzburg*, p. 2.
94 He was still unordained: Hauck (1954), 4, p. 122.
95 Rugger (d. 1125). On the disputed election see Meyer von Knonau (1909), pp. 188–9; Hauck (1954), 4, pp. 122–5; Wendehorst (1962), pp. 132–3; Schilling (1998), pp. 505–6.
96 Most German cathedral canons had been educated at their cathedral from childhood: Barrow (1989), 117–38.
97 See above, p. 253 n. 263.
98 See above, p. 248 n. 227.
99 Probably the legates mentioned in nn. 101, 102 below.
100 Abbot Erluf of Fulda, 1114–22. Stroll (2004), p. 384.

see, returned bringing with them the bishop of Ostia,[101] who possessed the authority of the lord pope in all matters, and two other cardinals who likewise had been sent from the seat of St Peter to reconcile the kingdom and the priesthood.[102] For this reason a royal council was announced throughout the provinces, the location of which was fixed for Würzburg on the occasion of the feast of St Peter.[103] As the time drew near the princes and crowds from the various provinces began to approach the appointed city, not without damage to the whole of Franconia. But as soon as trustworthy messengers reported that the lord emperor was not coming there because he was entangled in other business near the Rhine, each and everyone arranged to return home. Meanwhile, Gebhard, having allied himself firmly with the citizens and settled down inside the walls with copious forces, one afternoon took a strong detachment of his companions and, not suspecting anything ill, tried to attack some who had set up their camp almost a mile from the city and, as if to prune the enemies of the kingdom, either shamefully to expel them or, if they were off guard, to kill them. Startled by the cries of those advancing, however, those in the camp quickly formed a double line of battle and, bravely resisting, defended themselves and their camp; and with many on each side killed, wounded or captured, as the day drew to a close one side withdrew to the city and the other to its tents. Angered at this, the princes with one accord turned on the city in order to enthrone Rugger. But as they perceived that this could not proceed without bloodshed they turned aside to the monastery called Münsterschwarzach, where in the presence of the whole council, the metropolitan and other Roman legates, Rugger was consecrated bishop of the church of Würzburg and they returned to their own territories. Since then, Rugger has held that part of the bishopric around the River Neckar for his own use, while Gebhard has securely possessed the city and its surrounding area.

Meanwhile the bishop of Mainz, always seeking to take precautions against the anger of the emperor, began with impressive effort to fortify an old castle that had been almost completely derelict for many generations and which, because of the Aschaff stream that flows by it or – as some maintain – because of its founder Ascanius,[104] is named

101 Cardinal Bishop Lambert of Ostia (Pope Honorius II, 1124–30).
102 Gregory, cardinal deacon of S. Angelo (Pope Innocent II, 1130–43) and Saxo, cardinal priest of S. Stefano.
103 St Peter in Chains, 1 August.
104 The mythical son of the Trojan prince Aeneas who escaped to Latium (Italy) with

Aschaffenburg. The king resolved to oppose it and besiege it because he considered that it promoted injustice against himself and against the commonwealth. But the kind Jesus who loves men, through the industry of His servants the legates of the apostolic see, who were then staying at Mainz, began to remove by His Spirit the spirit of opposition to peace that dwelled within the princes and, moreover, to pour love into their hearts;[105] for without doubt it was truly believed that after so much rending of the *garment* of Christ,[106] after so much internal war among Christians, the *time of mercy for Sion*,[107] which is the church, had come albeit belatedly.

Consequently, a general assembly was held at the city of the Vangiones,[108] which is now called Worms.[109] It would be as tedious as it is unbelievable to recall how prudently, how eagerly and with how much concern the assembly of all the nobles struggled for peace and concord for more than a week, while He in whose *hand the heart of the king*[110] is bent all the impetuosity of the emperor into obedience to the reverend pope for the cause of Mother Church, even beyond the hopes of most. Soon afterwards both the emperor himself and his entire army were received back into communion by envoys of the apostolic see, and moreover, on apostolic authority, a general absolution was given for all who had been polluted by this schism. The manner in which he [Henry V], humbled for Christ in front of an enormous multitude, renounced ecclesiastical investiture and other spiritual business that had for so long been administered by the German kings (which he had resolved never to give up as long as he lived so as not to diminish the honour of the kingdom) and how, by his own hand and that of the lord bishop of Ostia, he gave them to our Lord Jesus Christ and His own in perpetuity according to the law of the church, as well as what the apostolic authority conceded to him to maintain the honour of the kingdom, can be shown more intelligibly by the following documents from both parties:[111]

---

his father at the fall of Troy.
105 An allusion to Romans 5.5.
106 An allusion to John 19.23.
107 See Psalm. 101.14.
108 A Germanic tribe, mentioned in Caesar's *De bello Gallico*, whose power centred on the area of Worms.
109 8 September. Stroll (2004), p. 388 suggests that the assembly might have been held at Mainz though Henry V remained at Worms.
110 Proverbs 21.1.
111 The Concordat of Worms (23 September 1122). See Classen (1973), pp. 411–60; Robinson (1990), pp. 437–40; Schilling (1998), pp. 500–33; Stroll (2004), pp. 388–98.

I,[112] *Henry, by the grace of God august emperor of the Romans, for the love of God and of the holy Roman church and of the lord Pope Calixtus and for the cure of my soul, do remit to God and to His holy apostles Peter and Paul and to the holy catholic church, all investiture through ring and staff, and grant that in all the churches there may be free election and consecration. The possessions and regalia of St Peter that have been removed* [from the church] *from the beginning of this discord until this day – whether in the time of my father or also in mine – and which I hold, I restore to that same holy Roman church; and, moreover, I shall faithfully aid in the restoration of what I do not hold. Likewise, the possessions that I hold of all other churches and princes, and of all others as well clergy as laity, I shall return according to the counsel of the princes and justice, and I shall faithfully aid in the restoration of that which I do not hold. And I grant true peace to Calixtus and to the holy Roman church, and to all those who are or have been on its side, and in those things for which the holy Roman church shall ask aid, I shall faithfully aid it.*

I,[113] *Calixtus, servant of the servants of God, do grant to his beloved son Henry, by the grace of God august emperor of the Romans, that the elections of the bishops and abbots of the German kingdom that pertain to the kingdom shall take place in your presence without simony or any violence, so that if any discord shall arise between the parties, with the counsel of the metropolitan and co-provincials or the judgement of the sounder part you may give assent and aid. The elect, moreover, may receive the regalia from you through the sceptre – excepting all things that are known to belong to the Roman church – and he should do what he ought lawfully to do before you for these. Those consecrated from other parts of the empire are to receive the regalia from you through the sceptre within six months. Moreover, concerning matters in which you make a complaint to me, according to the duty of my office I shall furnish my aid. I give true peace to you and to all who are or have been on your side in the time of this discord.* Given in the year 1122 on the ninth Kalends of October [23 September].

On account of the assembly's infinite multitude, these two documents were read, given and accepted in an open field by the Rhine; and after manifold praises had been rendered to the Ruler of things and the divine sacraments had been celebrated by the lord of Ostia, during which the lord emperor was fully reconciled [to the church] with the kiss of peace

---

112 Partial quotation of the oath sworn by Henry V to Calixtus II, *MGH Constitutiones* 1, pp. 159–60.

113 Partial quotation of the oath sworn by Calixtus II to Henry V with some rearrangement, *MGH Constitutiones* 1, p. 161. These distinctive versions of the oaths are also transmitted in a contemporary Bamberg manuscript (Bamberg, Staatsbibliothek, Msc. Can. 9, fol. 127r).

and Holy Communion, everyone departed with infinite joy.

Not long afterwards, that is at the feast of St Martin [11 November], the emperor held an assembly at Bamberg with the princes who had not been at the earlier one where,[114] in complete accordance with his vow, among many matters those that concerned the honour of both the royal and priestly power were arranged according to ancient custom. He sent his own legates with those of the Romans and he instructed both sets to take honourable messages and gifts to the lord Pope Calixtus, his kinsman, to whom he was now utterly united.

The year of the Lord 1123. Emperor Henry celebrated Christmas at Utrecht.[115] There arose during the days of that festival a certain dispute between the courtiers and the bishop's *ministeriales*, which developed into such a commotion that the whole court and the city simultaneously formed themselves into armed bands. There was such confused clamour, almost as if the people of Utrecht had organized a conspiracy against the emperor, that with one side charging headlong and the other resisting there resulted such a violent fight that many were killed, several of the townspeople were captured and the rest fled to a very strong tower that was situated there. Even the bishop[116] was alleged to have participated in this depraved scheme and because of that treachery was taken into custody, from which afterwards he could only with difficulty redeem himself by paying the fine of a great sum of money and through the intervention of the most important people of those parts, especially Archbishop Frederick of Cologne.[117] At that time also[118] the seed of discord begin to germinate when a certain noble woman whose name escapes me – but definitely the sister of Duke Lothar (on whose protection she relied) – presumed to rebel against the emperor.[119] This was ended only with difficulty and effort the following summer – to the

---

114 See Meyer von Knonau (1909), p. 217.

115 Henry spent Christmas 1122 in Speyer. This report may refer to Whitsun 1122 (14 May), which Henry spent in Utrecht. Cf. *Annals of Aachen* 1122, p. 685: 'At Whitsun, court was held at the further [city of] Trajan [Utrecht]. There occurred an uprising in which many were captured by the emperor while a few were killed.' See Meyer von Knonau (1909), pp. 193–4, 220–1.

116 Bishop Godebald of Utrecht, 1112–27.

117 After a royal expedition that besieged Godebald at Schulenburg (an island fortress on the River Ems), which took place after Whitsun (3 June) 1123. See Meyer von Knonau (1909), pp. 250–2.

118 Summer 1122.

119 Gertrude/Petronilla (d. 1144), sister of Lothar of Supplinburg and widow of Count Florentius II of Holland (d. 1121).

great damnation of that region, which is commonly called Holland – when at last the emperor himself led a large army there.[120]

At the same time, although external matters remained calm, first in Saxony and then in almost the whole of Germany the storm of civil war and sedition welled up and, as the prophet says, *lying and* perjury *overflowed and blood touched blood.*[121] Thieves who abounded everywhere under the name of knights attacked the villages and fields of the churches, plundered farmers at home and in the open, and – what a crime! – forced under torture those who were accustomed to nourish themselves only with bread and water to furnish them with luxuries; and since everybody now avenged the injuries done to himself with looting and arson, a want or rather a great scarcity of the year's produce began everywhere to become more serious.

In the locality of Worms there were seen for a few days a not insignificant multitude of armed knights coming together in formations and dispersing and, as if by agreement, forming troops now here and now there; at about the ninth hour[122] they returned to a certain mountain whence they had been seen to come. Finally, one of the residents of that area – not without great fear in the face of so prodigious an assembly – approached them armed with the sign of the cross; and soon one of those people came running towards him and swore by the name of our almighty Lord that he would reveal the reason for the appearance of these people. Among other things he said: 'We are neither phantoms as you suppose nor a host of knights as we appear to you, but the souls of knights who have been killed not long ago. Weapons and armour and horses, which were before instruments of sin for us are now the means of our torment and in truth everything that you can distinguish in us is fire, although your bodily eyes cannot discern it.' In connexion with this it is said that even Count Emico,[123] who had been killed a few years before, appeared and declared that he could be redeemed from this punishment by prayers and almsgiving.

Some report that on the night before Maundy Thursday, as they were hurrying to vigils[124] in the usual manner for churchmen, they saw as

---

120 Summer 1123. Another expedition followed in February 1124. See below, 1124, pp. 279–80. See Meyer von Knonau (1909), pp. 250, 260.

121 Hosea 4.2.

122 3 p.m.

123 See above, 1117, p. 263.

124 The Night Office (or Mattins), the longest of the divine offices observed by regular clergy.

it were such a countless number of stars falling from heaven that they seemed to imitate drops of rain in their number and manner of falling.[125]

At this time Bishop Dietrich of Zeitz shone forth.[126] He was extremely learned in letters, was always a champion for the catholics against the schisms that sprouted forth at various times in his day and exerted himself for the benefit of the church in all pastoral concerns committed to him. Not far from the surroundings or territory of his city he established over several years – with supreme effort and the greatest expense in costly buildings – a monastery or abbey on a hill that once long ago was called Bosau.[127] When the place was virtually completed, such that a not inconsiderable church had been consecrated and a congregation of monks had been placed there, there was found among those which we call the lay brothers a certain perverse man, born from the same race as the Sorbs, who was not subject to any holy rule but only to his own desires in all things.[128] Frequently was he rebuked by the abbot for his excesses, but not being improved he was handed over to the bishop for correction. Having been chastised, often harshly as was proper, he erupted into such violence that he stabbed the bishop with a knife as he stood in prayer before the altar, and after three days the venerable priest departed to Christ.[129]

The year of the Lord 1124. The emperor celebrated Christmas at Aachen. The moon appeared in eclipse on the Purification of St Mary [2 February]. Terrified by this, Conrad, a first cousin of the emperor,[130] pledged to change his life and to set out for Jerusalem, where he would devote himself to fighting for Christ; he thereby acquired substantial favour from all who had heard this. Several who had also previously been eagerly devoted to wickedness likewise professed to join his retinue.

Not long afterwards Emperor Henry commenced an expedition against those who opposed him[131] in the region of Holland and when, although

---

125 Cf. Cosmas of Prague, *Chronicle* 3.51, trans. Wolverton (2009), p. 238: 'In Lent, almost throughout the entire world, the powers of the air, like many stars, although they did not fall to the earth, still seemed to fall.'

126 Bishop Dietrich of Zeitz-Naumburg, 1112–23.

127 The monastery of Bosau, south of Merseburg, founded as part of the Hirsau reform movement in 1114. See Jakobs (1961), p. 55.

128 An allusion to the *Rule of St Benedict* 1: 'The third and worst kind of monks are the sarabites, who have never been tried under any rule nor by the experience of a master ... the pleasure of their desires is to them a law.'

129 27 September.

130 Conrad of Staufen, the emperor's nephew. See above, p. 248 n. 227.

131 Gertrude, the widow of Count Florentius of Holland. See above, 1123, p. 277.

slowly, he had conquered them he took himself to the more southerly regions, leaving the queen near the borders of Lotharingia. Around the middle of Lent he held an assembly at Worms with some of the princes; the others who were not there, that is the Saxons, Bavarians and Bohemians, he summoned to come to a council in Bamberg on the Nones of May [7 May], particularly because of the insolence of Duke Lothar, who had been observed to struggle afresh against the commonwealth because of the injustices that had been inflicted upon his aforementioned sister by the emperor.

This assembly was very large, for the dukes of the different provinces were there on account of the aforementioned Lothar and a few of the Saxon princes who conspired with him. The venerable Bishop Otto provided all or part of the necessary expenses for each participant in addition to the public and long-established aid for the imperial majesty,[132] which was demanded rather rudely by the courtiers. They also observed that this father had visited the palace less frequently than other bishops; in truth he would rather occupy himself in building or restoring monasteries,[133] in distributing alms, in staying awake at prayer or in becoming engrossed in other studies either practical or theoretical. There was no want of those who because of envy murmured and declared that he must devote himself more to public duties in an attempt to arouse the animosity of the emperor against that man of God. But since *the Lord keeps all them that love him*[134] *and destroys the ways of sinners*,[135] and Otto had not spared transitory goods at a time when every region was squeezed with want,[136] in a wonderful way everyone was supplied sufficiently, good overcame evil[137] and *in unfeigned charity*[138] by his services he won the devoted affection of the whole kingdom. When the business of the assembly had been completed, he announced both to the emperor and to all the princes that he had been frequently called upon through letters and messengers by Boleslav,[139] the duke of

---

132 The provision of hospitality (*gistum*) and food (*servitum*) to the royal entourage as it perorated through the kingdom by archbishops, bishops and royal abbots. See Metz (1971), 257–91; Bernhardt (1993), pp. 75–84; Robinson (1999), pp. 8–9.

133 Otto was an enthusiastic proponent of the Hirsau reform, founding or reforming some thirty institutions. See Jakobs (1961), pp. 140–5.

134 Psalm 144.20.

135 Psalm 145.9.

136 Famines in 1124: Curschmann (1900), p. 132.

137 See Romans 12.21.

138 2 Corinthians 6.6.

139 Boleslav III (1086–1138), duke of Poland 1102–38.

Poland, and, moreover, that even the lord Pope Calixtus had directed him with his permission and blessing to the Pomeranian people. These were Boleslav's neighbours whom that same duke had recently subjugated and compelled to seek refuge in Christianity. All who had convened from the church and from the court assented, praying for prosperity in this holy effort; only the sons of the church of Bamberg reluctantly let go of their beloved father, with great weeping for him as if they were following a funeral.[140]

After the confirmation of peace and after various legal cases and affairs of the kingdom had been resolved satisfactorily, the emperor, full of indignation against those who had disdained to attend the present assembly, proclaimed a general expedition for the following August, ostensibly against the Saxons but in reality against France and the kingdom of King Louis,[141] evidently to provide aid to his father-in-law, King Henry of England,[142] who was fighting against the same King Louis of France for the possession of the province of Normandy. After the appointed time, as the German army began to approach the border, scouts daily reported that the French had gathered a colossal army at home and expected to fight, or rather desired it recklessly. The emperor, however, was not then leading great numbers, for the Germans do not willingly fight against foreign peoples.[143] In the meantime it was reported from the rear that the citizens of Worms had with the help of Duke Frederick[144] restored Bishop Burchard[145] to his seat against the will of the emperor and were strengthening themselves in every way for rebellion behind the city walls. Hearing this the emperor returned and attacked the city with great ferocity and only lifted the siege when, as usual, after much effort had been expended there and many had been captured or killed before the walls, the citizens, who had finally run out of food, paid a fine of 5,000 talents and relinquished the bishop, making a pact according to the will of the emperor.[146]

The lord Pope Calixtus II, a man who was most excellent in origin and character, in wisdom as well as in the management of all divine and

---

140 The first of Otto's two missions to Pomerania (1124–5 and 1128). See Buske (2003), pp. 85–127; Buske (2007), pp. 143–55.

141 Louis VI 'the Fat' (1081–1137), king of France 1108–37.

142 Henry I (1068/9–1135), king of England 1100, duke of Normandy 1106.

143 See Meyer von Knonau (1909), pp. 273–4.

144 Duke Frederick of Swabia.

145 Bishop Burchard had been expelled from his city in 1121.

146 Cf. *Annals of Paderborn* 1124, pp. 144–5. See Meyer von Knonau (1909), pp. 280–1.

human affairs, ended his life in the Lord.[147] After his death one party of the Romans strove to have the archbishop of Ravenna[148] (sufficiently recommended by the testimony of his piety in all things) placed on the apostolic throne, while the other party, which favoured Lambert of Ostia,[149] was able to achieve its wish when he was afterwards elected by all in a unanimous election.[150] This man had long been proven for his service to the Roman church and was known on both sides [of the Alps] because of the legation in which he had recently laboured strenuously for the reconciliation of royal and priestly power in Germany. He was canonically consecrated according to the custom of that see with the unanimous acclamation of all clergy, whether nearby or far away, and as one truly worthy of the honour was called Honorius II.[151]

The year of the Lord 1125. Emperor Henry celebrated Christmas at the city of Argentaria, which is called Strasburg, and there the court was frequented by the princes of Alsace and Lotharingia, and the nobles of other areas across the Rhine. At that time, after a terribly severe winter, a stormy spring, a mighty famine and most cruel mortality there followed such great ruin in all provinces, but especially among the common people, that almost a third of the population is recorded to have died.[152]

At the same time, namely on that most holy Sabbath of Easter,[153] our most longed-for steward sent from heaven, Bishop Otto, revisited the flock entrusted to him after having been immersed in many tribulations for Christ's sake; and it was as with Christ Himself that the *Lord's anointed*[154] was received with gladness by his disciples, doubling the joy of the resurrection of the Lord. This same *faithful and wise steward*[155]

---

147 13 December.
148 Archbishop Walter of Ravenna. This, the only report of Walter's candidacy, is probably confusing him with Theobald Boccapecus, cardinal priest of S. Anastasia, who had been elected and was being installed as 'Celestine II' when the ceremony was interrupted and a new election held. See Robinson (1990), pp. 65–9.
149 See n. 101 above.
150 Lambert of Ostia was supported by the papal chancellor Haimeric and the Frangipani family; Theobald by the Pierleoni family.
151 Honorius II, 16 December 1124–13/14 February 1130.
152 Famine in 1125: Curschmann (1900), pp. 132–6.
153 24 March.
154 1 Kings 24.11.
155 Luke 12.42.

of Christ had recorded in letters the profit of the talent[156] entrusted to him as testimony of his faith and devotion, which we do not hesitate to add here for the edification of the reader:

'In the year of the Lord's Incarnation 1124, in the second year of the indiction, with Pope Calixtus II presiding over the Roman see, Otto, by the grace of God bishop of the church of Bamberg, at the instigation of divine command and corroborated by the authority and assent of the aforementioned pope, entered the pagan parts of Pomerania and certain towns in the country of the Liutizi[157] to call them away from their error and to lead them into the way of truth and the knowledge of the Son of God. Having baptized and converted them, he built and consecrated churches and he taught them how to serve these according to the institutions of the holy Fathers: namely, on the sixth day [Friday] to abstain from meat and milk in the manner of other Christians, on the Day of the Lord to refrain from all evil work and to go to church to hear the divine offices where they should persevere in ardent prayer. They should observe the feasts of the saints and their vigils with all diligence according to what they have been shown. They should strive diligently to observe the fasts, vigils, alms and prayers of the most holy Lent; they should bring their children to be baptized on the holy Sabbath of Easter or Pentecost with candles and capes, which are called white garments, accompanied by their sponsors, and they should bring them to church, clothed in the same garments of innocence, every day until the eighth day after the same Sabbath so that they may busy themselves in being present for the celebration of the divine offices. This also he enjoined upon them: that they ought not to kill their own children, for this great crime flourished among them; that they should not hold their sons and daughters at baptism but seek out sponsors and the sponsors must watch over them with faithfulness and friendship like natural parents. He forbade them also from taking a godmother as wife or from taking their own relations up to the sixth or seventh degree; and everyone was to be content with one wife. They ought not to bury Christian dead among pagans in woods or in meadows, but in cemeteries as is the custom with all Christians. They should not place cudgels on their graves and they should abandon all pagan rites and depravities; they should not construct temples for idols or go to soothsayers and there was to be no casting of lots. They were to consume nothing filthy, no carrion, nothing suffocated, nothing

156 See Matthew 25.13–30; Luke 12.42–8.
157 See above, p. 94 n. 76.

[offered to] idols and no animal blood. They should not communicate with pagans, they should accept no food or drink from them or in their vessels or in any of these things return to the customs of the pagans. He charged them also to do penance for perjury, adultery, murder and other crimes according to the institution of the canons and in all things obediently to observe the Christian religion. Women should come to church after giving birth and accept blessing from the priest according to the custom. The names of the cities: Pyritz, Stettin, Wollin, Kammin, Colberg, Belgard, Lubzen, Gartz.'[158]

During these times there were throughout the whole Roman empire many prodigies and frequent calamities of different sorts, so that their number and type could not be calculated by any mortal means. Some few, which came to our ears as reports, it is agreeable to note with our pen so that the example of the divine whip, which we have endured in lashes of many forms, will not be hidden from the succeeding generation.[159] On the fourth day [Wednesday] in the week of Whitsun[160] the cold from a most dreadful frost inflicted great damage on the new fruit and vines, which had already promised the hope of a most abundant [harvest] by the growth of their shoots, and not long afterwards, that is on the sixteenth Kalends of July [16 June], a storm so mighty that it seemed to threaten a flood cruelly devastated what had been left by the cold. Similarly, something extraordinary that broke out of the marshy areas destroyed the neighbouring crops, particularly the wheat, through mildew and blight. Even the breeding of bees, I know not through what portentous setback, almost entirely perished. In addition, signs of many sorts were attested to having been seen in the sun, moon and stars, so much so that they seemed to exceed the belief of some. The right calf of a certain boy born in the district of Tullifelt,[161] which had long been swollen and blue, at last burst in the place where the pus had collected and instead of discharge – wonderful to tell! – many grains of wheat – winter wheat, spelt, barley and oats – burst out.

Emperor Henry, the fifth of that name, wished to celebrate Whitsun[162] in the city of Utrecht but, overcome by a disease he had long concealed, he began to approach his last hour. Calling his companions to himself

---

158 A version of this letter is also transmitted in Ebo of Michelsberg's mid-twelfth-century *Vita Ottonis* 2.12, *MGH SS* 12, pp. 850–1.
159 The didactic purpose of history: see above, p. 20.
160 20 May.
161 On the River Werra.
162 17 May.

– that is his wife Queen Matilda as well as his relative Duke Frederick of Swabia and other princes – he gave them as far as he could his advice concerning the state of the kingdom, committed his property and the queen to Frederick as his faithful heir and ordered that the crown and other royal insignia be kept safe in a most secure castle that is called Trifels until the assembly of the princes could meet. Then having received the viaticum of the sacrament of Christ he at last ended his days on the tenth Kalends of June [23 May]. His body, arranged as is customary for a king, was taken to Speyer and in the presence of a great multitude of the nobles and lesser people, both clerical and lay, was honourably placed in the mausoleum of his ancestors in the twentieth year of his kingship and the fourteenth year of his emperorship.

First of all, as already described, he deprived his excommunicated father of the empire under the guise of religion, but once confirmed in the honour he changed his behaviour. After inflicting injuries on the apostolic see he always treated it as inferior to himself. To the business of the kingdom he gave little attention. He had a quick intelligence and was vigorous and daring, although he had little luck in battle and he excessively desired foreign things. They say that he amassed an infinite amount of money but since he died without children he knew not – alas! alas! as scripture says – for whom *he had accumulated it.*[163]

In this same year several of the nobles as well as an innumerable multitude of the common people were overtaken by a raging death. Among them Udalric of Eichstätt,[164] Rugger of Würzburg[165] and Arnold the son of Count Arnold,[166] a youth of good character; and many others were overwhelmed by the ultimate fate. For after divine will had accomplished an immense slaughter of the common people by famine and pestilence, a great plague began indiscriminately to ravage people everywhere, so that no condition, sex or age [of person] was spared from the threat of pallid death, and there were hardly sufficient [people] alive to tend to the dead bodies.

163 Luke 12.21.
164 Bishop Udalric II of Eichstätt, 1112–25 (d. 2 September).
165 See n. 95 above.
166 Probably Arnold of Loon, burgrave of Mainz.

BIBLIOGRAPHY

Primary sources

Actuarium Laudunense 928, 1052–1145, MGH SS 6, pp. 445–7.

Adam of Bremen, *History of the archbishops of Hamburg-Bremen*, ed. B. Schmeidler, *Magistri Adam Bremensis gesta Hamburgensis ecclesiae pontificum*, MGH SSrG 2 (Hanover and Leipzig, 1917).

— trans. F. J. Tschan, *History of the archbishops of Hamburg-Bremen*, new edn (New York, 2002).

Albert of Aachen, *Historia Ierosolimitana*, ed. and trans. S. B. Edgington, *Albert of Aachen: Historia Ierosolimitana. History of the journey to Jerusalem* (Oxford, 2007).

Ammianus Marcellinus, *Res gestae*, ed. and trans. J. C. Rolfe, 3 vols (Cambridge, Mass. and London, 1939–50; repr. 2000).

Annales Hildesheimenses. Continuatio Paderbornensis a. 1109–37, MGH SS 3, pp. 112–16.

Annalista Saxo, MGH SS 6, pp. 542–777.

— ed. K. Nass, *Die Reichschronik des Annalista Saxo*, MGH SS 37 (2006).

Annalium Ratisbonensium maiorum fragmentum, ed. G. Waitz, MGH SSrG [4] (Hanover, 1890), pp. 87–91.

Annals of Aachen = *Annales Aquenses*, MGH SS 16, pp. 684–7.

Annals of Augsburg = *Annales Augustani 973–1104*, MGH SS 3, pp. 123–36.

Annals of Disibodenberg = *Annales sancti Disibodi a. 891–1200*, MGH SS 17, pp. 4–30.

Annals of Hildesheim = *Annales Hildesheimenses*, ed. G. Waitz, MGH SSrG [8] (Hanover, 1878).

Annals of Magdeburg, MGH SS 16, pp. 105–96.

Annals of Niederaltaich = *Annales Altahensis maiores*, ed. E. L. B. von Oefele, MGH SSrG [4] (Hanover, 1890).

Annals of Paderborn, ed. P. Scheffer-Boichorst, *Annales Patherbrunenses. Eine verlorene Quellenschrift des 12. Jahrhunderts* (Innsbruck, 1870).

Annals of Rosenfeld = *Annales Rosenveldensis 1057–1130*, MGH SS 16, pp. 99–104.

Annals of St Alban (*Annals of Würzburg*) = *Annales Wirziburgenses*, MGH SS 2, pp. 238–47.

Annals of St James in Liège = *Annales Sancti Iacobi. Pars secunda* 1056–1174, *MGH SS* 16, pp. 638–42.

Annals of Weissenburg = *Annales Weissenburgenses*, ed. O. Holder-Egger, *MGH SSrG* [38] (Hanover and Leipzig, 1894), pp. 9–57.

Annals of Würzburg = *Annales Herbipolenses 1125–44, MGH SS* 16, pp. 1–12.

Anonymous imperial chronicle, 1095–1114, ed. and trans. F.-J. Schmale and I. Schmale-Ott, *Frutolfs und Ekkehards Chroniken und die Anonyme Kaiserchronik* (Ausgewählte Quellen zur deutschen Geschichte des Mittelalters 15; Darmstadt, 1972), pp. 212–65.

Anselm of Gembloux, *Chronicle* (a continuation of Sigebert of Gembloux), *MGH SS* 6, pp. 375–85.

Anselm II of Lucca, *Book against Wibert* = *Liber contra Wibertum, MGH Libelli* 1 (1891), pp. 517–28.

Anselm of St-Remi, *Historia dedicationis ecclesiae sancti Remigii* (*PL* 142.1415D–1440B).

Augustine, *De doctrina Christiana*, ed. J. Martin, *CCSL* 32 (Turnhout, 1962).

— *Ennarationes in psalmos*, ed. E. Dekkers and J. Fraipont, *CCSL* 38 (Turnhout, 1956).

— *Meditations* = *Meditationum liber unus, PL* 40.0901–42.

Balderic of Dol, *Historia Ierosolimitana, RHC Occ.* 4 (Paris, 1879), pp. 9–111.

Bede, *De ratione temporum*, ed. C. W. Jones, *CCSL* 123b (Turnhout, 1977).

Benedict, *Rule of St Benedict*, ed. and trans. T. Fry, *The Rule of St Benedict in Latin and English with notes* (Collegeville, Minn., 1981).

Beno, *Gesta Romanae aecclesiae contra Hildebrandum, MGH Libelli* 2 (1892), pp. 369–80.

Benzo of Alba, *Ad Heinricum IV imperatorem libri VII*, ed. H. Seyffert, *MGH SSrG* [65] (Hanover, 1996).

Bernold of St Blasien (of Constance), *Chronicon*, ed. I. S. Robinson, *Die Chroniken Bertholds von Reichenau und Bernolds von Konstanz, 1054–1100, MGH SSrG NS* 14 (Hanover, 2003), pp. 383–540.

— trans. I. S. Robinson, *Eleventh-century Germany: the Swabian chronicles* (Manchester, 2008), pp. 245–337.

Berthold of Reichenau, *Chronicon*, ed. I. S. Robinson, *Die Chroniken Bertholds von Reichenau und Bernolds von Konstanz, 1054–1100, MGH SSrG NS* 14 (Hanover, 2003), pp. 161–382.

— trans. I. S. Robinson, *Eleventh-century Germany: the Swabian chronicles* (Manchester, 2008), pp. 99–107 (first version), 18–244 (second version).

Boethius, *Consolation of philosophy*, ed. C. Moreschini, *Boethius. De consolatione philosophiae, Opuscula theologica* (Munich and Leipzig, 2000).

Bonizo of Sutri, *To a friend* = *Liber ad amicum*, ed. E. Dümmler, *Bonizonis episcopi Sutrini Liber ad amicum*, MGH Libelli 1 (1891), pp. 568–620.

— trans. I. S. Robinson, *The papal reform of the eleventh century: lives of Pope Leo IX and Pope Gregory VII* (Manchester, 2004), pp. 158–261.

Bruno of Merseburg, *Saxon war*, ed. H.-E. Lohmann, *Brunos Buch vom Sachsenkrieg*, MGH DM 2 (Leipzig, 1937).

Bruno of Segni, *Letters* = *Brunonis episcopi Signini epistolae quatuor*, MGH Libelli 2 (1892), pp. 563–5.

— *Letter 4*, ed. G. Fransen, 'Réflexions sur l'étude des collections canoniques à l'occasion de l'édition d'une lettre de Bruno de Segni', *Studi Gregoriani* 9 (1972), 529–32 (the full text of *Letter 4*, known in fragmentary form to Ernst Sackur, the MGH editor of Bruno's letters).

Caffaro of Genoa, *Annales Ianuenses*, ed. L. T. Belgrano, *Annali Genovesi* 1 (Fonti per la storia d'Italia 11; Genoa, 1890), pp. 3–75.

Catalogue of kings and emperors (twelfth century, Admont) = *Francorum imperatorum historia brevissime*, MGH SS 10, pp. 136–8.

Chronicle of Monte Cassino = *Chronica monasterii Casinensis*, ed. H. Hoffmann, MGH SS 34 (1980).

Chronicle of St Peter at Erfurt = *Cronica sancti Petri Erfordensis moderna*, ed. O. Holder-Egger, MGH SSrG [42] (Hanover and Leipzig, 1899), pp. 118–442.

Chronicon Suevicum Universale = *Swabian universal chronicle*: see *Reichenauer Kaiserchronik*.

Cicero, *In Pisonem*, ed. A. C. Clark, *M. Tulii Ciceronis Orationes* 4 (Oxford, 1922).

Codex Udalrici, book 2, ed. J. G. Eccard, *Corpus historicum medii aevi* 2 (Leipzig, 1723).

— ed. P. Jaffé, *Bibliotheca rerum Germanicarum* 5 (Berlin, 1869), pp. 17–469.

Cosmas of Prague, *Chronica Boemorum. Die Chronik der Böhmen des Cosmas von Prag*, ed. B. Bretholz, MGH SSrG NS 2 (Berlin, 1923).

— trans. L. Wolverton, *The Chronicle of the Czechs: Cosmas of Prague* (Washington, DC, 2009).

Cyprian, *Letter 55* (to Anthony), ed. W. Hartel, *Sancti Thasci Caecili Cypriani opera omnia*, CSEL 3/2 (Vienna, 1868).

De ordinando pontifice, ed. H. H. Anton, *Der sogennante Traktat 'De ordinando pontifice'* (Bonn, 1982), pp. 75–83.

Decree of the Council of Clermont, ed. R. Somerville, *The councils of Urban II, vol. 1: Decreta Claramontensia* (Amsterdam, 1972).

Die Ordines für die Weihe und Krönung des Kaisers und der Kaiserin, ed. R. Elze, MGH Fontes 9 (Hanover, 1960).

Donizo of Canossa, *Life of Matilda* = *Vita Mathildis comitissae metrica*, MGH SS 12, pp. 348–409.

Ebo of Michelsberg, *Vita Ottonis episcopi Babenbergensis*, MGH SS 12, pp. 822–83; partial translation by C. H. Robinson, *The Life of Otto, apostle of Pomerania, 1060–1139, by Ebo and Herbordus* (Translations of Christian literature. Series 2; London and New York, 1920).

Ekkehard of Aura, *Chronicle*, ed. G. Waitz, MGH SS 6, pp. 208–67 (1106–25).

— *Chronicle*, trans. W. Pflüger, *Die Chronik des Ekkehard von Aura. Nach der Ausgabe der Monumenta Germaniae* (Leipzig, 1879).

— *Chronicle* 1096–1125, ed. and trans. F.-J. Schmale and I. Schmale-Ott, *Frutolfs und Ekkehards Chroniken und die Anonyme Kaiserchronik* (Ausgewählte Quellen zur deutschen Geschichte des Mittelalters 15; Darmstadt, 1972), pp. 124–209, 268–377.

— *Vita sancti Burchardi*, MGH SS 15, 50–62 (partial edition).

— *Vita sancti Burchardi*, ed. F. J. Bendel, *Vita Sancti Burkardi. Die jüngere Lebensbeschreibung des heiligen Burkard, ersten Bischofs zu Würzburg. Mit einer Untersuchung über den Verfasser* (Paderborn, 1912).

— *Vita sancti Burchardi*, ed. F. J. Bendel and J. Schmitt, 'Vita sancti Burkardi Episcopi Wirziburgensis II.', *Würzburger Diözesangeschichtsblätter* 48 (1986), 19–89.

— *Vita posterior sancti Burchardi* = *Vita sancti Burchardi*, ed. D. Barlava, *Die Lebensbeschreibungen Bischof Burchards von Würzburg. Vita Antiquior – Vita Posterior – Vita Metrica*, MGH SSrG 76 (Hanover, 2005).

Erdmann, C. and N. Fickermann (eds), *Briefsammlungen der Zeit Heinrichs IV.*, MGH Briefe 5 (Weimar, 1950).

Eusebius of Caesarea, *Chronicle*, ed. R. Helm, *Eusebius Werke. Siebenter Band. Die Chronik des Hieronymus*, 2nd edn (Die griechischen christlichen Schriftsteller des ersten drei Jahrhunderte 47; Berlin, 1956).

Falco of Benevento, *Chronicle*, ed. G. del Re, *Cronisti e scrittori sincroni napoletani editi e inediti* 1 (Naples, 1845), pp. 160–276.

Frutolf of Michelsberg, *Breviarium de musica* and *Tonary*, ed. C. Vivell, 'Frutolfi Breviarium de musica et Tonarius', *Akademie der Wissenschaften in Wien. Philosophisch-Historische Klasse. Sitzungsberichte* 188/2 (1919).

— *Tonary* (facsimile edition), R. Maloy, *München, Bayerische Staatsbibliothek, Clm 14965b: the Tonary of Frutolf of Michelsberg* (Publications of medieval music manuscripts 32; Ottawa, 2006).

— *Chronicle*, ed. G. Waitz, MGH SS 6, pp. 33–211.

— *Chronicle*, 1001–1101, ed. and trans. F.-J. Schmale and I. Schmale-Ott, *Frutolfs und Ekkehards Chroniken und die Anonyme Kaiserchronik* (Ausgewählte Quellen zur deutschen Geschichte des Mittelalters 15; Darmstadt, 1972), pp. 48–121.

Frutolf of Michelsberg (?), *Rhythmomachia*, ed. R. Peiper, 'Fortolfi Rhythmimachia', *Zeitschrift für Mathematik und Physik 25. Supplement zur historisch-literarischen Abtheilung des XXXV. Jahrgangs* (1880), 167–227.

Fulcher of Chartres, *Historia Hierosolymitana*, ed. H. Hagenmeyer, *Fulcheri Carnotensis historia Hierosolymitana (1095–1127)* (Heidelberg, 1913).

— trans. F. R. Ryan, *A history of the expedition to Jerusalem 1095–1127* (New York, 1973).

Genealogia Zaringorum, *MGH SS* 13, pp. 735–6.

Gesta Francorum, ed. H. Hagenmeyer, *Anonymi Gesta Francorum et aliorum Hierosolimytanorum* (Heidelberg, 1890).

— ed. and trans. R. Hill, *The deeds of the Franks and the other pilgrims to Jerusalem* (London, 1962).

Gesta Treverorum, *MGH SS* 8, pp. 111–200.

Gregory I, *Sermons* = *Homiliae in Evangelia*, ed. R. Étaix, *CCSL* 141 (Turnhout, 1999).

Gregory VII, *Register*, ed. E. Caspar, *Das Register Gregors VII.*, *MGH Epistolae* 2/1–2 (Berlin, 1920, 1923).

— trans. H. E. J. Cowdrey, *The Register of Pope Gregory VII, 1073–1085: an English translation* (Oxford, 2002).

— *Epistolae vagantes* (unregistered letters), ed. and trans. H. E. J. Cowdrey, *The Epistolae vagantes of Pope Gregory VII* (Oxford, 1972).

Guibert of Nogent, *Historia quae dicitur gesta Dei per Francos*, *RHC Occ.* 4 (Paris, 1879), pp. 113–263.

Guido of Vienne, *Synodal letter* = *Epistola synodica concilii Viennensis*, PL 163.0465C–0466C.

Hagenmeyer, H. (ed.), *Die Kreuzungsbriefe aus den Jahren 1088–1100. Eine Quellensammlung zur Geschichte des ersten Kreuzzuges* (Innsbruck, 1901).

Hanover letter collection, ed. C. Erdmann and N. Fickermann, *Briefsammlung der Zeit Heinrichs IV.*, *MGH Briefe* 5 (Weimar, 1950).

Heimo of Bamberg, *De decursu temporum*, ed. H. M. Weikmann, *De decursu temporum*, *MGH Quellen* 19 (Hanover, 2004).

Helmold of Bosau, *Chronicle* = *Chronica Slavorum. Helmolds Slavenchronik*, ed. B. Schmiedler, *MGH SSrG* [32] (Hanover, 1937).

— trans. F. J. Tschan, *The Chronicle of the Slavs by Helmold, priest of Bosau* (Columbia records of civilization 21; New York, 1966).

Henry III, *Constitutiones*, *MGH Constitutiones* 1, pp. 93–105.

Henry IV, *Diplomas*, ed. D. von Gladiss and A. Gawlick, *Heinrici IV. Diplomata. Die Urkunden Heinrichs IV.*, *MGH DD* 6/1–3 (Berlin, Weimar and Hanover, 1941, 1959, 1978).

— *Letters*, ed. C. Erdmann, *Die Briefe Heinrichs IV.*, *MGH DM* 1 (Leipzig, 1937).

Henry V, *Diplomas*, ed. M. Thiel and A. Gawlick, *Die Urkunden Heinrichs V. und der Königin Mathilde*, *MGH DD* 7 (printed edition in preparation; digital edition: http://www.mgh.de/ddhv/index.htm).

Herman of Reichenau, *Chronicle* = *Herimanni Augiensis chronicon a. 1–1054*, *MGH SS* 5, pp. 67–133.

— trans. I. S. Robinson, *Eleventh-century Germany: the Swabian chronicles* (Manchester, 2008), pp. 58–98 (the annals for 1000–54).

Herrand of Halberstadt, *Letter* = *Epistola de causa Heinrici regis*, *MGH Libelli* 2 (1892), pp. 285–91.

Hesso of Strasburg, *Narrative of the Council of Rheims* = *Hessonis scholastici relatio de concilio Remensi*, *MGH Libelli* 3 (1897), pp. 21–8.

Historia belli sacri, *RHC Occ.* 3 (Paris, 1866), pp. 165–229.

Historia Hirsaugiensis monasterii, *MGH SS* 14, pp. 254–65.

Historia Welforum Weingartensis, *MGH SS* 21, pp. 454–71.

Hugh of Flavigny, *Chronicon*, *MGH SS* 8, pp. 288–502.

Humbert of Silva Candida, *Against simoniacs* = *Libri tres adversus simoniacos*, *MGH Libelli* 1 (1891), pp. 95–253.

— *Concerning the holy Roman church* = *De sancta Romana ecclesia*, ed. P. E. Schramm, 'Die beiden Fragmente "De sancta Romana ecclesia" des Kardinals Humbert von Silva Candida', in P. E. Schramm, *Kaiser, Rom und Renovatio. Studien zur Geschichte des römischen Erneuerungsgedankens vom Ende der karolingischen Reiches bis zum Investiturstreit* (Studien der Bibliothek Warburg 17; Leipzig and Berlin, 1929), pp. 120–36.

Ibn al-Qalanisi, *Chronicle*, ed. H. A. R. Gibb, *The Damascus chronicle of the crusades* (London, 1932).

Ineichen-Eder, C. E. (ed.), *MBDS 4/1. Bistümer Passau und Regensburg* (Munich, 1977).

Isidore of Seville, *Chronica maiora*, *MGH AA* 11, pp. 391–481.

— ed. J. C. Martin, *Isidori Hispalensis Chronica*, *CCSL* 112 (Turnhout, 2003).

— *Etymologies*, ed. W. M. Lindsay, *Isidori Hispalensis episcopi Etymologiarum sive originum libri XX*, 2 vols (Oxford, 1911); trans. S. A. Barney, W. J. Lewis, J. A. Beach and O. Berghof, *The Etymologies of Isidore of Seville* (Cambridge, 2006).

Jaffé, P. (ed.), *Monumenta Gregoriana* (Bibliotheca rerum Germanicarum 2; Berlin, 1865).

— *Monumenta Bambergensia* (Bibliotheca rerum Germanicarum 5; Berlin, 1869).

Jerome, *Letters*, ed. I. Hilberg, *CSEL* 54 (Vienna, 1910).

— *Chronicle* (see Eusebius of Caesarea).

— *Commentariorum in Danielem libri III*, ed. F. Glorie, *CCSL* 75a (Turnhout, 1964).

Johannes Trithemius, *De scriptoribus ecclesiasticis* (Basel, 1494).

— *Annales Hirsaugienses*, vol. 1 (St Gallen, 1690).

Josceran of Lyons, *Letter* = *Epistola ad Ioscerannum archiepiscopum Lugdunensem et responsio Ioscerani*, *MGH Libelli* 2 (1892), pp. 647–57.

Lampert of Hersfeld, *Annales*, ed. O. Holder-Egger, *MGH SSrG* [38] (Hanover and Leipzig, 1894), pp. 3–304.

Letter of the crusading princes (1099), ed. H. Hagenmeyer, *Die Kreuzungsbriefe aus den Jahren 1088–1100. Eine Quellensammlung zur Geschichte des ersten Kreuzzuges* (Innsbruck, 1901), pp. 167–74.

Liber de unitate ecclesiae conservanda, *MGH Libelli* 2 (1892), pp. 173–284; German translation by I. Schmale-Ott, *Quellen zum Investiturstreit. Zweiter Teil: Schriften über den Streit zwischen Regnum und Sacerdotium* (Ausgewählte Quellen zur deutschen Geschichte des Mittelalters 12b; Darmstadt, 1984), pp. 272–579.

Liber pontificalis, ed. L. Duchesne and C. Vogel, 3 vols (Paris, 1886–92); 2nd edn (Paris, 1955–7).

Liemar of Bremen, *Letter to Hezilo of Hildesheim*, ed. C. Erdmann and N. Fickermann, *Briefsammlungen der Zeit Heinrichs IV.*, *MGH Briefe* 5 (Weimar, 1950), pp. 33–5.

Life of Henry IV = *Vita Heinrici IV. imperatoris*, ed. W. Eberhard, *MGH SSrG* [58] (Hanover and Leipzig, 1899).

Lucan, *Civil war*, ed. J. D. Duff, *Lucan: the Civil war* (Cambridge, Mass. and London, 1928).

Manegold of Lautenbach, *Liber ad Gebhardum*, *MGH Libelli* 1 (1891), 308–430.

Matthew of Edessa, *Chronicle*, *RHC Documents arméniennes* 1 (Paris, 1869).

— ed. and trans. A. E. Doctourian, 'Matthew of Edessa: *Chronicle*' (Ph.D. dissertation; Rutgers University, 1975).

Maurus Servius Honoratus, *Commentary on Aenead* = G. Thilo and H. Hagen (eds), *Servii Grammatici qui feruntur in Vergilii carmina commentarii*, 3 vols (Leipzig, 1881–1902; Hildesheim, 1986).

Nospickel, J. (ed.), *Das Necrolog des Kloster Michelsberg in Bamberg*, *MGH LibM* NS 6 (Hanover, 2004).

Notae S. Emmerani, *MGH SS* 15/2, pp. 1093–9.

Odo of Ostia (Urban II), *Encyclical*, ed. C. Erdmann and N. Fickermann, *Briefsammlungen der Zeit Heinrichs IV.*, *MGH Briefe* 5 (Weimar, 1950), pp. 375–80.

Orderic Vitalis, *Historia ecclesiastica*, ed. M. Chibnall, *The Ecclesiastical history of Orderic Vitalis*, 6 vols (Oxford, 1969–79).

Orosius, *Histories against the pagans* = *Historiae aduersus paganos*, ed. and trans. M.-P. Arnaud-Lindet, 3 vols (Paris, 1990–1).

Otloh of St Emmeram, *Book of visions* = *Liber visionum*, ed. P. G. Schmidt, *MGH Quellen* 13 (Weimar, 1989).

Otto of Freising, *Chronicle*, trans. C. C. Mierow, *The two cities: a chronicle of universal history to the year 1146 A. D. by Otto, bishop of Freising* (New York, repr., 2002).

Ovid, *Metamorphoses*, ed. R. J. Tarrant, *P. Ovidi Nasonis Metamorphoses* (Oxford, 2004).

Paschal II, *Relatio registri Paschalis II*, *MGH Constitutiones* 1, pp. 147–50.

Passiones [of Archbishop Thiemo of Salzburg], *RHC Occ.* 5 (Paris, 1895), pp. 199–223.

Paul of Bernried, *The life of Pope Gregory VII* = *Vita Gregorii VII papae*, ed. J. M. Watterich, *Pontificum Romanorum vitae* 1 (Leipzig, 1862), pp. 474–545.

— trans. I. S. Robinson, *The papal reform of the eleventh century: lives of Pope Leo IX and Pope Gregory VII* (Manchester, 2004), pp. 262–364.

Peter Damian, *Letters*, ed. K. Reindel, *Die Briefe des Petrus Damiani*, 4 vols, *MGH Briefe* 4/1–4 (Munich, 1983, 1988, 1989, 1993).

— trans. O. J. Blum (vols 5 and 6 with I. M. Resnick), *The letters of Peter Damian*, 6 vols (Fathers of the Church, Medieval Continuation: Washington, DC, 1989, 1990, 1992, 1998, 2004, 2005).

Peter the Venerable, *On miracles* = *De miraculis* (*PL* 189.0851–0954).

Peters, E. (ed.), *The First Crusade: the Chronicle of Fulcher of Chartres and other source materials*, 2nd edn (Philadelphia, 1998).

Poetic chronicle of the canons of Liège = *Canonici Leodensis Chronicon rhythmicus*, *MGH SS* 12, pp. 415–21.

Protocol of the Synod of Quedlinburg (1085), *MGH Constitutiones*, pp. 651–3.

Pseudo-Isidorian Decretals = *Decretales Pseudo-Isidorianae et Capitula Angilramni*, ed. P. Hinschius (Leipzig, 1863).

Ralph of Caen, *Gesta Tancredi in expeditione Hierosolimitana*, *RHC Occ.* 3 (Paris, 1866), pp. 587–716.

Ranger of Lucca, *Vita metrica sancti Anselmi Lucensis episcopi*, *MGH SS* 30/2, pp. 1152–1307.

Raymond of Aguilers, *Historia Francorum qui ceperunt Iherusalem*, *RHC Occ.* 3 (Paris, 1866), pp. 231–309.

— trans. J. H. Hill and L. L. Hill, *Raymond d'Aguilers. Historia Francorum qui ceperunt Iherusalem* (Philadelphia, 1968).

— ed. J. H. Hill and L. L. Hill, *Le «Liber» de Raymond d'Aguilers* (Paris, 1969).

Regino of Prüm, *Chronicle*, trans. S. MacLean, *History and politics in late Carolingian and Ottonian Europe: the chronicle of Regino of Prüm and Adalbert of Magdeburg* (Manchester, 2009), pp. 61–231.

Reichenauer Kaiserchronik = Swabian universal chronicle = Chronicon Suevicum universale, MGH SS 13, pp. 61–72.

Robert of Rheims (the Monk), *Historia Hierosolymitana*, RHC Occ. 3 (Paris, 1866), pp. 717–882.

— trans. C. Sweetenham, *Robert the Monk's history of the First Crusade: Historia Iherosolimitana* (Aldershot, 2005).

Roman-German Pontifical = Pontificale Romano-Germanicum 1, ed. C. Vogel and R. Elze, 2 vols (Studi e Testi 226; Rome, 1963).

Ruf, P. (ed.), *MBDS 3/3. Bistum Bamberg* (Munich, 1939; repr. 1961).

Sallust, *War against Cataline, Jugurthine War*, ed. L. D. Reynolds, *C. Sallusti Crispi. Catilina, Iugurtha, Historiarum fragmenta selecta, Appendix Sallustiana* (Oxford, 1991).

Schmid, K. (ed.), *Die Klostergemeinschaft von Fulda im früheren Mittelalter*, 3 vols (Münstersche Mittelalter-Schriften 8/1–3; Munich, 1978).

Sigebert of Gembloux, *Chronicle*, MGH SS 6, pp. 268–374.

— *Letter = Epistola Leodicensium adversus Paschalem papam*, MGH Libelli 2 (1892), pp. 449–64.

Suger of St Denis, *Vita Ludovici grossi regis*, ed. and trans. H. Waquet, *Vie de Louis le Gros* (Les classiques de l'histoire de France au moyen âge; Paris, 1929).

Tegernsee necrology, *MGH NecG* 3, pp. 136–57.

Theoger of Metz, *Musica*, ed. and trans. F. C. Lochner, 'Dietger (Theogerus) of Metz and his "Musica"' (unpublished Ph.D. dissertation, University of Notre Dame, 1995).

Thietmar of Merseburg, *Chronicle*, ed. R. Holtzmann, *Die Chronik des Bischofs Thietmar von Merseburg und ihre Korveier Überarbeitug*, MGH SSrG NS 9 (Berlin, 1935).

— trans. D. A. Warner, *Ottonian Germany: the Chronicon of Thietmar of Merseburg* (Manchester, 2001).

Translatio S. Modoaldi, MGH SS 12, pp. 289–310.

Vita Leonis IX papae, ed. J. M. Watterich, *Pontificum Romanorum vitae* 1 (Leipzig, 1862), pp. 127–70.

— ed. M. Parisse and M. Goullet (Les Classiques de l'histoire de France au moyen âge 38; Paris, 1997).

— trans. I. S. Robinson, *The papal reform of the eleventh century: lives of Pope Leo IX and Pope Gregory VII* (Manchester, 2004), pp. 97–157.

Walram of Naumberg, *Letter = Epistola de causa Heinrici regis*, MGH Libelli 2 (1892), pp. 285–91.

Wenrich of Trier, *Letter written in the name of Bishop Theoderic of Verdun* = *Epistola sub Theoderici episcopi Virdunensis nomine composita*, MGH Libelli 1 (1891), pp. 280–99.

Wido of Ferrara, *Concerning the schism of Hildebrand* = *De scismate Hildibrandi*, MGH Libelli 1 (1891), pp. 529–67.

Widukind of Corvey, *Deeds of the Saxons*, ed. P. Hirsch, *Res gestae Saxonicae*, MGH SSrG [60] (Hanover, 1935).

William of Malmesbury, *Deeds of the English kings* = *Gesta regum Anglorum*, vol. 1, ed. and trans. R. A. B. Mynors, R. M. Thomson and M. Winterbottom, *The history of the English kings* (Oxford, 1998; repr. 2006).

Wipo, *Deeds of Emperor Conrad* = *Gesta Chuonradi II. imperatoris*, ed. H. Bresslau, MGH SSrG [61] (Hanover, 1915).

— trans. T. E. Mommsen and K. F. Morrison, *Imperial lives and letters of the eleventh century* (New York, 1967; repr. 2000), pp. 52–100.

Wolfger of Prüfening (?), *De scriptoribus ecclesiasticis*, ed. E. Ettlinger, *Der sogenannte Anonymus Mellicensis De scriptoribus ecclesiasticis* (Strasburg, 1896).

— *Vita Theogeri abbatis S. Geogrii et epispoci Mettensis*, MGH SS 12, pp. 449–79.

Würzburg Chronicle, ed. G. Waitz, 'Chronicon Wirziburgense ad a. 1057', MGH SS 6 (Hanover, 1844), p. 17–32.

Secondary sources

Allen, M. I. (2003), 'Universal history 300–1000: origins and western developments', in D. Mauskopf Deliyannis (ed.), *Historiography in the middle ages* (Leiden), pp. 17–42.

Alphandéry, P. (1929), 'Les citations bibliques chez les historiens de la première croisade', *Revue d'histoire des religions* 99, 139–57.

Althoff, G. (2006), *Heinrich IV.* (Gestalten des Mittelalters und der Renaissance; Darmstadt).

Amouroux-Mourad, M. (1988), *Le comté d'Edesse 1098–1150* (Paris).

Arbusow, L. (1963), *Colores rhetorici. Eine Auswahl rhetorischer Figuren und Gemeinplätze als Hilfsmittel für akademische Übungen an mittelalterlichen Texten* (Göttingen).

Arnold, B. (1985), *German knighthood, 1050–1300* (Oxford).

— (1997), *Medieval Germany 500–1300: a political interpretation* (Toronto).

Barrow, J. (1989), 'Education and the recruitment of cathedral canons in England and Germany 1100–1225', *Viator* 20, 117–38.

Becker, A. (1964, 1988, 2012), *Papst Urban II.*, 3 vols (Schriften der MGH 19; Stuttgart).

Benson, R. L. (1968), *The bishop-elect: a study in medieval ecclesiastical office* (Princeton).

Bernhardt, J. W. (1993), *Itinerant kingship and royal monasteries in early medieval Germany, c. 936–1075* (Cambridge).

Beumann, H. (1973), 'Tribur, Rom und Canossa', in J. Fleckenstein (ed.), *Investiturstreit und Reichsverfassung* (Vorträge und Forschungen 17; Sigmaringen), pp. 33–60.

Black-Veldtrup, M. (1995), *Kaiserin Agnes (1043–1077). Quellenkritische Studien* (Cologne, Weimar and Vienna).

Blake, E. O. and C. Morris (1985), 'A hermit goes to war: Peter and the origins of the First Crusade', *Studies in Church History* 22 (Oxford), 79–107.

Bloch, H. (1986), *Monte Cassino in the middle ages*, 3 vols (Rome and Cambridge, Mass.).

Blöndal, S. (1978), *The Varangians of Byzantium: an aspect of Byzantine military history*, trans. and rev. B. S. Benedikz (Cambridge).

Blumenthal, U.-R. (1977), '*Patrimonia* and *regalia* in 1111', in K. Pennington and R. Somerville (eds), *Law, church and society. Essays in honor of Stephan Kuttner* (Pennsylvania), pp. 9–22.

— (1978a), 'Opposition to Pope Paschal II: some comments on the Lateran council of 1112', *Annuarium historiae conciliorum* 10, 82–98.

— (1978b), *The early councils of Pope Paschal II, 1100–1110* (Toronto).

— (1988), *The Investiture Controversy: church and monarchy from the ninth to the twelfth century* (Philadelphia). Originally published as *Der Investiturstreit* (Urban-Taschenbücher 335; Stuttgart, 1982).

— (2004), 'The papacy, 1024–1122', in D. Luscombe and J. Riley-Smith (eds), *The new Cambridge medieval history* 4/2 (Cambridge), pp. 8–39.

Borst, A. (1984), 'Ein Forschungsbericht Hermanns des Lahmen', *DA* 40, 379–477.

Boshof, E. (1978) 'Lothringen, Frankreich und das Reich in der Regierungszeit Heinrichs III.', *Rheinische Vierteljahrsblätter* 42, 63–100.

— (1986), 'Das Reich und Ungarn in der Zeit der Salier', *Ostbairische Grenzmarken* 28, 178–94.

— (1991), 'Bischöfe und Bischofskirchen von Passau und Regensburg', in S. Weinfurter (ed.), *Die Salier und das Reich* 2 (Sigmaringen), pp. 113–54.

Bosl, K. (1972), 'Adel, Bistum, Klöster Bayerns im Investiturstreit', in *Festschrift für Hermann Heimpel zum 70. Geburtstag am 19. September 1971*, vol. 2 (Veröffentlichungen des Max-Planck-Instituts für Geschichte 36/2; Göttingen), pp. 1121–46.

Bresslau, H. (1879, 1884), *Jahrbücher des Deutschen Reichs unter Konrad II.*, 2 vols (Leipzig).

— (1896), 'Bamberger Studien', *NA* 21, 140–234.

Brett, M. (1995), 'The battles of Ramla (1099–1105)', in U. Vermuelen and D. de Smet (eds), *Egypt and Syria in the Fatimid, Ayyubid and Mamluk eras* (Leuven), pp. 17–37.

— (2004), 'Abbasids, Fatimids and Seljuqs', in D. Luscombe and J. Riley-Smith (eds), *The new Cambridge medieval history* 4/2 (Cambridge), pp. 675–720.

von den Brincken, A.-D. (1957), *Studien zur lateinischen Weltchronistik bis in das Zeitalter Ottos von Freising* (Dusseldorf).

Brooke, C. N. L. (1951), 'The composition of the chapter of St Paul's, 1086–1163', *Cambridge Historical Journal* 10, 111–32.

— (1956), 'Gregorian reform in action: clerical marriage in England, 1050–1200', *Cambridge Historical Journal* 12, 1–21.

Brühl, C. (1968), *Fodrum, Gistum, Servitium regis* 1 (Cologne and Graz).

Buchholz, G. (1879), *Die Würzburger Chronik. Eine quellenkritische Untersuchung* (Leipzig).

Buske, N. (2003), 'Erinnerungen an Bischof Otto von Bamberg in Pommern', in A. Albrecht and N. Buske (eds), *Bischof Otto von Bamberg. Sein Wirken für Pommern* (Schwerin), pp. 85–127.

— (2007), 'Erinnerungen an die Missionreisen des Bischofs Otto von Bamberg', in L. Göller, W. F. Reddig, R. Hanemann and W. Taegert (eds), *1000 Jahre Bistum Bamberg, 1007–2007. Unterm Sternenmantel* (Petersberg), pp. 143–55.

Büttner, H. (1973), 'Erzbischof Adalbert von Mainz, die Kurie und das Reich in den Jahren 1118 bis 1122', in J. Fleckenstein (ed.), *Investiturstreit und Reichsverfassung* (Vorträge und Forschungen 17; Sigmaringen), pp. 395–410.

Cahen, C. (1969), 'The Turkish invasion: the Selchükids', in K. M. Setton and M. W. Baldwin (eds), *A history of the crusades, vol. 1: the first hundred years*, 2nd edn (Madison, Wis.), pp. 135–76.

Cate, J. L. (1969), 'The crusade of 1101', in K. M. Setton and M. W. Baldwin (eds), *A history of the crusades, vol. 1: the first hundred years*, 2nd edn (Madison, Wis.), pp. 343–67.

Cazzani, E. (1955), *Vescovi e arcivescovi di Milano* (Milan).

Cheney, C. R. (ed.) (2000), *A handbook of dates for students of British history* (London, 1945); rev. edn by M. Jones (Royal Historical Society Guides and Handbooks 4; Cambridge).

Chibnall, M. (1993), *Empress Matilda: queen consort, queen mother and lady of the English* (Oxford).

Chodorow, S. (1971), 'Ecclesiastical politics and the ending of the Investiture Contest: the papal election of 1119 and the negotiations at Mouzon', *Speculum* 46, 613–40.

Classen, P. (1973), 'Das Wormser Konkordat in der deutschen Verfassungsgeschichte', in J. Fleckenstein (ed.), *Investiturstreit und Reichsverfassung* (Vorträge und Forschungen 17; Sigmaringen), pp. 411–60.

— (1982), 'Res gestae, universal history, apocalypse: visions of past and future', in R. L. Benson and G. Constable (eds), *Renaissance and renewal in the twelfth century* (Oxford), pp. 387–420.

Constable, G. (2008), *Crusaders and crusading in the twelfth century* (Farnham).

Cordiolani, A. (1961), 'Le computiste Hermann de Reichenau', *Miscellanea di Storia Ligure* 3, 167–90.

Costick, C. (2008), *The social structure of the First Crusade* (Leiden).

Cowdrey, H. E. J. (1966), 'Archbishop Aribert II of Milan', *History* 51, 1–15.

— (1968), 'The papacy, the Patarenes and the church of Milan', *Transactions of the Royal Historical Society*, 4th series 18, 25–48.

— (1970), 'The Peace of God and the Truce of God in the eleventh century', *Past and Present* 46, 42–67.

— (1978), 'Two studies in Cluniac history (1049–1126); II. Abbot Pontius of Cluny (1109–22/26)', *Studi Gregoriani* 11, 178–298.

— (1982), 'Pope Gregory VII's "crusading" plans of 1074', in B. Z. Kedar, H. E. Mayer and R. C. Smail (eds), *Outremer: studies in the history of the crusading kingdom of Jerusalem presented to Joshua Prawer* (Jerusalem), pp. 27–40.

— (1983), *The age of Abbot Desiderius: Montecassino, the papacy and the Normans in the eleventh and early twelfth centuries* (Oxford).

— (1990), 'The papacy and the Berengarian controversy', in P. Ganz, R. B. C. Huygens and F. Niewöhner (eds), *Auctoritas und Ratio. Studien zu Berengar von Tours* (Wiesbaden), pp. 109–38.

— (1998), *Pope Gregory VII, 1073–1085* (Oxford).

— (2004), 'The structure of the Church, 1024–1073', in D. Luscombe and J. Riley-Smith (eds), *The new Cambridge medieval history* 4/1 (Cambridge), pp. 229–67.

Cram, K.-G. (1955), *Iudicium belli. Zum Rechtscharakter des Krieges im deutschen Mittelalter* (Beihefte zum Archiv für Kulturgeschichte 5; Münster and Cologne).

Curschmann, F. (1900), *Hungersnöte im Mittelalter. Ein Beitrag zur deutschen Wirtschaftsgeschichte des 8. bis 13. Jahrhunderts* (Leipzig).

Cushing, K. G. (1998), *Papacy and law in the Gregorian revolution: the canonistic work of Anselm of Lucca* (Oxford).

— (2005), *Reform and spirituality in the eleventh century: spirituality and social change* (Manchester).

Dale, J. (2011), 'Imperial self-representation and the manipulation of history in twelfth-century Germany: Cambridge, Corpus Christi College MS 373', *German history* 29, 557–83.

Deér, J. (1972), *Papsttum und Normannen. Untersuchungen zu ihren lehnsrechtlichen und kirchenpolitischen Beziehungen* (Studien und Quellen zur Welt Kaiser Friedrichs II. 1; Cologne and Vienna).

Dengler-Schreiber, K. (1979), *Scriptorium und Bibliothek des Klosters Michelsberg in Bamberg* (Studien zur Bibliotheksgeschichte 2; Graz).

Diepolder, G. (1964), 'Die Herkunft der Aribonen', *Zeitschrift für bayerische Landesgeschichte* 27, 74–119.

Dussand, R. (1927), *Topographie historique de la Syrie antique et médiévale* (Paris).

Eads, V. (2010), 'The last Italian expedition of Henry IV: re-reading the *Vita Mathildis* of Donizone of Canossa', *Journal of Medieval Military History* 8, 23–68.

Edgington, S. B. (2010), 'Oriental and occidental medicine in the crusader states', in C. Kostik (ed.), *The crusades and the Near East: cultural histories* (London), pp. 189–215.

Egger, J. (1897), 'Das Aribonenhaus', *Archiv für österreichische Geschichte* 83, 385–525.

Engel, P. (2001), *The realm of St Stephen: a history of medieval Hungary, 895–1526*, trans. T. Pálosfalvi (London).

Erdmann, C. (1927), 'Mauritius Burdinus (Gregor VIII.)', *Quellen und Forschungen aus italienischen Archiven und Bibliotheken* 19, 205–61.

— (1932), 'Die Briefe Meinhards von Bamberg', *NA* 49, 332–431.

— (1935), *Die Entstehung des Kreuzzugsgedankens* (Forschungen zur Kirchen- und Geistesgeschichte 6; Stuttgart); trans. M. W. Baldwin and W. Goffart, *The origin of the idea of crusade* (Princeton, 1977).

— (1936), 'Die Bamberger Domschule im Investiturstreit', *Zeitschrift für bayerische Landesgeschichte* 9, 1–46.

— (1938), *Studien zur Briefliteratur Deutschlands im elften Jahrhundert* (Schriften der MGH 1; Leipzig; repr. 1962).

— (1939), 'Untersuchungen zu den Briefen Heinrichs IV.', *Archiv für Urkundenforschung* 16, 184–253.

— (1940), 'Zum Fürstentag von Tribur', *DA* 4, 486–95.

Fenske, L. (1977), *Adelsopposition und kirchliche Reformbewegung im östlichen Sachsen* (Veröffentlichungen des Max-Planck-Instituts für Geschichte 47; Göttingen).

Fingernagel, A. (1991), *Die illuminierten lateinischen Handschriften deutscher Provenienz der Staatsbibliothek Preußischer Kulturbesitz Berlin, 8.–12. Jahrhundert. Teil 1: Text* (Wiesbaden).

Fink, H. S. (1969) 'The foundation of the Latin states, 1099–1118', in K. M. Setton and M. W. Baldwin (eds), *A history of the crusades, vol. 1: the first hundred years* (Madison, Wis.), pp. 386–409.

Fleckenstein, J. (1968), 'Heinrich IV. und der deutsche Episkopat in den Anfängen des Investiturstreits', in J. Fleckenstein and K. Schmid (eds), *Adel und Kirche. Festschrift für Gerd Tellenbach* (Freiburg, Basel and Vienna), pp. 221–36.

Fliche, A. (1924–37), *La réforme grégorienne*, 3 vols (Spicilegium sacrum Lovaniense: études et documents 6; Louvain and Paris).

Flori, J. (1999), *Pierre l'Ermite et la première croisade* (Paris).

France, J. (1994), *Victory in the East: a military history of the First Crusade* (Cambridge).

— (1998a), 'The anonymous *Gesta Francorum* and the *Historia Francorum qui ceperunt Iherusalem* of Raymond of Aguilers and the *Historia de Hierosolymitano itinere* of Peter Tudebode: an analysis of the textual relationships between primary sources for the First Crusade', in J. France and W. G. Zajac (eds), *The crusades and their sources: essays presented to Bernard Hamilton* (Aldershot), pp. 39–69.

— (1998b), 'The use of the anonymous *Gesta Francorum* in the early twelfth-century sources for the First Crusade', in A. V. Murray (ed.), *From Clermont to Jerusalem: the crusaders and crusader societies 1095–1500* (International medieval research: selected proceedings of the International Medieval Congress, University of Leeds 3; Turnhout), pp. 29–42.

Fransen, G. (1972), 'Réflexions sur l'étude des collections canoniques à l'occasion de l'édition d'une lettre de Bruno de Segni', *Studi Gregoriani* 9, 515–33.

Fried, J. (1973) 'Der Regalienbegriff im 11. und 12. Jahrhundert', *DA* 29, 450–528.

Fuhrmann, H. (1982), 'Pseudoisidor, Otto von Ostia (Urban II.) und der Zitatenkampf von Gerstungen (1085)', *Zeitschrift der Savigny-Stiftung für Rechtsgeschichte. Kanonistische Abteilung* 68, 52–69.

Gabriele, M. (2007), 'Against the enemies of Christ: the role of Count Emicho in the anti-Jewish violence of the First Crusade', in M. Frassetto (ed.), *Christian attitudes towards the Jews in the middle ages* (New York and Oxford), pp. 61–82.

Ganshof, F. L. (1964), *Feudalism*, trans. P. Grierson, 3rd edn (London; repr. 1996).

Gernhuber, J. (1952), *Die Landfriedensbewegung in Deutschland bis zum Mainzer Reichslandfrieden von 1235* (Bonn).

Giese, W. (1979), *Der Stamm der Sachsen und das Reich in ottonischer und salischer Zeit* (Wiesbaden).

von Giesebrecht, W. (1890) *Geschichte der deutschen Kaiserzeit* 3, 5th edn (Leipzig).

Gil, M. (1992), *A history of Palestine 634–1099*, trans. E. Broido (Cambridge).

Goetz, H.-W. (1999), *Geschichtsschreibung und Geschichtsbewußtsein im hohen Mittelalter* (Vorstellungswelten des Mittelalters 1; Berlin).

— (2002), 'The concept of time in the historiography of the eleventh and twelfth centuries', in G. Althoff, J. Fried, P. J. Geary (eds), *Medieval concepts of the past: history, memory, historiography* (Cambridge), pp. 139–65.

Goez, E. (1996), 'Der Thronerbe als Rivale. König Konrad, Kaiser Heinrichs IV. älterer Sohn', *Historisches Jahrbuch* 116, 1–49.

Goez, W. (1962), *Der Leihezwang. Eine Untersuchung zur Geschichte des deutschen Lehnrechts* (Tübingen).

— (1968), 'Zur Erhebung und ersten Absetzung Papst Gregors VII.', *Römische Quartalschrift für christliche Altertumskunde und Kirchengeschichte* 63, 117–44.

Golden, P. B. (1990), 'The peoples of the south Russian steppes', in D. Sinor (ed.), *The Cambridge history of early inner Asia* (Cambridge), pp. 256–84.

Göller, L. (2007), 'Domstift und Kollegiatstifte', in L. Göller, W. F. Reddig, R. Hanemann and W. Taegert (eds), *1000 Jahre Bistum Bamberg, 1007–2007. Unterm Sternenmantel* (Petersberg), pp. 43–9.

Gottlob, T. (1936), *Der kirchliche Amtseid der Bischöfe* (Kanonistische Studien und Texte 9; Bonn).

Green, R. P. H. (1982), 'The genesis of a medieval textbook: the models and sources of the *Ecloga Theoduli*', *Viator* 13, 49–106.

Gresser, G. (2007), *Clemens II. Der erste deutsche Reformpapst* (Paderborn).

von Guttenberg, E. (1937), *Das Bistum Bamberg* (Germania sacra 2/1; Berlin).

von Hacke, C. B. (1898), *Die Palliumverleihungen bis 1143. Eine diplomatisch-historische Untersuchung* (Marburg).

Hagenmeyer, H. (1890). See *Gesta Francorum*.

Hägermann, D. (1970) 'Untersuchungen zum Papstwahldekret von 1059', *Zeitschrift der Savigny-Stiftung für Rechtsgeschichte. Kanonistische Abteilung* 56 (1970), 157–93.

Hallam, E. M. (1989), *Chronicles of the crusades: eye-witness accounts of the wars between Christianity and Islam* (London).

Haller, J. (1951), *Das Papsttum. Idee und Wirklichkeit* 2, 2nd edn (Stuttgart).

Hallinger, K. (1950, 1951), *Gorze-Kluny. Studien zu den monastischen Lebensformen und Gegensätzen im Hochmittelalter*, 2 vols (Studia Anselmiana 22/23; Rome).

Hamilton, B. (1980), *The Latin church in the crusader states: the secular church* (London).

Hauck, A. (1954), *Kirchengeschichte Deutschlands*, 4 vols, 8th edn (Berlin and Leipzig).

Hay, D. J. (2008), *The military leadership of Matilda of Canossa, 1046–1115* (Manchester).

Healy, P. (2006), *The Chronicle of Hugh of Flavigny: reform and the Investiture Contest in the late eleventh century* (Aldershot).

Hechelmann, A. (1866), 'Burchard der Rothe, Bischof von Münster und kaiserlicher Kanzler, 1098–1118', *Zeitschrift für vaterländische Geschichte und Altertumskunde* 26, 281–332.

Heidrich, I. (1991), 'Bischöfe und Bischofskirche von Speyer', in S. Weinfurter and H. Seibert (eds), *Die Salier und das Reich* 2 (Sigmaringen), pp. 187–224.

Herrmann, K.-J. (1973), *Das Tuskulanerpapsttum (1012–1046). Benedikt VIII., Johannes XIX., Benedikt IX.* (Päpste und Papsttum 4; Stuttgart).

Hiestand, R. (1972), 'Legat, Kaiser und Basileus: Bischof Kuno von Praeneste und die Krise des Papsttums von 1111/1112', in H. Fuhrmann, H.-E. Meyer and K. Wriedt (eds), *Aus Reichsgeschichte und Nordischer Geschichte. Karl Jordan zum 65. Geburtstag* (Kieler Historische Studien 16; Stuttgart), pp. 141–52.

Hillenbrand, C. (2000), *The crusades: Islamic perspectives* (New York).

Hlawitschka, E. (1974), 'Zwischen Tribur und Canossa', *Historisches Jahrbuch* 94, 25–45.

— (1991), 'Zur Herkunft und zu den Seitenverwandten des Gegenkönigs Rudolf von Rheinfelden', in S. Weinfurter (ed.), *Die Salier und das Reich* 1 (Sigmaringen), pp. 175–220.

— (2006), *Die Ahnen de hochmittelalterlichen deutschen Könige, Kaiser und ihrer Gemahlinnen. Ein kommentiertes Tafelwerk. Band I: 911–1137*, 2 vols (MGH Hilfsmittel 25; Hanover).

Hoesch, H. (1970), *Die kanonischen Quellen im Werk Humberts von Moyenmoutier. Ein Beitrag zur Geschichte der vorgregorianischen Reform* (Forschungen zur kirchlichen Rechtsgeschichte und zum Kirchenrecht 10; Cologne and Vienna).

Hoffmann, H. (1964), *Gottesfriede und Treuga Dei* (Schriften der MGH 20; Stuttgart).

— (1986), *Buchkunst und Königtum im ottonischen und frühsalischen Reich* (Schriften der MGH 30; Stuttgart).

— (1995), *Bamberger Handschriften des 10. und des 11. Jahrhunderts* (Schriften der MGH 39; Hanover).

Hollister, C. W. (2001), *Henry I* (New Haven and London).

Holtzmann, R. (1941), *Geschichte der sächsischen Kaiserzeit (900–1024)* (Munich).

Holtzmann, W. (1963), 'Maximilla regina, soror Rogerii regis', *DA* 19, 149–67.

Höss, I. (1950), 'Die Stellung Frankens im Investiturstreit unter besonderer Berücksichtigung Würzburgs', *Mainfränkisches Jahrbuch* 2, 303–15.

Houben, H. (2002), *Roger II of Sicily: a ruler between east and west*, trans. G. A. Loud and D. Milburn (Cambridge).

van Houts, E. (1995), 'The Norman conquest through European eyes', *English Historical Review* 110, 832–53.

Hüls, R. (1977), *Kardinäle, Klerus und Kirchen Roms 1049–1130* (Bibliothek des Deutschen Historischen Instituts in Rom 48; Tübingen).

Jakobs, H. (1961), *Die Hirsauer. Ihre Ausbreitung und Rechtsstellung im Zeitalter des Investiturstreites* (Kölner historische Abhandlungen 4; Cologne and Graz).

Jasper, D. (1986), *Das Papstwahldekret von 1059. Überlieferung und Textgestalt* (Beiträge zur Geschichte und Quellenkunde des Mittelalters 12; Sigmaringen).

Jenal, G. (1974, 1975), *Erzbischof Anno II. von Köln (1056–75) und sein politisches Wirken*, 2 vols (Stuttgart).

Joranson, E. (1928), 'The great German pilgrimage of 1064–65', in L. J. Paetow (ed.), *The crusades and other historical essays* (New York), pp. 3–43.

Kappner, H. (1931), 'Die Geschichtswissenschaft an der Universität Jena vom Humanismus bis zur Aufklärung', *Zeitschrift des Vereins für thüringische Geschichte und Altertumskunde, Neue Folge* 14, 68–204.

Kennedy, V. L. (1938), 'The *De officiis divinis* of MS. Bamberg, Lit. 134', *Ephemerides liturgicae* 52, 312–26.

Klaar, K.-E. (1966), *Die Herrschaft der Eppensteiner in Kärnten* (Klagenfurt).

Klewitz, H.-W. (1957), 'Die Entstehung des Kardinalkollegiums', in H.-W. Klewitz, *Reformpapsttum und Kardinalkolleg* (Darmstadt), pp. 11–134 (originally published in *Zeitschrift der Savigny-Stiftung für Rechtsgeschichte. Kanonistische Abteilung* 25 [1936], 115–21).

— (1971), 'Das alemannische Herzogtum bis zur staufischen Epoche. Aufgaben und Probleme der Erforschung seiner inneren Entwicklung und ihrer geschichtlichen Voraussetzungen', in H.-W. Klewitz, *Ausgewählte Aufsätze zur Kirchen- und Geistesgeschichte des Mittelalters* (Aalen), pp. 231–62 (originally published in F. Maurer and K. S. Bader [eds], *Oberrheiner, Schwaben, Südalemannen. Räume und Kräfte im geschichtlichen Aufbau des deutschen Südwestens* [Arbeiten vom Oberrhein 2; Strasburg, 1942], pp. 79–110).

Köhler, M. A. (1991), *Allianzen und Verträge zwischen fränkischen und islamischen Herrschern im Vorderen Orient. Eine Studie über das zwischenstaatliche Zusammenleben vom 12. bis ins 13. Jahrhundert* (Berlin).

Kost, O.-H. (1962), *Das östliche Niedersachsen im Investiturstreit* (Göttingen).

Kottje, R. (1978), 'Zur Bedeutung der Bischofsstädte für Heinrich IV.', *Historisches Jahrbuch* 97–8, 131–57.

Krause, H.-G. (1960), *Das Papstwahldekret von 1059 und seine Rolle im Investiturstreit* (Studi Gregoriani 7; Rome).

Kubach, H. E. and W. Haas (1972), *Der Dom zu Speyer*, 3 vols (Die Kunstdenkmäler von Rheinland-Pfalz 5; Munich).

Ladner, G. (1968), 'Das Reich Kaiser Heinrichs III. und die Kirchenreform', in G. Ladner, *Theologie und Politik vor dem Investiturstreit. Abendmahlstreit, Kirchenreform, Cluni und Heinrich III.*, 2nd edn (Darmstadt), pp. 60–84.

Lange, K.-H. (1961), 'Die Stellung der Grafen von Northeim in der Reichsgeschichte des 11. und frühen 12. Jahrhunderts', *Niedersächsische Jahrbuch für Landesgeschichte* 33, 1–107.

Latowsky, A. A. (2013), *Emperor of the world: Charlemagne and the construction of imperial authority, 800–1229* (Ithaca, NY).

Leitschuh, F. and H. Fischer (1887), *Katalog der Handschriften der Königlichen Bibliothek zu Bamberg* 1/2 (Bamberg; rept. 1966).

Lilie, R.-J. (1993), *Byzantium and the crusader states 1096–1204*, trans. J. C. Morris and J. E. Ridings (Oxford).

Loibl, R. (1997), *Der Herrschaftsraum der Grafen von Vornbach und ihrer Nachfolger* (Historischer Atlas von Bayern: Altbayern 2/5; Munich, 1997).

Loud, G. A. (2000), *The age of Robert Guiscard: southern Italy and the Norman conquest* (Harlow).

— (2002), 'The papacy and the rulers of southern Italy, 1058–1198', in G. A. Loud and A. Metcalfe (eds), *The society of Norman Italy* (The medieval Mediterranean. Peoples, economies and cultures, 400–1500 38; Leiden), pp. 151–84.

— (2007), *The Latin church in Norman Italy* (Cambridge).

Luchaire, A. (1890), *Louis VI le Gros. Annales de sa vie et de son règne (1081–1137)* (Paris).

Maloy, R (2002). 'The roles of notation in Frutolf of Michelsberg's tonary', *Journal of Musicology* 19, 641–93.

Martin, G. (1994), 'Der salische Herrscher als *Patricius Romanorum*. Zur Einflußnahme Heinrichs III. und Heinrichs IV. auf die Besetzung der *Cathedra Petri*', *Frühmittelalterliche Studien* 28, 257–95.

Märtl, C. (1985), 'Zur Überlieferung des *Liber contra Wibertum* Anselms von Lucca', *DA* 41 (1985), 192–202.

— (1991), 'Die Bamberger Schulen – ein Bildungszentrum des Salierreichs', in S. Weinfurter and H. Seibert (eds), *Die Salier und das Reich. Band 3. Gesellschaftlicher und ideengeschichtlicher Wandel im Reich der Salier* (Sigmaringen), pp. 327–45.

Masnovo, O. (1922), 'Pier Grosolano e il suo epitafio', *Archivio Storico Lombardo* 5/49, 1–28.

Maurer, H. (1978), *Der Herzog von Schwaben* (Sigmaringen).

McCarthy, T. J. H. (2002), 'Literary practice in eleventh-century music theory: the *colores rhetorici* and Aribo's *De musica*', *Medium aevum* 71, 191–208.

— (2004), 'The identity of Master Henry of Augsburg (d. 1083)', *Revue bénédictine* 114, 140–57.

— (2008), 'Biblical scholarship in eleventh-century Michelsberg: the *Glosa in vetus et novum testamentum* of MS Karlsruhe, Badische Landesbibliothek, 504', *Scriptorium* 62, 3–45.

— (2009), *Music, scholasticism and reform: Salian Germany 1024–1125* (Manchester).

— (2011), 'Frutolf of Michelsberg, the schools of Bamberg and the transmission of imperial polemic', *Haskins Society Journal* 23.

McCormick, M. (1975), *Les annales du haut moyen âge* (Typologie des sources du moyen âge occidental 14; Turnhout).

McKeon, P. R. (1966), 'The Lateran council of 1112, the "heresy" of lay investiture and the excommunication of Henry V', *Medievalia et Humanistica* 17, 3–12.

Mellinkoff, R. (1973), 'Riding backwards: theme of humiliation and symbol of evil', *Viator* 4, 153–76.

Melve, L. (2007), *Inventing the public sphere: the public debate during the Investiture Contest (c. 1030–1122)* (Brill's studies in intellectual history 154; Leiden).

Metz, W. (1971), 'Tafelgut, Königsstraße und Servitium Regis in Deutschland vornehmlich im 10. und 11. Jahrhundert', *Historisches Jahrbuch* 91, 257–91.

Meyer von Knonau, G. (1890, 1894, 1900, 1903, 1904, 1907, 1909), *Jahrbücher des Deutschen Reichs unter Heinrich IV. und Heinrich V.*, 7 vols (Leipzig).

Miccoli, G. (1966), *Chiesa gregoriana. Ricerche sulla riforma del secolo XI* (Storici antichi e moderni. Nuova serie 17; Florence).

Minninger, M. (1978), *Von Clermont zum Wormser Konkordat. Die Auseinandersetzungen um den Lehnsnexus zwischen König und Episkopat* (Forschungen zur Kaiser- und Papstgeschichte des Mittelalters 2; Cologne and Vienna).

Möhring, H. (1992), 'Graf Emicho und die Judenverfolgungen von 1096', *Rheinische Vierteljahrsblätter* 56, 97–111.

Morin, G. (1896), 'Note sur un *Liber hermeneumatum* ou commentaire biblique en forme de glosse de l'époque carolingienne', *Revue bénédictine* 13, 66–71.

— (1910), 'Le glossaire biblique du moine Albert de Siegburg', *Revue bénédictine* 27, 117–21.

Morris, C. (1984), 'Policy and visions: the case of the Holy Lance found at Antioch', in J. Gillingham and J. C. Holt (eds), *War and government in the middle ages: essays in honour of J. O. Prestwich* (Woodbridge), pp. 33–45.

Morrison, K. F. (1962), 'Canossa: a revision', *Traditio* 18, 121–48.

Moyer, A. E. (2001), *The philosophers' game: rithmomachia in medieval and Renaissance Europe* (Ann Arbor, Mich.).

Mulinder, A. (1996), 'The crusading expeditions of 1101–2' (unpublished Ph.D. dissertation, University of Wales at Swansea).

— (1998), 'Albert of Aachen and the crusade of 1101', in A. V. Murray (ed.), *From Clermont to Jerusalem: the crusades and crusader societies* (International medieval research: selected proceedings of the International Medieval Congress, University of Leeds 3; Turnhout), pp. 69–77.

Munier, C. (2002), *Le Pape Léon IX et la réforme de l'Eglise, 1002–1054* (Strasburg).

Murray, A. V. (1992), 'The army of Godfrey of Bouillon: structure and dynamics of a contingent on the First Crusade', *Revue belge de philologie et d'histoire* 70, 315–22.

— (2000), *The crusader kingdom of Jerusalem: a dynastic history 1099–1125* (Oxford).

Nelson, J. (1988), 'Kingship and empire', in J. H. Burns (ed.), *The Cambridge history of medieval political thought c. 350–c. 1450* (Cambridge), pp. 211–51.

Neocleous, S. (2010), 'Byzantine-Muslim conspiracies against the crusades: history and myth', *Journal of Medieval History* 36, 253–74.

Ní Chléirigh, L. (2010), 'The impact of the First Crusade on western opinion towards the Byzantine empire: the *Dei gesta per Francos* of Guibert of Nogent and the *Historia Hierosolymitana* of Fulcher of Chartres', in C. Kostick (ed.), *The crusades and the Near East: cultural histories* (London), pp. 161–88.

Nicholson, R. L. (1940), *Tancred: crusading leader and lord of Galilee and Antioch* (Chicago).

North, W. L. (2000), 'Negotiating public orthodoxy in the "Pravilegium" dispute of 1111/1112: the evidence of Bruno of Segni', in S. Elm, E. Rebillard and A. Romano (eds), *Orthodoxie, christianisme, histoire* (Collection de l'École française de Rome 270; Rome), pp. 199–220.

Pizarro, J. M. (2003), 'Ethnic and national history ca. 500–1000', in D. Mauskopf Deliyannis (ed.), *Historiography in the middle ages* (Leiden), pp. 43–87.

Pohl, W. (1994), 'Tradition, Ethnogenese und literarische Gestaltung: eine Zwischenbilanz', in K. Brunner and B. Merta (eds), *Ethnogenese und Überlieferung. Angewandte Methoden der Frühmittelalterforschung* (Vienna), pp. 9–26.

Pokorny, R. (2001), 'Das *Chronicon Wirziburgense*, seine neuaufgefundene Vorlage und die Textstufen der Reichenauer Chronistik des 11. Jahrhunderts', *DA* 57, 63–93, 451–500.

Rassow, P. (1960), *Die geschichtliche Einheit des Abendlandes* (Cologne and Graz).

Reuter, T. (1991), *Germany in the early middle ages, 800–1056* (London).

— (2006), 'Peace-breaking, feud, rebellion, resistance: violence and peace in the politics of the Salian era', in T. Reuter, *Medieval polities and modern mentalities*, ed. J. L. Nelson (Cambridge), pp. 355–87. Originally published as 'Unruhestiftung, Fehde, Rebellion, Widerstand. Gewalt und Frieden in der Politik der Salierzeit', in S. Weinfurter (ed.), *Die Salier und das Reich* 3 (Sigmaringen, 1991), pp. 297–325.

Riley-Smith, J. (1984), 'The First Crusade and the persecution of the Jews', *Studies in Church History* 21, 51–72.

— (1986), *The First Crusade and the idea of crusading* (London).

Robinson, I. S. (1978a), *Authority and resistance in the Investiture Contest: the polemical literature of the late eleventh century* (Manchester).

— (1978b), '"Periculosus homo": Pope Gregory VII and episcopal authority', *Viator* 9, 103–31.

— (1979), 'Pope Gregory VII, the princes and the *pactum*, 1077–1080', *English Historical Review* 94, 721–56.

— (1980), 'Die Chronik Hermanns von Reichenau und die Reichenauer Kaiserchronik', *DA* 36, 84–136.

— (1988), 'Church and papacy', in J. H. Burns (ed.), *The Cambridge history of medieval political thought* (Cambridge), pp. 252–305.

— (1989), 'Bernold von Konstanz und der gregorianische Reformkreis um Bischof Gebhard III.', in H. Maurer (ed.), *Die Konstanzer Münsterweihe von 1089 in ihrem historischen Umfeld* (Freiburg im Breisgau), pp. 155–88.

— (1990), *The papacy 1073–1198: continuity and innovation* (Cambridge).

— (1999), *Henry IV of Germany, 1056–1106* (Cambridge).

— (2004a), 'Reform and the church, 1073–1122', in D. Luscombe and J. Riley-Smith (eds), *The new Cambridge medieval history* 4/1 (Cambridge), pp. 268–334.

— (2004b), *The papal reform of the eleventh century: lives of Pope Leo IX and Pope Gregory VII* (Manchester).

— (2008), *Eleventh-century Germany: the Swabian chronicles* (Manchester).

Rubenstein, J. (2004), 'How, or how much, to reevaluate Peter the Hermit', in S. J. Ridyard (ed.), *The medieval crusade* (Woodbridge), pp. 53–69.

— (2008), 'Godfrey of Bouillon versus Raymond of St Gilles: how Carolingian kingship trumped millenialism at the end of the First Crusade', in M. Gabriele and J. Stuckey (eds), *The legend of Charlemagne in the middle ages: power, faith and crusade* (New York), pp. 59–76.

— (2011), *Armies of heaven: the first crusade and the quest for apocalypse* (New York).

Ryan, J. J. (1956), *St Peter Damian and his canonical sources: a preliminary study in the antecedants of the Gregorian reform* (Pontifical Institute of Mediaeval Studies: Studies and texts 2; Toronto).

Savvides, A. G. C. (1993), 'Late Byzantine and western historiographers on Turkish mercenaries in Greek and Latin armies: the Turcopoles/Tourkopoloi', in R. Beaton and C. Roueché (eds), *The making of Byzantine history: studies dedicated to Donald M. Nicol* (Aldershot), pp. 122–36.

Schieffer, R. (1972), 'Spirituales latrones. Zu den Hintergründen der Simonieprozesse in Deutschland zwischen 1069 und 1075', *Historisches Jahrbuch* 92, 19–60.

— (1981), *Die Entstehung des päpstlichen Investiturverbots für den deutschen König* (Schriften der MGH 28; Stuttgart).

— (1987), 'Meinhard von Bamberg', *Verfasserlexikon* 6, cols 310–13.

Schiffmann, S. (1931), 'Heinrich IV. und die Bischöfe in ihrem Verhalten zu den deutschen Juden zur Zeit des ersten Kreuzzugs' (dissertation, Berlin).

Schilling, B. (1998), *Guido von Vienne – Papst Calixt II.* (Schriften der MGH 45; Hanover).

Schlesinger, W. (1973), 'Die Wahl Rudolfs von Schwaben zum Gegenkönig 1077 in Forchheim', in J. Fleckenstein (ed.), *Investiturstreit und Reichsverfassung* (Vorträge und Forschungen 17; Sigmaringen), pp. 61–85.

Schmale, F.-J. (1957), 'Fiktionen im Codex Udalrici', *Zeitschrift für bayerische Landesgeschichte* 20, 437–74.

— (1959), 'Die Glaubwürdigkeit der jüngeren Vita Burchardi. Anmerkungen zur Frühgeschichte von Stadt und Bistum Würzburg', *Jahrbuch für fränkische Landesforschung* 19, 45–83.

— (1961), *Studien zum Schisma des Jahres 1130* (Cologne and Graz).

— (1966), 'Zur Abfassungszeit von Frutolfs Weltchronik', *Bericht des Historischen Vereins für die Pflege der Geschichte des ehemaligen Fürstbistums Bamberg* 102, 81–7.

— (1971), 'Überlieferungskritik und Editionsprinzipien der Chronik Ekkehards von Aura', *DA* 27, 110–34.

— (1979), 'Die "Absetzung" Gregors VI. in Sutri und die synodale Tradition', *Annuarium Historiae Conciliorum* 11, 55–103.

— (1980), 'Ekkehard von Aura', *Verfasserlexikon. Die deutsche Literatur des Mittelalters* 2 (Berlin and New York), cols 443–7.

— (1986), 'Ekkehard von Aura', *Lexikon des Mittelalters* 3, cols 1765–6.

Schmale-Ott, I. (1956), 'Die Recenzion C der Weltchronik Ekkehards', *DA* 12, 363–87.

— (1971), 'Untersuchungen zu Ekkehard von Aura und zur Kaiserchronik', *Zeitschrift für bayerische Landesgeschichte* 34, 403–62.

Schmid, A. (1989), '"Auf glühendem Thron in der Hölle". Gebhard III., Otloh von St. Emmeram und die Dionysiusfälschung', in P. Morsbach (ed.), *Ratisbona sacra: das Bistum Regensburg im Mittelalter. Ausstellung anlässlich des 1250jährigen Jubiläums der kanonischen Errichtung des Bistums Regensburg durch Bonifatius 739–1989. Diözesanmuseum Obermünster Regensburg, 2. Juni bis 1. Oktober 1989* (Munich), pp. 119–21.

Schmid, K. (1988), 'Frutolfs Bericht zum Jahr 1077 oder der Rückzug Rudolfs von Schwaben', in D. Berg and H.-W. Goetz (eds), *Historiographia Mediaevalis. Festschrift für Franz-Josef Schmale* (Darmstadt), pp. 181–98.

— (1994a), 'Die Salier als Kaiserdynastie. Zugleich ein Beitrag zur Bildausstattung der Chroniken Frutolfs und Ekkehards', in H. Keller and N. Staubach (eds), *Iconologia sacra. Mythos, Bildkunst und Dichtung in der Religions- und Sozialgeschichte Alteuropas. Festschrift für K. Hauck zum 75. Geburtstag* (Arbeiten zu Frühmittelalterforschung 23; Berlin), pp. 461–95.

— (1994b), 'Ein verlorenes Stemma "Regum Franciae". Zugleich ein Beitrag zur Entstehung und Funktion karolingischer (Bild-)Genealogien in salisch-staufischer Zeit', *Frühmittelalterliche Studien* 28, 196–225.

Schmidt, T. (1977), *Alexander II. (1061–1073) und die römische Reformgruppe seiner Zeit* (Päpste und Papsttum 11; Stuttgart).

Schneidmüller, B. (1999), 'Widukind', *Lexikon des Mittelalters* 9 (Stuttgart), cols 74–6.

Schramm, P. E. (1968), 'Böhmen und das Regnum. Die Verleihungen der Königswürde an die Herzöge von Böhmen', in. J. Fleckenstein and K. Schmid (eds), *Adel und Kirche. Gerd Tellenbach zum 65. Geburtstag dargebracht von Freunden und Schülern* (Freiburg, Basel and Vienna), pp. 346–64.

— (1983), *Die deutschen Kaiser und Könige in Bildern ihrer Zeit, 751–1190*, 2nd edn (Munich).

Schreiner, K. (1989), 'Gregor VIII. nackt auf einem Esel. Entehrende Entblößung und schandbares Reiten im Spiegel einer Miniatur der "Sächsischen Weltchronik"', in D. Berg and H.-W. Goetz (eds), *Ecclesia et Regnum. Beiträge zur Geschichte von Kirche, Recht und Staat im Mittelalter. Festschrift für Franz-Josef Schmale zu seinem 65. Geburtstag* (Karlsruhe), pp. 151–202.

Semmler, J. (1959), *Die Klosterreform von Siegburg. Ihre Ausbreitung und ihr Reformprogramm im 11. und 12. Jahrhundert* (Veröffentlichungen des Instituts für geschichtliche Landeskunde der Rheinlande an der Universität Bonn 53; Bonn).

Servatius, C. (1979), *Paschalis II. (1099–1118). Studien zu seiner Person und seiner Politik* (Päpste und Papsttum 14; Stuttgart).

Somerville, R. (1974), 'The Council of Clermont (1095) and Latin Christian society', *Archivium Historiae Pontificiae* 12, 55–90.

— (1980), 'Anselm of Lucca and Wibert of Ravenna', *Bulletin of Medieval Canon Law* n.s. 10, 1–13.

— (2011), *Pope Urban II's Council of Piacenza* (Oxford).

Steindorff, E. (1874, 1881), *Jahrbücher des Deutschen Reichs unter Heinrich III.*, 2 vols (Leipzig).

Stoclet, A. J. (1984), 'Zur politisch-religiösen Tendenz der Chronik Frutolfs von Michelsberg', *DA* 40, 200–9.

Störmer, W. (1977), 'Aribonen', *Lexikon des Mittelalters* 1 (Stuttgart), cols 929–30.

— (1991), 'Bayern und der bayerische Herzog im 11. Jahrhundert', in S. Weinfurter (ed.), *Die Salier und das Reich* 1 (Sigmaringen), pp. 503–47.

— (1997), 'Kaiser Heinrich II., Kaiserin Kunigunde und das Herzogtum Bayern', *Zeitschrift für bayerische Landesgeschichte* 60, 437–63.

Stroll, M. (2004), *Pope Calixtus II (1119–1124): a pope born to rule* (Studies in the history of Christian traditions 116; Leiden).

Struve, T. (1985), 'Die Romreise der Kaiserin Agnes', *Historisches Jahrbuch* 105, 1–29.

— (1995), 'Mathilde von Tuszien-Canossa und Heinrich IV. Der Wandel ihrer Beziehungen vor dem Hintergrund der Investiturstreites', *Historisches Jahrbuch* 115, 41–84.

Stürner, W. (1972), 'Der Königsparagraph im Papstwahldekret von 1059', *Studi Gregoriani* 9, 37–52.

Taviani-Carozzi, H. (1996), 'Une bataille franco-allemande en Italie: Civitate (1053)', in C. Carozzi and H. Taviani-Carozzi (eds), *Peuples du moyen âge. Problèmes d'identification* (Aix-en-Provence), pp. 181–211.

Tellenbach, G. (1993), *The church in western Europe from the tenth to the early twelfth century*, trans. T. Reuter (Cambridge).

Tierney, B. (1964), *The crisis of church and state 1050–1300* (Englewood Cliffs, NJ).

Toussaint, I. (1982), *Die Grafen von Leiningen. Studien zur leiningischen Genealogie und Territorialgeschichte bis zur Teilung von 1317/18* (Sigmaringen).

Tritz, H. (1952), 'Die hagiographischen Quellen zur Geschichte Papst Leo IX.', *Studi Gregoriani* 4, 191–364.

Tyerman, C. (2006), *God's war: a new history of the crusades* (Cambridge, Mass.).

Vivell, C. (1913), 'Vom uneditierten Tonarius des Mönches Frutolf', *Sammelbände der Internationalen Musik-Gesellschaft* 14, 463–84.

Vogel, J. (1983), *Gregor VII. und Heinrich IV. nach Canossa* (Arbeiten zur Frühmittelalterforschung 9; Berlin and New York).

Volkert, W. and F. Zoepfl (1974), *Die Regesten der Bischöfe und des Domkapitels von Augsburg* 1/3 (Augsburg).

Vollrath, H. (1991), 'Oral modes of perception in eleventh-century chronicles', in A. N. Doane and C. B. Pasternack (eds), *Vox intexta: orality and textuality in the middle ages* (Madison, Wis.), pp. 102–12.

Waas, A. (1957), *Heinrich V. Gestalt und Verhängnis des letzten salischen Kaisers* (Sigmaringen).

Wadle, E. (1973), 'Heinrich IV. und die deutsche Friedensbewegung', in J. Fleckenstein (ed.), *Investiturstreit und Reichsverfassung* (Vorträge und Forschungen 17; Sigmaringen), pp. 141–73.

Ware, R. D. (1992), 'Medieval chronology: theory and practice', in J. M. Powell (ed.), *Medieval studies: an introduction*, 2nd edn (Syracuse, NY), pp. 252–77.

Wattenbach, W. and R. Holtzmann (1948), *Deutschlands Geschichtsquellen im Mittelalter. Deutsche Kaiserzeit*, 3 vols (Tübingen).

Wegener, W. (1959), *Böhmen/Mähren und das Reich im Hochmittelalter* (Cologne and Graz).

Weinfurter, S. (1986), 'Die Zentralisierung der Herrschaftsgewalt im Reich durch Kaiser Heinrich II.', *Historisches Jahrbuch* 106, 241–97.

—— (1999), *The Salian century: main currents in an age of transition*, trans. B. M. Bowlus (Philadelphia).

Wendehorst, A. (1962), *Das Bistum Würzburg 1. Die Bischofsreihe bis 1254* (Germania Sacra, NF 1; Berlin).

Werner, E. (1978), *Zwischen Canossa und Worms. Staat und Kirche 1077–1122*, 3rd edn (Berlin).

Wilks, M. J. (1971), '*Ecclesiastica* and *regalia*: papal investiture policy from the Council of Guastalla to the First Lateran Council, 1106–23', in G. J. Cummings and D. Baker (eds), *Councils and assemblies: papers read at the eighth summer meeting and the ninth winter meeting of the Ecclesiastical History Society* (Studies in church history 7; Cambridge), pp. 69–85.

Wisplinghoff, E. (1975), *Die Benediktinerabtei Siegburg* (Germania sacra, NF 9; Berlin).

Wolfram, H. (2006), *Conrad II, 990–1039: emperor of three kingdoms*, trans. D. A. Kaiser (Philadelphia).

Wollasch, J. (1973), *Mönchtum des Mittelalters zwischen Kirche und Welt* (Münstersche Mittelalter-Schriften 7; Munich).

Woody, K. M. (1970), '*Sagena piscatoris*: Peter Damiani and the Papal Election decree of 1059', *Viator* 1, 33–54.

Yeomans, D. K. (1991), *Comets: a chronological history of observation, science, myth and folklore* (New York).

Zerbi, P. (1965), 'Pasquale II e l'ideale della povertà della chiesa', *Annuario dell'Università Cattolica del Sacro Cuore 1964–5* (Milan).

Ziese, J. (1982), *Wibert von Ravenna, der Gegenpapst Clemens III. (1084–1100)* (Stuttgart).

Zimmermann, H. (1968), *Papstabsetzungen des Mittelalters* (Vienna, Cologne and Graz).

Zoepfl, F. (1952), 'Die Augsburger Bischöfe im Investiturstreit', *Historisches Jahrbuch* 71, 305–33.

INDEX

1106 Continuation
   alterations to Frutolf's *Chronicle* 44–6
   authorship 41–3, 46–8, 57–8, 82
   crusading movement 48–53
   Henry IV, attitude towards 44, 53–5, 60
   Henry V, attitude towards 54, 55–6, 60, 64
   papacy, attitude towards 44, 53–6, 63
   portents 49
1125 Continuation
   authorship 74, 82, 83
   dating 75
   Henry V, attitude towards 75–6, 77, 78–81
   papacy, attitude towards 75–80
   sources 74 n. 336, 78, 266 n. 45, 276 n. 113, 284 n. 158

Acre, siege (1104) 50, 175, 183 n. 329, 183 n. 331, 256, 256 n. 293
Adalbero, bishop of Würzburg 97, 108, 111, 115, 116, 124, 126, 127, 128
Adalbert, archbishop of Hamburg-Bremen 9, 108, 109 n. 205, 109 n. 206
Adalbert, archbishop of Mainz 71, 75, 76, 79, 81, 213 n. 194, 215, 216, 241, 243, 245 n. 206, 247, 263 n. 14, 265, 270, 272 n. 87, 273
Adalbert of Babenberg (*fl.* late ninth century) 90, 90 n. 47
Adalbert of Babenberg, margrave of the East March 96, 97, 102
Adalbert, bishop of Worms 111, 117
Adalbert of Eppan/of Tyrol, count 203, 224, 225
Adelaide, daughter of Henry IV 184, 184 n. 336
Adelaide, second wife of Henry IV *see* Eupraxia-Adelaide
Adelaide of Susa, margravine of Turin 108, 114 n. 249, 177 n. 295, 195 n. 67
Adelgoz, archbishop of Magdeburg 79, 246 n. 220, 267
Adhemar, bishop of Le Puy 147
Agnes, daughter of Henry IV 184 n. 336, 201, 248 n. 228
Agnes of Poitou, empress 3, 36, 97, 98, 104, 104 n. 164, 104 n. 171, 105, 109, 109 n. 207
Albert of Aachen 52
Alexander the Great 23, 24, 27, 67
Alexander II, pope 3–4, 10, 39, 40, 106–7, 111, 111 n. 223, 112, 119, 125, 148
Alexius Comnenus 51, 122 n. 308, 143, 145 n. 68, 146, 153, 153 n. 125, 154, 163, 164, 165, 166, 183, 184, 184 n. 333
   hostility towards in western sources 52–3
Almus, brother of King Coloman I of Hungary 210, 236
Amel, prior of Aura 66, 220
Andreas I, king of Hungary 98 n. 120, 100 n. 133
Anno, archbishop of Cologne 3, 9, 38, 104, 109 n. 207, 111, 113, 117 n. 269
Anonymous imperial chronicle
   authorship 41, 42–4, 57–8, 82

INDEX

classical literature, influence of
  61–3
crusading movement 59, 63
  dating 56
  Henry IV, attitude towards 60–1
  Henry V, attitude towards 61–3
  imperial panegyric 59, 61–3
  papacy 63–6
  sources 58–9, 58 n. 263, 83
  surviving manuscript 56, 58 n.
    263, 217 n. 232
Anselm IV, archbishop of Milan 51,
  162 n. 194
Anselm I, bishop of Lucca *see*
  Alexander II
Anselm II, bishop of Lucca 33, 40,
  119
Antioch, siege (1097–8) 132, 133,
  134 n. 411, 140, 154, 155,
  156, 160, 165
Arian heresy 250
Aribert II, archbishop of Milan 95
  n. 81
Aribo, archbishop of Mainz 89, 91
Aribo II, count palatine of Bavaria
  172, 175, 176
Aribo, margrave (d. 909) 175, 175
  n. 276
Aribones, dynasty 46, 53, 58, 175–6
Armenia, Armenians 144, 154 n. 128,
  160
Arnold, bishop of Speyer 103
Arnold of Loon, burgrave of Mainz
  285
Arnulf of Choques, patriarch of
  Jerusalem 168
Ascalon, battle (1099) 45, 135, 156–7
Aschaffenburg 274–5
Aura, monastery 47, 66, 219–20
Azo, bishop of Acqui 72

Baldwin of Boulogne (of Edessa),
  king of Jerusalem 50, 52,
  73, 142, 147, 159 n. 167,
  160, 167, 169, 172, 173,
  183, 191, 255, 256, 263–4

Baldwin of Bourcq, count of Edessa,
  king of Jerusalem 161, 263
Baldwin V, count of Flanders 99, 102
Bamberg 1, 2, 11, 15, 16, 21, 32, 33,
  34, 35, 38, 45, 46, 66, 74, 74
  n. 336, 85, 87, 87 n. 30, 89,
  90 n. 47, 91, 95, 98, 99, 100,
  107, 111, 113, 120, 136,
  137, 197, 210, 217, 237,
  245, 277, 280–1, 283
Bardo, archbishop of Mainz 99
Basel, council (1061) 3
Beatrice of Lotharingia, margravine
  of Tuscany 3, 97 n. 105,
  102, 102 n. 156
Beatrice of Schweinfurt 176–7, 194
Benedict VIII, pope 38, 88, 89
Benedict IX, pope 2, 98 n. 114
'Benedict X', antipope 3
Berengar I, count of Sulzbach 177,
  211 n. 184, 272
Berengar of Tours 118
Bern, abbot of Reichenau 15, 17
Bernold of St Blasien, chronicler 9
  n. 33, 34 n. 137, 38, 39, 41,
  49, 55, 63 n. 282, 80, 125 n.
  338, 126 n. 346
Bertha of Turin, first wife of Henry
  IV and empress 9, 34, 108,
  123, 127, 129, 184 n. 336,
  201 n. 107
Berthold of Reichenau, chronicler 22,
  31, 32, 36, 37, 39, 41, 54,
  69, 81
Berthold I of Zähringen, duke of
  Carinthia 105, 106, 115,
  116, 177 n. 298
Berthold II of Zähringen 106
Bethlehem 143, 161 n. 182, 258 n.
  309
Bohemia 85, 87, 96, 113, 117, 120,
  130, 138, 151, 180, 198,
  211, 211 n. 183, 237, 280
Bohemund, prince of Tarranto and
  Antioch 133 n. 405, 134 n.
  410, 136, 142, 154 n. 134,

139 n. 155, 158, 159 n. 167, 173, 184, 255
Boleslav Chrobry, duke of Poland 85, 87
Boleslav III, duke of Poland 280, 281
Boniface II of Canossa, margrave of Tuscany 97 n. 105, 102
Borivoi II, duke of Bohemia 180 n. 314, 181, 198 n. 93, 211 n. 183
Boto of Pottenstein, count 53, 175–6
Bretislav I, duke of Bohemia 96, 100 n. 131
Brixen, synod (1080) 11, 33, 39, 40, 112 n. 234, 118
Bruno, archbishop of Trier 64, 186, 202, 206 n. 147, 223, 224
Bruno, bishop of Augsburg 32, 86, 91, 93
Bruno, bishop of Segni 13, 72–3, 250
Bruno, bishop of Speyer 270 n. 74
Bruno, bishop of Toul *see* Leo IX
Bruno, bishop of Würzburg 97
Bruno, duke of Saxony 90
Bruno of Querfurt, missionary 88
Burchard, bishop of Halberstadt 127
Burchard, bishop of Lusanne 128
Burchard, bishop of Münster 79, 269
Burchard II, bishop of Worms 270 n. 75, 281
Burchard, librarian of Michelsberg 16, 17–19
Burdinus *see* 'Gregory VIII'

Cadalus, bishop of Parma *see* 'Honorius II'
Calixtus II, pope 75, 76, 77, 78, 80, 243 n. 187, 248 n. 231, 264 n. 31, 265, 266, 267, 270, 276, 277, 281, 283
Canossa 33, 114, 125
Canossa-Lotharingia, house 3, 4, 97 n. 105, 102, 130 n. 382
'Celestine II', antipope *see* Theobald, cardinal priest of S. Anastasia

Charles, bishop of Constance 9–10
Charles the Great 13, 23, 24, 30, 58, 59, 61, 64, 67, 150, 176, 187, 188, 209, 219, 235
Cicero 60, 61, 62, 187
Civitate, battle (1053) 101 n. 146
Clement II, pope 2, 115
'Clement III', antipope *see* Wibert of Parma
clerical marriage *see* nicholaitism
Clermont, council (1095) 12, 34, 146–7
Cluny 76, 208, 235, 264, 265, 268
Cnut, king of the Danes 92, 93 n. 62, 94
Codex Udalrici 24, 115 n. 252, 118 n. 276, 266 n. 45
Cologne, siege
  (1106) 70, 203, 204, 205, 225, 226–7
  (1114) 71, 218, 245
Coloman I, king of Hungary 131, 139, 152, 209, 210, 236
comets 108, 132, 140, 149, 189, 203, 211, 225, 238
compilation 14, 24–7
Concordat of Worms 13, 14, 69, 75, 77, 78, 79, 80, 266, 275–7
Conrad, archbishop of Salzburg 206 n. 144, 233
Conrad of Beichlingen 53, 174, 193
Conrad, bishop of Speyer 103
Conrad, bishop of Utrecht 137, 158, 189
Conrad I, duke of Bavaria (1049–53) 7, 102, 103
Conrad I, king 30
Conrad II, king and emperor 5, 32, 61, 91–5, 128 n. 364
Conrad, king and son of Henry IV 45, 50, 54, 55, 129, 130 n. 382, 136, 140–2, 162, 191–2, 256
Conrad, margrave of Moravia 120
Conrad, *ministerialis* of King Conrad 141

INDEX

Conrad of Palestrina, cardinal and papal legate 73, 76, 77, 246 n. 219, 251, 252, 263 n. 13
Conrad of Staufen (King Conrad III) 79, 184 n. 337, 248, 253, 265, 273, 279
Conrad of Vohburg, count palatine of Bavaria 121
Conrad 'the Younger' (d. 1039) 92 n. 60
Constantine VI, Byzantine emperor 29
Constantine the Great 7, 30, 147, 242, 248, 251
Constantinople 6, 23, 30, 50, 51, 131, 140, 143, 145, 146, 153, 163, 242, 269
Cornelius, pope 119
Crescentii, Roman family 2, 3, 121
Crusade of 1101 46, 48, 50–3, 73, 162–71
Cunigunde, wife of Henry II, queen and empress 1, 85, 90, 95
Cunigunde, wife of Henry III *see* Gunhild
Cyprian, bishop of Carthage 119

Daimbert, archbishop of Pisa 34, 45, 133 n. 402, 136, 158, 159 n. 167, 161 n. 182, 191 n. 34
Damasus II, pope 3, 98, 99
David, *scholasticus* of Würzburg 57, 59, 65, 212
Dedi I, margrave of the Lower Lausitz 8, 36, 109
Dedi II, son of Dedi I 109
Desiderius, abbot of Monte Cassino *see* Victor III
Diepold III of Cham-Vohburg, margrave of the Bavarian Nordgau 177, 180, 198, 211 n. 184
Dietrich, bishop of Zeitz-Naumburg 80, 279
Dietrich III of Kaltenburg, count 205, 227

Donatist heresy 234
Dorylaeum, battle (1097) 133 n. 403, 154 n. 132

Eberhard, bishop of Augsburg 93
Eberhard, bishop of Bamberg 1, 15, 32, 35, 85 n. 9, 87, 88, 89, 91, 95
Eberhard, bishop of Eichstätt 186, 202, 223
ecclesiastica 64, 65, 272
Egilbert, archbishop of Trier 137
Ekbert II, margrave of Meißen 124, 127 n. 351, 128
Ekkehard of Aura
  biography 46–8
  chronicle 25, 44
  dating 66
  Henry IV 54, 60, 69–70
  Henry V 55, 70–2, 80, 81
  Hierosolimita 73–4
  manuscripts 66–9
  papacy 55, 72–3
  relationship with other continuations 21, 31 n. 123, 41–3, 44, 46–7, 57–8, 74, 82–3
  sources 67–8
Emehard, bishop of Würzburg 127, 173, 179, 197
Emico, count (d. 1117) 263, 278
Emico, count of Flonheim 34, 131, 139, 151
Erkembert, abbot of Corvey 25, 43, 44, 48, 66, 67, 68, 73, 74, 83, 219, 254 n. 267
Erluf, abbot of Fulda 273 n. 100
Erlung, bishop of Würzburg 57, 66, 71, 75, 79, 179, 180, 181, 197–8, 200, 207, 234, 248, 273
Ernest I, duke of Swabia 88, 91 n. 51
Ernest II, duke of Swabia 92 n. 60, 93
Eupraxia-Adelaide, second wife of Henry IV 9, 128, 159
Eustace of Boulogne 147

Eutychean heresy 250
exceptio spolii, legal doctrine 125
    n. 335, 125 n. 338

famine 31, 87, 102, 103, 133, 134,
    143, 148, 154, 155, 159,
    190, 280, 282, 285
Fire of Easter 170 n. 237, 259 n. 326
First Crusade 34–5, 45, 48–50, 129,
    131–2, 139–40, 142–58
    German antipathy towards 49,
        148–9, 152
    Jews 34, 130, 131, 132, 133–6,
        138, 140, 152
    'People's Crusade' 34, 49, 130–1,
        138–9, 150–2
    portents 49, 130, 138, 149–50
First Lateran Council (1123) 80
Flarchheim, battle (1080) 117
Folkmar, leader in the People's
    Crusade 130, 138, 151
Forchheim, election (1077) 36, 40,
    106 n. 182, 114 n. 250, 116
fortuna 62–3, 195, 200, 204, 217, 225,
    226, 230
Frangipani, Roman family 77, 282
    n.150
Frederick, archbishop of Cologne
    137, 158, 189, 218, 245, 277
Frederick of Arnsberg, count 213 n.
    194, 245, 267
Frederick, bishop of Halberstadt 63,
    179, 197, 207 n. 149
Frederick I (of Büren), duke of
    Swabia 121 n. 298, 184, 201
Frederick II, duke of Swabia 184 n.
    337, 201, 253, 263, 273,
    281, 285
Frederick II, duke of Upper Lotharingia 92 n. 60, 102 n. 154
Frederick of Gleiberg 105
Frederick of Lotharingia, cardinal *see*
    Stephen IX
Frederick of Somerschenburg, Saxon
    count palatine 80, 216, 244,
    268

Frederick I of Tengling, count 175
    n. 278
Friderun, wife of Count Palatine
    Hartwig II 176
Frutolf of Michelsberg
    autograph manuscripts 16–17, 21
    biography and works 15–19
    Chronicle 14, 19–20
    Bamberg 1, 35
    calculation of the date of
        creation 25–7
    continuations of 14, 20, 41–4,
        44–6, 56, 57, 58, 74, 82–3
    date of composition 20, 104
    dating systems 29–31, 67–8
    exempla 20, 35, 39
    First Crusade 34–5
    Gregory VII 32, 33, 38–40
    Henry IV 31, 33–4, 35–8, 54
    manuscripts 21
    papacy 14, 54, 38–41
    political outlook 14, 29–31,
        35–41, 62
    sources 22, 24–5, 31–3, 34–5
    synchronous history 27–9

Gebhard, archbishop of Salzburg
    111, 124–5
Gebhard, bishop of Constance 172
    n. 250, 177, 184, 186, 195,
    196, 202, 221, 223, 224
Gebhard I, bishop of Eichstätt *see*
    Victor II
Gebhard I, bishop of Regensburg 90
Gebhard II, bishop of Regensburg
    90, 94
Gebhard III, bishop of Regensburg
    94, 99, 100 n. 131, 103
Gebhard IV, bishop of Regensburg
    127, 198
Gebhard, bishop of Speyer 182, 183
    n. 328, 200
Gebhard, bishop of Trent 203, 206 n.
    144, 225, 233
Gebhard (of Henneberg), imperial
    bishop of Würzburg 75, 79,

INDEX

273, 274
Gelasius II, pope 75, 76, 77, 250, 251, 263, 264, 265
Gerard, abbot of Schaffhausen 52, 169
Gerard, bishop of Angoulême 242
Gerard, bishop of Florence *see* Nicholas II
Gerstungen-Berka, conference (1085) 12, 33, 124–5
Gertrude of Brunswick 174 n. 267, 244
Gertrude/Petronilla, sister of Lothar of Supplinburg 277 n. 119, 279 n. 131
Gisela, daughter of Henry III 98
Gisela, sister of Henry II 86
Gisela, wife of Conrad II, queen and empress 91, 92 n. 60, 95, 96
gistum and *servitium* 280 n. 132
Gleichen, siege (1089) 34, 128
Godebald, bishop of Utrecht 277
Godfrey, abbot of Fulda 210, 237
Godfrey 'the Bearded', duke of Upper Lotharingia and margrave of Tuscany 3, 98, 99, 100 n. 140, 102, 103, 105
Godfrey V (of Bouillon), duke of Lower Lotharingia and Advocate of the Holy Sepulchre 34, 45, 50, 131–2, 133, 136, 139, 142, 147, 152–3, 157, 158, 159–60, 167, 190–1, 255, 256, 264
Godfrey I of Leuven, duke of Lower Lotharingia 245
Godfrey of Namur, count 62
Gorrizim 52, 144, 165
Gottschalk, leader in the People's Crusade 34, 130, 138, 151
Gozelo I, duke of Upper and Lower Lotharingia 95, 98 n. 111
Gozwin, count of Grabfeld 107–8
'Great Saxon Rebellion' (1073–5) 8, 10, 111 n. 217, 111–13, 125 n. 334
Gregory, cardinal deacon of S. Angelo *see* Innocent II
Gregory VI, pope 2, 98 n. 114
Gregory VII, pope 7, 12, 13, 39, 72, 107, 112–15, 118–19, 122, 123, 126, 161, 162, 172, 191, 242, 250 n. 248, 251
allegations against 39–40, 112, 113, 118–19
Henry IV 9, 10–11, 12, 32, 33
letters 24, 33, 112 n. 235, 114 n. 245, 115 n. 252
'Gregory VIII', antipope 75, 76, 77, 80, 264, 266 n. 40, 267, 267 n. 49, 270, 274, 282
Guastalla, council (1106) 12, 63, 64, 65, 206–7, 232–4
Guido, archbishop of Vienne *see* Calixtus II
Gunhild, first wife of Henry III 92, 94 n. 79
Gunther, bishop of Bamberg 107

Hadrian I, pope 64, 209 n. 163, 235 n. 122
Hartwig, archbishop of Magdeburg 127 n. 362, 128 n. 366, 172, 193, 199
Hartwig, bishop of Regensburg 76, 181
Hartwig of Bogen, count 180
Hartwig II, count palatine of Bavaria 175, 176
Harzburg (royal fortress) 112
Helmold of Bosau 69
Henry, abbot of Michelsberg 89
Henry, archbishop of Magdeburg 179, 186, 197, 202, 223, 228
Henry, bishop of Augsburg 36
Henry, bishop of Paderborn 179, 197
Henry, bishop of Würzburg 88
Henry 'the Black', duke of Bavaria 132 nn. 400, 401, 272
Henry, duke of Bavaria (d. 955) 90
Henry I of Eilenburg, margrave of the Lower Lausitz and Meißen, 174, 194

Henry III of Eppenstein, duke of
    Carinthia 163
Henry 'the Fat', margrave of Frisia
    53, 174, 193
Henry, first-born son of Henry IV
    112 n. 227
Henry I, king 30, 90, 176 n. 281
Henry II, king and emperor 1, 23,
    32, 35, 85, 87, 88, 89, 90, 91
Henry III, king and emperor 32, 61,
    91, 92, 93, 94, 95–104, 105
  autocratic rule 3, 7–8, 53, 102 n.
    150
  and papacy 2–3, 11
Henry IV, king and emperor 1, 14,
    20, 24, 31, 32, 34, 35, 37, 38,
    40, 45, 50, 53, 54, 55, 56,
    57, 58, 60, 68, 69, 70, 80,
    81, 103, 104–37, 139, 140,
    143, 171, 173, 174, 189–94,
    245 n. 212, 255
  accusations of sexual immorality
    against 9, 70, 111, 159, 192
  burial 61, 205, 231, 241
  episcopal appointments 9–10, 66,
    123–4, 127, 137, 172, 193,
    197–8
  excommunication 11, 33, 44,
    171–2, 185
  Gregory VII 10–11, 33, 39, 112,
    113–15, 118–19, 120, 121–2
  imperial coronation 123
  investiture 1–2, 6, 11–12, 65, 70
  minority 3, 8, 104–6, 108–9
  papacy 8–12, 39, 56, 111
  rebellion of Henry V 12, 54, 55–6,
    60, 61, 62, 68, 177–85,
    195–205, 221–32
  Saxony 8–9, 32, 36, 106, 108–12,
    113, 116, 117, 119–20, 121,
    125, 126, 128
Henry V, king and emperor 1, 14, 25,
    41, 42, 44, 46, 57, 58, 61,
    63, 66, 67, 68, 69, 70, 75,
    81, 82, 136, 140, 187, 188,
    189, 194, 210, 211, 212,
    217, 219, 221, 236, 245–53,
    262–85
  excommunication 65, 73, 76, 77,
    243, 246, 252, 263, 267 n.
    49
  imperial coronation 56, 65, 209,
    211, 214–15, 235, 237, 240
  investiture 1–2, 12–13, 56, 64–5,
    73, 75, 76, 77–9, 81, 208–9,
    213, 234, 235, 242–3,
    249–50, 266–7, 275–7
  Italian expedition
    (1110–11) 59, 61, 63, 211–15,
      237–41
    (1116) 71–2, 75, 247, 248, 261,
      263, 264
  papacy 12–13, 64, 65, 70, 72,
    76, 81, 206, 207, 208–9,
    213–15, 233, 234–5,
    239–41, 241–2
  rebellion against Henry IV 12,
    54, 55–6, 60, 61, 62, 68,
    177–85, 195–205, 221–32
  Saxony 70–1, 79, 80, 81, 216, 216
    n. 224, 244, 246
Henry I, king of England 217, 245,
    281
Henry II of Laach, count palatine of
    Lotharingia 129
Henry of Limburg, duke of Lower
    Lotharingia 137, 203, 204,
    210, 225, 226, 230, 237,
    245
Henry 'the Quarrelsome', duke of
    Bavaria 90
Henry of Regensburg, count 166
Henry of Schweinfurt, margrave
    85, 87
Henry of Stade, margrave of the
    North March 128 n. 363
Heribert, archbishop of Cologne 89
Herman II, archbishop of Cologne
    94
Herman III, archbishop of Cologne
    137, 158, 189
Herman Billung, count 117

INDEX

Herman, bishop of Bamberg 107, 111, 113
Herman IV, duke of Swabia 95
Herman of Reichenau, chronicler 7, 15, 17, 18, 22, 24, 27 n. 111, 29, 31, 38, 53
Herman of Salm, anti-king 33, 37, 120 n. 295, 121, 124 n. 330, 127
Hesso, *scholasticus* of Strasburg 78, 266
Hezilo, bishop of Hildesheim 39
Hildebrand, archdeacon of Rome *see* Gregory VII
Hildulf, archbishop of Cologne 113
historical *exempla* 20, 35, 39
Höchstädt, battle (1081/2) 121
Hohenmölsen, battle (1080) 33, 37, 106 n. 185, 119
Hoier of Mansfeld, count 216 n. 225, 244 n. 202, 246
Homburg, battle (1075) 8, 113, 232 n. 92
'Honorius II', antipope 3
Honorius II, pope 75, 77, 266, 274 n. 101, 282
Hugh Candidus, cardinal priest of S. Clemente 118
Hugh III, count of Tübingen 116
Hugh of Flavigny, chronicler 39
Hugh the Great, abbot of Cluny 114 n. 249, 228
Hugh of Vermandois 147
Humbert, deacon of Mainz 101
Humbert of Moyenmoutier, cardinal bishop of Silva Candida 5–6, 11

Ida of Cham, margravine of the East March 166 n. 219
Innocent II, pope 274 n. 102

Jaffa 52, 158, 165, 166, 167–70, 172
  battle (1102) 50, 52, 173
Jaromir, duke of Bohemia 87 n. 27
Jerusalem 34, 43, 46, 48, 53, 66, 68, 107, 129, 130, 134, 135, 136, 138, 142, 143, 145, 146, 151, 153, 155, 156, 157, 162, 166, 188, 192, 252, 254–60 *passim*, 279
  crusader kingdom of 48, 49, 50, 53, 73, 158, 159–61, 166–71, 172–3, 175, 190–1, 263–4
  siege (1099) 45, 134–5, 137, 155, 156, 189
Jews 34, 130, 131, 132, 138, 139, 140, 152, 189
John I, bishop of Speyer 176
John, cardinal bishop of Sabina *see* Silvester III
John, cardinal bishop of Velletri *see* 'Benedict X'
John of Crema, cardinal priest of S. Grisogono 269 n. 69
John of Gaeta, cardinal *see* Gelasius II
John Gratian, archpriest *see* Gregory VI
John IV, patriarch of Grado 243
John XIX, pope 93 n. 62
Jordan of Clivio, archbishop of Milan 249, 252

Kaiserswerth 104
Kilij Arslan, sultan of Rum 144 n. 66, 153 n. 126, 154 n. 127

Ladislav, king of Hungary 129
Lambert, cardinal bishop of Ostia *see* Honorius II
Lampert of Hersfeld, chronicler 7–8, 37
Lateran synod
  (1102) 12, 171, 192–3
  (1112) 63, 65, 70, 72, 76, 241–3
  (1116) 72, 76, 248–53
Leo IX, pope 3, 4–5, 15, 38, 39, 99–102
Leopold II, margrave of the East March 120, 129, 166 n. 219

Leopold III, margrave of the East March 180 n. 314, 181, 198 n. 93
Liemar, archbishop of Bremen 39, 128 n. 368, 137
Liudolf, duke of Saxony 90
Liutizi 94, 103, 105, 283
Liutold of Eppenstein, duke of Carinthia 106
Lothar of Supplinburg, duke in Saxony 207, 216, 234, 244, 269, 277, 280
Louis VI, king of France 281
Ludwig (Louis) IV 'the Child' 30, 90
Ludwig II of Thuringia, count 216, 243, 244
Luitpold, archbishop of Mainz 99, 101, 107
lunar cycle 131, 139, 188

Maccabees 63, 204, 226
Maginulf, archpriest of S. Angelo *see* 'Silvester IV'
Magnus Billung, duke in Saxony 110 n. 216, 117, 184, 201, 207, 221, 234
Mailberg, battle (1082) 120 n. 297
Mainz coronation *ordo* 35
Mainz, council
 (1085) 35, 123–4
 (1097) 132, 140, 189
 (1098) 34, 132, 136 n. 424, 140, 189, 191 n. 38
 (1105–6) 54, 69, 182–3, 184–6, 200–2, 221–3, 227
 (1114) 217, 245
 (1115) 71, 247
Manegold of Lautenbach 35–6
Marcward, abbot of Corvey 220
martyrdom 38, 63, 80, 166 n. 218, 258, 259
Matilda, countess of Tuscany and margravine of Canossa 40, 72, 102, 114 n. 249, 122 n. 310, 126, 129 n. 376, 141 n. 34, 162, 191, 212, 224, 238, 247
Matilda, empress, wife of Henry V 56, 61, 217, 245, 248, 265, 280, 285
Matilda, queen, wife of Henry I 176
Matilda, sister of Henry IV 37, 105
Maurice, archbishop of Braga *see* 'Gregory VIII'
Meinhard I, bishop of Würzburg 94
Meinhard II, *scholasticus* of Bamberg and imperial bishop of Würzburg 24, 66, 124, 126, 127, 197
Mellrichstadt, battle (1078) 117, 232 n. 92
Menfö, battle (1044) 97 n. 109
Merzifon, battle (1101) 51, 163 n. 200
Melfi, council (1089) 12
Melfi, treaty (1059) 4
Michelsberg, monastery 1, 15–16, 17, 19, 21, 24, 32, 35, 41, 44, 47–8, 86, 89
Milan, archbishopric 6, 10–11, 249, 252
ministeriales 127 n. 351, 141, 174, 194, 218, 223, 223 n. 39, 277
Mosonmagyaróvár *see* Wieselburg
Münsterschwarzach, monastery 75, 273, 274

Nicaea, siege (1097) 133, 153–4, 183
nicholaitism 5, 7, 178, 196
Nicholas II, pope 3, 4, 106 n. 186, 274
Nicophorus III Botaniates, Byzantine emperor 164 n. 208
Nordhausen, council (1105) 178, 196
Novatian heresy 119 n. 287, 234
Nuremberg, siege (1105) 179–80, 198

Odo of Châtillon, cardinal bishop of Ostia *see* Urban II
Odo II, count of Blois-Champagne 94, 95

INDEX

Odo, count of Savoy 108
Oppenheim, assembly (1076) 114
Otbert, bishop of Liège 203, 207 n. 149, 225, 231
Otloh, monk of St Emmeram 7, 15
Otto, bishop of Bamberg 43, 46–7, 57, 58, 66, 74, 74 n. 336, 80, 172, 186, 193, 202, 223, 224, 245, 265 n. 36, 272, 280–1, 282–4
Otto, bishop of Regensburg 127
Otto II, duke of Swabia 99
Otto of Kastl-Habsberg, count 177, 195 n. 67
Otto I, king and emperor 90, 176
Otto II, king and emperor 90
Otto III, king and emperor 83, 90
Otto 'the Illustrious', duke of Saxony 90
Otto of Northeim, duke of Bavaria 8, 36, 53, 104 n. 167, 106, 109–11, 115, 174, 193
Otto III (of Schweinfurt), duke of Swabia 99, 105, 177
Ovo (Aba/Samuel), king of Hungary 96, 97

Papal Election Decree (1059) 40, 112 n. 233
papal elections 2, 3, 76, 77, 126, 264, 265, 266, 282
papal primacy, doctrine 6–7, 39
Paschal II, pope 12, 14, 44, 46, 51, 53, 54, 55, 63, 75, 76, 77, 137, 159, 171–2, 177, 186, 190, 195, 196, 202, 206–9, 212–15, 223, 232–6, 239–41, 248–53
  capture by Henry V 13, 65, 70, 214–15, 240
  criticism of 72, 73, 241–3, 249–51, 262, 263, 264
  investiture 12–13, 56, 64–5, 72, 209, 215, 235, 240, 242, 249–50
Peace of God 7, 45, 97 n. 101, 124, 132, 136–7, 140, 178, 189, 196, 253, 265 n. 38, 281
Pechenegs 145, 163, 164
'People's Crusade' *see* First Crusade
Peter Damian, cardinal bishop of Ostia 2 n. 6, 4, 6, 8 n. 29, 40 n. 171
Peter Grosulan, archbishop of Milan 249, 252
Peter the Hermit 51, 130, 138, 153, 255
Peter, king of Hungary 96, 97, 98
Peter Pierleoni 213 n. 193, 239 n. 153, 251
Peter the Venerable, abbot of Cluny 20
Piacenza, council (1095) 9, 60, 146 n. 79, 159, 172 n. 250
Pilgrim, archbishop of Cologne 89, 94
Philip I, king of France 147
Photinan heresy 250
Pleichfeld, battle (1086) 33, 126
Poland, Poles 87 n. 28, 210, 237, 281
Pomerania 74, 80, 281, 283–4
Ponte Mammolo, treaty (1111) 13, 61, 63, 65, 72, 73, 76, 214–15, 240, 249, 262
Pontius, abbot of Cluny 78, 248, 266
Poppo of Henneberg, count 117
Poppo, patriarch of Aquileia *see* Damasus II

Quedlinburg, synod
  (1085) 125
  (1105) 54, 177–8, 195

Rainald of Bar and Mousson, count 71, 217, 244
Rainer of Bieda, cardinal priest of S. Clemente *see* Paschal II
Ramla 167
  first battle (1101) 50, 52, 169
  second battle (1102) 172–3
  third battle (1105) 183
Rapoto IV, count of Cham 120

Rapoto V, count of Cham 136, 158, 189
Rato, abbot of Michelsberg 89
Raymond of St Gilles, count of Toulouse 35, 45, 133 n. 402, 134 n. 410, 136, 142, 147, 155 n. 139, 157, 158, 166, 173, 255
regalia 64, 65, 76, 79, 213, 239, 272, 276
Reginbold, bishop of Speyer 95
Reichenau imperial chronicle 31
Reinhard, bishop of Halberstadt 244, 246
Retting II, Bavarian count 285
Rheims, council (1119) 77–8, 266–7
Richard of Aversa, prince of Capua 4, 101 n. 146
Richard, cardinal bishop of Albano 184, 201, 221
Robert II, count of Flanders 35, 134 n. 410, 136, 142, 147, 154, 155 n. 139, 157, 209, 236, 255
Robert II, duke of Normandy 136, 142, 147, 157, 255
Robert Guiscard, duke of Apulia and Calabria 4, 101 n. 146, 122 nn. 308, 314, 123 n. 319
Roger I, count of Sicily 141, 256
Roman empire 30, 31, 35, 36, 59, 62, 102, 105, 108, 142, 178, 187, 188, 196, 205, 210, 217, 228, 236, 284
Rudolf III, king of Burgundy 89 n. 37, 93 n. 62, 94
Rudolf of Rheinfelden 8, 105, 106, 113, 117, 125
  election as anti-king 33, 40, 114–16
  Henrician propaganda against 33, 36–8, 105, 106, 119–20
Rudolf I of Stade, margrave of the North March 216, 244
Rugger, archbishop of Magdeburg 79, 267

Rugger, Gregorian bishop of Würzburg 75, 79, 81, 273, 274, 285
Rumold, bishop of Constance 105
Ruothard, archbishop of Mainz 56, 127, 132, 140, 177, 179, 182, 185, 189, 196, 198, 200, 202 n. 115, 210, 222 n. 27, 237
Rupert, bishop of Bamberg 113, 172, 193
Rupert, bishop of Würzburg 179, 180, 181, 198, 200, 207, 234

Sabellian heresy 250
sacral kingship 12, 14, 35–6, 50, 62
Saracens 133, 134, 135, 143, 145, 154, 155, 156, 161, 167, 172, 183
Saxo, cardinal priest of S. Stefano 274 n. 102
Saxon rebellion
  (1073–5) 8, 9, 10, 111–13, 125
  (1112–13) 70, 216, 243–4
  (1115) 71, 246
Seljuk Turks 51, 52, 130, 132 n. 397, 133, 138, 140 n. 20, 144, 145, 154, 156, 161, 163, 164, 165, 173, 183–4, 188, 255, 259
Sennes, archbishop of Capua 243
Siegfried, archbishop of Mainz 10, 38, 107, 111, 115, 116, 121 n. 300, 123
Siegfried of Ballenstedt, count palatine of Lotharingia 182, 200, 210, 215, 216, 237, 241, 243, 244, 246
Siegfried, imperial bishop of Augsburg 122, 127
Sigebert of Gembloux, chronicler 12, 22, 55, 58, 62
Sigehard of Burghausen, count 53, 174, 175, 194
Silvester III, pope 2, 98 n. 114
'Silvester IV', antipope 70, 224

simony 2, 5, 6, 7, 9, 10, 11, 13, 56,
    111 n. 223, 276
six ages of history 25–6, 29, 142 n.
    45
solar eclipse 94, 95, 129
Sorbs 182, 279
Stephen of Blois 166
Stephen I, king of Hungary 86, 93,
    94, 95, 98 n. 120
Stephen IX, pope 3–4, 100, 105, 106
Suidger, bishop of Bamberg *see*
    Clement II
Sutri, synod (1046) 2, 98 n. 114
Swabian universal chronicle see
    Reichenau imperial chronicle

Tancred, prince of Galilee 173
Theobald, cardinal priest of S.
    Anastasia 77, 282 n. 148
Theoderic II, bishop of Münster 79,
    269
Theoderic, cardinal priest of S.
    Grisogono 71, 76, 246, 247,
    248, 263 n. 13
Theoger, abbot of St Georgen and
    bishop of Metz 80, 268
Thiemo, archbishop of Salzburg 166
translatio imperii (translation of
    empire) 30
Troyes, council (1107) 12, 64, 78,
    208, 235
Turcopoles 145, 165
Tusculani, Roman family 2, 3

Udalric, archbishop of Benevento
    102
Udalric II, bishop of Eichstätt 285
Udalric, bishop of Regensburg 180,
    181, 198, 199
Udalric II of Passau, count 136, 158,
    190
Udalric of Wiemar, count 70, 216 n.
    224, 243
Udo, archbishop of Trier 117
Udo, bishop of Hildesheim 179, 197
Udo II of Stade, margrave of the
    North March 128 n. 363
Udo III of Stade, margrave of the
    North March 207, 234
universal history 21–2
Urban II, pope 12, 13, 34, 40, 46,
    50–1, 54, 55, 72, 125, 126,
    137, 141 n. 34, 146, 159,
    162 n. 187, 172, 190, 242

Varangians 145
Victor II, pope 3, 102, 103, 104–5
Victor III, pope 39, 40, 126
Visé, battle (1106) 62–3, 204, 226
Vladislav I, duke of Bohemia 217
Vratislav II, duke of Bohemia 117,
    120 n. 297, 129
Vsevolod, prince of Kiev 128 n. 364,
    159 n. 163

Walram, bishop of Naumburg 37–8
Walter, archbishop of Ravenna 77,
    282
Welf II, count 93
Welf III, duke of Carinthia 100 n.
    131, 103
Welf IV, duke of Bavaria 46, 51, 110,
    122, 127 n. 352, 130, 132,
    138, 140, 163, 166, 188, 189
Welf V, duke of Bavaria 129 n. 375,
    132, 140, 189, 203, 225
Welfesholz, battle (1115) 71, 246 n.
    216
Werner, archbishop of Magdeburg
    117
Werner I, bishop of Strasburg 89
Werner (Wezilo), count of Kyburg
    and Thurgau 93
Werner, *ministerialis* of Henry IV,
    duke of Spoleto 223
Wezilo (Werner), archbishop of
    Mainz 123 n. 326, 124–5,
    127
Wibert of Parma, archbishop of
    Ravenna, antipope 'Clement
    III' 11, 33, 54, 69, 118–19,
    123, 137, 161–2, 191, 223

Widelo, bishop of Minden 63, 207 n. 149
Wido, bishop of Chur 186
Wido, bishop of Ferrara 12
Widukind (d. 807) 176
Wieselburg, Hungarian border fortress 131, 139, 152
Wigold, Gregorian bishop of Augsburg 123, 127
William, abbot of Hirsau 15, 17, 24–5
William, bishop of Pavia 162 n. 195
William, bishop of Utrecht 107
William of Champeaux, bishop of Châlons-sur-Marne 78, 266
William the Conqueror 108
William V, duke of Aquitaine 97
William IX, duke of Aquitaine 51, 162, 163, 164, 166
William of Malmesbury 59, 65, 212 n. 186, 240 n. 166
William, margrave of the North March 103
Wipo, imperial chaplain and historian 5, 62
Wiprecht II of Groitzsch, count 182, 216, 224 n. 47, 244
Wiprecht III of Groitzsch, count 211 n. 183
Wolfgang of Regensburg, canonisation 100
Wolfhelm, abbot of Fulda 210, 237
Worms, council (1076) 11, 33, 39, 113–14
Würzburg Chronicle 24, 31–2
Würzburg, siege (1086) 33, 126

EU authorised representative for GPSR:
Easy Access System Europe, Mustamäe tee 50,
10621 Tallinn, Estonia
gpsr.requests@easproject.com